Energy
Psychology
and EMDR

The Norton Energy Psychology Series
A Norton Professional Book

Energy Psychology and EMDR

Combining Forces to
Optimize Treatment

John G. Hartung and Michael D. Galvin

W. W. Norton & Company
New York · London

For information about permission to
reproduce selections from this book, write to
Permissions, W. W. Norton & Company, Inc.,
500 Fifth Avenue, New York, NY 10110

Book design by Leeann Graham
Manufacturing by Haddon Craftsmen, Inc.

Library of Congress Cataloging-in-Publication Data

Hartung, John, Psy.D.
   Energy psychology and EMD : combining forces to optimize treatment / John
Hartung and Michael Galvin.
       p.   cm. — (The Norton energy psychology series)
      Includes bibliographical references and index.
"A Norton professional book."
ISBN 0-393-70378-9
1. Bioenergetic psychotherapy.   2. Eye movement desensitiziation and reprocessing.
I. Galvin, Michael, Ph. D.   II. Title..   III. Series

PC489.B5   H376   2003
616.85'210651—dc21   2002038678

W. W. Norton & Company, Inc., 500 Fifth Avenue, New York, N.Y. 10110
www.wwnorton.com

W. W. Norton & Company Ltd., Castle House, 75/76 Wells St., London W1T 3QT

1   2   3   4   5   6   7   8   9   0

Dedicated to the patients and trainees around the world who, having endured even more than is reflected in the following pages, humbled and enriched us.

Contents

Foreword

Since the advent of energy psychology and eye movement desensitization and reprocessing (EMDR), cross-fertilization between the systems has proliferated. Certainly this has been the norm throughout the history of science and technology, as practitioners of various trades—not only psychotherapy—attempt to cleave and synergistically recombine elements of different systems to produce more vigorous hybrids. Joining the understandings and methodologies of energy psychology with those of EMDR affords such a possibility. John Hartung and Michael Galvin have pioneered this mission in their work and in this book.

Not long ago I discovered the tremendous value of EMDR. In addition to resolving my own long-standing trauma via energy psychology and EMDR, described in *Energy Diagnostic and Treatment Methods* (2000a), I have successfully treated a number of clients with these methods.

An early attempt of mine to integrate these approaches was with a client who suffered from social phobia to such an extent that she remained practically mute during our sessions, unable to talk comfortably with me even after months of treatment. To no avail, I tried a wide range of therapeutic approaches with her. In every respect, except for rapport and comfort, she was compliant. Being moderately obese, she also wanted to lose weight and I was not helping her to get results in that area either.

After I received training in thought field therapy (TFT) and EMDR, my client agreed to give these therapies a try in hopes of resolving her social phobia. At first I attempted the basic EMDR protocol diligently for an entire session, and nothing seemed to happen. Her discomfort did not reduce or increase and she did not appear to get anything out of the varied sets of eye movements that I was using at that time. No movement. No insight. Nothing! Could it be that EMDR was not as effective as I thought?

Then several days later she called me to ask if "that eye movement therapy" could have made her recall things from her past that she had forgotten or repressed. I told her it was my understanding that this could happen. Although I inquired, she would not discuss any details over the phone. I was left wondering until our next session, which we moved up because she was experiencing much discomfort.

During most of the follow-up visit my client remained reticent except to say that what she recalled was very upsetting. It was only during the final few (safe) minutes of the session, after I helped her to relieve some of the discomfort via the TFT "tapping therapy" that she agreed to relay some "details." In her typical style, our definitions of *details* were polar opposite. She simply said that her mother had embarrassed and shamed her. She preferred not to report any further about the embarrassment. "Maybe next time," she said. It was the proverbial cliff-hanger!

Finally during the next session I got the details I was hoping for, after helping her to relieve her embarrassment at telling me through some additional tapping therapy. But my imagination failed to determine what had happened to her as a child. It turns out that her mother was from, as she said, "the old country" and believed that children needed to eat everything on their plates—"clean their plates"—at meals. Like many children, my client did not hold cleaning her plate with the same high regard as her mother did. Therefore, when she did not eat to her mother's liking, she had to sit at the table alone until she cleaned her plate. If the "dillydallying" went on for too long, her mother called everyone who was immediately available—brother, father, even visiting neighbors—to stare at her and berate her. My client recalled that the spectators "yelled and laughed" at her, causing her to become very embarrassed.

Could this have been the hidden reason for her social phobia? Could being observed by others somatically remind her of these frightfully embarrassing events? What if we were to relieve the "child's" trauma with EMDR? Would that catapult her into a more comfortable state of being?

Actually I ended up using a combination of EMDR and TFT, which no doubt other practitioners were working on at the time. Joining these forces resulted in neutralizing the traumatic events and alleviating the embarrassment and shame that interfered with my client's enjoyment of social interactions. She also started to lose weight without struggle. Was her eating disorder an integral aspect of the social phobia, integrated into her psyche from the plate-cleaning traumas?

Interestingly and perhaps expectedly, these changes threatened her husband, since his now socially comfortable and increasingly trimmer spouse was quite different from the person he had married. This led the way for some needed joint sessions that helped them to create a much more interesting and satisfying life together. That was in 1993.

In 1995, two years after I began presenting TFT in various areas of the United States, Michael Galvin invited me to bring TFT to Colorado Springs and Denver. At that time I also met John Hartung. John and Michael readily embraced the conviction that TFT was an important tool in the service of people suffering from trauma and other clinical problems.

To say the least, these two psychologists are a rare breed. Schooled in the traditional methods of research, assessment, and therapy, they took the leap (never recklessly though) and received training in EMDR, a most revolutionary and controversial approach to treatment. Soon they became facilitators and then EMDR trainers, ones who brought this amazing method to Spanish-speaking countries that had been ravaged by natural disasters and civil war. When I met them, they were ready to take another leap—a quantum leap—into the even stranger universe of subtle energies and kinesiology. And what fueled this for them? Why would they go from the strangeness of EMDR to the bizarreness of TFT? In my experience John and Michael are compassionate, scientifically minded professionals who eagerly seek to relieve human suffering and to investigate more about what makes us tick. And if that means delving into out-of-the-ordinary ways, they would say, "Why not?"

After years of experience with EMDR and energy psychology, these gentlemen have arrived at a well-grounded integrative approach that enhances the power of both modalities. Their psychotherapeutic acumen in Gestalt, solution focused, behavioral and cognitive methods, transactional analysis, the range of energy psychology, common sense, and many more areas becomes readily apparent in these chapters. What we have here is more than energy psychology with EMDR or vice versa. Here we have seasoned clinicians with the courage and willingness to step outside the box and to transform it into a needed evolutionary shape.

Psychotherapists and researchers trained in EMDR and energy psychology, as well as students of human behavior change will find the wealth of clinical knowledge and technique in this book to be of tremendous value. I would encourage all therapists to explore this work and to integrate these tools into their repertoire. This is the dawning of the new age in psychological therapy. Enjoy the sunrise.

Fred P. Gallo, Ph.D.
Energy Psychology Series Editor
April 2002

Preface

As clinical and consulting psychologists, we have continually searched for ever better ways to help people. At this point after almost 60 years of combined practice, we have come to rely on energy psychology (EP) and eye movement desensitization and reprocessing (EMDR) as our preferred methods. In this book we present the clinical findings that have led us to believe that these methods excel—especially in combination—in helping clients achieve profound change and growth, usually quickly and with stable results. While clinical impressions eventually must be verified by scientific evidence, advances in practice almost always precede scientific validation. We expect to modify these methods as what we learn from research catches up with or surpasses what we learn from clinical practice.

Some 60,000 individuals have been trained in EMDR (Robbie Dunton, personal communication, August 8, 2001). We have found no estimate of the number of those trained in all of the EP methods, or even in those based on meridian theory. Sandmeier and Cooper (2000) write that over 30,000 have been trained in TFT alone.

We hope to persuade energy therapists to look at the richness that EMDR has to offer, keeping in mind that the interests of some clients sometimes might be better served by treatment with EMDR than EP. We also hope to convince EMDR clinicians to consider using energy techniques as additional resources for those times when EMDR stalls. For readers yet untrained in either, we offer an overview of the two brief therapies that have transformed our professional lives.

We have collaborated on various projects since we first worked together in a community mental health agency in 1974, and we have continued to share ideas, often on long bicycle trips, on how to broaden our traditional graduate school training. For over a dozen years we have worked together as executive coaches. We became so impressed with the healing power of EP and EMDR that we began to train others in both approaches. Either together or separately we have conducted therapy sessions and training courses for both professional and nonprofessional participants in 13 countries, in Europe, Asia, and the Americas.

The case studies in this book are true stories about our trainees, supervisees, or clients (we use the terms *client* and *patient* interchangeably). Many of the examples are disguised to protect the identities of the individuals mentioned. In some cases we pieced together data from more than one individual to protect confidentiality further. To limit confusion, we use the pronoun *I*, followed by J. H. or M. G., when we are describing particular clients or a project of special interest to only one of us. When discussing our collaborative projects, we use the pronoun *we*.

ABOUT JOHN

In my early professional years, I looked for more effective treatment strategies among the traditional psychotherapies. I spent long hours observing and listening to many of the "masters." I learned about optimism while listening to Abe Maslow and Victor Frankl and about intuition while watching Virginia Satir and Arnold Lazarus. I reflected on my thinking errors in the presence of Albert Ellis, then Aaron Beck, Christine Padesky, and Don Meichenbaum. It was moving to watch Alexander Lowen perform his bioenergetic magic on his 80th birthday, and unsettling to have my questions challenged by Joseph Wolpe and Thomas Szasz. I experienced the warm power of Mary Goulding and Carl Rogers, put up with the provocative Sal Minuchin, and endured many analytic interpretations. I meditated, punched pillows, ran long distances, fasted, and dissected dreams on my pilgrimage in search of ways to be of use to my clients.

Each time I found something useful from one of my teachers and experiences, and I shared my discoveries: I told friends, taught what I was learning in university courses, conducted off-campus trainings, and offered what seemed to be useful strategies to my patients.

But it was not enough. Too many of my clients did not seem to benefit much for very long. Growing increasingly doubtful of the promises of psychotherapy as I knew it, I took a sabbatical in 1989 from my private practice and traveled around Europe on my bicycle. I then taught for a semester with the Fulbright program in Peru, telling my students about the latest in psychotherapy and about the frustrations that caused me to question its efficacy.

In 1992 I heard about the unusual approach to psychotherapy called EMDR. This preposterous-sounding method seemed too good to be true, but I always have that glimmer of naïve hope that psychology might yet prove useful in helping people to change within a reasonable period of time. I signed up for EMDR training and was hooked after my first hour with the inspirational Francine Shapiro. I began to use EMDR in my practice the day after that training ended, and since then my clients have consistently reported more benefit from psychotherapy than I had ever heard before.

EMDR has also been a blessing in my personal life. About six years ago I had been mountain biking with my buddy Michael Merrifield, who writes books about "gonzo rides in Colorado." Just trying to follow him down a particularly gnarly ravine got me in over my head—quite literally—as I flipped twice that day and landed upside down each time. My helmet protected my skull, but the rest of my body suffered. The next morning I could not lift my head from the pillow because of a muscle spasm in my neck and shoulder. Consulting with my primary care physician, a chiropractor, and a physical therapist did little to relieve the pain. Three months later I still felt significant muscle pain, and on awakening in the morning, I still had to use a hand to lift my head off the pillow.

At about that time I volunteered to supervise someone who was completing her training to become an EMDR facilitator. Since there was no client available, I agreed to be the treatment subject. I felt emotionally fine that day, I said, and could recall no unfinished business in my life. However, I did remember that a week earlier I had butterflies in my stomach as I introduced myself to a group of corporate leaders. At the moment it had been unpleasant; now, however, it was but a vague memory.

The trainee did a nice job having me imagine back to the previous week. I was able to get a picture and negative belief about myself, but not much emotion. She then asked me to notice the picture, repeat the negative belief, and then simply to "notice what comes up" as she moved her hands back and forth in front of me and I followed her fingers with my eyes. At one point I noted that my neck and shoulder hurt. "I fell off my bike," I explained. There was no traumatic memory maintaining it, I assured her. It had a purely mechanical explanation, I insisted. She asked me for a bit of detail, then suggested that I simply pay attention to what I had just reported, and move my eyes again as she waved her hands in front of me. Much to my surprise I drifted back to a memory of presenting myself at another time in my life, a time I was reciting a poem to a group of peers in high school. I recalled being very nervous. Apparently I had been reciting too fast because the face of the teacher then flashed into my memory as he shouted, "SLOW DOWN," startling everyone in the room and giving me a pretty good scare. The tears that then welled up in me, and the shame and anger that I had not fully admitted to before, further surprised me. And with the apparent randomness that so characterizes EMDR, I began processing memories that connected the butterflies from the previous week, with the recitation from decades before, with the physical back pain that I would not have tied to either of these memories prior to this EMDR experience.

Within 45 minutes I was able to recall both memories without feeling any upset. I then put my hand to my neck and shoulder. No pain. I bent and twisted. Still no pain. Six years later I remain pain free and grateful to my colleague who more than reciprocated for the help I had offered her.

Then Michael Galvin told me about another odd-sounding psychotherapy called thought field therapy (TFT), and I took a course taught by psychologist Fred Gallo. As I applied TFT, I noticed it seemed to work as well as EMDR and had additional virtues.

After a few months, however, I was using TFT infrequently. I was finding it had minimal impact on the clients I treated. I had also become rather skeptical about the claims being made about its efficacy.

To humor my old friend Michael, I signed up for advanced TFT training, again with Fred Gallo. Fred opened his Level 2 training by asking those of us in attendance to report our success rates with TFT. I confessed that my clients did not respond very favorably, certainly not as positively to energy therapy as they did to EMDR. The other trainees in attendance that day, to the contrary, reported both high rates of success and much enthusiasm. Fred then invited me to the front of the training room to be checked out energetically.

Fred offered to muscle test me for the possibility of an energy interference, called a *psychological reversal* or *energy reversal*, that might account for the trouble I had been having using the basic energy techniques effectively (see Chapters 1 and 3). These reversals will sometimes show up in the middle of treatment and interfere with therapy, much as a negative belief (e.g., "I really don't deserve to be feeling this good") might appear and disrupt treatment that is based on positive thinking. To check on his hypothesis, Fred asked me to make certain statements as he tested my muscles by pressing down on my extended arm. He and I then went through every possible energy reversal statement in the training manual, for example: "I deserve to use energy methods effectively," "It's possible for me to be effective," "I will do the work necessary . . . ," "I will allow myself to . . . ," and so forth. Alas, nothing turned up that looked like an energy reversal. Being the sensible educator he is, Fred then turned to me:

Fred: I'm confused, John. What do you think is going on?
John: I don't know if this makes sense, but I have this odd idea that I can't get too good at using TFT. Somehow being highly effective using energy therapy might make me disloyal to the people in the EMDR community, and I feel such commitment to them. Does that sound crazy?
Fred: Energy reversals take strange forms at times. Let's test for what you said.

Fred muscle tested me for this hunch and finally found something that looked like it could account for the trouble I had been having using TFT effectively. On an energy level and quite unconsciously, I had come to associate success using TFT with disloyalty to EMDR. Fred then corrected me for that particular psychological reversal and the subsequent muscle test suggested that I was "cured" of that particular interference.

The end of this short story is that later in that training I worked with another participant who had been trying for several months to resolve a gruesome memory of having been tortured as a child. For several months prior to the TFT workshop, the participant had been using EMDR and other therapies with a very experienced and well-trained private practitioner but would dissociate every time he began to work on the memory. Because of earlier feedback from his regular therapist and his ease at dissociating from his truly horrible memory of abuse, he was beginning to think he might have multiple personalities. I began to use some energy techniques I learned the same day that Fred corrected my disloyalty psychological reversal, and the participant finally was able to resolve the traumatic emotions associated with this particularly difficult memory, without dissociating.

After this and similar experiences, I was finally able to make use of TFT. Not only did the techniques begin to work consistently, but also I was able to appreciate the ways that reversals can occur, and be corrected, on the energy level. I was reminded again of how we sometimes learn more under conditions of failure, and how we invent when the basic tools we already have no longer suffice.

ABOUT MICHAEL

My graduate training involved an interesting range of schools of thought, as some professors in the department, including H. S. Penny-packer, were very active in investigating and teaching basic behavioral psychology while Sidney Jourard and others pioneered humanistic psychology. Vernon Van De Riet returned from a strange-sounding place in California—Esalen—with a new method, Gestalt therapy, which he taught to a group of students, including me. I settled on Gestalt therapy as my principal modality. During my internship, I was introduced to a method that was fast becoming popular among psychotherapists, but of which I had heard not a word in graduate school, transactional analysis. Though a brilliant intellectual therapy, it lacked in emotional content, and so I, along with many others, combined it with Gestalt therapy (James & Jongeward, 1971). On be-ginning practice, I founded and directed the Pikes Peak Area Transac-tional Analysis Seminar. This Gestalt-enhanced transactional analysis and its advances, such as redecision therapy (Goulding & Goulding, 1997), was my main modality for years. An important concept in transactional analysis is that under parental influence, each of us makes decisions in early childhood that form a life "script" (Berne, 1972). I have found understanding the nature of these decisions to be helpful in planning and carrying out treatment, and I still use life script analy-sis to help choose targets for therapeutic intervention.

I learned much from many of the same teachers as John and have also incorporated elements from many sources including Harold Greenwald's *Direct Decision Therapy* (1989), Frank Farrelly's *Provocative Therapy* (1989), and the varieties of solution-focused therapy (O'Hanlon & Weiner-Davis, 1989). For years I have been using the framework in Lazarus's *Practice of Multimodal Therapy* (1989) to conceptualize and guide my work.

Soon after he became involved with EMDR, John told me about it. At first I was quite skeptical: "This woman in California is curing serious disorders in people by moving her fingers in front of their faces and having them follow with their eyes?" John admitted that skepticism was also his first reaction, and it is similar to the one we now often get when we introduce the method to others. Nevertheless, I was persuaded by John's continuing enthusiasm and that of other trusted colleagues, including Jim Knipe and Bob Tinker. After a few months, I took Level I training in EMDR.

At about the same time I saw an ad for a "five-minute phobia cure" in a publication from a division of the American Psychological Association. Immediately skeptical, I turned the page, but then turned back, considering that if it really would help, I owed it to my clients to investigate. The tape and documents I received began my introduction to Roger Callahan's thought field therapy (TFT). This form of psychotherapy was even more peculiar than EMDR, but I got good results from simply studying and applying the techniques described. Interested in more training, I was referred by Dr. Callahan to Fred Gallo, who agreed to come to Colorado to conduct an early TFT Level 1 training. I told John, who was open enough to take the first training presented by Fred in the region. As we applied it, TFT seemed to work as well as EMDR, and both had complementary virtues.

I readily took to the energy concepts and soon was practicing them with the bulk of my clients.

Case example:

Early on, I described the case of a client who was fearful about an upcoming computed axial tomography scan (Galvin, 1995). In fact, she had called off a previous scan halfway through, in spite of having been given Vicodin intravenously. In the office, we lowered her anxiety to negligible levels with some tapping therapy and she left confident of being able to undergo the procedure, which had been re-scheduled for that Friday. Her anxiety returned in the days before the appointment, however, and she asked me to go to the hospital to work with her there if need be. We met before the procedure and did some tapping therapy to lower her fear again. In the examination room, I sat with her as she went into the scanner. A couple of times she asked to be pulled out, we did a little more tapping, and she continued the examination. About halfway through the procedure, my schedule required me to leave. The client said she thought she would be all right. When I returned to the office the following Monday, I found a message the client had left on my answering machine: "Thank you for helping me; it was about the most relaxing time I have ever had." She later reported that over the following weeks other symptoms of a long-standing claustrophobia had disappeared, though we had not specifically addressed them.

COMBINING THE METHODS

The final step for us was to begin blending energy approaches with EMDR. The first impetus for this arose when we independently discovered that using an energy exercise during an EMDR session could help a client to process trauma more efficiently. With time we experimented more and more with using energy techniques with EMDR to contain an emotionally upsetting experience, help to finish a session where the subjective units of disturbance (SUD) score was still too high, or slow down the dissociative process. We also began to notice that clients who were reworking the same issue over and over without much resolution were often helped after we corrected for a psychological reversal—much as Fred did with John in his advanced energy training course. We found we could introduce these strange energy procedures in the midst of EMDR processing with very little resistance from patients, and the techniques worked wonderfully.

Case example:

In an EMDR session, a client with a history of being verbally abused determined that her target issue had a subjective units of disturbance (SUD) score of 9. (SUD is determined by a 0 to 10 scale, where 0 means "no disturbance" and 10 means "highest disturbance.") After different "channels," or aspects, of the issue had been processed, the SUD level was down to 6. After a few more minutes of work it was at 5. The next couple of sets of bilateral stimulation had very little effect. When I asked, "What do you get now?" the client repeatedly responded, "It's the same thing. He's still standing there yelling how stupid I am."

This treatment block could be targeted with EMDR techniques that Shapiro (2001a) calls interweaves. I instead decided to conceptualize the problem as a psychological reversal (see Chapter 3), so I asked the client to tap the side hand point while saying three times, "I deeply accept myself even though I still have some of this problem." No changes were immediately apparent in the client, but when bilateral stimulation was reinitiate—still targeting "the same thing"—treatment progressed rapidly and the SUD rating was soon at 0.

A second impetus for combining the methods came from administrators of forensic treatment programs. Early efforts using EMDR with criminals produced two distinct problems. One was that many offender-clients refused to use EMDR, or to continue to do so when they realized it would likely require them to relive traumatic memories, a particularly discouraging proposition for a person who has survived by suppressing or diverting certain emotions. Another problem was created by a group of newly trained and very enthusiastic EMDR clinicians who had been using EMDR rather inappropriately with offenders. In some cases a client left what appeared to be a successful EMDR session, only to return to his community corrections halfway house talking about wanting to commit suicide. After several threats of this sort (no deaths, we are happy to report), program administrators began to believe that EMDR, far from being the treatment of choice for this population, was too dangerous to be considered at all. As detailed in Chapter 9, we were able to continue by blending energy therapy into EMDR for the sake of both clients and administrators. Eventually we worked as therapists in a research program with an offender population.

A third motive arose from discussions with student-trainees. The first trainings we conducted were in EMDR. We then began to offer training in energy methods, either to our EMDR students who wanted to learn more about the innovative therapies or to paraprofessionals who would not have been eligible for EMDR training. In both our EMDR and energy therapy seminars we began to hear from students who were frustrated in their work with certain clients who responded to neither of these methods alone. Since our trainees' experiences paralleled our own, we began to tell them how we were combining EMDR with energy therapies with positive results. Eventually we organized a training format that included blending strategies.

Our experiences in discovering EMDR and energy therapies, then blending them, are not particularly unique. Many of our colleagues have been on their own pilgrimages in search of better solutions to psychological problems. Some, like Michael, learned the two methods and took to them immediately. Others, as in John's experience with TFT, began or became skeptical of the new paradigm, and needed to revisit them before they felt legitimate. Still others, however, began using the methods enthusiastically but eventually slipped back to old habits. One of our colleagues, for example, referred a client for a consult:

Colleague: I just don't seem to be very good at using EMDR.
Question: What has been your experience so far?
Colleague: Well, I get the usual miracles, quick responses, problems resolved, client is happy with the therapy, that sort of thing. But it just does not seem to fit my style.

What does "not fit my style" mean? we wonder. Could this be a case of a psychological reversal, accessible to muscle testing and correctable with energy treatment? Could the client's problem be triggering something similar in the therapist, perhaps an unresolved traumatic memory? Part of our purpose in this book is to suggest ways for healing distress. And part is to encourage therapists to apply the techniques from EMDR and the energy therapies to themselves.

Sometimes by resolving their own personal issues (traumas, energy blocks, blocking beliefs), therapists can eliminate what has been interfering with their ability to use the treatment strategies effectively with others. We know that many of our colleagues have had experiences similar to the one John described earlier, and that by attending to them, they find the problem is not so much a "matter of style" but rather unfinished personal business that limits them and their work. From time to time in the book, we will visit the issue of therapist variables and will mention ideas for how therapists can use both EMDR and energy techniques on themselves. The old adage "Physician heal thyself" has become more meaningful to us since learning these new methods and raising our standards for treatment efficacy.

ACKNOWLEDGEMENTS

We first thank our teachers—Francine Shapiro, Fred Gallo, Gary Craig, Tapas Fleming, Greg Nicosia, and Larry Nims—both for sharing their knowledge and for allowing us to carry on their work in our own trainings.

Many individuals in different countries have sponsored, collaborated with, and educated one or both of us through the years. Pablo and Raquel Solvey invented their own integrative approach in Argentina and have hosted us marvelously, and María Elena Lesmi often leaves her Buenos Aires home for international trainings with our team. Ligia Barascout de Piedrasanta has been brilliant in establishing an advanced therapies institute in Guatemala, where we have been her frequent houseguests. Emre Konuk, from his veranda overlooking the Bosporus, has coordinated dozens of Turkish therapists working with trauma victims. Esly Carvalho inspired a postgraduate training program in the innovative therapies in Quito, Ecuador, where she is psychodramatist extraordinaire. And Reginaldo Hernandez, having used his years in political exile to prepare himself as a psychiatrist and acupuncturist, headed up an interdisciplinary team in his native El Salvador prior to his untimely death. Others on this very short list include Luciana Weissmann and Ignacio Jarero in Mexico; Vilma Castilla and Yamilett Mejía Palma in Nicaragua; Visal Tumani supporting the Turkish team from Germany; François Bonnet who coordinates EMDR France from Aix-en-Provence; Reyhanna Raabat Sedat in South Africa; and team members from Colombia, Venezuela, and various parts of Indonesia.

Words are inadequate to express the depth of our appreciation for the initiative and energy of the U.S.-based international team, whose members include, in order of appearance, Liz Snyker, Christie Sprowls, Cathy Wickham, Laurel Parnell, Priscilla Marquis, Barbara Zelwer, Michael Keller, and Nancy Errebo. Without the support of Robbie Dunton, much of this work would have died on the vine.

We have benefited immensely from long discussions with other energy psychology and EMDR practitioners in Colorado Springs, especially Nikki Brooker, Collette Sheets, Beverly Schoninger, Nancy Bowers, Ellie Corriel, and Peter Philbrick. Our colleagues Bob Tinker, Jim Knipe, and Sandra Wilson supported us from the beginning in EMDR and continue significant work in the method.

We wish to thank our illustrator, Langdon Foss (www.lllama.com) for his patience and skillful work.

Our editors, Regina Dahlgren Ardini, Mary Babcock, Deborah Malmud, Michael McGandy, and Casey Ruble, provided insightful commentary and support that helped us clarify the content.

Ideas in this book came to us almost exclusively during our contacts with clients, supervisees, and trainees, and we apologize for not being able to remember all the instances in which individuals offered a particular insight or lesson that we describe herein.

Finally we acknowledge the dedication of Professor Lee Becker, initially skeptical but then a dedicated and valuable researcher of EMDR. An inspirational supporter of the scientist-practitioner model, he lived to see patients benefit from his careful work but not to see the publication of this volume.

John Hartung, Psy.D.
Michael Galvin, Ph.D.
Colorado Springs
September, 2002

Chapter 1

The Basics

ENERGY PSYCHOLOGY

Energy psychology (EP) has a long history and a short history. The long history is of the discovery and use of the subtle but potent human energy system and it seems to have begun at many times and in many places. Gallo (1999) cited ancient knowledge of such an energy system among the peoples of Arabia and Brazil, the Bantu tribes of Africa, and the Eskimos. The development of yoga in India brings us the knowledge of chakra energy centers. An Egyptian papyrus of 1150 BCE seems to refer to the meridian system.

The general concept of energy systems has been used and investigated for millennia, and exists in the healing lore of many if not all cultures. Early in Western history Hippocrates called it *vis medicatrix naturae*. It is known as *chi* or *qi* in China, *prana* in the yoga tradition of India and Tibet, *yesod* in the Jewish cabal tradition, *ki* in Japan, *baraka* by the Sufis, *wakan* by the Lakota Indians, *orenda* by the Iroquois, and *megbe* by the Ituri Pygmies (Eden, 1998).

1

History and Theory

The number of energy systems recognized by a given culture or practitioner varies considerably. Eden (1998) wrote that there are eight
major systems: the aura, the chakras, the meridians, the Celtic weave,
the basic grid, the five rhythms, the triple warmer, and the strange
flows. The systems are said to have in common a vital energy that
influences health and well-being. The first three are used in EP.

The energy field which surrounds all living things is called the aura
or, as pertains to EP, the human biofield. It has been depicted as a
radiance around Buddha, light coming from the fingers of gods of India,
and as halos behind or above the heads of Christian holy figures. Persons able to see the aura sometimes describe it as extending out for
several inches, composed of many layers, corresponding to aspects of
the human being such as physical, emotional, mental, and spiritual. The
state of the (parts of the) aura is said to be diagnostic of the state of
these aspects. Devices have been invented which purport to photograph
the aura, including Kirlian photography (Lambrou & Pratt, 2000) and
the Coggins aura camera (http://www.auraphoto.com).*

Bioenergy is said to enter the body through seven energy centers
called chakras, described as spinning circles or funnels. *Chakra* is a
Sanskrit word meaning "wheel." Six are located along a line paralleling
the spinal column, and the seventh is said to extend out of the top of
the head (Mentgen & Bulbrook, 1996). The chakras connect with the
meridians and other energy levels. Pert (2000) believes she has found
neurophysiological correlates with the first six chakras, and considers
them to be "minibrains," points of electrical and chemical concentration that receive, process, and distribute information within what she
calls the *bodymind*. Chakras are first mentioned in the Hindu Vedas
perhaps as early as the 15th century BCE, and appear in the Upani-
shads, Sutras, and other writing to the present. Part of the function of
chakras is to connect energy with the meridians.

The meridian energy system is said to involve 14 energy pathways:
2 central vessels that run vertically on the center of the front and back
of the body, plus 12 primary meridians that exist bilaterally. Each
meridian is said to have two channels of energy. One flows close to

---

* The first aura phot was made by Nicola Tesla in 1891. The method was popularized
  by Semyon Davidovich Kirlian whose method was announced in the 1930s. There
  has been much refinement, including the technology of Guy Coggins who developed
  a camera to videotape and capture on computer the aura as it changes in real time.

the skin and is presumably the one accessible to an acupuncturist and an energy psychotherapist. The other, flowing deeper inside the torso, passes through the organ with which it is associated. In our practice and teaching we are concerned only with the surface channels. Along each of the meridians are the acupuncture points, some 365 in the 12 primary meridians alone (Wildish, 2000).

Most people associate acupuncture with China, and indeed the great majority of the development and use of this meridian healing system was carried out there. The tradition may have started with Qigong masters who learned to sense and move energy, and gave rise to disciplines including Tai Chi, Kung Fu, and acupuncture. The definitive text on acupuncture was written about 2600 BCE; it remains the earliest documentation of any type of energy system. Since an oral tradition doubtless preceded this work, practitioners had been developing the field for considerable time before the 27th century BCE. It is often assumed, therefore, that the discovery of a network of energy pathways in the body occurred in China. However, history is often not that easy or clear. Concurrently, though not testified to by written documents, work was underway in Europe. In 1991, the mummified body of a man was discovered after it emerged from the alpine glacier that had preserved it. This man lived about 3200 BCE in the area that is now the Tyrol region of Austria and Italy. Among the many findings emerging from detailed examinations were the facts that he suffered from rheumatism and that there were tattoos on his skin. Acupuncturists noticed that the marks coincide significantly with the locations they use today to treat rheumatoid arthritis. Unfortunately (according to some of us), the energy therapy tradition was not continued in the Western world. Westerners went their "scientific," rational, objective way, leading to outward exploration, while Eastern compatriots looked inward, expanding different but valuable paradigms. Recently Westerners have rediscovered energy therapy, largely through exposure to acupuncture which is now recognized by the National Institutes of Health (NIH) as an effective treatment for a growing number of medical disorders. Shortly thereafter, therapists began to think in terms of these concepts, which brings us to the short history, the bringing of energy theory into the field of psychotherapy.

Our condensed recitation of the short history begins in the 1960s, when chiropractor George Goodheart, building on the knowledge of manual muscle testing (Kendall & Kendall, 1949), developed applied kinesiology. Among the many discoveries incorporated into applied kinesiology was the joining of muscle testing with meridian theory to promote physical health.

In the following decade, psychiatrist John Diamond was trained in applied kinesiology. Applying muscle testing to psychiatry, he discovered that the different meridians and their associated organs were related to different emotions. He used muscle testing to determine which meridian was involved in a client's problem, by directing the client to place a hand over the corresponding organ and state affirmations intended to restore balance. He concluded that the order in which the meridians were addressed was crucial in treatment. His first system of diagnosis and treatment was called behavioral kinesiology (Diamond, 1979). He also found that clients sometimes think and act in ways contrary to their own good and own intentions. He called this phenomenon "reversal of the body's morality" but found few ways to address it. Diamond's work continues to evolve significantly as he refines and modifies the theory and therapy procedures.

Building on Diamond's early work, psychologist Roger Callahan, after training in applied kinesiology, developed a method he called the Callahan techniques, later thought field therapy (TFT), and currently Callahan Techniques-TFT (Callahan & Callahan, 1996). Callahan uses muscle testing in assessment but developed new procedures for treatment. Having found the organ involved with the negative emotional state, he treats a related meridian rather than the organ itself. There is little documentation on the process of discovery Callahan went through to develop TFT. He probably got the idea of percussing (tapping) from applied kinesiology (Walther, 1988). Initially, he tapped on *both* ends (or near the end points) of meridians and on *both* pairs of the bilateral meridians. He next realized that tapping is necessary only on one end of one meridian of the pair, and that the *client* can (and should) do it. He found that tapping a meridian point was as effective as, and less intrusive than, stimulating the point with one of the acupuncture techniques (e.g. the insertion of needles, burning of herbs on the acupoint site, focusing of laser light or electricity, manipulation of muscles associated with specific meridians).

Callahan also believes that the order in which the points are treated is essential, a position no longer held by all energy therapists. The process of uncovering these points is called *diagnosing*. By this Callahan does not mean reaching a diagnosis according to the *Diagnostic and Statistical Manual of Mental Disorders* (American Psychiatric Association, 2000) but rather using muscle testing to determine which points need to be tapped and in what order. He added a procedure called *eye roll* at the end of successful treatment, probably again incorporating elements from applied kinesiology.

Another of Callahan's innovations was the *nine gamut treatments* (9g), so named because the client runs through a gamut of nine quick actions while tapping a meridian point. These procedures, derived from applied kinesiology, are also said to potentiate treatment.

As he treated many clients with different problems, he discovered that many problems could be resolved using a typical tapping sequence. He called these *algorithms* and made them available in books and videos. Without knowing Callahan's "diagnostic" procedure, clinicians and laypersons could treat problems with a very high rate of success, simply by having the client tap a predetermined sequence of points for a given problem.

Callahan also identified what he terms the *collarbone breathing problem*, called *neurological disorganization* by most energy therapists, as well as a treatment for it. He expanded Diamond's notion of the reversal of the body's morality into what he calls *psychological reversal*, and identified various aspects of it. Moreover, he developed treatments for these reversals, making progress possible in heretofore untreatable cases. Callahan identified another set of blocks to treatment, *energy toxins*. These "toxins" are ingested, inhaled, or absorbed substances such as corn, perfume, or laundry detergent. He cites many cases to show how identification and elimination of such a substance from a client's environment can allow previously blocked treatment to proceed.

Finally, in what he claims is a significant advance over the diagnostic method, Callahan invented a method called the *voice technology*. By sampling the client's voice over the telephone, this machine "diagnoses" which points need to be treated and in what order. Callahan considers his muscle testing procedure and voice technology to be proprietary information and trade secrets, and charges sums that seem unusually high to many practitioners for training in the diagnostic method and much higher for the voice technology. He believes the exceptional effectiveness of the techniques justifies the fees.

He imposed restraints on his trainees against divulging the methodologies to others. Gregory Nicosia uses the term *Thought Energy Synchronization Therapy* for his method and Callahan brought legal action against him believing the name was too similar to *Thought Field Therapy*. As a result of the proceedings, the term *Thought Field Therapy* is ruled generic. Later, Sheila Bender, Victoria Britt, and John Diepold (the

BDB Group) were sued by Callahan. After an out-of-court settlement the three have been able to write and go on teaching thought field therapy diagnostic and treatment models which they continue to modify. Their work is now called *Evolving Thought Field Therapy* (EvTFT).

In the mid-1990s Callahan authorized Fred Gallo to offer programs that taught the TFT algorithms, and these methods began to be widely practiced. Gallo went on to write extensively in the field and to elaborate his own method in *Energy Diagnostic and Treatment Methods* (2000a). Gallo's approach includes elements of Diamond's and Callahan's systems as well as innovations, including the use of muscle testing to determine if there is more than one point on a meridian to treat.

Another of Callahan's early trainees was a layperson, Gary Craig. He and his partner, Adrienne Fowlie, even bought the voice technology machine, but after years of successfully using it, they began to suspect that the complicated procedure was not necessary, nor was the order in which the points were tapped. They consequently developed a procedure in which the client taps almost all the TFT points. Craig claims as high a success rate with his new emotional freedom techniques (EFT) as with voice technology. He generously offers his basic treatment manual and additional assistance at no cost on the EFT Web site (see Appendix B). His method is a "comprehensive algorithm," possibly the most frequently practiced energy technique. We teach it in all our EP training courses and reports from our trainees and practitioners who have learned the technique elsewhere are consistently positive. Inclusion of the word *comprehensive* means that the same basic form of EFT can be applied to just about every problem presenting in practice. This does not include learning socialization techniques, improving communication with one's spouse, or parent training, though EFT can be applied to any related disturbing emotion, thought, or body sensation that comes up in these situations. Craig (1998) added sophisticated techniques to his method, but we believe most clinicians practice basic EFT, or even an abbreviation of it.

Larry Nims (1998), another early student of Callahan's, independently developed a different comprehensive algorithm which clinicians also enthusiastically received. His algorithm went through rapid changes to the point that it is now a form of suggestion to the unconscious. Most recently Nims (2002) eliminated all energy tapping from his model. Many clinicians continue to practice the earlier comprehensive algorithm and claim success.

John Diepold (2000) developed an alternative to tapping. In his touch-and-breathe (TAB) technique, instead of tapping the meridian point a few times, the client simply touches it, usually with one to four fingers depending on the location, for the duration of one natural breath. Diepold offers a solid rationale for TAB, and many practitioners have found it as effective as tapping though research on differential effectiveness has not yet been done. Whenever we refer to *tapping* in this book, the TAB technique can be equally applied. This is also true for the "gamut spot" but not for the "sore spot," which is rubbed not tapped. One meridian whose end point is not tapped in most energy therapies is the bladder (Bl) meridian. The point tapped on that meridian is the second, Bl-2 (eyebrow) (see Figure 3.4). It is tapped instead of the end point, Bl-1 (inside eye), because clients sometimes accidentally hit their eyeball while trying to tap the inside eye point. With TAB, point Bl-1 can be used for treatment.

A final technique popular among energy therapists comes from the acupuncture tradition, but not from the line of development of psychotherapies just described. In 1993, acupuncturist Tapas Fleming happened on a technique that involves simultaneously touching meridian points, a chakra, and the occipital region of the head. It arose from an insight she had while pondering the fact that often the allergies her clients had were related to trauma. A couple of years later she introduced the procedure to the EP community as "making peace with your trauma," soon changing the name to Tapas acupressure technique (TAT) and developing it into a seven-step procedure (2001a, 2002). If tapping in a given sequence is an algorithm, techniques such as TAT might be seen as "chords" in that several points are stimulated at once. Originally brought to bear on the effects of trauma, TAT has gained considerable popularity as clinicians have found it rapidly effective for a wide variety of problems.

There is one relatively popular form of EP that includes work with the chakras, the Seemorg matrix work of Asha Nahoma Clinton (2001a, 2001b, 2001c, 2002). Eden and Feinstein (2002) also include chakra work in their training courses, as does Shaw (2002).

Although not widely known in the United States, aura work has apparently been underway in this country for some time. One of us (M. G.) remembers seeing a psychiatrist demonstrate his use of the aura at a meeting of the American Association of Humanistic Psychology in Estes Park in the mid-1970s. Hover-Kramer (2002) described psychotherapeutic work with both the chakras and aura.

The "heritage" of these and other energy treatments that have been developed is presented in Figure 1.1. We do not have space to discuss all the energy therapies represented in the figure, nor are all energy

FIGURE 1.1 ENERGY PSYCHOLOGY HERITAGE TREE

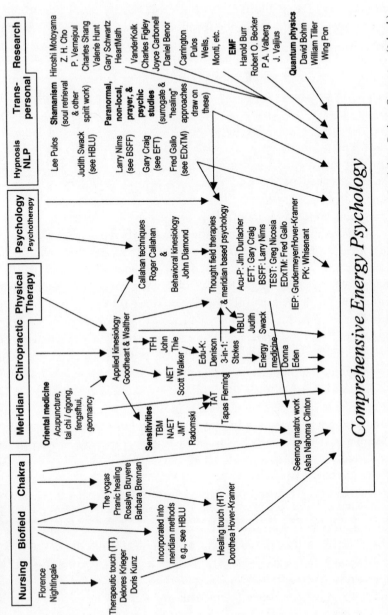

Figure courtesy of David Grudermeyer and Rebecca Grudermeyer (2002). *The Energy Psychology Desktop Companion*, (2d ed.). (Del Mar, CA: Willingness Works).

therapies included in this overview. Interested readers are referred to the publications by the Grudermeyers (2000) and by Gallo (2000a). For a more detailed account of the history of EP, consult Gallo's *Energy Psychology* (1999).

Although endowed with a long history, EP is a recently elaborated, fast-evolving field—even its name is still not settled. It is often called *energy therapy*. The name *energy psychotherapy* has been proposed to dispel the implication that it belongs to psychologists exclusively. We use the term *energy psychology* because it has entered the literature (Gallo, 1999).

According to the founding president of the Association for Comprehensive Energy Psychology, David Grudermeyer, and his colleague Rebecca Grudermeyer (2000), "Energy Psychology is the generic name for an emerging family of experimental rapid-effectiveness tools that utilize the body's energy pathways (meridian acupoints system), energy centers (chakras) and biofield (aura) to assist in addressing psychological, spiritual, mind-body, and peak performance goals" (p. vi).

Legend for Figure 1.1 Energy psychology heritage tree

BSFF   = Be set free fast
HBLU   = Healing from the body level up
TBM   = Total body modification
NAET   = Nambutripad allergy elimination technique
JMT   = Jaffe-Mellor Technique
TAT   = Tapas acupuncture technique
Edu-K   = Educational kinesiology
TFH   = Touch for health
NET   = Neuro Emotional Technique
Acu-P   = Acu-Power
EDxTM   = Energy diagnostic and treatment methods
IEP   = Individualized Energy Psychotherapy
PK   = Psychological kinesiology
NLP   = Neuro-linguistic programming
EMF   = Electromagnetic fields
TEST   = Thought energy synchronization therapy

(Adapted from David Grudermeyer and Rebecca Grudermeyer [2002] *Energy Psychology Desktop Companion* [2d ed.] [Del Mar, CA: Willingness Works]. Used with permission of the authors.)

Principles

The theory and practice of EP rest on several principles. At the foundation is the assumption that there is a complex subtle energy system in the human body. (There is evidence that it also exists in animals and plants.) There are many manifestations of it, but all are characterized by a flow of energy.

One of the ways the energy flows is through the meridians described earlier. When energy flows normally, a person is in a state of health; when the flow is blocked, disorders result. Physical factors can disrupt the flow of energy, but so can psychologically traumatic events. Disturbing thoughts and emotions triggered by traumas affect the meridians, which then affect the sense of well-being, especially when the originally disturbing event, or a similar event, is later brought to mind.

Each meridian is related to an organ, which in turn is related to a set of emotions (see Table 3.2). On each meridian is a number of acupoints that can be treated. If the correct points are treated, the blockage or disturbance in the meridian will be removed and the accompanying emotional disturbance will clear. Practically any problem presented in therapists' offices can be dealt with in this way. There are several methods of treatment, but our version of EP generally uses only tapping or light pressure. Patients can usually reliably report on their own internal state by means of the subjective units of disturbance (SUD) 0 to 10 scale, where 0 means "no disturbance," and 10 means "highest disturbance."

Some problems have several aspects, and not until the presenting one is cleared is an underlying one apparent and accessible to treatment. Unlike the treatment of physical disorders, the patient must be thinking of the problem for it to be treatable. Once brought to mind, the problem will "resonate," or remain accessible for some time.

Treatment can be blocked by a number of factors, including neurological disorganization, psychological reversal, and energy system toxins. These blocks can also be addressed by procedures including tapping or touching the correct acupoints or performing related activities such as rubbing a neurolymphatic reflex and stating affirmations. By means of muscle testing, the therapist can determine which acupoints to treat and the nature of the treatment blocks.

Practice

Using the paradigm just described, we suggest that EP therapists follow a series of seven steps. The therapist's relationship with the client is established in Step 1. Although EP procedures can be carried out with little or no rapport, in the context of ongoing psychotherapy the therapist should assure that all elements of the therapeutic relationship are in place. In Step 2 the therapist informs the client about EP. Because EP is not like typical psychotherapy, when obtaining informed consent, clinicians should include an explanation of the essentials of the method in a manner appropriate to the patient. During history taking, Step 3, clinicians should listen for the possibility of underlying aspects and inquire about possible energy toxins in the patient's environment. In Step 4, when the energy system is readied for treatment, the practitioner treats blocks that are suspected or are discovered through muscle testing. Step 5 involves targeting specific problems for treatment. The practitioner monitors SUD levels and verifies from time to time that the problems are properly held in mind.

Treatment begins with Step 6. Using knowledge of the properties of the meridians, the therapist applies treatments designed to address the targeted problems. They may involve single meridian points, series of them, or a few selected nonmeridian points. The practitioner also can make use of muscle testing or voice technology to locate treatment points. If treatment blocks reappear, they are corrected. By the end of the session the SUD score is usually 0 or 1. If it is not, energy-based strategies for quickly bringing it to that level are employed, or relaxation exercises are used to remove the client's focus from the targeted problems and produce calm. Step 7 closes the session. The therapist briefs the client about future sessions and requests the client to keep a journal of experiences. Journal entries are reviewed during the following session, with particular attention to the appearance of new aspects and the influence of treatment blocks.

EP Compared with Other Psychotherapies

EP stems from a paradigm very different from the approaches used in the rest of psychology and from other disciplines practiced in the Western world. One way to compare the different psychotherapeutic approaches is to examine the level of functioning at which one intervenes. The *behavior* of an individual is the function probably most easily accessed, and behavioral therapists have developed theory and a panoply of techniques for intervening at this level. Other therapies intervene at the *interpersonal* level, either as a principal focus, such as with *family and systems* therapies, or as part of the overall approach, such as in psychoanalysis. Transactional analysis, as its name implies, is another approach based on analytic theory, although it addresses many other aspects of functioning. A "deeper" level of analysis is the *cognitive* level. Rational emotive behavioral therapy and cognitive therapy are among the most well-known methods available for changing thoughts in order to improve emotional well-being. Fewer methods exist for intervening on the *emotional* level itself, with Gestalt therapy perhaps the most well known.

At the *chemical* level a comparison can be made between EP and pharmacological approaches in psychotherapy. For the treatment of posttraumatic stress disorder (PTSD), for example, a psychiatrist might prescribe any of several psychotropic drugs, perhaps Zoloft, which has been shown effective in the treatment of PTSD symptoms (Brady, Healy, Norcross, & Guy, 2000). Whether or not practitioners are aware of the exact molecular dynamics, they can be confident that the drug will inhibit the uptake of serotonin at neurotransmitter sites by adding molecules to the patient's system. An energy therapist, aware of poor compliance on the part of many patients (30% in the study by Brady et al.) and of the influence of side effects, might choose to treat the same symptoms by focusing on the functioning of molecules that already exist in the body (see Chapter 2).

Energy psychologists believe, as do practitioners of acupuncture and other energy-based healing practices, that the meridian, chakra, and aura systems underlie, affect, and are affected by cognitive, emotional, sensory, and chemical events. In essence, energy practitioners believe that they are intervening at the most basic level of functioning.

There does not need to be a competition between established and alternative methods. They can be complementary or supplementary. Pharmacological interventions, for example, are very helpful, both to make patients available for EP treatment and to help patients who do not respond to nonpharmacological treatment. Alternative methods should be given fair consideration when a therapist plans treatment for a patient.

EP Therapy as Used in This Book

We refer primarily to meridian-derived techniques when we speak of EP therapy in this book. In our practices we are much more inclusive, and from time to time we use techniques based on other energy systems, such as the chakras. Our reasons for limiting ourselves to the meridian system, both in this book and in our training courses, are three: utility, simplicity, and face validity.

By *utility* we mean that we have been able to help the vast majority of our clients, often rapidly, by relying solely on treatment of the meridian points. The percentage further increases when we combine EP with EMDR. What we teach has been useful to us, and our students report that these techniques have helped them to be more effective with their clients.

By *simplicity* we mean that the concepts of the meridian system are not difficult to learn or use. They can be taught effectively in a two-day course, allowing us to reach a fairly extensive group of students economically. This criterion implies that an EP practitioner is made, not born, and that effective therapy should be taught to willing trainees rather than confined to a few gifted guru-types. In our training we rely more on tools and skills (such as muscle testing) rather than special gifts (such as intuition), special relationships, or other factors not easily teachable. In our own development we continue to study other forms of EP, and recommend to our students that they expand their skills beyond the meridian therapies (see Appendix B). In this way the meridian-derived therapies can form a base for further training experiences, which often require more commitment in both time.

By *face validity* we simply mean that most clients will give the meridian point techniques a try (perhaps because of knowledge of acupuncture or acupressure), whereas techniques involving other energy systems seem to have less appeal. This will probably change over time. Gallo (2001) has said that the focus on the meridian system in EP is largely an accident, perhaps because Callahan based TFT on the meridians instead of the chakras or strange flows, or perhaps because acupuncture is much more widely known than other energy-based treatments.

What we present in this book is but a fragment of a much larger picture. Practitioners (and their clients) interested in using exercises from the energy systems other than the meridians will find *Energy Medicine* (Donna Eden with David Feinstein, 1998) practical and inclusive. Paul Wildish's The *Book of Ch'i* (2000) is one source for additional practices based on the Asian concept of the life force.

EMDR

History and Theory

Eye movement desensitization and reprocessing (EMDR) is the innovative psychotherapy method developed by Francine Shapiro (1995, 2001a) from whom we learned the approach during Level I and II (Now called Part I and Part II) training courses. Though applied to almost all disorders, EMDR is recommended particularly for the treatment of traumatic memories and the mental, emotional, behavioral, and interpersonal problems associated with traumatic experiences.

The phrase *eye movements* in the name has a curious history. Shapiro (2001a) discovered EMDR at a time she was looking for forms of psychotherapy that would help people heal from stress and related physical illness. She became motivated by her own experience with cancer in 1979. Although radiation eliminated the cancer, she was interested in how a patient might use body-mind tools to promote prevention and healing. While walking in a park one day in 1987, she noticed that as she thought about something disturbing, her eyes spontaneously made rapid movements from lower left to upper right, which seemed to cause the thought to lose its disturbing quality. When she brought up another disturbing thought and made the eye movements deliberately, she found the same positive result. Eager to share her discovery, she asked friends to try the procedure; it worked for them too. Most, however, needed help in keeping their eyes moving, so Shapiro assisted them by moving her hands and asking them to follow with their eyes. Subsequently other forms of bilateral, alternating stimulation in addition to the eye movements have been used effectively, but *eye movement* has been retained in the name of the method because of its historical precedence.

Shapiro noticed that most of the disturbing thoughts her subjects reported were related to anxiety, so she used the word *desensitization*, a term originated by Joseph Wolpe (1969), to describe the anxiety-reducing effects of the eye movements. Therefore in its earliest form the technique was called eye movement desensitization, or EMD, and it was the effect of this method that Shapiro (1989) described in her pioneering study of victims of trauma.

Though the people she worked with in those early days showed great improvement, they retained some of their anxiety and other trauma symptoms, so Shapiro designed strategies to resolve symptoms further and taught her clients coping skills. With these additions to the method, subjects learned new ways to think about the past and the future and new ways to look at themselves—hence the term *reprocessing* was added to the name EMD. Trial-and-error experimentation produced continuing advances in the model, and what is taught today in EMDR courses is quite different from the version that guided early research and therapy.

Principles

What follows are the salient principles and assumptions of EMDR. Further discussion can be found in the works of Lipke (2000) and Shapiro (2001a).

1. It is first assumed that humans can heal themselves. In psychological terms, each person has a natural ability to process disturbing life events to the point where these events become simple memories, no longer bothersome. Most of the time the natural healing mechanism functions well: We talk about something that troubles us, think about it, dream about it, perhaps pray over it; time passes; eventually we no longer feel troubled and may even have learned from the experience. According to Shapiro (2001a), an "adaptive information processing" (AIP) mechanism stimulates "the presumed self-healing mode" of the individual (pp. 27 and 28).

2. The self-healing system, the AIP, can become blocked or "stalled." When someone experiences an overly severe trauma, for example, "an imbalance may occur in the nervous system, caused perhaps by changes in neurotransmitters, adrenaline, and so forth," causing the natural information-processing system to stop functioning (Shapiro, 2001a, p. 31). In this sense, a person can get "stuck" in a specific traumatic memory.

3. Blocked processing affects individuals in past, present, and future time. They not only feel disturbed when thinking about the unprocessed traumatic memory but also experience various problems (symptoms) in the present that are directly related to the traumatic memory. Most symptoms, in fact, are rooted in old unresolved traumas. The unresolved past, and present symptoms, then, interfere with future functioning. EMDR follows a three-pronged treatment approach which involves healing the past, removing present symptoms, and addressing possible future manifestations of the issue.

4. EMDR can reactivate the AIP by jump-starting the system so that it can begin to function effectively once more. Critical to EMDR processing are the eye movements or other bilateral alternating stimulations such as tones and taps. As Shapiro (2001a) has noted, a definitive neurobiological explanation of

the effects of EMDR has not yet been offered, though several theoretical explanations have been suggested.

   a. Clients pay "dual attention" (Shapiro, 2001a), reviewing the past trauma while simultaneously noting present-day resources in themselves and the therapist. Perhaps this is what allows the previously avoided traumatic memory to be faced and updated.

   b. The AIP system is then reactivated and functions as it was intended.

   c. Bilateral simulation maintains and accelerates the AIP as clients revisit the trauma long enough to reprocess it adaptively.

   d. This adaptive and accelerated processing proceeds in a positive, curative direction because of the principle of self-healing.

   e. Since it is assumed that self-healing is inherent to humans, AIP often continues to remain activated after EMDR and available to manage future traumatic events.

5. As clients revisit the traumatic past, they will often report reexperiencing an event in its original form, with similar intensity, emotions, thoughts, and visual memories. These "abreactions" can surprise clients, sometimes because the intensity of a known memory is unexpected and sometimes because a known memory triggers another memory hidden in the memory network (metaphorically called "childhood file folders"). Though abreactions are neither required nor evident in all EMDR sessions, their appearance is sufficiently frequent for us to suggest that they comprise another principle of EMDR. Abreactions are the primary reason for the rule that only professionals be trained in EMDR (on the assumption that they will be equipped to manage abreactions). We believe that the way EMDR invites and utilizes abreactions poses both a risk and an opportunity, and consider both of these possibilities from time to time in this book.

Procedure

Treatment procedures are organized according to eight phases. In Phase 1 a careful history is taken, with special attention given to the patient's history of trauma. Because of the possibility of abreactions, care is taken to assess the client's ability to manage them. Phase 2, preparation, involves education of the client regarding the EMDR method, and instruction in the specific procedures to be used. The client is also taught how to maintain safety and control during EMDR processing. In Phase 3, assessment, the client is asked to describe the traumatic event that will be the treatment target, with its accompanying visual aspects, beliefs, feelings, and body sensations. Eye movements (or another form of bilateral stimulation) begin immediately thereafter, in Phase 4, desensitization. No one phase is more important than the others, though in this phase the clinician often must have unusually high levels of skill and experience to guide the client through processing of the traumatic memory that comprises the treatment target.

If the desensitization phase is successful, the patient moves to Phase 5, installation, to strengthen positive thoughts and feelings that can be more readily accessed now that the negative interference has been eliminated. Phase 6 then involves a body scan for any remaining physical symptoms, and the session ends with Phase 7, closure. If Phases 4 and 5 have not been entirely successful, Phase 6 is omitted, and closure is modified accordingly. Phase 8, reevaluation, is a very important follow-up procedure conducted during the subsequent session, when previous work is double-checked, and issues that may have been uncovered can be targeted for continuing treatment.

EMDR Compared with Other Psychotherapies

Shapiro coined the word "syncletic," or "synthesis of the eclectic," to reflect her view that EMDR is consistent with aspects of other psychotherapies and, indeed, borrows from other psychological orientations. EMDR and the psychoanalytic tradition share, for example, the view that traumatic memories have not yet been incorporated into more reality-based perceptions, and that treatment must be directed at updating earlier events in the client's life, often from childhood. The free association of psychoanalysis, however, is accelerated in EMDR to a degree that renders obsolete most of the assumptions of analytic treatment (such as the need for long-term therapy, the reliance on the healing relationship between client and therapist, the requirement that the therapist analyze the client's statements, and the preeminence of client insight over emotional or behavioral change).

Behavioral terms are used frequently in EMDR training courses, though often with a different connotation. Mainly, the EMDR assumption that past trauma needs to be reexperienced—a psychoanalytic theme—is at odds with the traditional behavioral focus on the present. The *desensitization* that occurs in EMDR, for example, refers to the reduction of negative emotions through confronting and reprocessing of traumatic memories. As used by Wolpe (1969), desensitization was said to result from relearning by reciprocal inhibition, that is by the pairing of a presently experienced anxiety response with an incompatible physiological mechanism, usually relaxation, also in the present. Memories might supply information, but were largely seen as irrelevant to treatment. Comparisons have also been made between EMDR and behavioral exposure, but the relatively greater speed of change with EMDR and other distinctions suggest EMDR is radically different from exposure alone (Perkins & Rouanzoin, 2002). Strict behaviorists also question the emphasis on cognitive change in EMDR. Wolpe, for example, tried EMDR and found it to be a promising behavioral technique (Wolpe & Abrams, 1991), but when he spoke at an EMDR awards ceremony (where we were present) he thanked the "EMD" Institute. Wolpe went on to suggest, in his gentle manner, that changes in a client's thinking (the R in EMDR) were interesting but largely superfluous correlates of the only important changes—the neurophysiological responses.

Shapiro did not follow Wolpe's suggestions, but rather further emphasized the cognitive features of the EMDR model. Shapiro (2001a) seemed to imply that changes in thinking are more likely to precede and cause, rather than accompany or result from, changes in other aspects of functioning, such as emotional, sensory, imaginal, or behavioral. In this sense EMDR is a cognitive therapy.

An apparent discrepancy occurs if we allow that competing hypotheses and therapies can all have validity. Lazarus (1989) resolved this by concluding that apparently contradictory models of change may all have merit in different contexts, and that any aspect of human functioning can at one time be a cause, at another an effect. In this sense the "syncletic" feature of EMDR mimics the multimodal approach of Lazarus. EMDR clinicians whose clients seem to experience emotional changes prior to updating their ways of thinking will conclude that EMDR, at least some of the time, is more consistent with Wolpe's formula. Cognitive therapists may pay more attention to times when clients first correct thinking errors and only then proceed with emotional healing. Until cause-effect relationships have been researched, EMDR effects can be used as "evidence" for any number of theoretical orientations.

There is overlap between EMDR and other psychotherapies in terms of informed consent, history-taking, use of homework, and follow-up. Rapport between therapist and client is also seen as essential, though EMDR therapists are more likely to attribute treatment benefit to the EMDR method than to the therapist or the presumed healing power of the therapeutic relationship.

EMDR is built on both earlier research and clinical precedents from the field of psychotherapy and is also distinctive from previous discoveries. Advances offered by EMDR allow clinicians either to segue from their present therapeutic orientation to EMDR or to utilize techniques from EMDR within their present approach. We know of one psychoanalytically oriented clinician, for example, whose patients lie on a Freudian couch as they freely associate from one idea to another. When a patient happens upon a memory that interferes with analytic "uncovering" because it is particularly upsetting or tends to recur at a certain level of disturbance no matter how often the patient revisits it, the analyst may opt to use EMDR to help resolve that memory. Another friend who is an excellent psychodrama therapist continues to use the psychodrama group setting to stimulate reactions in clients, and then combines psychodrama techniques with alternating bilateral tapping from EMDR to process past issues. The combined use of psychodrama and EMDR is further enriched by having one of the group participants, in the role of "assistant therapist," conduct the tapping while the director monitors reactions. In a similar manner, Gestalt practitioners may use a double-chair to stimulate an emotional reaction, then add bilateral stimulation to help a client process the experience; and couples therapists use EMDR to help each spouse individually with traumatic memories, then meet with the couple to talk about communication skills to improve their present relationship.

OBJECTIONS TO USING EP
AND EMDR, EITHER IN COMBINATION
OR AT ALL

It is rare for us to conduct a training in either of the two methods without encountering some degree of skepticism among our participants, and we have found it is helpful to discuss objections and questions as we begin. In this spirit we list 10 frequent criticisms of each method, and add our comments.

Criticisms of EP

1. "Where is the scientific support for EP? The so-called 'evidence' is based on case studies. How many other psychotherapy fads started on the basis of 'miraculous cases,' only to be shown later to have been overmarketed?"

We concur that the research on EP is just beginning. Research almost always lags behind practice in our field. Nonetheless we believe that clinical impressions need to be substantiated by empirical science. The Association for Comprehensive Energy Psychology (ACEP) has formed a committee that is encouraging, coordinating, and helping to fund research efforts. We are making our own very modest contributions to research and will report on some of our projects later. Chapter 2 provides a brief overview of the support from the scientific community.

2. "For many people EP has no face validity. It looks odd and, at least in the United States, seems mystical. It isn't necessary to argue over whether it works if people won't try it in the first place. In sum, energy psychotherapy doesn't look like psychotherapy."

In our work with a few clients, we have had to say that it's hard to argue with this However, we continue to be surprised at how many of our clients, if given the chance and questioned, will talk not only about their openness to alternative therapies but also of their past experiences and familiarity with energy treatments, especially acupuncture.

For those potential clients for whom energy concepts are unfamiliar and who are reluctant to try them, we suggest in Chapter 3 several ways to introduce the energy paradigm within a framework that reflects Western scientific discoveries.

3. "Okay, it works, but there just doesn't seem to be much to it."

Even after trying out the energy model and finding it to be useful, a person may not allow the concepts into his or her view of how things ought to be. For some this would constitute too challenging a paradigm shift. Energy therapists might consider this an example of a psychological reversal, and one that can be corrected or perhaps an example of what has come to be called "the apex problem" (Callahan, 2001) which is a sort of cognitive dissonance: people experience benefit from energy treatment but credit the gains to something more familiar such as "distraction." As far as there not being "much to it," we are reminded of the tale recounted by Gallo (1999) of the plumber who submitted a bill for $1,000 for solving a long-standing boiler problem that others had failed to solve; he had simply tapped on the boiler. When an itemized bill was demanded, he detailed that $5 was for tapping, and $995 for knowing where to tap. The techniques and algorithms of energy therapy can indeed be applied in cookbook fashion, but the underlying theory is quite complex, involving concepts from the unconscious to quantum physics. Advances in the practice of energy psychotherapy have been made by those familiar with these concepts.

"Secondary gain" issues may also be at work, such as the one a colleague confessed to us: "I just finished $40,000 worth of graduate studies to get my Ph.D. I can't afford to believe in the energy psychology model!" Since this sounds so much like the initial experience of one of us (J. H.) described in the Preface, we will not pretend that this kind of reluctance is rare or that it is immediately or easily modified.

4. "It also seems way too odd to my academic colleagues, and at times I wonder if I will continue to be regarded as a serious scholar."

Research is the best way out of this predicament in our experience. Many of our academic colleagues seem to have a relatively high standard of proof for energy therapies (as well as EMDR, by the way) and a relatively low standard for other more traditional therapies. A number of untested and unsubstantiated psychotherapies continue to be taught at the undergraduate and graduate level, and not simply for historical interest but because the professors actually believe in them. Given some of the criticisms that leveled against EMDR research, we wonder whether solid empirical support for EP is really what some academicians are seeking. Some who have invested years of scholarly research and writing in earlier theories are not naturally predisposed to accept the EP or EMDR models. We are talking about paradigm shifts, which are matters of passion more than reasoning, and which do not necessarily submit to the cold facts of science, as the following story exemplifies.

Once at an international conference outside the United States, I (J. H.) agreed to demonstrate EP techniques to a group of about 100 psychologists and psychology students. I invited to the front of the hall anyone who might be willing to work publicly on a problem for which treatment success or failure would be obvious: the social phobia called *public speaking anxiety*. Five anxious but courageous participants raised their hands and came forward. They all insisted that they could not give a short speech to the rest of the group without experiencing intense anxiety; several even refused to face the audience. After about 45 minutes of energy work, including corrections for certain psychological reversals, each of the five in turn gave brief speeches to the audience, with none reporting anxiety. It was fairly hard to discount the lowering of SUD rating, the obvious behavior changes, and the self-reported experiences, and comments from the audience were respectful and cordial. I then left the conference for lunch. Halfway through I was interrupted by two cognitive-behavioral professors visiting from other countries; one had given a lecture earlier on social phobia diagnosed according to the *DSM*. They did not protest what they had just seen but insisted that the changes in the participants' anxiety levels must have had to do with principles of cognitive behaviorism, not this so-called energy. (EP practitioners would call this another example of the apex phenomenon.) I said I could not disprove their hypothesis and asked them to invite me to their countries for further discussion and to sponsor an EP seminar so their students could also observe the method. After four years neither of the professors has as yet offered an invitation.

We recognize that institutions of higher learning are both repositories of knowledge and expanders of that knowledge, but wonder if an emphasis on the former is at the expense of the latter.

5. "Like it or not, academics are largely in charge of accrediting continuing education programs, and recently the American Psychological Association took energy therapies off their list. How am I going to earn continuing education units?"

We cannot currently offer a remedy. We believe it is simply a matter of time before the American Psychological Association's requirements for these credits are met by replicated studies of energy therapies. A task force of the ACEP is working on the issue. In the meantime, a growing number of State accrediting bodies grants continuing education credit for energy psychology programs. On the other hand, we would humbly point out that some of our own personal life-changing experiences would not have been approved for continuing education credit either.

6. "The outrageous claims made by some practitioners about curing long-standing problems in minutes are embarrassing, and take the energy model beyond odd."

We are disheartened by claims of success that are not supported by follow-up data, as well as by professional ads predicting miraculous results. One of us (M. G.) was once president of the Colorado Psychological Association, and the other (J. H.) has examined those seeking to be licensed as Colorado psychologists, so we note with particular interest any claim that might be a breach of psychology ethics. To date, we are aware of only one psychologist in the United States who was reprimanded for making claims for EP; the licensing board determined that his claims for EP efficacy were not supported by research. The most disconcerting of the ads we read are those implying that "my therapy is better than your therapy," indeed "better than anyone else's therapy." First, the practitioners who cannot back up such claims with careful research run a good chance of committing an ethical violation. Second, other energy practitioners could be seen as charlatans by association; some academicians we know rely on instances such as these to keep energy discussions off their campuses. Third, there is a good chance that at least some of those claims are, in fact, false. We have seen a number of clients who were declared "cured" by EP clinicians, only to reexperience some of their previous symptoms. Some redefinition of "cure" is required for that context. However, when a client with a long-standing problem is free of that problem months after EP treatment and attributes the benefit to EP, then we believe there is justification to say the treatment was effective, even if it only required a few minutes of time.

7. "There is virtually no standardization among the energy psychotherapies or the energy trainings. What we have is a series of trainers and training models, and the consumer is pretty much left with the task of investigating each one. It

also seems that the different trainers are quite competitive with each other, proclaiming one training superior to another. Additionally, how is research to be conducted when so little effort has been made to define what energy psychotherapy is and is not?"

We would disagree with the flavor of this criticism, as we see relatively little competitiveness among energy practitioners and trainers. Instead, there seems to be a spirit of sharing, of cross learning, that is refreshing. The competitiveness we do see is uncharacteristic.

Regarding standardization of training, the brochure describing a particular training course should mention course content, practicum activities, demonstrations, and possible uses of the methods taught. The specific energy system on which the training is based (e.g., meridians, charkas) should also be identifiable. There is no group that certifies EP training in general (although individual trainers have their certification requirements, which vary in rigor), but this is also true for many other methods. It behooves the consumer to be informed, and we address the matter in Chapter 11.

Regarding research, we agree that one cannot scientifically investigate the general effect of energy psychology in any meaningful way. However, just as the general description of EP is redefined by individual practitioners, so can one study specific therapies based on EP. For example, in Chapter 2 we mention studies of the impact of selected TFT algorithms for specific client problems. We also cite an example of the use of the EP approach called EFT. Meridian charts used in EP show a limited number of meridian points, each of these fairly easy to locate for purposes of defining independent variables and for suggesting random (sham) meridian points for comparison. The effects of tapping charted versus sham points can be measured. One could also measure differential effects of tapping versus touching of meridian points, for example.

8. "There is also no standardization when it comes to trainee selection. Virtually anybody can learn these techniques."

We see the accessibility of the energy model as one of its virtues. Formal psychotherapy will never reach more than a small portion of people in the world, and there really is no alternative to enlisting nonprofessionals to join the healing community. This now seems rather conventional, in fact, as the concept of "giving energy therapy away" has already been taken to the next level in the publication of inexpensive self-help books, such as those by Callahan (2001), Gallo and Vincenzi (2000), and Lambrou and Pratt (1999). We also note that since EP treatment rarely produces abreactions or retraumatization, any liability related to including untrained individuals in an EP course is minimal.

9. "It seems awfully mechanical. 'Tap here, tap there.' I end up feeling more like a plumber than priest. I prefer being a priest."

We offer two views on this issue. On the one hand, a mechanical approach has benefits. The first is that many clients prefer the simple and straightforward approach with the tapping sequences. In addition, trainees, including those with limited formal education, can learn this model easily. Without a well-defined set of instructions and patterns, the self-help books just cited could not have been written. Also, there is a variation in that some approaches involve repeated applications of specific algorithms, whereas others consist of a single "comprehensive" algorithm, repeated over and over until a problem is resolved.

On the other hand, the repetition of a specific sequence of taps has definite limits. For example, some practitioners who take courses on TFT algorithms complain about the monotony of the sequences and cease using them in their practices. Relatively few of our colleagues trained in energy diagnostics continue to use this approach, even though it produces highly effective results. And clients in particular may report feeling like they are being treated anonymously; they may dislike the cookbook approach and prefer to be treated more individually. Fortunately, EP practitioners and trainers can offer either predesigned or tailor-made treatments, depending on the preference of the client or student.

10. "I don't find the EP therapies to be rich enough, and by that I mean cognitively rich. Clients change, feel better, say goodbye, and that's it. Many of my clients would like to be able to put words to their experience once in a while, but that doesn't happen often with EP."

We tend to agree with this criticism, and wonder if it reflects the style of the EP practitioner, many of whom practice in a routine way, prescribing the same algorithm over and over again for a given problem. When the energy work allows the client to reflect more, to talk, to raise hunches, and to depend on intuition as to where to go next, indeed richer cognitive processes do take place. We have witnessed many extremely powerful EP sessions during which the client developed insight after insight and was eventually able to put words to the experience. In general, however, we do find EMDR to be more powerful than EP in eliciting the conceptual material that links the client's treatment experiences. EMDR clients not only vocalize more during a session but also are better able to access their therapy work afterward.

On the other hand, many of our clients do not come for the insight so prized by therapists. Many simply want to have their distress alleviated and are not interested in dream analysis or exploration of childhood experiences. Energy therapy is preferable for clients who simply want to be healed, and who do not necessarily care if they can put their experience into words.

We have to be careful to maintain a focus on what the client wants and needs, and not what pleases us. Some therapists have entered the field wanting to help others with emotional, behavioral, or cognitive problems; these therapists may find the rapid results of EP (without the negative connotations of a "quick fix") refreshing. Others have entered the field because they enjoy the world of the psyche, exploring the unconscious, examining the therapeutic relationship, interpreting dreams, intuitively weaving connections between childhood events and current functioning. While there is nothing inherently wrong with these activities, they should be provided only if the patient gives informed consent to be treated in this manner. Sometimes it may be the therapist who wishes for the perceptive richness while the client may just want to be relieved of distress.

Criticisms of EMDR

Let us now respond to 10 complaints we commonly hear about EMDR.

1. "EMDR can only be taught to professional therapists, either licensed or working toward a professional psychotherapy license. Natural healers who would be eligible for energy training are excluded from EMDR courses. We can never expect to help all those who suffer if healing is monopolized by those who are formally trained."

This comment about trainee selection is generally accurate. Persons not formally schooled in psychotherapy are usually excluded from training. EMDR uses a sort of free association that quickly homes in on relevant historical issues that can lead to abreactions, and it is thought that only formally trained clinicians can predict and handle these episodes. We have observed, however, that both those with professional degrees and those without formal psychotherapy training have trouble managing abreactions. The problem is not only with trainee selection but also with training. In later chapters we mention some of the experiments we have conducted to develop procedures to help practitioners manage abreactions using EMDR, EP, or the two in combination.

2. "EMDR seems to invite abreactions, while clients treated with energy methods seem to enjoy benefits similar to those of EMDR but without so much suffering. Indeed, abreactions are relatively rare with energy therapy. Why allow such suffering? Why not use EP instead?"

Client preferences guide us. Some clients prefer to use EMDR even after they have experienced abreactions. Some will tell us, "After comparing EP and EMDR, I find that energy work isn't satisfying enough." Abreactions during EMDR tend to be rather short-lived, a matter of minutes, and there are techniques for handling and preventing them, including energy techniques (see Chapters 4 and 5).

3. "One of the dangers of abreactions is dissociation, a risk with EMDR."

Some clients do escape from intense emotional suffering by dissociating, that is, by retreating into a part of themselves where they are so isolated from their suffering that they no longer feel it. The challenge for the therapist is to proceed with such care that the clients can pace themselves slowly, containing the experience, working bit by bit on an issue, keeping their emotional intensity within a tolerable range, a process that has been called *fractionated abreaction* (Kluft & Fine, 1993). Other suggestions for handling abreactions are presented in Chapters 4 and 5.

4. "In the training we were treated like infants and told to read from the manual. The trainer said we would be relying on everything we had ever learned about psychotherapy, but in the practicum we were not allowed to deviate at all from the EMDR training manual, as if our clinical intuition and experience were of no value whatsoever. EMDR is entirely too rigid for me."

Indeed, guidelines in EMDR training are rather strict, and in our initial training we too were put off at times by our unyielding practicum facilitators. After watching hundreds of our own trainees practice EMDR, however, we have come to endorse the rigor of EMDR training, for two reasons. First, we find that many clinicians veer off too quickly from the EMDR model, then often find that their more "personalized" form of EMDR does not work very well. Unfortunately, they attribute their treatment failures to EMDR rather than to the changes they made in the model. After witnessing too many failed experiments of this sort, we have become quite conservative as trainers and facilitators and now practically plead with our trainees to "conserve" the EMDR model as it has been developed. "The model we teach, works," we say. "We cannot say what will happen if you change it around. It may be better, but it is also possible that you will break something if you try to fix what isn't broken."

A second reason for the rigid training is related to research. As we suggest in Chapter 2, some of the published studies that showed negative or modest EMDR effects may have involved less-than-optimal EMDR treatment, which makes it virtually impossible to determine whether EMDR or other factors were at fault. However, if studies use EMDR in strict accordance to the model, then we can be confident of what produced the study results.

5. "EMDR is just a lot of smoke and mirrors: cognitive therapy with a bit of behaviorism, some Gestalt techniques, irrelevant eye movements, and a lot of hype."

It is true that EMDR contains pieces from many psychotherapy schools (Shapiro's word *syncletic* implies that). As we described in the Preface, we studied and practiced traditional therapies before learning and using EP and EMDR. We found that the various ingredients of the other therapies never worked as well as EMDR, and we sincerely doubt that these ingredients in combination are solely responsible for the effects we see using EMDR. We were particularly impressed when we used EMDR with former clients whom we had not helped very much with cognitive, behavioral, or Gestalt methods. Virtually all of these clients responded much more favorably to EMDR than they did to pre-EMDR treatments.

Until EMDR is further dismantled and its various components analyzed, we will not be able to say for sure which pieces are essential to the method. Though some parts later may be shown to be nonessential, for now we are content to accept the entire package.

6. "I don't see how you can justify using EMDR under emergency conditions, especially where you might have only one contact with a victim."

This objection raises some important ethical issues. What is our responsibility for follow-up with clients? If a client "opens up" as a result of our treatment, we would be expected to help the client contain the experience prior to ending the session, then to be available by phone, and finally to follow up for a period of time to finish the work. Under emergency conditions, in a refugee camp with displaced victims, at a natural disaster site, and in similar settings, follow-up is often a luxury, so we must be careful not to encourage people to open up what cannot be resolved fairly quickly. We are not aware of any long-term follow-up data on any of the emergency interventions done by EMDR therapists. For the most part we recommend EP in these situations because of the low likelihood for abreactions and for discovering related painful issues. An exception is the limited use of EMDR with children that has been pioneered by Lucina Artigas (Jarero, 1999).

7. "In EMDR training we were taught how to use different containment and relaxation exercises to end unfinished sessions. I would rather use energy techniques at that point to help my clients to work through some of their unfinished business before leaving. In some cases the EMDR containment exercises don't work very well, or for very long. The question I have is this: Why risk having a client reopen issues between sessions, or leave with a high level of distress at the end of a session, when energy techniques could be used to take treatment further?"

We believe there are many situations where EMDR and energy techniques can be used to complement each other. Treatment with EMDR usually will produce a completed session. In Chapter 4, we suggest ways to use EMDR even more efficiently and with less risk. However, when time is running out and the client still reports feeling highly distressed, energy techniques can be blended into the EMDR work for quicker and deeper resolution of the client's problems (see Chapter 5).

8. "I'm pretty sure psychological reversals are sometimes causing EMDR treatment to fail. Therefore, I think they should be corrected up front in EMDR work."

We agree. We suggest that EMDR practitioners consider beginning an EMDR session with a simple psychological reversal correction. Without switching paradigms, EMDR practitioners can present energy exercises to clients in several palatable ways (see Chapter 5).

9. "I know EMDR techniques are recommended for self-use, but it seems to me the energy techniques are much safer, more friendly, work faster, and can be taught to a client during the first contact."

We agree that energy techniques can usually be taught earlier in the course of treatment, can easily be practiced at home, and can usually be used more effectively by clients in emergency situations. We also believe that clients need to be asked what they perceive as "friendly" and "safe," and whether "faster" is a priority for them or simply the therapist's value. Later we examine the role of face value with these methods. Although energy work meets the criteria of friendliness, safety, and speed, we are surprised at how many of our clients, even those who ask for energy treatment in our office, simply will not use energy techniques when they are on their own, but may be willing to practice forms of bilateral stimulation, even though these may appear to be less efficient or more cumbersome.

10. "It seems to me that the EMDR Institute has created a real money-maker here, with elaborate, expensive training and formidable prohibitions against anyone practicing EMDR without the institute's own training."

In the early days of EMDR practice, Shapiro considered the method to be "experimental" and wanted to ensure client safety by verifying that those applying the method were as well prepared as possible. Therefore, a condition of training was that participants agreed not to teach the method they learned to anyone else. The training involved Level I lasting two and one-half days, and Level II of another two and one-half days. Fees were (and are) in line with those charged by others for programs of similar length, in spite of the fact that EMDR training is more costly (each training includes one licensed therapist for every nine participants to facilitate the two practica). With the publication of Shapiro's textbook in 1995, the prohibition of teaching EMDR to others was lifted, and as research began to validate the method, it was no longer considered experimental. The EMDR International Association took over the function of certifying trainers, and the EMDR Institute is now one of many sanctioned sources of training. Interestingly enough, all certified trainers provide programs of about the same length as those of the institute.

Using these comments as background, we now discuss use of EP and EMDR for different treatment conditions.

WHEN TO USE EP OR EMDR

Based on our work with clients, as well as input from program administrators and training participants, we prefer to use EP over EMDR, or vice versa, in certain circumstances. Here we list major treatment issues and other factors that help us decide which method to use where in our treatment plan. The reader may well use a different or longer list. This section provides a basis for our later discussion on using the two methods in combination, when we suggest leveraging the relative merits of one method to increase the reach or impact of the other. Our rule of thumb is as follows: if what we are doing is not working, or if for any reason our client objects to what we are doing, we offer to try something else from the EMDR or EP repertoire.

We limit our set of guidelines to what we can defend from our own experience or the available research. Hence, we do not include diagnoses such as manic-depression and schizophrenia. Some uses of EP and EMDR are absent from the list because the intervention required involves a holistic, comprehensive effort. For example, although both EP and EMDR are useful in helping a borderline personality client to reduce the effects of traumatic memories, adequate treatment for this client is long term and complex and depends on a

therapist with unusual patience, tenacity, relationship skills, and training. EP and EMDR can assist in reducing certain anxiety responses
and perhaps in developing a more positive self-image in a person with
anorexia, but the responsible eating-disorder therapist should also utilize medical resources, possibly hospitalization, family systems treatment, and close supervisory monitoring of diet and exercise. And while
we have used both EP and EMDR effectively in helping perpetrators
of violent and sexual assault to resolve their traumas and reduce their
urges to act out, simply eliminating such symptoms will not automatically enable the client to exhibit new skills, attitudes, and habits.

These comments speak in part to the limitations of EP and EMDR
and to the need for the clinician neither to overstate the power of the
methods nor to underrate the value of specialty training. On the other
hand, sometimes adding EP or EMDR, or both, can transform a weak
treatment protocol into an effective one. Extant treatment programs
for eating-disordered persons, addicts, sex offenders, domestic violence perpetrators, and individuals with borderline personality diagnoses produce modest results. So often a dedicated patient who works
hard, learns and practices new skills, and tries to change seems to be
thrown off track by the most trivial provocation, or fails just as success
seems within reach. Often EP or EMDR can help to eliminate a traumatic memory that causes the client to keep stumbling, or can help to
reduce the urge to use a prohibited substance, thereby enabling a well-
intentioned client finally to respond to an otherwise good treatment
program.

With these cautions in mind, we now offer our guidelines, which
are listed in Table 1.1.

Preparatory Considerations

1. Client choice is paramount. If a client requests EMDR or EP, that
request should be honored. Based on our experiences, either method
will work effectively 90% or more of the time with the majority of
clients, provided the client has given consent to the method used.

Of course we recommend that clients be told about both EP and
EMDR and how each approach might be able to help. The ethical
principles of psychologists state, "Psychologists obtain appropriate
informed consent to therapy or related procedures" (American Psychological Association, 1992). In this regard we mention the energy model
to those who ask for EMDR, just as we mention EMDR to those who
first request energy methods. Often clients who prefer EMDR or EP

TABLE 1.1 WHICH THERAPY FOR WHICH PROBLEM?

	EP	EMDR
Preparatory considerations		
1. Client choice	3	3
2. Client asks for empirically supported treatment	1	3
3. Client asks for method with face validity	2	3
4. Therapist choice	3	3
5. Preparation of the therapist for a session	3	2
Presenting problems		
6. Anxiety	3	3
7. Phobia	3	2
8. Depression	2	2
9. Trauma	3	3
10. Emergencies, one-session-only contacts	3	0
11. Dissociation	3	1
12. Medical conditions affecting treatment	3	2
13. Dilemmas	2	3
14. Insomnia and other sleep disturbances	1	2
15. Addictions	1	1
16. Physical pain	3	2
17. Blocks to optimal performance	3	3
During treatment		
18. Abreactions, elevated SUD, "looping"[a]	3	2
19. When images are not reported	2	3
20. When self-referent beliefs are not reported	2	3
21. When little or no emotion is reported	2	3
22. Running out of time, high SUD at end of session	3	1
23. Resistance and other forensic uses	3	2
Miscellaneous		
24. Children	3	3
25. Group use	3	1
26. Client self-care following a session	3	2
27. Client self-care without formal therapy	3	0
28. Paraprofessional training	3	1
29. Cross-cultural use	3	2

Note. The rating scale is as follows: 0 = not recommended for this particular purpose; 1 = limited usefulness for this purpose; 2 = useful; 3 = very useful and a treatment of choice.

[a] A term from EMDR indicating an issue's processing is blocked and repetitious.

initially will consent to use the other method at specific times in treatment if they understand it, though client consent should be carefully rechecked if a switch is suggested.

Some clients will remain reluctant to try the alternative even after we give additional information. Persons who subscribe to certain religious beliefs, for example, may report that they find the energy paradigm to be weird, scary, or even satanic. Others agree to "something more traditional, like EMDR" (which brings a smile to our faces), but shun anything that sounds like "a journey into metaphysics" (in the words of one client).

2. Empirical support for EP is modest. The *concept* of energy enjoys more scientific support than does the *practice*. Case studies that are relied on to defend EP therapy are suggestive but do not constitute a body of research. There is much scientific support for EMDR, at least in the treatment of PTSD (see Chapter 2).

3. The face validity of EMDR is still superior to that of EP. Scientific support, integration of techniques from earlier methods, a theory that fits nicely with Western concepts of the brain and body, the special attention given to abreactive experiences, the emphasis on changes in thinking, and similar matters persuade the average client that EMDR looks more like "real psychotherapy" than do the EP methods.

Within another 10 years this may not be the case; there are many who foresee energy becoming a component of all forms of psychotherapy and other healing alternatives by then. In the meantime EP will be limited by the reality that we do not yet have research data to substantiate the rather exuberant claims about the power of EP, nor have we translated chi concepts into terms more familiar to those skeptical clients who want more than our assurance that these new therapies are legitimate. This last problem may be partially corrected by explaining the energy model within a U.S.-based frame of neuroscience that westerners may find more familiar (See Chapter 3).

4. Therapist choice implies that a kind of placebo effect often characterizes the work we do. No matter how effective others might find a therapy to be, if we do not believe it, we may very possibly limit, albeit unconsciously, its usefulness. Therapists who are uncomfortable with a method, or who, even after competent training, do not have confidence in it, may unwittingly communicate their doubts to the client.

Some therapists are open enough to attend trainings in these new therapies. They leave convinced by the theoretical discussions and clinical demonstrations, but on returning to their offices, they are uncomfortable with them, unwilling to carry them out, or even to think about carrying out in practice. I (J. H.) once finished an EP training in Europe and was about to leave for dinner with the training team when a patient knocked on the clinic door with an urgent problem: her chronic pain had become unbearable; could she see someone? Physical therapy and other efforts simply had not worked, and the patient's employment was in jeopardy because of missed workdays. I agreed to conduct EP therapy with the patient, and after about 30 minutes half of the pain had gone. I then asked my translator, who had been one of the better students both in the EP course and in an earlier EMDR training, to take over for me while I worked with yet another emergency patient. The trainee continued what I had been doing, and after another half-hour the patient left, free of pain and very grateful. Seven months later I ran into the trainee, who said he was using EMDR with excellent results, but "could not get myself to use the energy stuff." I asked about the patient. He smiled and said, "Still okay. I just talked with her and she said she still hasn't gotten any of her pain back." I smiled back: "I'll invite you back when I do another energy course."

Initially we all practice the therapies favored by our graduate or medical school professors. Along the way, we add and discard therapies and techniques we read about or are trained in, perhaps even discarding the ones learned in school. We each end up, therefore, with an eclectic mixture in which we have the utmost confidence (or else we would not practice it) but which, in its exact form, has no empirical support. Admittedly, some or many of the elements of what we practice are supported by research, and perhaps that is enough. In any case, this is the customary manner of building up a psychotherapeutic panoply, as far as we can tell. Practitioners seem to believe that just one method is not enough for all situations.

Yet, many dedicated practitioners of either EP or EMDR seem to get very good results with one of the methods alone and don't resort to using the other. Nicosia (1997) wrote about using TFT and EMDR on the same patient, but he applied them sequentially rather than in combination. Phillips (2000) has a more elaborate approach but also usually uses methods in a sequential, rather than combined way. Lane (2001) also alternates between EP and EMDR.

We have observed, in person and on film, many demonstrations by experts in various methods. In those demonstrations, the masters seem to use nothing but their method, client centered, Gestalt, rational-emotive therapy, and so on. We have not seen Ellis using the double-chair (or especially the double-pillow) technique, the Gouldings using intentional reciprocal inhibition, Rogers talking about his value as a social reinforcer, or Perls doing script redecision work, even though all these procedures are useful. And their writings seem to bolster our impression. Similarly, when Shapiro runs into difficulty in the course of treatment, she will not search for a psychological reversal but rather for a blocking belief or feeder memory. When Gallo, on the other hand, encounters difficulty, he will not resort to these proven EMDR techniques but will search for other more effective points on the meridian, a psychological reversal, a neurological disorganization, or an interfering toxin. These experts seem to achieve effective results adhering exclusively to their chosen methods. Yet the large majority of therapists, whether or not they describe themselves as eclectic, usually say that they try to use the best technique to address a given problem. This is an approach that Lazarus (1989) has expertly systematized.

So whereas a few trainees in EP and EMDR seem to go back to their previous (probably eclectic) manner of working, on the other end of the continuum are those who seem to practice nothing but the new method. Therapist choice has very much to do with the method chosen.

5. Therapists are encouraged to prepare themselves for treatment sessions. While we have found both EP and EMDR to be useful as self-help exercises, in Chapter 8 we recommend energy exercises in particular because we find these to be relatively more efficient and portable than EMDR.

Presenting Problems

6. Anxiety is very successfully addressed by both EP and EMDR, especially compared to the methods we had relied on through decades of practice. For targeting anxiety, EMDR has a simple yet comprehensive protocol that is very effective. A TFT algorithm is also very successful with anxiety.

Because of their portable nature, EP techniques can be used by patients who suffer from panic attacks. Relaxation strategies are usually prescribed for them, but effective EP treatments are more easily applied when the client is in the middle of such a disorienting attack.

For treatment of obsessive-compulsive anxiety disorder (OCD), clinicians are encouraged to include a combination of exposure and response prevention which requires that the patient resist engaging in the compulsive behavior that has reduced anxiety in the past. Unfortunately, the methods traditionally employed (e.g., relaxation, self-talk, rhythmic breathing) require persistent repetition and produce modest results. Both EP and EMDR techniques can be used during a session so the client can resolve, much more efficiently and effectively, the anxiety that results from exposure. Because EP techniques are more portable than EMDR exercises, we recommend that the client use EP between sessions to manage OCD symptoms as they arise.

7. Phobia was the focus of the first documented use of TFT, and the phobia algorithm has been used successfully thousands of times. Callahan's publishing of the *Five Minute Phobia Cure* (1985) was one of the early impetuses in the spread of knowledge of the method. When a patient presents with a phobia, other factors notwithstanding, our inclination is to try the algorithm. We have indeed lowered SUD scores to 0 after five minutes of tapping, although preparation and closure are always attended to. EP is successful with both recently acquired and long-standing phobias. EP also is rated higher because EP treatment can be conducted over the phone, which is critical in the treatment of agoraphobic patients who have great difficulty leaving home.

There are EMDR protocols for phobias of objects that might be encountered in the environment, such as snakes and thunder, and for phobias of situations into which clients must deliberately put themselves, such as public speaking and flying. The latter is encountered surprisingly often in our executive population and is usually quickly treated with EP. EMDR protocols take longer to administer than the EP algorithm but are routinely successful and probably more effective when one specific incident originated the phobia and is a layer or aspect that has to be treated.

8. Depression can range from a mild case of the blues to a recurrent major depressive disorder. Cummings (1999) wrote that some mood disorders are more psychological (such as reactive depression) and others are more biological (such as bipolar disorder). Psychotherapy and antidepressants are roughly equally effective in treating depressed people, but together these two methods produce greater effect because subjects unreachable by one of these treatments benefit from the other. Cummings concluded that if we selected subjects more carefully (i.e., assigning psychological problems to psychotherapists and pharmacological problems to medical practitioners), then both treatments would be seen as more efficient and effective. For similar

reasons, when we use EMDR and EP to treat affective problems, we need to consider what caused the problems in a specific individual so that we can treat factors relevant to that person and that person's future functioning.

With severe depression, psychopharmacology is usually involved, but some psychological treatment is helpful as well. Milder cases of depression can clear in a session or two with EP therapy, but in clinical practice, treatment typically is significantly longer. EMDR is very effective with trauma-based disorders, depression being one of them.

9. Trauma is assumed to underlie the majority of psychological problems, and both EP and EMDR are treatments of choice for relatively simple as well as severe and complicated trauma, even trauma resulting from politically motivated torture (Gorman, 2001). Although only EMDR has been researched extensively as a treatment trauma, the thousands of case studies showing successful use of EP parallel the early clinical impressions of EMDR on which we relied before peer-refereed articles supporting EMDR were published.

An EP algorithm has been discovered for treating PTSD, and we use it when we do not want to take the risk of increasing a client's distress. As usual, if the algorithm is initially unsuccessful, other techniques such as EFT, be set free fast (BSFF), and TAT can be brought to bear. When dissociative tendencies are a concern in the treatment of anxiety, we are more likely to turn to EP techniques.

The standard EMDR protocol has proved very successful in treating PTSD (see Chapter 2), and additional protocols have been developed for special circumstances such as recent traumas. We use EMDR to treat PTSD when clients need to make sense of the disaster in the context of their view of the world.

10. For emergencies and one-session-only contacts, we clearly favor EP because of the potential complications of abreactions that EMDR might elicit. EMDR might also uncover issues that are related to the emergency, but which do not have to be treated at that very moment in order for the client to experience relief.

As stated earlier, the theory underlying EMDR is that alternating visual or other bilateral stimulation activates the AIP in the client (Shapiro, 2001a). Whatever information appears next is processed. Sometimes it is positive; sometimes it is a mixed account of nostalgia; often it is an unfinished memory of terror or rage or despondency that the client has kept hidden for years, a memory that has been intruding intermittently in the client's life and now leaps to the forefront of consciousness. Trainees are taught to be respectful of the "mindfulness" of the AIP, which goes where it needs to go; frequently it leads to an extremely disturbing traumatic memory.

Sometimes these memories, intrusive as they are, have been fairly well camouflaged, so their appearance during EMDR can be quite surprising to both client and therapist. They also might be connected to many "channels," an EMDR term for chains of associated memories contained in the same childhood memory file. To begin work on such a complex memory when there is only one session to treat the client is not advised. Clinicians are asked not to use EMDR when insufficient information about the client is available and when there is little time to deal with the related traumatic memories that may appear.

EP therapists consistently report that abreactions during energy treatment are rare and usually quickly subside. Additionally, traumatic material that appears is almost always manageable and resolvable during the same session. One-session treatments are fairly common, in fact. EP treatment under emergency conditions is also common, because the focus is maintained on an isolated problem, resolution is usually straightforward, and follow-up is rarely necessary.

Where EMDR is used at sites of natural disasters (e.g., hurricane or earthquake) or human-caused violence (as it was in Oklahoma City and Bosnia), care should be given to preparing the treatment staff well, ensuring that ongoing therapy is possible for victims, providing follow-up support and supervision as necessary, and then offering training in advanced treatment strategies for local clinicians.

We are aware of no research that compares EMDR with EP methods under such conditions. However, a group of Turkish therapists that works with earthquake victims has been trained in both methods and is planning a study to compare individual EMDR, group EMDR with children utilizing the technique called the *butterfly hug* (Jarero, 1999b), energy techniques for both individuals and groups, and an art therapy.

We also note that paraprofessionals can be more easily trained in EP methods than in EMDR and can be an important resource at disaster sites where professionally trained EMDR clinicians are not available. A caveat is in order here: not all victims of natural disasters were free of trauma prior to the disaster, and even with EP a paraprofessional can happen on old psychic wounds that can overwhelm the containment strength of the energy technique. Persons using EP methods exclusively need to recognize when they have reached the limits of their healing abilities, and to have access to professional clinicians who can assist in dealing with preexisting trauma and other exceptional problems.

11. Dissociation can occur when the client wants to escape from severe abreactive experiences. Persons trained in EMDR are taught techniques that can help the client to contain a troubling emotional reaction so that it does not lead to the level of terror that triggers dissociation. We believe these EMDR interventions are underutilized; we address this theme in Chapter 4.

Even with advanced training in using EMDR with dissociative clients, clinicians may find that EMDR processing moves too quickly for the client. In Chapter 5 we describe EP interventions that can be used for those times when even cautious use of EMDR therapy overstimulates the client. Generally find that energy techniques are more rapid and effective in lowering the level of anxiety that triggers dissociation.

12. Medical conditions affecting treatment require careful investigation. Because of the abreactions that occur with EMDR, any medical problems that can be exacerbated by heightened emotional arousal need to be monitored carefully. We tend to be conservative and encourage clients with heart problems and other conditions that put them at medical risk to consider trying energy techniques, either exclusively or at least as a supplemental tool to lower distress during an EMDR session.

Pregnant clients deserve special consideration too. While some people like to say that "pregnancy is not an illness," this comment ignores the real risk that pregnant clients take when experiencing emotionally upsetting therapy. And even though the vast majority of pregnant women who have been treated with EMDR have not had negative side effects, we are aware of several incidents that suggest practitioners be particularly cautious when considering using EMDR with pregnant clients.

- In one study on EMDR (we do not cite the study in order to protect the identity of the individuals involved), pregnant women were not accepted as subjects. After the study began, one pregnant woman who had been excluded as a subject suffered a miscarriage. While the miscarriage was not attributable to EMDR, we wonder what might have happened had this subject participated in the study and then miscarried. There would be no proof that EMDR precipitated the miscarriage, but researchers could not have ruled out the possibility.

- One of our colleagues, a psychologist, was pregnant for the second time when she participated in a practicum at a Level II EMDR training. During that experience she worked on a trauma that involved "pushing" something out of consciousness, and following that she gave birth prematurely. Since her first delivery had occurred after a normal gestation period, she said she felt certain that the premature delivery was triggered by her EMDR work.
- Consideration at least should be given to consulting with the attending physician to ensure that the client is not at special risk for an abreactive therapeutic experience (e.g., from using EMDR). Sometimes the client will know when she is at risk, but at other times she may not be aware that she should avoid extraordinary experiences that stimulate her own and the fetus's physiological responses

In practice, we have used EMDR with a number of pregnant clients with no negative consequences as far as we know. Colleagues find EMDR helpful and risk free if the focus is exclusively on the positive (e.g., visualizing a happy birth and a future positive relationship with the baby). I (J. H.) used EMDR with one client whose pregnancy reminded her of a previous abortion and sexual abuse and whose previous experience with EMDR had convinced her that this would be the best way for her to understand the links between memories and her pregnancy. I took special care to inform her of the possible risks from abreactions and related accompanying stimulation of the fetus, checked out her medical condition, then suggested that the likely benefit from using EP techniques might be similar to that expected from EMDR. She said the fetus was already overstimulated from preoccupations with her memories of having been abused, and she opted for EMDR, so I responded to her request. She delivered a healthy baby with peace and joy.

Both EP and EMDR practitioners have informally reported improvements in or elimination of the symptoms of asthma and allergies related to psychological factors. According to the many case studies we have heard, no negative side effects have accompanied the reported benefits. Research would be particularly welcome in this area to investigate which treatments appear promising, whether effects are maintained, and how any risk factors, particularly any associated with medical factors, might be further reduced.

13. Dilemmas appear frequently in therapy. Synonyms for a dilemma might be *ambivalence, reluctance, resistance, hesitation,* and *confusion.* All imply an attraction to or fleeing from two opposing sides of an issue, a "yes-but" tug of war between options. The concept helps us better to appreciate the "neurotic paradox," New Year's resolutions made and broken, and the relapses that so often occur with an addict committed to sobriety. EMDR is a particularly powerful tool for these issues. In Chapter 6 we describe an EMDR technique for dilemmas that can be used during an EP session (or, for that matter, as part of an EMDR session).

14. Insomnia and other sleep disturbances deserve special attention in therapy. These symptoms are fairly common side effects of unresolved trauma and further complicate healing by disrupting the sleep cycles needed to manage the stresses that accrue from daily life. A trauma victim, then, feels a growing accumulation of problems, quite the opposite of what we have been taught to expect with the dictum "Time heals all wounds."

Sleep disturbances should always be investigated for possible chemical, neurological, or other organic causes (Pallesen, Nordhuis, Havik, & Nielson, 2001). Some sleep disturbances are due to the cycling of unfinished emotional business, preoccupation with the future, and various unidentified worries. EP and EMDR interventions are useful both for targeting nightmares or the content of nighttime preoccupations and for installing images and thoughts conducive to undisturbed sleep.

Because none of the EP exercises produce a consistent benefit in our experience, we rate EP techniques less positively than the EMDR procedure.

15. Addictions are an especially important application of both EMDR and the energy model. A psychotherapist does not need to specialize in addictions in order to provide effective treatment for a patient's substance abuse problems. Whether a client volunteers the information or not, many presenting problems in psychotherapy are associated with some form of substance use. A careful clinician will investigate substance use during the history taking and give appropriate attention to this issue.

Several EMDR protocols have been developed for use with addicts (Omaha, 1998; Popky, 1999; Shapiro, Vogelmann-Sine, & Sine, 1994).

The long-term benefits of the protocols have not been substantiated so far, though Popky (1999) wrote of planning a multiple-site research project. Most practitioners have described specific applications of energy-based treatments for addicts (Callahan, 1987a; Britt, Diepold, & Bender, 1998; Gallo & Vincenzi, 2000; Lambrou & Pratt, 2000; Nicosia, 1999). A common EP stance is that addictions are anxiety related, and that aspect is stressed in treatment. In addition, many addictive substances are toxic and produce psychological reversals, so correction of these reversals is recommended along with specific algo-rithms. As with EMDR, it is difficult to decide from the available liter-ature whether EP treatment produces sustained improvement.

Addictive habits are notoriously determined by many factors (e.g., physical addiction, habit strength, secondary gain, pleasure, environ-mental cues, peer pressure) and a holistic, multifaceted approach is necessary. While EMDR or EP can help to reduce addictive urges, process traumatic memories that trigger urges, and strengthen a per-son's non-addictive self-view, these efforts are not likely to prove very useful outside of a comprehensive treatment program that takes the many possible causes of addiction into consideration. For these rea-sons we rate both methods relatively low.

We do not specialize in addictive work, but the offender research project we mention in Chapter 9 addresses substance use. As we are only in the third year of the project, we do not yet have any indica-tion as to long-term benefits. Some of the case studies suggest that combined use of EP and EMDR is promising in reducing addictive behavior, but we will await follow-up data before making any stronger statements.

16. Physical pain can often be alleviated or even eliminated with EP, EMDR, or both. In the Preface one of us (J. H.) reported on his experience using EMDR to heal muscle pain that seemed to have been the result of a fall but actually was being maintained by an unresolved memory. Thus, when physical pain is partly or completely the result of psychological factors, successful treatment resolves not only the psychological symptoms but also the physical ones, including pain, to the extent that the psychological factors were causal. We generally encourage a combined use of the two methods because of the frequent complexity of pain.

As with all medical issues, special attention needs to be paid to possible organic, chemical, and other factors that could cause or ag-gravate a pain response. Some of our medically trained EP students remind us that pain may serve as a warning signal of a condition that requires medical attention, and they warn against eliminating physical pain before it is thoroughly assessed.

Minimal traumatic brain injury (MTBI) is particularly unresponsive to treatment. After relief is experienced, the client often reports later that the pain has returned. Environmental (mold, smoke, certain lights), personal (stress, sleep disturbance), and many other factors exacerbate MTBI symptoms. These patients, whose condition can be undetected by traditional neuropsychological and neurological testing, frequently blame themselves for their situation and may even think they are "imagining" their pain. It is important not to give them false expectations from EP or EMDR.

17. Treating individuals experiencing blocks to optimal performance involves a shift from the more usual focus on trauma to an emphasis on the positive, often called performance enhancement. In Chapter 9 we describe our experiences using EP and EMDR in executive coaching and illustrate the use of the two methods with other high-achieving clients.

During Treatment

18. Abreactions during treatment can be healing. They can also frighten a client into terminating therapy. In Chapter 4 we cover a number of EMDR interventions that are quite useful at helping clients to contain and then to resolve abreactive experiences. We rate EP somewhat higher than EMDR because certain energy techniques enable the client to move more rapidly through abreactions (see Chapter 3). This is an especially important consideration when clients feel overwhelmed by emotion, ask to end their suffering during an abreactive episode, or are at risk to dissociate.

We hasten to point out that efficient recovery from an abreaction is not the only value that clients endorse. Frequently our clients who have tried both EP and EMDR have opted to continue through intensely disturbing emotions with EMDR because they feel more completed after such a therapy experience. These are the persons who report that EMDR "feels more like therapy." Some find their EMDR therapy work to be more "memorable." Others say that suffering in treatment explains the pain of the problem they had endured for so long, and that to terminate that intense suffering with energy exercises would not give justice to their history. We do not argue in these cases, but again respect each client's choice.

19. Sometimes images are not reported because the patient is unable to identify the original incident that is maintaining present symptoms. A technique taught in EMDR seminars, sometimes called the *floatback procedure*, is often quite useful in helping the client to search for "feeder memories"—that is, early events that are thought to be "feeding" the present symptoms (see Chapter 4).

20. Although both methods are useful, we prefer EMDR when self-referent beliefs are not reported or when insight is desired because of the way EMDR structures cognitive processes into assessment and treatment. Asking clients to identify what they have learned from a traumatic event that reflected an unfriendly attitude towards themselves can add power to treatment. Cognitive changes often occur throughout EMDR processing, and an attentive therapist can track subtle variations in how clients talk about themselves, and later discuss these changes with clients who can then put words to the healing experience.

The benefit of using energy therapies to generate insight or intellectual understanding is not widely appreciated, perhaps because, as we noted earlier, too many energy practitioners take a "recipe" or "one-size-fits-all" approach to treatment, relying on algorithms or other prearranged strategies to guide their work. This kind of treatment is likely to be smooth, systematic, and successful—an excellent strategy if the client wants only to feel relief from symptoms. In such a case, it would be enough for the therapist simply to repeat the same tried-and-true formula over and over until the symptoms diminish. We have observed any number of energy therapists doing precisely this, with rather high levels of success.

Other clients report that simply repeating an algorithm over and over, while effective in relieving symptoms, feels mechanical and almost "too efficient"; they feel detached from the process. Some express disappointment at moving through their struggle too easily and not having come to "understand" themselves, of not having put words to the treatment process to make it more "memorable" afterward. Clients feel dissatisfied and incomplete when they heal too quickly after so many years; too rapid a resolution seems to trivialize their suffering.

When EP therapists personalize treatment, the client is more likely to add insight and words to the healing experience. Often the therapist and client together can invent a sequence of corrections and taps that will parallel the textbook algorithm, giving the client the experience of being taken more seriously and feeling empowered by helping choose the steps of treatment.

21. EMDR can be effective for clients who say they feel little emotion, reporting instead a general kind of malaise, a "sense" of meaninglessness or emptiness, without being able to identify very clearly whether what they feel is sadness, anger, or fear. They seem to be bothered by events but in an oddly intellectual way. Another group, for no particular reason they can identify, does not experience feelings very deeply, like the nonemotional man who assured his wife that he loved her, since he had told her so when they married 40 years earlier. "And if I change my mind," he added, "I'll send you a memo." A third rather different subgroup of patients does not report feeling because of fear of their emotional side. They act as if their feelings, their emotional memories, are themselves phobic objects, which they avoid as surely as a person with acrophobia would avoid looking over a cliff.

Some clients appear to be genetically predispositioned to be nonemotional and will not respond significantly to either EMDR or EP therapy. On the other hand, those who have learned to avoid feeling will often respond to an EMDR intervention.

Some EP practitioners would point out that with muscle testing the SUD level can be detected, and the problem then treated with the client having little awareness of the problem,but reporting benefits following a session. We would concur somewhat with this, as we have conducted and witnessed sessions where clients were treated successfully without ever exhibiting the level of emotional upset that might normally be expected given the severity of the problem. On the other hand, in our experience, there are many clients who would find this kind of work to be decidedly abstract and cold. Additionally, we would propose to clients who have trouble feeling emotion that with EMDR they have an opportunity to safely discover the rich emotional side of life.

22. Not infrequently we run out of time in an EMDR session, and the SUD level reported by the client remains high. One choice at that point would be to use EMDR techniques to close an incomplete session, which essentially means helping the client to contain the problem until the next session.

An option available to those who know EP is to introduce energy exercises to reduce the SUD, perhaps even resolving the remaining aspects of the problem. In any case, a careful follow-up in the next session would indicate whether other aspects or holons (energy terms) or channels (an EMDR term) remain to be treated. In Chapter 5 we discuss the use of EP to close an unfinished EMDR session.

23. Resistance and other issues with forensic populations can be targeted effectively with both methods, either in closed prison units or in the open community (probation or parole, community corrections, halfway housing). Because EP can be demonstrated so readily, and because the demonstration itself is often so intriguing that otherwise skeptical clients will be encouraged to try out the treatment, we rate EP higher than EMDR.

Off and on through our careers we have worked with forensic clients in outpatient, half-way, and prison settings. In Chapter 9 we discuss the offender population, one of those groups psychotherapists have largely ignored or declared unreachable. As with addiction, we are speaking only of intervention with EP or EMDR at certain limited points or stages of treatment. The traumas that characterize most offenders can indeed be processed, but whether this work produces lower recidivism is a question yet to be answered.

Miscellaneous

24. Children respond well to both EP and EMDR, whether used separately or together. Several very readable books have been written about applications of EMDR with children (Greenwald, 1999; Lovett, 1999; Tinker & Wilson, 1999). We know of none yet written specifically for those who wish to use EP with children. It generally is suggested that children being treated for trauma are particularly vulnerable because of limited coping skills and intellectual limits, and therapists who treat children should have special training and be prepared to offer appropriate nurturing, safety, and control (Tinker & Wilson, 1999).

Children are still being shaped and affected by their home environment, and it would be a serious error to think of EP and EMDR simply as techniques that can be employed without involvement of the parents, siblings, and other persons who influence the child. In this sense the notion of secondary gain is particularly salient: the child's apparently positive changes in therapy may disrupt a family system, which in turn may resist change or even punish the child. Involving significant others before, during, and after treatment often determines whether EMDR or EP (or any effective child treatment procedure) will produce stable benefit.

For those already skilled in working with children, it is not complicated to adapt the techniques we mention in this book to these
younger clients. Translating terms to a suitable vocabulary level, allowing for a child's limited attention span, and being especially aware
of reinforcers in the child's environment are some of the special steps
we take with children. The question of how much to involve the parents in treatment is also critical: Should I invite a parent to be present
during a session to support and better understand the child? Or would
the parent's presence discourage the child from speaking honestly?
Even the explanation of the treatment needs to be modified, as consent needs to come from both parent and child, albeit with different
levels of comprehension.

25. When a clinician wishes to reach many clients at once, EP can
be used effectively in group therapy, with all ages and populations.
Muscle testing and treatment techniques can be demonstrated, and
group members can follow along with the therapist who models the
treatment procedures. Abreactions are rare. The therapist can take
SUD ratings after each set of treatments, without being too concerned
that one or more persons will be negatively affected. In Chapter 9 we
describe how to introduce EP in a group setting, and to treat several
clients at once. Some therapists have experimented with using EMDR
in a group context. Forte (1999) suggested that EMDR with children
in a group therapy setting not only is cost effective, but also can be
done safely, as children tend to resolve traumatic issues more directly
and rapidly than adults. Lucina Artigas was working at an EMDR
emergency site with Mexican children rendered homeless by Hurricane Pauline, when it occurred to her that the children might be able
to tap themselves in an alternating bilateral fashion while she guided
them in visual exercises (Jarero, 1999). She had the children touch
each of their shoulders with the opposite hand in an alternating fashion, thereby inventing what she called the butterfly hug (abrazo de la
mariposa). Wilson and her EMDR team (Wilson et al., 2000) reported
using the butterfly hug successfully with Kosovo refugees living in a
refugee camp in Germany. And Korkmazlar and Pamuk (2000) used
the butterfly hug effectively in one-session treatment of children affected by the 1999 earthquakes in Turkey.

We do not recommend EMDR for adult groups. One or more persons in the group could experience elevated SUD levels or even abreactions, and the group therapist would not be able to monitor all

group members continuously and adequately. EMDR as we use it requires careful attention to the client, especially during the desensitization phase. Many clinicians already have more than enough trouble
during the desensitization phase with only one client. Group EMDR
has been used mainly with adults who could not otherwise afford individual treatment (e.g., offenders). Clearly in these cases we would encourage the group therapists to use EP rather than EMDR.

Artigas and Jarero (1999a, 2000) have reported as has Boèl (1999),
safe and effective use of the butterfly hug with adults traumatized by
natural disasters and treated under emergency conditions, particularly
when the TAT pose is combined with the butterfly hug.*

26. Self-care for clients following and between sessions is the focus
of Chapter 7. It is possible and valuable to teach clients how to treat
themselves as soon as possible. Because more preparation is required
before an EMDR client can be taught to use the method at home, we
rate EP higher on this issue.

27. Self-care without formal therapy has been mentioned on an
electronic discussion list available to graduates of EMDR Institute
trainings, but we recommend only EP methods for persons who wish
to treat themselves with no formal therapeutic support. Our reasons
have already been noted: the possibility for abreactions is too high
with EMDR, and we would not want a client to run the risk of opening old wounds with self-applied EMDR unless an EMDR-trained
clinician were available in the event of a psychological emergency.

28. Paraprofessional training has long been one of our interests,
especially as we work with persons from cultures where formal psychotherapy training is not readily accessible. In Chapter 10 we discuss
training of paraprofessionals. One of us (J. H.) is just beginning a pilot
project teaching EMDR to a group of carefully selected paraprofessionals, hence, the rating of 1 to indicate that we are hopeful but so
far have no results to report. Our experience teaching energy methods
to those not formally trained as psychotherapists is relatively extensive, and so far the results have been very positive.

29. Cross-culturally, both EP and EMDR seem to be marketable.
After teaching both methods to persons from quite a few countries,
we are left with few predictions about where EMDR or EP will or will
not be embraced. Many cultures do not have a tradition of formal

* Their results are available at: http://www.amamecrisis.com.mx/proing.htm.

psychotherapy training, so we rate EMDR slightly below EP for the same reasons mentioned for paraprofessional training.

A FLOW CHART FOR COMBINING EMDR OR EP

Figure 1.2 depicts *in a very general way* how the observations we have just made play out in practice. The figure represents the "big picture" of how we use energy techniques along with EMDR, and charts a course for deciding when to switch from one to the other. It is not meant to be comprehensive; we leave many of the moment-to-moment clinical decisions to the therapist.

An EMDR session without complications would flow down the right side of the chart through the first seven phases of treatment. It is assumed that no looping, dissociation, or severe abreactions will appear. This is usual for EMDR in our experience. A similarly smooth EP session, from readiness through muscle testing and treatment, is represented by progression down the left side of the chart. The activity in the middle is what we mostly focus on in this book.

The flow chart begins in one of the two upper corners. If, for example, you begin a session with EMDR (upper right), you will start with Phases 1 and 2. If you decide that your client is not likely to dissociate (no dissociation), you may proceed to Phase 3 of EMDR. However, if dissociation is detected, you have two options: either move on to EMDR resource installation or consider switching to the EP model. You can also note that if the client reports that the "SUD is too high" during the evaluation of Phase 3 you have the option of using EP to lower the SUD score prior to initiating EMDR. The rest of the chart is read in a similar way.

COMBINING EP AND EMDR

We have yet to read of a coherent theory that explains both EP and EMDR. While ultimately they may be shown to produce similar changes at a basic level, they do not share the same assumptions about problems, the same postulated mechanisms for change, or similar treatment strategies. When we speak of combining the two as treatment methods we refer simply to their practical utility, in the way that Lazarus (1989) speaks of "technical eclecticism." If our therapeutic efforts with one of the methods are not helping the client to move forward in healing, then we try something else, often a technique from the other method and sometimes two simultaneously. We have not

FIGURE 1.2. FLOW CHART FOR USING EP AND EMDR

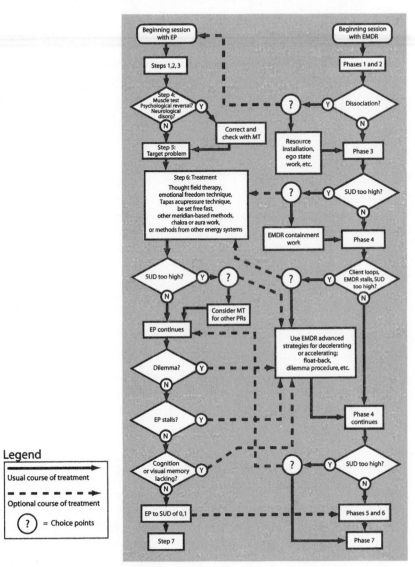

Figure courtesy of Langdon Foss.

seen conflicts between the two approaches when we use them in this way.

Shapiro speaks of neurophysiological change and of change occurring on every level of being. EP therapists speak of perturbations in the thought field, changes in energy flow and changes at the level of energetic vibrations in the cells, molecules, and atoms. Someday research may point to the most basic elements of change in each method, and these basic elements may be shown to coincide.

Chapter 2

Research

Scientific support lags far behind what EP and EMDR therapists claim to know from clinical experience and case studies. While the *concept* of subtle energy is supported, the clinical use of EP methods has little scientific backing so far. And whereas trauma is the only client problem for which EMDR is scientifically supported, therapists use EMDR methods for many others. Lack of empirical evidence is not unusual in the field of psychotherapy. Chambless and colleagues (1998) noted that there are no well-established, empirically supported psychotherapies for most of the problems that clients report and that are described in the *Diagnostic and Statistical Manual of Mental Disorders* (American Psychiatric Association, 2000). This does not mean that findings in the clinic are not valid, only that they need to be tentatively recommended until they enjoy scientific standing—that is until treatment effects are controlled for, predicted, empirically tested, and replicated.

In this brief overview of the research available on EP and EMDR, we comment from both scientific and clinical perspectives, as we remain active in both areas. Our careers have included teaching research methodology (J. H.), conducting original research (M. G.), and participating as therapists in clinical pilot studies and controlled outcome studies (M. G. & J. H.). We continue to consult with active clinical researchers.

EP

In this review of the EP literature we first introduce the general concept of subtle energy and then discuss separately the three energy systems included in the Grudermeyers' definition of EP: the meridians, chakras, and auras. As much as possible we use language that allows the concept of energy to be discussed in scientific terms and to be subject to the kind of analysis endorsed by the scientific community. Use of a common language helps to reduce the isolation from the scientific community that so many energy practitioners feel, and makes it less easy for those in the scientific community to ignore the work from alternative healing practitioners.

This information on EP is taken largely from James Oschman's *Energy Medicine: The Scientific Basis* (2000); the references to scientific parallels to the chakra system are from Candace Pert's *Molecules of Emotion* (1999). Oschman's career in academic science, and Pert's position as research professor in the Department of Physiology and Biophysics at Georgetown University School of Medicine make them particularly credible commentators on the subject of subtle energy, energy medicine, and EP.

Evidence for the Existence of Subtle Energy

Most people are familiar with the electrical fields that are generated by tissues and organs in living bodies. One familiar device used to measure the biological electrical fields is the electrocardiogram (EKG), which reads the pulse of electricity through the heart muscle that begins each heartbeat (Oschman, 2000). Another is the electroencephalogram (EEG),which detects brain electricity.

Unfortunately, electrical signals become distorted and weakened as they pass through tissues, so researchers have turned their attention to another of the biological energy fields: the magnetism created in the space surrounding the electrical currents. The relationship between electricity and magnetism can be attested to by any primary school student who has wrapped a bolt with insulated electrical wire, sent electricity through the wire, and then observed the bolt attract metal paper clips. A similar electricity-magnetism or electromagnetic relationship occurs in the living body.

The phenomenon of magnetism in a living body, or biomagnetism, allows for a more precise representation of activity in the body than electrical signals do, as biomagnetic signals pass undistorted through fluid, tissue, and even bone (Oschman, 2000).

While the concept of biomagnetism is becoming more acceptable, until the early 1960s the mainstream scientific community considered it nonsense, in part because available devices could not measure biomagnetism. Biomagnetic waves are quite weak (hence the term *subtle energy*) and much more difficult to detect than the body's more powerful electrical impulses. Among those who investigated biomagnetism were Gerhard Baule and Richard McPhee (1963) at the department of electrical engineering at Syracuse University in New York, who predicted that the heart produces magnetic fields, and developed a device which enabled them to measure those fields. Eventually the field of the heart was able to be detected 15 feet away from the body.

With further advances in quantum physics, more sophisticated devices were invented. One of the more interesting is the superconducting quantum interference device or SQUID, developed by James E. Zimmerman and his colleagues (Zimmerman, Thiene, & Hardy, 1970; Zimmerman, 1972). The SQUID makes it possible to conduct even more sensitive measurements of the faint magnetic fields produced by the body while screening out interference from other more powerful fields. The magnetic field of the earth, for example, is a million times more powerful than the magnetism produced by a person's heart. Brain fields, which are hundreds of times weaker than the heart's field, are even more susceptible to interference from background magnetism (Oschman, 2000). Hence, human subjects studied with a SQUID must be housed in a special medical laboratory that screens out background magnetism from the earth or from the typical urban environment, and they can wear no magnetic material, such as zippers or nails in shoes. Great care is also taken to control for other sources of magnetic interference, as every muscle movement, visual stimulus, and thought produces its own magnetic current (Oschman, 2000).

SQUIDs are now used to measure magnetic waves in brains and the rest of the body, and in the energy fields that spread around the body. Additional methods are being invented to measure magnetic fields, with promising results. The implications for healing are significant. Certain medical problems, such as tumors, do not show up on EEGs or computed axial tomography scans but can be detected by biomagnetic recordings (Modena et al., 2001; Oschman, 2000).

Evidence That Energy Can Be Harnessed for Intentional Healing

Pulsed electromagnetic field (PEMF) therapy is used to heal fractured bones that have not repaired themselves spontaneously. Oschman (2000) credited a number of researchers for the discovery of PEMF: Bassett (1995); Bassett, Mitchell, and Gaston (1982); and Brighton, Black, Friedenberg, Esterhai, and Connolly (1981). Treatment involves placing a small direct current generator next to the bone injury for 8 to 10 hours a day, producing PEMF. This magnetic field in turn causes currents to flow in nearby hard tissues (i.e., bone), triggering the process that heals the fractured bone. Clinical tests have proved that PEMF treatment will "jump-start" bone healing, even in patients whose fractures have gone unhealed for as long as 40 years (Bassett, 1995).

The physics principle underlying the use of PEMF is that energy within the living body is characterized by vibrations or oscillations. These vibrations occur at many frequencies. Each atom, molecule, cell, tissue, and organ has an ideal frequency that coordinates its activities (Fröhlich, 1968). The frequency generated by the PEMF device mimics the natural vibratory frequency required for bone healing. This sympathetic resonance (much as two tuning forks of the same frequency would affect one another) generates the correct vibrations for repairing the fracture, essentially re-calibrating the appropriate frequency (Oschman, 2000).

To date we are not aware of any research showing that a similar healing process can be produced by an energy practitioner. However, there are intriguing reports that energy fields emanating from the hands of practitioners of therapeutic touch and other energy methods can be detected. In the 1980s, John Zimmerman (1990) of the University of Colorado School of Medicine, using a SQUID, detected strong biomagnetic signals emitted by the hands of a practitioner of healing touch. The practitioner, relaxing into the healing state that is the focus of the therapeutic touch method, was able to produce a range of energy frequencies, as if scanning for the proper frequency. The practitioner was not always able to produce the desired energy current: Recordings were repeated eight times, and strong biomagnetic signals were recorded five times. The frequencies detected were similar to those emitted by the PEMF device.

Seto and colleagues (1992) conducted similar studies in Japan, replicating and refining the work of Zimmerman to the point where practitioners were shown to emit pulsing biomagnetic fields in the same frequency range that the biomedical researchers using PEMF treatment had found necessary to initiate healing in bones. Persons untrained in energy healing were unable to produce the biomagnetic pulses.

These studies do not prove that energy practitioners can effect healing by manipulating subtle energy fields. So far, though, the findings are consistent with what energy practitioners believe.

Evidence That the Meridian System Exists and Can Be Used in Healing

The energy basis for most of our EP work is the meridian system. As stated in Chapter 1, this system consists of pathways that carry the flow of energy (*chi* in Chinese) through the body. The pathways have been compared to utility lines that carry electricity along copper wires. Just as electrons can slow down owing to the resistance in the copper, so can energy slow down in the meridians. And just as transformers are placed on utility poles to recharge electrons so they can continue to flow along electrical wires, so there are points along the meridian lines thought to serve as mini-transformers (Becker & Sheldon, 1985). These points are known in Chinese medicine as acupuncture points, and for several thousand years have been the sites for acupuncture treatments. The points are named according to their location on a specific meridian segment, such as bladder-1 and liver-3.

While meridians are taken for granted in many countries, Western medicine has been slow to accept the concept. McNally (2001), for example, referred to the meridian system as prescientific folk medicine and implied that it is inappropriate to use physics terms such as *energy* and *fields* when discussing the concept. Lohr (2001) concluded that no convincing scientific evidence has been found for the existence of meridian lines.

Several publications in English suggest that acupuncture meridians are low-resistance pathways for the flow of electricity (Becker, 1990). Becker and his team found about 25% of the postulated meridian points using an electrode device that could be rolled along the meridian lines. He speculated that energetic background noise might have interfered with finding more meridians.

Zang-Hee Cho (1998), a physicist at the University of California-Irvine, was a pioneer in the development of positron emission tomography (PET) and magnetic resonance imaging (MRI). After finding relief from a back injury through acupuncture, he began using MRI technology to measure the effects of acupuncture treatment. He reported that specific acupuncture stimulation at the site of the little toe affected blood flow to the brain, even though no known nerve, blood, or other direct connection existed between those two specific sites. Acupuncture theory, however, predicted this effect as a function of energy concepts. Today many insurance companies reimburse acupuncture treatment, not necessarily because all of the theoretical components are endorsed but because treatment consistent with the theory is effective.

At the 2001 Association for Comprehensive Energy Psychology (ACEP) conference, Lambrou and Pratt (2001) reported unpublished data on the effect of stimulating specific meridian points. In one study they used functional MRI to measure pain arousal. When a subject immersed a finger in hot water, he reported pain, and increased activation was noted at the site of the anterior cingulate cortex and thalamus, as predicted. When stimulation was then applied to the subject's liver-3 meridian point on the arch of the foot, he was able to put his finger in the hot water without experiencing pain, and there was no increased activation of the anterior cingulate or thalamus. Stimulation applied to sham (random) sites on the subject's body produced neither anesthesia nor brain changes.

Evidence for the Effectiveness of Meridian-Based Psychotherapy Methods

We found 12 reports on the effects of meridian-based treatment for clinical problems, 11 on thought-field therapy (TFT) and 1 on the emotional freedom techniques (EFT). Three of the 12 are experimental studies. The others are collections of case studies.

Joyce Carbonell and Neta Mappa at Florida State University (Carbonell, 1996) conducted an experimental study on the use of TFT for acrophobia. They used the Cohen Acrophobia Questionnaire (Baker, Cohen, & Sanders, 1973) to identify 49 university students as having a fear of heights. Subjects were randomly assigned to receive either TFT (TFT group) or placebo TFT (control group); subsequent analysis indicated that pretreatment measures in the two groups were equivalent. Those in the TFT group were treated with the algorithm for phobia; subjects in the control group received a treatment consisting of tapping sham points (i.e., points on the body, whether meridian locations or not, that are not used in TFT).

Posttest assessment included the SUD scale and paper and pencil measures that were not described. Subjects were also asked to ascend a stepladder following treatment to provide a realistic test of effects. Both groups showed improvement on the measures, with the TFT group demonstrating significantly more improvement than the control group.

The study was reported in the TFT newsletter (Carbonell, 1996), and while the authors indicated plans to publish the entire study, we have not found a later publication. The brief report we reviewed for these purposes is difficult to interpret because no statistics were given, and some of the measures used were not described. As both groups were treated for psychological reversal, the control group was exposed to some of the TFT method, and the authors did not explain their rationale for this apparent contamination. Finally, it is not clear whether subjects were tested with the Cohen Acrophobia Question-naire following treatment, or whether follow-up was conducted. We therefore have no way to tell if the initial scores used to select subjects improved to where they were no longer considered acrophobic. Some of these issues may be resolved through the process of publication in a peer-reviewed journal.

Three studies were published in a special edition of the *Journal of Clinical Psychology* (JCP) (Beutler, 2001). They were criticized in that same issue for various flaws, but they remain fascinating preliminary reports from a clinical standpoint. The first was an investigation at a health maintenance organization (HMO) site by a group of clinicians interested in exploring the range of problems that might be amenable to TFT (Sakai et al., 2000). Seven therapists used TFT with 714 pa-tients for 31 different problems, including physical pain, addictive cravings, a variety of anxiety disorders, posttraumatic stress disorder (PTSD), relationship and work stress, trichotillomania, and depres-sion. Appropriate TFT algorithms were applied for each specific prob-lem. Patients were asked to rate their level of distress before and after treatment on the SUD scale. Results were significant for all problems reported by five or more subjects. Differences in the ratings before and after treatment for alcohol cravings, major depressive disorder, and tremors were significant at the .01 level, certainly a respectable clinical finding. More surprisingly, the positive changes in all the other problem areas reached a significance level of .001. Long-term effects were not evaluated systematically; several clients were followed by telephone for up to six months, and all reported that their symptoms had not returned.

Sakai and colleagues intended only to test the potential reach of TFT for different presenting problems, and recognized that their study did not control for many variables. In their conclusion they recommended randomized control studies comparing TFT with other treatments, using standardized measures and more systematic follow-up to see if the effects of TFT are maintained over time.

In the second *JCP* article, Johnson, Shala, Sejdijaj, Odell, and Dabishevci (2001) reported on a field study of TFT with victims of violence. In 1999 the ethnic Albanian residents in Kosovo were terrorized by invading Serbian forces. In 2000, TFT clinicians from Sweden, the United Kingdom, and the United States treated 105 persons who had been tortured or raped or who had witnessed the massacre of loved ones. The treatment team estimated that the 105 patients had suffered a total of 249 separate traumas. Working through translators and attempting to respect taboos against the expression of emotional suffering the team treated the patients for two weeks during each of five different months in 2000; the report did not mention the average time spent conducting TFT with each patient. Relying on informal reports, the team determined that 247 of the 249 traumas were resolved. Follow-up contacts from one to nine months following treatments uncovered no reports of relapse. Scientists can criticize this study's lack of randomization of subjects, use of nonstandardized measures, failure to account for competing hypotheses, and the like. Practicing psychotherapists, on the other hand, aware that the rate of spontaneous remission of PTSD symptoms during the first year is around 30% (Kessler, Sonnega, Bromet, Hughes, & Neslon, 1995) or at most 50% (Ehlers, 1999) will more likely feel exhilarated when reading about this work. A report of 98% recovery from trauma, even if informal, is likely to encourage a clinician who is dedicated to alleviating the suffering of trauma victims.

In the third *JCP* study Pignotti and Steinberg (2001) described 39 patients they treated with TFT. Their sample was not random, as they planned only to show what TFT might accomplish in clinical practice. Unfortunately they go well beyond the data in interpreting their results. They claimed, for example, that patients' symptoms were "completely eliminated" even though they attempted follow-up for only 4 patients (10%). They also defended their results by citing changes in heart rate variability (HRV), even though the meaning of HRV is controversial and the relationship between HRV and relief of clinical symptoms is unknown (Herbert & Gaudiano, 2001).

Callahan (2001) summarized two studies in *Tapping the Healer Within*. The first was by Robert Bray at San Diego State University, who used TFT to treat 29 immigrants and refugees with PTSD. Following treatment, 23 (79%) of the patients reported significant declines in the frequency of their symptoms.

The second, by Ian Graham, involved TFT treatment of 179 patients in the United Kingdom for a variety of psychological problems. All but 11 responded positively, with the average SUD rating dropping from 8.29 to 2.17 after an unreported amount of TFT treatment.

Callahan (1987b) and Leonoff (1996) authored two additional reports. In both studies people called in to radio programs to complain of phobias, anxiety, addictive cravings, guilt, and marital problems, and Callahan and Leonoff treated the callers with TFT over the phone. Callahan reported a "success" rate of 97%; Leonoff's reported rate was 100%. The data presented should be questioned for accuracy, purported benefits should be examined to see if they endured, and conclusions should be considered tentative until their work has been replicated under controlled conditions. However, we applaud these practitioners for being willing to demonstrate their psychotherapeutic technique so publicly. After all, it might have turned out the other way: ninety percent of the callers could have announced to thousands of listeners that they did not feel any better after treatment, and that TFT is a hoax.

The last three reports on TFT are dissertations, two of them case studies and one a controlled experiment. The first dissertation evaluated the effects of TFT treatment on phobia and self-concept (Wade, 1990). An experimental group of subjects 28 and a wait-list control group of 25 was administered tests which identify elements of self-concept. Two- to three-month follow up showed significant improvement in three scales for the experimental subjects: self-acceptance, self-esteem, and self-incongruency. There was an average decrease of 3.4 points in SUD level for the experimental group compared to a decrease of less than half a point in the control group.

In his critique of the study, Lohr (2001) noted that only 2 of 14 measures favored TFT compared to a wait group, and that even these results could have been explained with alternative hypotheses.

The other two dissertations recount studies conducted by two of our colleagues, Dale Darby and Beverly Schoninger, who have shared their preliminary data with us. These two researchers (and two others also conducting TFT studies) attend nontraditional universities (which has us wondering whether mainstream campuses are involved in this kind of research) and are largely self-funded. (All four have taken on tasks far beyond the minimum that would have been required had they simply wanted to finish their doctoral work. They are, in our view, true scholar-practitioners.)

Darby (2001) had completed a study of TFT with persons who had been unable to receive necessary medical attention because of intense needle phobias. His study has obvious methodological problems. For example, the author conducted the TFT treatment and also collected the pretreatment and posttreatment data, there was no independent control group, and the follow-up was after only one month. Nonetheless, what he found deserves our attention.

The treatment sample consisted of 20 men and women with blood-injection-injury phobia. Baseline values were established with a fear inventory and the SUD measure. Darby intended to test the power of minimal EP interventions, so subjects were treated for only one hour each with the diagnostic version of TFT. All completed treatment within the allotted hour. A month following treatment the measures were administered again. While not all subjects showed improvement, the differences between pretreatment and posttreatment measures were statistically significant in the positive direction.

Regardless of the statistical outcome, the study had personal meaning for many of the participants. Following treatment, subjects were exposed to a hypodermic needle and syringe, and those whose phobia had improved made comments such as "It's just a needle," "No big deal," "It doesn't bother me," "More curiosity about it than fear," "It's just an instrument now," and "Now I can watch myself receive an injection." After only an hour of TFT diagnostic treatment, some overcame what could have been a life-threatening phobia. Might more subjects have benefited had treatment been longer than one hour?

Schoninger (2001) conducted a study of EP with persons hampered by public speaking anxiety, a social phobia. Thirty-eight women and 10 men were assigned to either a treatment group or a wait-group control. All 48 were videotaped while giving an extemporaneous speech in front of a small audience and then completed self-report instruments to measure their emotional responses to the public speaking experience. Among the measures used were the SUD scale, Spielberger's State-Trait Anxiety Inventory, and the Clevenger and Halvorson

Speaker Anxiety Scale (see McCrosky, 1970, and Clevenger & Halvorson, 1992). No significant differences in pretreatment measures were found between the two groups.

Subjects in the treatment group were then treated with TFT for up to one hour, which was also videotaped, and immediately gave another speech, after which their anxiety was measured with the same instruments. Scores on all three instruments were dramatically lower compared to the pretreatment scores ($p < .001$).

Subjects in the wait group returned two weeks later, gave another speech, and completed the same instruments. Scores at this time were slightly higher than earlier, but not significantly so. This group was then treated with up to an hour of TFT and again completed the self-report instruments. Scores were significantly lower than pretreatment scores and comparable to the posttreatment scores of the treatment group; no significant post-treatment differences between the two groups were measured by any of the instruments. Of particular interest were changes on positive and negative factors measured by the Speaker Anxiety Scale. Following TFT treatment subjects reported less shyness, confusion, physiological activity, and postspeech anxiety, and more interest in giving a future speech, increased positive anticipation, and more poise.

Schoninger then invited all subjects to be interviewed by her four months later. This follow-up did not include further measurement with the instruments already mentioned. In the summary report we received, she listed "comments from some of the participants." One subject said a friend commented on the difference in how the subject acted after treatment. After the subject spoke "off the cuff" at a meeting, the friend said laughingly, "You're like the mouse that roared." A second subject reported, "I am more relaxed when I have to speak in front of people." A third one reported, "At staff meetings at the hospital I don't have trouble speaking up. I am planning to teach a parenting class and I don't have any anxiety about it." Additional anecdotal reports will be available from the author once she has completed her dissertation.

The last of the 12 meridian-derived treatment studies we review compared EFT with diaphragmatic breathing in the treatment of children with animal phobias. This unpublished report was presented at an ACEP conference (Carrington, 2001). Based on the graphs shown at the presentation, the deep-breathing group fared about as well as those who received EFT, and in neither case were the benefits very positive. SUD scores were somewhere in the midrange for both groups following treatment. (See Chapter 3 for comparisons of EFT with TFT algorithms.)

Evidence on Muscle Testing Used in Healing

Muscle testing is often used before and during EP treatment, though there is much controversy as to its reliability. That is, sometimes a practitioner may seem extremely accurate in "reading" a client in this way and sometimes not accurate at all. Britt, Diepold, and Bender (1998), Gallo (1999), and Lambrou and Pratt (2000) generally regard muscle testing as useful and dependable. Monti, Sinnott, Marchese, Kunkel, and Greeson (1999) performed research on muscle testing which they reported in the reputable scientific journal *Perceptual and Motor Skills*. Their research showed the effect of true and false statements on muscle strength.

Evidence That the Chakras Exist and Can Be Used in Healing

The locations of the chakras or energy centers in the body appear to be coterminous with points of electrical and chemical concentration. Pert (2000) reported finding concentrations of neuropeptides (which she termed the "molecules of emotion") at the sites of six of the traditional seven chakras. At the seventh (the crown of the head), she detected no such concentration. She speculated that the dense concentration of neuropeptides in the brain is transformed into a phenomenon that is not yet measurable with available instrumentation. She then noted that in the chakra tradition of many cultures, "the seventh chakra, the seat of intention, is actually above the head in the body's energy field" (Pert, 2000, p. 9). The implication is that proper stimulation of the chakra sites may effect changes in the body's neurochemistry, which in turn improve communication among the various components involved in physical and emotional health.

Healing touch practitioners have attempted to show evidence for their work, though study results can be difficult to interpret in terms of observable and behavioral benefits. For example, in *The Healing Touch Level I Notebook* used in basic training (Mentgen & Bulbrook, 1996), only about half of the approximately dozen studies summarized indicated benefit to healing touch patients. Symptoms measured before and after treatment included tension headaches, stress, anxiety, and diastolic blood pressure. The 2001 edition for Level II (Mentgen & Bulbrook, 2001) does not update the earlier list of research studies.

A recent study reported in the *Healing Touch Newsletter* (Diener, 2001) involved chakra work with five adult female subjects suffering from fibromyalgia. During the week before treatment, subjects rated their low and high pain levels on a scale from 0 to 9, with 9 being maximum pain. Average scores were 3.7 for one subject and between 5.2 and 5.7 for the other four. Ten sessions of chakra work and other healing touch procedures were then conducted on a massage table. In about two-thirds of the sessions, subjects reported some improvement, and though the benefits were not maintained for more than a few days, even temporary relief is welcome to sufferers of this chronic pain syndrome. After the final session the average decrease in pain scores for the five subjects was 1.54. The author noted that this number "seems barely significant," but then observed that "the Chakra Connections corrected all imbalances found in the chakras and Magnetic Unruffling cooled 76% of the warm astral fields" (Diener, 2001, p. 8). One of the challenges facing EP practitioners and researchers is exemplified here: given that changes in energy dynamics are not always or immediately accompanied by positive experiences in the physical plane, how might the EP proponent translate articles of faith (e.g., that energetic changes have practical importance) into language and "evidence" acceptable to the scientific and pragmatic community?

Evidence That the Auras Exist and Can Be Used in Healing

In the 1960s the Russian scientist Semyon Kirlian became known for his camera that was able to detect energy emitted by living tissue when subjected to certain electronic frequencies (Lambrou & Pratt, 2000). When he cut off a part of a freshly plucked leaf and photographed the remaining leaf, the developed photograph would show a distinct radiation pattern of light that depicted the shape of the original leaf, including the part that had just been cut off. The implication was that the energy that surrounded the original leaf remained even after a material part of the leaf had been removed. Those who work with auras in healing often use Kirlian photography as support for their assumptions.

In an intriguing report, Pavek (2001) described a two-year-long effort to prove that the biofield (i.e., aura) exists and can be accurately detected with the hands of an experienced energy practitioner. The study is particularly noteworthy because the author first described failures, then learnings, and finally a successful ending.

After much trial-and-error experimentation, Pavek decided to utilize brass screening material that is commonly used in electronic isolation rooms. Two isolating sleeves allowed the experimenter and subject to place their hands inside without touching, and while being visually blocked from each other. Presumably, the subject would then place a hand in the sleeve or not, at random, and the experimenter would state whether an energy field was detected or not. Twenty-two energy healers who do not normally detect auras were then trained, after which they were tested a total of 220 times using the sleeves. They were able to detect when a subject's hand was in the sleeve or not with 93% accuracy. Pavek noted that when testing was conducted in the open air (i.e., without the brass screen to keep the biofield from spreading), the percent of accurate readings dropped significantly. He concluded that this was consistent with the view that the biofield is part of the electromagnetic spectrum.

We already reviewed Zimmerman's discovery that experienced therapeutic touch practitioners can emit biomagnetic fields similar to those produced by machines that activate the healing functions in nonunion bone fractures. Findings like these do not prove that the person who can detect or create a certain energy field can manipulate that field to effect physical and emotional healing in a patient; we must await clinical research to evaluate the applicability of these phenomena.

EMDR

EMDR remains at the center of a spirited debate as to the coherence of its theoretical foundations, necessity of its components, and effectiveness of its use (e.g., Rosen, 1999). Claims have been made that research supportive of EMDR has been faked (as cited in Beutler & Harwood, 2001), and EMDR has been dismissed as such an improbable treatment that "further research on EMDR qua EMDR is unnecessary" (McNally, 1999, p. 3). Persons willing to read the following reports of what science actually says about EMDR will probably be open-minded about its possibilities.

Evidence That EMDR Is Effective

In 1995 a committee of the Division of Clinical Psychology of the American Psychological Association (APA) reviewed the degree to which psychotherapies in use were supported by empirical evidence (Chambless et al., 1998). EMDR was judged to be "probably effica-cious" for civilian patients with PTSD. Subsequently, the International Society for Traumatic Stress Studies designated EMDR as effective for PTSD (Chemtob, Tolin, van der Kolk, & Pitman, 2000). While Muris and Merckelbach (1999) cautioned against using EMDR for conditions other than PTSD, clinicians realize that this indication still allows broad use of EMDR, as traumatic stress can produce flashbacks, anxi-ety, depression, hopelessness, anger, difficulty concentrating, recur-rent nightmares, emotional numbing, and other symptoms for which clients seek help.

In the first meta-analysis of the EMDR literature, van Etten and Taylor (1998) found EMDR to be as effective as any of the other behavioral treatments for PTSD and more efficient, requiring less treatment time overall. They further concluded that the effects of EMDR were more positive than those of both placebo and supportive therapy. A second metaanalysis examined the relationship between ef-fect size estimates and the quality of research conducted on EMDR (Maxfield & Hyer, 2002). The authors found that studies of higher-quality research tended to produce stronger benefits for clients. In a third meta-analysis, Marzano and Marzano (2001) concluded that EMDR is a viable therapy for PTSD as determined by a wide variety of dependent measures. An extensive, up-to-date bibliography of re-search on the efficacy of EMDR can be found on the EMDR Institute's Web site (see Appendix B).

To give a sense of the benefit that can be expected when EMDR is used and studied optimally, we review one of the studies on which the APA relied to determine that EMDR is useful for PTSD. Our col-leagues Sandra Wilson, Lee Becker, and Bob Tinker (1995) performed a study which showed positive EMDR results that parallel our experi-ences working clinically with hundreds of patients. Briefly, 40 men and 40 women volunteered to be treated for traumatic memories of an event that had occurred three months to 54 years earlier. Half of the men and half of the women were treated with three 90-minute EMDR sessions. Their symptoms improved significantly, and their gains were stable at the 15-month follow-up (Wilson, Becker, & Tinker 1997). The rest of the men and women were on a delayed-treatment wait list. The trauma symptoms of this group did not change during the month they waited. After treatment with EMDR, the delayed treat-ment group showed equivalent gains that also held up over the 15

months. Overall, there was an 84% reduction in the incidence of
PTSD symptoms at the 15-month follow-up. The authors noted that
this finding compared reasonably well with the 75% to 80% reduction
in PTSD symptoms that Richards, Lovell, and Marks (1994) found
with a longer behavioral exposure method (60 hours of exposure compared with the 4½ hours allowed in the study conducted by Wilson
and colleagues). Wilson's group also reported that no individuals
showed worse symptoms on any of the posttreatment measures, which
is noteworthy given that exposure methods used in the treatment of
PTSD sometimes produce a worsening of symptoms (Pitman et al.,
1991). Because five persons still met PTSD criteria at the 15-month
follow-up, the authors cautioned, "For some individuals, three sessions
of EMDR do not constitute complete treatment" (Wilson et al., 1997,
p. 1054).

In a review critical of EMDR, Lohr, Lilienfeld, Tolin, and Herbert
(1999) concluded that Wilson and colleagues "did not compare
[EMDR treatment] effects with any control condition" (p. 197). However, the delayed-treatment group acted as a control for itself; the 40
persons in this group did not show improvement during the month
they waited for EMDR treatment, were then treated, and reported
positive benefits similar to those in the first treatment group. Perhaps
the delayed-treatment subjects would have improved had they been
asked to wait for 15 months, or perhaps they would have remained
equally traumatized. The researchers decided that it would be unethi-
cal to deny treatment for so long, and were willing to forego the
opportunity for an equivalent control group. The Lohr group also ar-
gued that the effective components of EMDR are nothing other than
certain cognitive, behavioral, and guided imagery techniques that are
already in wide use in existing therapies. They did not explain, however, how 4½ hours of EMDR was as effective as the 60 hours of the
behavioral exposure method reported by Richards and fellow researchers (1994).

In their metaanalysis, Marzano and Marzano (2001) noted that
while studies have generally supported the efficacy of EMDR, a report
by Jensen (1994) did not. However, they noted that in Jensen's study
persons assigned to a control group were given a list of alternative
treatment sources where they might receive mental health treatment
during the duration of the study. Additionally, Lipke (1999) reviewed
the Jensen treatment tapes and concluded that EMDR treatment was

terminated prematurely, while clients were in the midst of improving (as measured by SUD scores).

Evidence That EMDR Is Superior to Other Treatments

Cahill, Carrigan, and Freuh (1999) stated that it is important to know not only whether a new treatment works for a particular client problem but also whether the new treatment is better than existing treatments. Marzano and Marzano (2001) reviewed 12 studies in which EMDR was compared to some other form of therapy. EMDR generally fared well. In the study by Marcus, Marquis, and Sakai (1997), for example, EMDR was compared to standard-care treatments typically offered in an HMO setting. The authors concluded that EMDR was much more efficient, and that the provision of EMDR as a treatment of choice could save HMOs several million dollars annually.

Marzano and Marzano found one study to be a glaring exception to the general rule that EMDR was superior to other therapies. This study compared EMDR and a specific cognitive-behavior therapy approach called trauma treatment protocol (TTP). This method involves prolonged imaginal exposure, cognitive restructuring, and guided self-dialogue (Devilly & Spence, 1999). The authors reported that TTP was superior to EMDR immediately following treatment, and that this relatively greater efficacy increased at a three-month follow-up.

Perkins and Rouanzoin (2002) reviewed the article by Devilly and Spence and found extensive problems in how EMDR was conducted. They concluded that these problems compromised the conclusions drawn in the study. Marzano and Marzano also noted the possibility of experimenter bias, as the first author was the designer of TTP and had conducted all of the TTP therapy and EMDR therapy for all subjects except three.

We compared the results of Devilly and Spence's study with those from Wilson and colleagues based on self-report measures that were used in both studies: the Spielberger State-Trait Anxiety scale (Spielberger, Gorsuch, Lushene, Vagg, & Jacobs, 1983) and the SCL-90-R Global Distress Index (Derogatis, 1992). In Devilly and Spence's study, on both measures TTP was superior to EMDR. In the study by Wilson and colleagues, however, on both measures the posttreatment scores were more positive than the scores of both the EMDR and TTP subjects in Devilly and Spence's. Pretreatment data show little difference between the subjects in the two studies so one cannot say that the PTSD subjects in Devilly and Spence's study were worse off at the start.

Of the 12 original EMDR subjects in Devilly and Spence's study, 6 "dropped out of treatment before completion" (Devilly & Spence, 1999, p. 151). Other studies have not shown such a high dropout rate of EMDR subjects. In the study by Wilson and colleagues, for example, all of the original 80 subjects who began EMDR completed treatment. In a comparison of EMDR with prolonged exposure, there were likewise no dropouts in the EMDR group, but the exposure group had a 30% dropout rate (Ironson, Freund, Strauss, & Williams, 2002).

Interestingly, the 6 subjects who terminated EMDR prematurely in Devilly and Spence's study were included in the outcome data. Measuring the effects of EMDR on clients who drop out reflects a misunderstanding of EMDR theory and practice. As Shapiro (2001a) noted, "The client's level of disturbance can get much worse before it gets better" (p. 40). Experienced EMDR clinicians understand well that the processing of memories often will uncover other disturbing memories. Sometimes as one is resolved, another is uncovered. The EMDR subjects in Devilly and Spence's study who terminated treatment prematurely left possibly in the midst of an abreaction, probably in the midst of desensitization, and almost certainly prior to completing their work.

The divergent data from different research articles parallel what we see in clinical practice. Some EMDR clinicians report relatively little risk to clients, low dropout rates, positive benefits, and stable results on follow-up. Others find EMDR to be unimpressive, to cause harm, or to produce high dropout rates. One of our interests as scientist-clinicians is to examine more closely the procedures and styles of these two groups of clinicians. This information could be made available so that more therapists learn and benefit from the "best practices" of EMDR work.

Brain Changes Following EMDR Treatment

A study by Levin, Lazrove, and van der Kolk (1999) provided preliminary information about how the brain changes as a result of EMDR treatment. A PTSD client treated with three 90-minute EMDR sessions was evaluated before EMR with psychological testing, self-reports, and neuroimaging using single photon emission computed tomography; then was reevaluated with the same tests. After treatment, when the client recalled the traumatic memory that had been the target of EMDR, neuroimaging showed increased activity in the anterior cingulate gyrus and the left frontal lobe, which the authors interpreted as signs that the client had learned to differentiate real from imagined threat. Positive changes were also noted on psychological testing (the subject was no longer diagnosable as PTSD following treatment) and in the client's self-report. These data suggest that the brain changes with EMDR treatment so that it can begin to respond to *past* events as just a memory, and to think about the *present* as something new.

EP AND EMDR COMPARED

EP and EMDR have not been compared under rigorous methodological parameters. However, in 1993, at Florida State University, Charles Figley and Joyce Carbonell (1995) invited 10,000 members of the APA to nominate highly effective and efficient PTSD treatments of PTSD. They selected four: EMDR, TFT, visual/kinesthetic dissociation (V/KD) (Bandler & Grinder, 1979), and traumatic incident reduction (TIR) (Gerbode, 1989). Even though the purpose of the project was to identify the active ingredients of psychotherapy for trauma, some reviewers have seen it as a comparison of the therapies involved. Wylie (1996), for example, suggested that the greater efficiency of TFT would make it superior to the other three therapies. We summarize the study because it provides preliminary outcome data that can serve as a tentative baseline for the future and because the findings are interesting clinically.

In their study, 51 PTSD subjects reported average initial SUD ratings of between 8 and 9 related to their traumatic experiences. They then were treated for a maximum of four sessions each. Follow-up data were gathered on 40 of the subjects four to six months after treatment. Gallo (1999, p. 19) summarized the follow-up data (Table 2.1).

The EP treatment, TFT, was most efficient: barely an hour of treatment time was required. This finding is consistent with clinicians' reports about the efficiency of TFT. On the other hand, the group that enjoyed the most sustained benefit was the group treated by EMDR, which produced the lowest SUD score at follow-up.

Taking a closer look at the data, Gismondi (2000) noted that TFT "worked well on more fragile dissociative clients that the EMDR team refused to treat" (p. 9). This comment is intriguing to us as it parallels our clinical experience and encourages us: perhaps we can combine EP (represented by TFT here) and EMDR to improve the efficiency,

TABLE 2.1 GALLO'S SUMMARY (1999) OF DATA FROM FIGLEY
AND CARBONELL'S STUDY

Method	No. of Subjects	Treatment Time (min)	Follow-up SUD Score
V/KD	11	113	3.30
EMDR	6	172	2.64
TIR	9	254	5.67
TFT	14	63	3.60

Results of an early demonstration study showing the efficiency of TFT and the effectiveness of EMDR.

safety, and many other positive effects of treatment for the greater benefit of our clients!

We consider this a pilot study, heuristic in that it stimulates further investigation and pioneering in that it raises expectations about how much better psychotherapy can and must become.

"PERSONALIZING" RESEARCH

Lambert, Okiishi, Finch, and Johnson (1998) observed that practicing clinicians have remained rather skeptical about the usefulness of psychotherapy research (which suggests that what we have reviewed so far may not sway clinicians very much!). They suggested an alternative way for clinicians to defend their work, whether in response to third parties or as some indication of what future clients might expect. Recognizing both the constraints of applied practice and the growing call for accountability, they recommended that individual psychotherapists use standardized, self-report rating scales to provide ongoing information about the progress of their clients. They discuss the Outcome Questionnaire (OQ), which measures client functioning on three dimensions: emotional state, social role, and interpersonal relations. The OQ can be acquired at a nominal fee from the authors, and then copied as needed once a licensing agreement is signed.

Few psychotherapists ever conduct formal research after graduate school, so we welcome the ideas of Lambert and his team (1998), which allow clinicians to gather their own data. We also speculate that clients are more interested in what a particular clinician has accomplished with past clients than in what research data say. Clients ask not so much whether EP and EMDR are effective but rather how likely it is that the clinician will be able to help them. Related questions are "How much better am I likely to feel after working with you?" "How long is this likely to take?" and "How much will it cost to work with you?" Based on the research we just summarized, the answer to even a simple question such as "How many people who start EMDR actually complete treatment?" could be "50%" or "100%," depending on the practitioner.

In this spirit, one of us (J. H.) gives an information sheet to prospective clients (see Appendix A). Though he has used the OQ with clients when third parties request feedback on treatment progress, he more commonly employs SUD measures. As part of an informed consent package, this sheet provides information about previous clients' experiences. Since different presenting problems are associated with different rates of change, rather than indicating the "number of clients who benefit," the data are tied to the type of problem(s) for which a client seeks treatment. It is recommended that a disclaimer be included, or discussed, to indicate that the numbers are historical only and do not predict or guarantee that future results will match past results. Past behavior is predictive but not perfectly so. Clients can use the data to clarify their expectations for therapy but only in a general sense.

This way of presenting historical data is beneficial to both therapists and clients. Therapists become more cognizant of how well they are doing with different presenting problems and can refine their practices as a result. They will not be likely to overstate their expertise or effectiveness since they are holding themselves accountable for future results. Clients benefit because they have more information on which to base their informed consent. Were a number of clinicians willing to offer similar data, clients could have even more information available to help them to choose between clinicians in a competitive market. As a result, clinicians might eventually specialize according to their best skills and refer clients to experts in different specialties.

Chapter 3

Conducting EP

There is a fairly structured eight-phase process to be followed in EMDR. No equivalent exists for EP practice, except for conducting the treatment itself. This lack of standardization is a cause for concern since many EP trainees do not have extensive experience carrying out formal psychotherapy sessions and are relatively unfamiliar with even basic procedures such as opening a session, introducing oneself and EP, and learning the history of the presenting problem. As a result, some trainees leave an EP course with a wealth of theory and technique but when faced with a patient, realize that they are not sure exactly where to start, or how or when to proceed logically from one stage of treatment to the next. We now describe seven steps that serve as a guide for our EP work and cover the essentials of adequate EP treatment. Though the work sometimes seems simple, instruction and supervised practice are recommended for maximum effectiveness.

STEP 1: RAPPORT

Relevance

A well-known EP therapist recently stepped on stage during a training program. He had agreed to use his particular model to treat a client publicly. The energy therapist boasted that the energy model is superior to the others, and that he would soon prove his claim to be true. His client arrived, somewhat anxious and hesitant, presumably a perfect subject for energy methods. The energy clinician immediately instructed the client to touch here, tap there, do this, then that. The client complied but appeared to become more and more distressed rather than relieved. The therapist raised his voice, ever so slightly, repeating the instructions. The client seemed to become even more skeptical rather than persuaded. Treatment went on and on until the client, eventually losing patience, left the stage more anxious than before and now also disappointed and angry. The demonstration of the energy model was a decided failure.

The therapist was of the school that the real therapy is the tapping and related procedures. He saw no real need to provide warmth, trust, support, and the like but simply stimulated the correct points in the correct order. The therapist doubtless had had consistent success simply applying the techniques correctly without having established a conventional therapeutic relationship. Perhaps in this instance, he was too distant.

Indeed, in some cases, EP techniques (as well as EMDR, see Chapter 4) will work in the absence of a long-term, trusting therapeutic relationship. The following are examples:

- At times life-changing experiences occur in training practica where virtually no time is available to establish a rapport between therapist-trainee and client-trainee.
- An EP therapist asked to consult on specific problems with a client may also become a co-therapist and provide time-limited treatment, usually with no relationship building other than a brief introduction by the primary therapist. Even with this little time to build rapport, results are almost always positive.
- In disaster response situations, therapists have provided valuable services to clients seen only once with minimal introduction and under considerable stress.

Commonly a therapist is first exposed to EP in a training workshop. To see a trainer work effectively with a person about whom the trainer knows almost nothing, and with whom there appears to be no relationship, can give the impression that everything in EP depends on technique. However, the trainees who volunteer to be treated by us publicly are carefully self-selected and generally appear on stage somewhat convinced of the efficacy of the therapy and already wishing to heal (thereby accounting for motivation), perhaps wanting to be a good demonstration subject (thereby accounting for demand characteristics), and already trusting the trainer (thereby accounting for adequate rapport).

The reality in the therapy office is often quite different from training, consultation, and disaster response situations. Many formal therapy clients arrive asking to be helped but often are burdened by skepticism, fear, ambivalence, and a past filled with contributory traumatic events. Though they seem to present with a circumscribed problem for which the energy therapist has a ready, reliable treatment, more complex underlying disorders are not unusual. They therefore benefit from the support and understanding of an empathic relationship.

We have observed EP therapists who seemed rather cold, rather odd, somewhat nervous, even pessimistic or obnoxious, who nevertheless helped their clients with specific problems. Yet the example at the beginning of this section shows that sometimes the client needs to trust the clinician and feel cared about enough to be willing to try the method. Therefore, at times the relationship is indeed essential, and other times the treatment tool may eclipse or render largely irrelevant the relationship variables.

Transference

Most therapists view transference—that tendency of a client to "transfer" beliefs and feelings from outside the therapy office onto the therapist—as a treatment opportunity. They differ on how the transference is interpreted to the client and whether it should be interpreted at all. Most EP therapists we know (not all by any means) move fairly rapidly in transferring the transference (so to speak) back to the client. They look immediately for a way for the client to experience personally and internally what has just been done or said to the therapist. Gestalt therapists, psychodrama practitioners, and other body workers would have little trouble with this kind of immediacy.

EP therapists tend to bypass discussion of the past events in the client's life that might explain the transference, and work directly with thoughts or emotions that the client presently exhibits. (EMDR therapists may use ego state concepts to uncover earlier situations that require attention.)

We have seen less of a tendency for our clients to become enmeshed in transference issues compared to what we experienced when we did more traditional therapy. Part of the explanation has to do with the lower emphasis on the therapy relationship in EP, and part has to do with the time-limited nature of the treatment not allowing therapist and client to get to know one another as well. Even when a client seeks to draw the therapist personally into the client's therapy work, EP strategies can help the client to detach from the therapist and return to work on what is directly relevant in the client's life.

Countertransference

Countertransference refers to a therapist's reacting to the client with beliefs and feelings from past situations, as when the client does something minor and unpleasant that causes an exaggerated negative reaction in the therapist. EP clinicians we know tend not to analyze and discuss countertransference feelings with the client, but instead consider how the client's behavior might cause problems with persons outside of the therapy office, and target those situations. In order to stay centered and not be drawn in by a client's unpleasant behaviors, therapists need to attend to their own equanimity. Techniques described in Chapter 8 are helpful in this regard.

General Consensus

Although EP techniques are often quick both in demonstrations and in therapy, they are usually employed in the context of a multifaceted treatment relationship. The therapist will take a history, explain procedures, discuss treatment goals, and address peritherapeutic issues such as marriage and employment.

Most practicing psychotherapists follow the general guideline that a warm, empathic, genuine therapeutic relationship facilitates or even enables effective treatment. Depending on the needs and history of the client the therapist will, of course, dedicate more or less attention to establishing rapport. Gallo (1999, 2000a) reviews the issue of rapport in psychotherapy and considers it essential in EP. "In short, in most instances, before the client is willing to follow therapeutic directives, he or she needs to feel understood and accepted by the therapist" (2000, p. 23). Britt and colleagues (1998) concur: "Effective psychotherapy requires a trusting relationship" (unnumbered second page of manual, 2 pages before p. 1). The skills and commitment therapists have developed in this area should not be left behind when embarking on energy treatment.

STEP 2: INFORMED CONSENT

An early part of any treatment is the process of informed consent (Handlesman & Galvin, 1988). Here therapists review the process of psychotherapy in a way appropriate to the particular client—and in some states, according to legal dictates. They cover legal and ethical considerations including limitations of confidentiality, and information about themselves and their practice including fee information, the risks and benefits of treatment methods, and alternative treatment approaches. It is incumbent on therapists to let the client know when there are efficacious treatment alternatives and, if the client is curious about them, to provide further information. This can be problematic when a client requests or is referred for a specific modality. It is our custom to provide the requested treatment method, but if treatment stalls, we inform again about available options.

Gallo (1999, pp. 132–133; 2000a, pp. 22–23, 30) suggested ways to present energy therapy to clients. Clinicians will tailor wording to fit their own practices. Our explanations vary in length and scholarliness depending on the interest and sophistication of the client. A surprising number of clients have heard of acupuncture, and since meridian theory is at the root of the energy therapy we practice, we usually start with that: "You have heard of acupuncture, where Chinese doctors have been curing people for thousands of years. And now the National Institutes of Health (NIH) is certifying it for a growing number of disorders. Well, I won't stick any needles in you; I'll just have you touch or tap or rub various places on yourself [demonstrating on self] and do some other things which at first might seem odd, but which all have their reasons. I'll be happy to explain them if you want. Although the scientific research is just starting, we're having very good results with this approach and I think it can help you. Would you be willing to give it a try?" Refusal here is rare, and we typically propose a demonstration of the method on a problem the client has already mentioned.

We also might emphasize the electrical nature of the body, since almost everyone is familiar with EKG and EEG examinations. We mention that the energy that flows in the meridians is probably electromagnetic, and that acupuncturists believe it sometimes gets blocked.

In one case, an electrician came in to work on his anger, and ended by teaching me (J. H.) more about possible parallels between household electricity and subtle energy. I had suggested that he try energy techniques as he said it was urgent that he learn to control his emotions. I mentioned that the energy in his body might be somewhat like the electricity in the wires he handles every day, and that the transformers on electrical lines might be similar to the points I would teach him to tap. "They're called *step-up transformers*," he quickly informed me. He then explained that the electrons in a copper wire will eventually stop flowing because of resistance in the wire, resistance he measures in ohms, and the transformers step up the flow of electrons and send them on to the next transformer, and eventually to where the electricity will be used. When I said that some think the meridian points have a similar function, he understood how tapping the meridian points could facilitate the energy flow in his own body in the same way. Pulos (1999) used a similar analogy, speaking of rubbing the neurolymphatic reflex or "sore spot" (see below) as an "electrical reset button." Until more is known about the subtle energies, speaking of them metaphorically seems to us to be valid.

The notion of chakras can also be presented in familiar ways. The following example incorporates information from Pert's *Molecules of Emotion* (1997) and two of her audiotapes (2000) and frames EP in Western scientific terms.

Case Example:

The client, a financial consultant, is in his first psychotherapy session ever. He has been taking drugs prescribed for insomnia and worry but continues to sleep poorly and feel anxious. He has asked for psychotherapeutic help to try to eliminate both these symptoms and to learn coping skills that will make it possible to live without taking medications. A discussion of EMDR and related research findings has just ended. He is very agreeable to try EMDR, and especially liked the research I presented.

Therapist: *How about if I tell you now about that term energy psychology which you just read on that information sheet?*
Client: *Yes. I must admit it sounds a little peculiar to me.*
Therapist: *Maybe I can begin by talking about your medication. Even though you said you don't like the idea of depending on drugs, you also said it helps you to feel somewhat better. Well, the reason they work for you is that there are receptors in your body that act like a lock, and make room for the medications, which are like a key. When the two connect—the key into the lock so to speak—you feel a sense of well-being. There are a lot of receptors in the body, perhaps 200 to 300*

different kinds, that link up with chemicals we take in, whether it is aspirin, alcohol, or morphine. So why are these receptors there at all? According to neuroscientists, the receptors were originally meant to receive chemicals the body manufactures, but for some reason they began to be used for these artificial chemicals that come in from the outside. Take morphine, for example. Do you know what the natural morphine in the body is called?

Client: Actually, no.

Therapist: Have you ever heard of endomorphine or endorphin?

Client: Well, yeah. That's what comes from a "runner's high." So you're saying the body can produce its own morphine, its own marijuana, and its own alcohol?

Therapist: That is roughly the idea, that the receptors that accept the outside chemicals are also designed to accept something similar that the body makes, or at least that the body can make.

Client: Well, that makes sense.

Therapist: We used to think these receptors were only in the brain, but scientists have found them throughout the body—in the organs, the muscles, the joints. So the substances that fill up these receptors or locks, things called peptides or neuropeptides, end up everywhere in the body, and when they create a sense of well-being or pleasure, they do so throughout the body. It gives a new dimension to the concept of body-mind, doesn't it?

Client: Well, that's the way I feel, like my whole body feels better, not just my brain. But now I'm wondering why haven't I been producing my own chemicals?

Therapist: That's a good question, and one we can get to as we work together. I also hope we can talk about ways to get those chemicals manufactured again. But first let me tell you about some other discoveries that might interest you. I was recently reading about the work of Candace Pert, a neuroscientist at Georgetown University. She was involved in the discovery of the opiate receptor, among other things. You can imagine how important that was. She talks about how these receptors and their peptides tend to be found in concentrations in certain places in the body. One day she was giving a lecture, as I understand it, about where these receptors are concentrated, and she placed her hand on where the places might be in her own body. She put her hand on her forehead, then over her throat, then on the center of her chest, and so forth—and later one of the people in the audience went up to her and said she had been covering the exact places where the ancient chakras were said to be located. This spooked her at first, she said, because she thought the chakras were unscientific, mystical notions, and she didn't want to believe they were related in any way to what she was finding in her empirical research. Eventually, however, she began to wonder if what she had been studying in her lab might be the scientific explanation for the energy systems called chakras. And to shorten a *long story, she now writes about the similarities between the specific neuropeptide accumulations she was finding at a molecular and cellular level on the one hand, and the chakras on the other.*

Client: *So using chakras is just a way to somehow restart the chemicals that the body has stopped producing?*

Therapist: *That's an interesting way to describe it, and I don't know why that wouldn't be true. Those of us who work in this field of energy psychology think of the meridian points, which we teach our clients, as being part of the same energy system as the chakras. Are we teaching clients to stimulate their natural neuropeptides? Perhaps that's the way it is. I don't know. There are certainly interesting connections here. In any case, energy techniques work, so I do this because clients seem to benefit, not because I can explain exactly how they work.*

This sort of dialogue is fairly typical for us. Engineers, scientists, clients who subscribe to evangelical Christian dogma, and others tell us that this type of explanation helps them give the energy model a try by anchoring it in a base that feels solid and familiar.

We are confident in this method of explanation and believe it helps encourage clients to try the technique. Often in the initial description, or at a later time when the client expresses curiosity or skepticism about the methods, we hand out articles to read or (increasingly) give Web sites to investigate, especially Altaffer's energy therapy home page and Craig's emotional freedom technique (EFT) (see Appendix B). Interestingly enough, many clients, knowing which therapies we practice, arrive for the initial appointment already having read something or browsed a Web site.

STEP 3: CLIENT HISTORY

For clinicians already skilled at taking a client history, we do not undertake to reteach the topic. For practitioners unaccustomed to taking a thorough history (and there are many), we simply draw attention to a few points especially relevant to EP.

Client history is more emphasized in EMDR trainings than in EP. Perhaps because energy techniques can work even at cocktail parties, an EP therapist can become casual with regard to knowing a client's history. Sometimes, however, it is critical to know a client fairly well before initiating treatment, particularly where medical factors, severe trauma histories, and a tendency toward dissociation could complicate treatment.

Aspects

A thorough understanding of the patient's circumstances can help prepare for the unexpected appearance of what are called *aspects*. Although in EP the SUD usually becomes lower (or sometimes remains unchanged), on occasion it will rise. This increase is almost always due to the appearance of underlying emotions, aspects of a problem of which the patient is not aware until they are uncovered by the resolution of the presenting problem.

We sometimes introduce this concept of aspects to clients, now or in the previous step, in a metaphor along these lines:

> If I had a bunch of weeds in my backyard, I might go out there and grab the tops of the weeds and pull them right out. Now it might be that I get all the weeds that way, but I might also find that there were shorter weeds underneath, and I just got the tallest. I couldn't see those shorter ones until I had taken care of the biggest weeds. So I grab the ones I now see and I pull, only to discover yet another layer of shorter weeds. I might have to pull quite a few layers before I finally clear the place out. It's like that with therapy work sometimes. We clear out one aspect of a problem, only to discover that it was covering another that needed to be processed. Finding the new aspect doesn't mean the previous therapy was a failure. Quite the contrary. It just means there's more to do.

In treating a rape victim, for example, we initially might target the associated fear. The algorithm for trauma is often effective in similar cases, and the SUD score might go from 9 to 7 to 4 to 2—and then to 8. The newly elevated score is not a sign that treatment is a failure, but that a new aspect has been uncovered. On inquiry we find the patient now experiences guilt much more than the fear, which really *is* scored at 2 or below. As the guilt is treated with tapping of the appropriate points, the score again lowers—and again rises. Now it is anger and resentment that need to be addressed.

One middle-aged Asian man presented for treatment of a driving phobia, but during history taking it became apparent he was suffering from a generalized anxiety disorder, of which the phobia was but one aspect. Another client had called with the same presenting problem. She had developed it soon after moving from her native Germany. Her husband had transferred to his company's U.S. office and was working long hours getting "up-to-speed" with his new responsibilities. Her phobia forced him to spend a stressful (for him) amount of time driving her to various appointments but produced significant secondary gain for her. Needless to say, these driving phobias proved impervious to the algorithm for phobias until the underlying issues were addressed. In both cases, careful assessment revealed what would only have become obvious after fruitless treatment of what the client deemed the major problem, but was in reality only an aspect of it. In addition, the considerable depth to which treatment eventually went required an empathic, supportive relationship, not simply the skillful application of brief meridian treatments.

Thus, aspects are often uncovered in treatment—sometimes to the distress of therapist and patient. A careful history may avoid the surprise. Clarisse came in stating that she needed to work on a phobia of crossing bridges. Initially I (M. G.) was fairly confident that treatment would be brief and effective, but as I learned more about the patient's life, it became apparent that the specific phobia was but one manifestation of general low self-esteem. Further investigation revealed that the low self-esteem stemmed from abuse through her childhood by a father who struck—or threatened to strike—her without warning. As might be expected therefore, when we tried the usually successful phobia algorithm on the idea of driving over bridges, targeting an upcoming summer trip to the Pacific Northwest, results were disappointing. Distress lessened only slightly. After a few "rounds" of tapping, the general fearful lifestyle and then various traumatic situations with her father surfaced. Knowledge of the etiological nature of the abusive childhood helped me guide treatment more effectively than if I had simply reacted to the aspects as they appeared. After archaic issues were resolved over the course of many sessions, phobia treatments became successful, and the patient reported increased self-esteem in social interactions as well.

Other Factors to Evaluate

A thorough history should include an evaluation of other factors as well. The therapist can determine if the client avoids significant matters or is especially sensitive to others. In addition, the clinician can assess the client's ability to handle emotional upset including the client's ability to manage stress between sessions as well as the availability of supportive people in the environment.

History taking can reveal issues of secondary gain. A man who had been married five years presented for treatment for a fear of flying.

Again, this fear is usually quickly responsive to treatment, and I (J. H.) could have simple applied the phobia algorithm. Inquiry revealed, however, that the only times the patient took airplane flights was to New England, where his in-laws lived. In addition, the phobia began five years ago. This fear of flying would have been impervious to the usually highly effective phobia algorithm until feelings about the relationship with wife's family were resolved.

As explained in more detail in Step 6, energy toxins can block treatment. During history taking, inquiries should be made about allergies, use of tobacco, exposure to chemicals, and the like. Initially the therapist should be alert to circumstances where symptoms occur, when the patient is in a certain place or is exposed to or ingests a certain substance. The inquiry should be resumed if treatment is later blocked and toxins are suspected.

STEP 4: PREPARING THE ENERGY SYSTEM FOR TREATMENT

In this Step we introduce the client to some of the techniques of EP and screen for conditions that commonly block treatment. We find that addressing them at this point is efficient, as work proceeds relatively quickly and can save considerable time in Step 6.

Muscle Testing

Muscle testing is a technique that can be used at many stages of EP. We introduce it at this point and use it with most of our clients; some energy practitioners use muscle testing more frequently, and others little or not at all.

To conduct muscle testing, the clinician first gets permission to touch the patient. Then the therapist selects an indicator muscle and makes inquiries of the client to determine that there are no problems with it. Usually the deltoid muscle of the shoulder is involved in testing the arm. To test this indicator muscle, most commonly the clinician and client stand facing each other, offset a bit to the right. The client then extends the left arm out to the side perpendicular to the body. Some examiners rest the left hand on the client's right shoulder. Using the right hand, the clinician presses downward the client's wrist, having instructed the client to resist consistently on each test. In general, the indicator muscle is strong when the client has something positive or true in mind and weak in the opposite condition.

One of us (J. H.) varies the procedure by standing directly in front of the client, whose upper arms are held next to the body and forearms are parallel to the ground. He then pushes the client's wrists inward. Another variation has the client standing with arms down at the sides; the therapist holds the inside of the client's wrist and gently tries to pull the arm away from the side of the body. The other of us (M. G.) uses a technique learned from Diepold (Britt et al., 1998) in which he stands at 90 degrees to the client, so as to avoid direct visual interaction. The client is instructed to gaze downward and the examiner looks across in front of the client but can monitor the client's state by peripheral vision. He then tests the client's left arm with his right hand.

In order to calibrate—that is to get an idea of the client's general response strength—we first test "in the clear"—in other words with the client not concentrating on anything in particular. Next, to calibrate what is a strong response and what is a weak response, we ask the client to state something true while we perform muscle testing, and then something false during another test. A common test is to ask the client to state his or her name, then a false name. Other tests include saying, "Today is [correct day of the week]" versus "Today is [incorrect day of the week]," or "Two plus two is four" versus "Two plus two is seven." There is usually a notable difference, with the first test resulting in a strong arm and the second, weak. Often at this point, the client is impressed with the unexpected results. This is helpful in building credibility for EP, with initially resistant subjects, including those skeptical about psychotherapy in general or EP in particular and those "sent" for therapy such as adolescents, spouses, and forensic patients.

It should be noted that skill in muscle testing is acquired with training and practice, though beginners often have many successes.

Neurological Disorganization

After introducing the client to muscle testing and calibrating responses, we often use the muscle test to check for neurological disorganization. This condition, called "the collarbone breathing problem" by Callahan and "polarity switching" by kinesiologists, is believed to be caused by disturbances in the usual electrical polarity of the brain. This condition "involves the central nervous system's misinterpreting and misconstruing nerve impulses" (Gallo, 2000a, p. 216). We suspect neurological disorganization at any point in treatment when the client seems clumsy, uncoordinated, dyslexic, or mentally confused; stutters; or is hyperactive.

In the most common muscle test for neurological disorganization, the client holds one hand just above the head, palm down, while the examiner performs muscle testing. A second test is done with the palm up. If the first test shows a strong response and the second is weaker, neurological disorganization is probably not present; if both results are strong, it probably is. A weak response and then a strong one indicates massive psychological reversal, while weak on both tests indicates general system weakness. Treatments of psychological reversal are presented later. For general system weakness, the client can drink water or do the "thymus thump" (Diamond, 1979), a rhythmic tapping of the sternum with a fist.

Practitioners of Callahan Techniques-TFT will treat neurological disorganization with a fairly involved process called *collarbone breathing*. Many others use an "over-energy correction," which is one of "Cook's hookups" (Dennison & Dennison, 1989) in which the client places the left ankle over the right; extends the arms, crossing the right one over the left; turns the palms together and interlaces the fingers; brings the hands in to rest against the chest; and breathes with the tip of the tongue touching the roof of the mouth behind the teeth. (Some practitioners will advise this tongue position only for breathing in, and a position with tongue down behind the teeth for breathing out.) A minute or two of breathing in this position is usually enough to correct the neurological disorganization. If it does not, there are other treatments (Gallo, 2000a).

If a client expresses undue skepticism at this point, we may tell about an experience with Cook's hookups. I (J. H.) had just completed an EP training course outside the US and was invited by the local sponsor, a psychiatrist, and acupuncturist, to visit an alternative treatment clinic along with the rest of the training team. Among the unfamiliar devices there was a machine purported to measure subtle energies along the meridian lines, and naturally we all wanted to try it. When it came time for me to be measured, the attending physician (trained in Germany and using a South Korean-manufactured machine) used a metal probe to touch certain acupuncture points on my hands and torso and looked to a computer monitor as results were recorded. He then gave the "bad" news: "Every one of the points I tested is overenergized." I looked at the monitor: the computer had indeed printed out a score well above what was considered the normal range for human subjects, and well above what my team members had scored. I asked to take a five-minute break, during which I sat among the palm trees on his patio and did Cook's hookups. When I returned, he retested me: all of the points now registered normal. The physician was accustomed to prescribing homeopathic remedies in such circumstances and was surprised that a simple hand position and breathing procedure could cause such dramatic and immediate changes in an energy reading. He was able to find the source for my over-energy condition: a pendant I had been wearing that was designed to reflect electromagnetic field contamination (see below) but which I apparently was using for too many hours in the day. That was indeed useful information, as I had been having trouble regulating my own energy levels during the EP course.

Massive Psychological Reversal

Psychological reversal is thought to be a kind of energy disruption that prevents us from making full use of our energy resources. It is not fully understood; some hypothesize that it is a result of energy flowing in the wrong direction in one or more meridians, although acupuncturists do not use that concept. Nevertheless, a useful way to explain psychological reversal to clients is to ask how a perfectly good tape recorder would work if perfectly good batteries were put in backward. This metaphor helps normalize the phenomenon and minimize client self-blame. Lambrou and Pratt (2000) renamed the phenomenon, calling it an "internal disagreement," as well as saying it involves "self-sabotaging thoughts and beliefs" (p. 39). Whatever its nature, the effects of reversal are well known. When a reversal is present, people act contrary to their own intentions (Callahan & Perry, 1991; Diamond, 1988). They say they want to lose weight, let go of their anxiety, or stop smoking, but they continue with the problematic symptom. In addition, when reversal is present, the therapeutic process is blocked. Craig (1999) stated, "When it is present it will stop any attempt at healing, including EFT, dead in its tracks" (p. 23). This means all therapies, including EMDR.*

* How then to explain the fact that EMDR usually works so well? Theory states that all of us go in and out of reversal during the day. We conjecture that this accounts for some of the success of EMDR. If treatment is attempted when a psychological reversal is present it will be blocked, but if tried later when the client is not reversed, it will be successful. Moreover, it is possible that particular elements of EMDR are

Many types of psychological reversals have been identified (Britt et al., 1998; Durlacher, 1994; Gallo, 2000a; Grudermeyer & Grudermeyer, 2000; Lambrou & Pratt, 2000; Nicosia, 1999), but the massive psychological reversal (MPR) is one of the most common (Callahan & Callahan, 1996).

As noted, if the test for neurological disorganization yields a weak then a strong result, we already believe MPR is present and we will correct for it before proceeding. Otherwise we test specifically for MPR. Table 3.3 presents the tests and corrections for MPR. We ask the patient to say, "I want to be happy" (or "I want a happy life") and then test, followed by "I want to be miserable" (or "I want a miserable life") and a muscle test. A strong then weak result is negative for MPR; a weak then strong indicates its presence. If MPR is found, we correct. This entails rubbing the Sore Spot /Neurolymphatic Reflex in a clockwise direction, or tapping the side hand point (Figure 3.1) while saying three times, "I deeply accept myself with all my problems and limitations."

Since correction is so quick and effective, and since no harm is done if it is administered when MPR is not present, we very often apply it at the beginning of treatment, even if we don't specifically suspect the presence of MPR. If later during the course of treatment the client seems blocked by an MPR, or muscle testing indicates the presence of psychological reversal, we will again ask the client to correct for it.

The many practitioners of EFT will recognize the MPR correction as the "Setup," the first step in the EFT "recipe." The originator of EFT, Craig (1999) hypothesizes that about 40% of clients have a psychological reversal affecting the problem the problem they present. He therefore has all clients perform the Setup as a routine step in EFT on the premise that if a reversal is present, the correction needs to be performed, and if not, only a little time is spent and no harm is done.

sometimes effective corrections for reversal. The direction of eye movement, for example, is itself sometimes changed from horizontal to vertical, diagonal, circular, or other configurations. Physical tapping on one side and then the other of the body can be substituted for the eye movement, as can tones in one ear and then the other. Two of these modes of stimulation—or even all three—can be administered concurrently. Clients can be asked to change focus of attention to different aspects of the situation being processed or to a past instance of the situation. It is possible that any of these, or other, EMDR techniques may possess an as-yet-undiscovered ability to correct reversals.

As mentioned, there are many types of reversals. The most common ones, their diagnosis and correction procedures, and related affirmations are presented in Tables 3.3 and 3.4 and discussed below. We could—and some practitioners do—rule out more of these reversals before starting treatment, but most patients are well enough prepared for treatment after screening for neurological disorganization and MPR. If treatment stalls later, then we consider other psychological reversals.

STEP 5: TARGETING THE PROBLEM

Early in therapy, patient and clinician review the problems revealed during history taking and set overall goals. These goals may be (and often are) renegotiated during the course of treatment. They should cover not only the alleviation of current pain but also the creation of more effective functioning in the future.

At each session, the client and clinician choose one problem as an initial focus of treatment. When a problem has been identified, we—as do almost all energy psychotherapists—use the SUD scale extensively to monitor progress in resolving emotional disturbance. Some patients may complain fairly strongly about a problem or troubling emotion but give a surprisingly low SUD rating for it. In these cases, we suspect there is more internal upset than the patient is aware of. Muscle testing proves very useful here. The client is instructed to say something like, "My disturbance is at a three" while the therapist tests an indicator muscle. The number which tests strong (or strongest) is assumed to be valid for use in Step 6, treatment.

Unlike with acupuncture for physical problems, where the patient's mind may be on anything during therapy, EP requires the patient to keep the problem in mind during treatment. EP will not function unless the patient is thinking about or feeling the targeted issue. Often after the process of identifying the problem during this step, the problem will continue to "resonate"—be sufficiently fixed in mind—until step 6. If the therapist suspects that focus has been lost, it is enough to remind the patient to "think of the problem," or to use words to that effect.

As mentioned, when some parts of the problem are resolved, hidden aspects may come to light. The therapist should track all aspects and ensure that by the end of Step 6 the SUD rating of the initially targeted problem (as well as the SUD scores of other aspects that have surfaced) is addressed.

We usually find ourselves targeting emotions, but EP can address cognitions as well. Durlacher (1994) was one of the first to write about applying the tapping therapies to what he called "negative life beliefs." Nicosia (1999) called them "life beliefs" and Gallo (2000a), "core beliefs." All have developed treatments for them. Instead of a SUD scale, scales appropriate to the believability of positive self-beliefs are used. The irrational self-beliefs are targeted and treated with energy techniques very much as disturbing emotions are. We less frequently refer to cognitive energy work in this book, but it can readily be accomplished with EP.

Obviously, not all problems dealt with in psychotherapy will be appropriate for EP—or EMDR. Other skill sets are required for dealing with such issues as career planning, assertiveness, many marital problems, effective interactions with dysfunctional families during and after therapy, and so forth, as well as with specialty areas.

By the end of this step, the patient has the problem in mind, and all is in place for treatment to begin.

STEP 6: TREATMENT

Energy therapists who work with meridians have patients tap on meridian points. Some simply apply "algorithms" (see below), directing patients to tap sequences of points that they know to be useful for given conditions. But as demonstrated earlier, the real secret is in "knowing where to tap." We too utilize algorithms but believe the effectiveness of an EP therapist is increased with a deeper understanding of the properties of the meridians being tapped.

The Meridian-Emotion Relationship

It is theorized that the organs and their meridians are associated with corresponding emotions. The therapist who knows these relationships will understand the patient and guide treatment in a much more informed manner than the one who simply applies formulas. Table 3.1 shows these relationships as well as treatment points (Figure 3.1) and affirmations that can be used while tapping.

It should be mentioned that there is some variability among authorities as to the "meanings" of the various meridians. The reader can consult Diamond (1985), Durlacher (1994), Gallo (1999), Teeguarden (1996), and Whisenant (1990). The information in Table 3.1 is adapted from what we have learned from various trainers and it seems to work well for us and our trainees.

As we described in Chapter 1, the meridians exist bilaterally (with two vessels centrally), each including the many points which are treated by acupuncturists. Figures 3.2 through 3.9 show the meridians and both midline vessels as well as the treatment points relevant to our practice of EP. Each point is labeled with a meridian point number and treatment point abbreviation. The points are no bigger than a pencil eraser and are represented by the white area inside the circle.

Energy therapy only requires tapping of one end point (or sometimes a point near the end) of either of the two meridians (or of a mid-line vessel), yielding a relatively small number of treatment points (whose locations and associated emotions practitioners can memorize). These, as well as the sore spot, or neurolymphatic reflex, are illustrated on Figure 3.1.

Gallo's *Energy Diagnostic and Treatment Methods* (2000a) uses some points in addition to the end points. Those we have adopted for use are included in Figures 3.2 through 3.9 and listed in Table 3.2. Although a given end point of a meridian is usually treated, the other end point of the meridian can also be used, as well as the supplementary points we list. These extra points are sometimes effective when the end points are not; they are also helpful if the part of the body of the patient where the usual point is located is missing or injured. For example, a person with one arm could tap the lateral edge of the eyebrow point (TH-23) instead of the usual gamut point (TH-3) (see below). Abbreviations and further specifications for treatment point location are listed in Table 3.2.

In TFT and the majority of meridian energy therapies, treatment is as follows:

1. The patient brings the problem to mind.
2. A "sequence" of meridian points is tapped. A sequence may be a selected point or points, may be an algorithm, or the points may be determined by the diagnostic procedure or Voice Technology (VT).
3. The nine gamut treatments (9G) are performed. The client taps the gamut spot (G) (see Figure 3.3) on the back of the hand, between the last two metacarpals (point 3 on triple-heater meridian), while performing nine steps: close eyes, open eyes, hold head still and point eyes down to the side, point eyes down to the opposite side, roll eyes in a complete circle, roll eyes in a complete circle in the opposite direction,

TABLE 3.1 MERIDIAN TREATMENT POINTS AND RELATED EMOTIONS

Meridian	Treatment Point Location	Negative Emotions	Affirmations
Bladder (Bl)	Radial end of eyebrow (eb) (or when using touch and breathe, inside eye [ie])	Trauma, frustration, fear, impatience, restlessness	I am in peace and harmony. Every issue within me has been resolved.
Gallbladder (GB)	Outside orbit of eye socket (oe)	Rage, loss of power, fury, wrath	I extend myself with love and forgiveness.
Stomach (St)	With the eye looking straight, directly below the pupil on the intra-orbital ridge (ue)	Anxiety, fear, phobia hunger, deprivation, disgust, bitterness, disappointment, greed	I am content. I am tranquil. I am satisfied.
Governing vessel (GV)	Under nose (un)	Powerlessness, embarrassment, hopelessness	I am hopeful. I can.
Conception (central) vessel (CV)	Under lip (ul)	Shame, defectiveness, worthlessness, undeserving	I am deserving. I am worthwhile.
Kidney (K)	Under the collarbone on either side of the sternum) (uc)	Sexual or creative indecision, anxiety, extrapunitiveness, lack of possibilities	I am sexually secure. I am creatively secure. My sexual/creative energies balanced. I have possibilities.

Meridian	Location	Negative emotions	Positive affirmation
Spleen/pancreas (Sp)	About four inches under armpit (ua)	Future anxiety, worry, addictive urges	I have faith and confidence in my future. I feel secure. My future is secure.
Liver (Lv)	Top edge of 8th rib, below nipple (r)	Anger, lack of joy, resentment	I am joyful. I have a positive attitude and humor.
Lung (Lu)	Radial nail point of thumb (t)	Grief, intolerance, scorn, prejudice, disdain, criticalness	I have humility. I am tolerant. I am modest.
Large intestine (LI)	Radial nail point of index finger (if)	Guilt, cannot let negatives go, self-punitiveness	I forgive myself. I am pure and good. I am deserving of unconditional love.
Circulation/sex (CX)	Radial nail point of middle finger (mf)	Jealousy, regret, sexual tension, stubbornness	I am free of the past. I am relaxed. My body is relaxed. I am generous.
Heart (Ht)	Radial nail point of little finger (lf)	Anger (specific)	I love (specifically, I forgive) [a specific person].
Small intestine (SI)	Outer edge of hand, on crease formed when making fist (sh)	Vulnerability, sadness, sorrow	I am full of happiness.
Thyroid/triple warmer/triple energizer/tri-heater (TH)	Back of the hand between metacarpal bones of two smallest fingers "gamut spot" (g)	Depression, despair, sadness, grief, hopelessness, loneliness, despondency. Also, physical pain	I am light and buoyant. I feel encouraged and hopeful.

FIGURE 3.1 TREATMENT END POINTS AND SORE SPOT

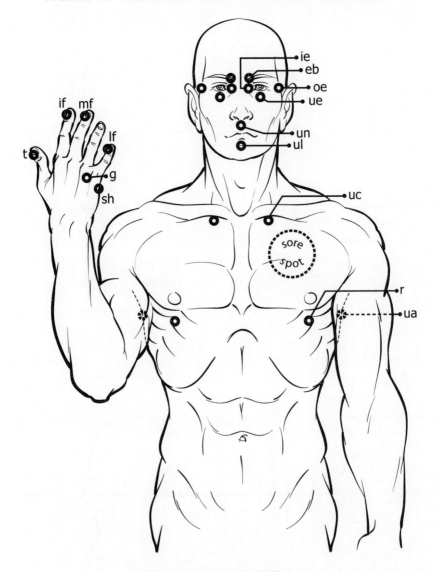

Abbreviations explained in Table 3.1.

Figure courtesy of Langdon Foss.

FIGURE 3.2 CENTRAL VESSEL AND LIVER MERIDIANS

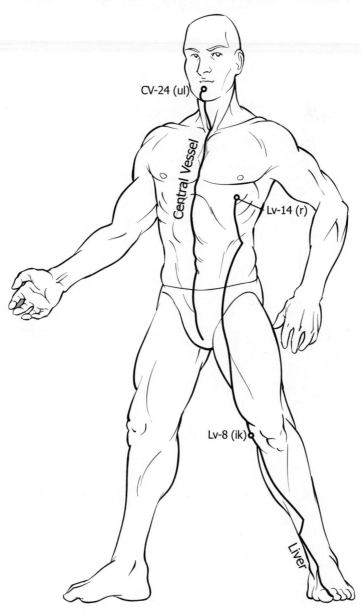

Abbreviations explained in Tables 3.1 and 3.2.

Figure courtesy of Langdon Foss.

FIGURE 3.3 GOVERNING VESSEL AND TRIPLE HEATER (OR THYMUS) MERIDIANS

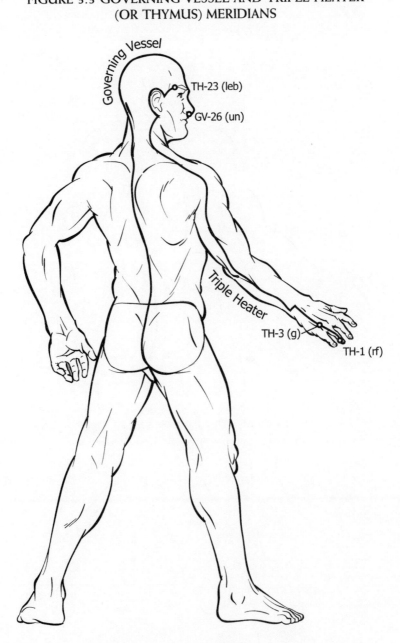

Abbreviations explained in Tables 3.1 and 3.2.

Figure courtesy of Langdon Foss.

FIGURE 3.4 GALL BLADDER AND SMALL INTESTINE MERIDIANS

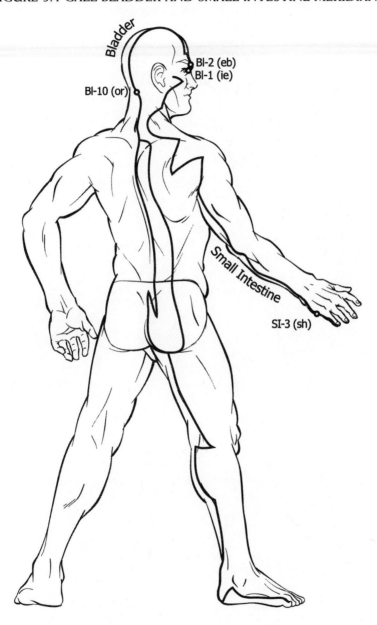

Abbreviations explained in Tables 3.1 and 3.2.

Figure courtesy of Langdon Foss.

FIGURE 3.5 GALL BLADDER AND HEART MERIDIANS

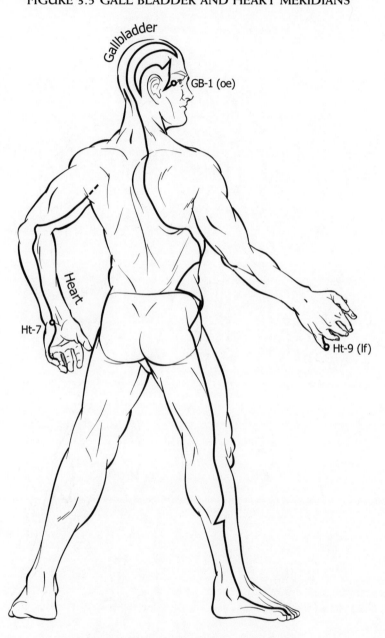

Abbreviations explained in Tables 3.1 and 3.2.

Figure courtesy of Langdon Foss.

FIGURE 3.6 CIRCULATION-SEX AND STOMACH MERIDIANS

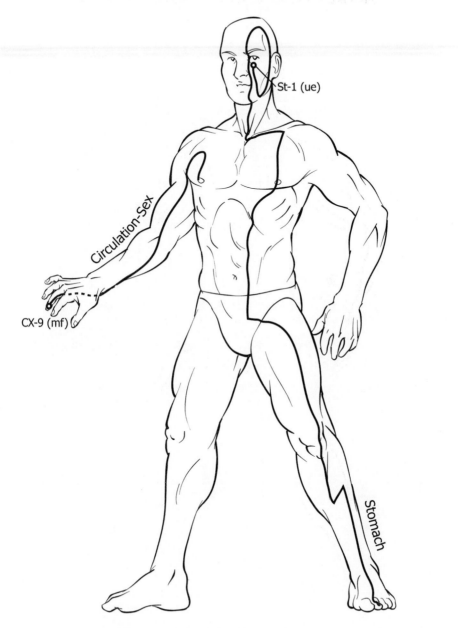

Abbreviations explained in Tables 3.1 and 3.2.

Figure courtesy of Langdon Foss.

FIGURE 3.7 KIDNEY AND SPLEEN MERIDIANS

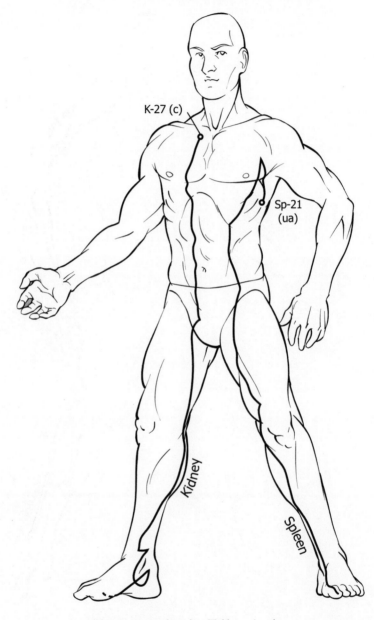

Abbreviations explained in Tables 3.1 and 3.2.

Figure courtesy of Langdon Foss.

FIGURE 3.8 LARGE INTESTINE AND LUNG MERIDIANS

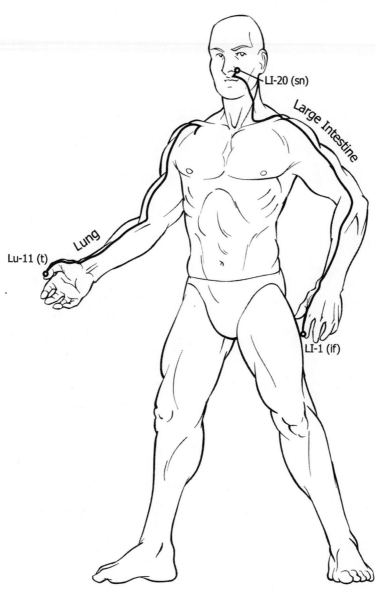

Abbreviations explained in Tables 3.1 and 3.2.

Figure courtesy of Langdon Foss.

FIGURE 3.9 ALARM POINTS

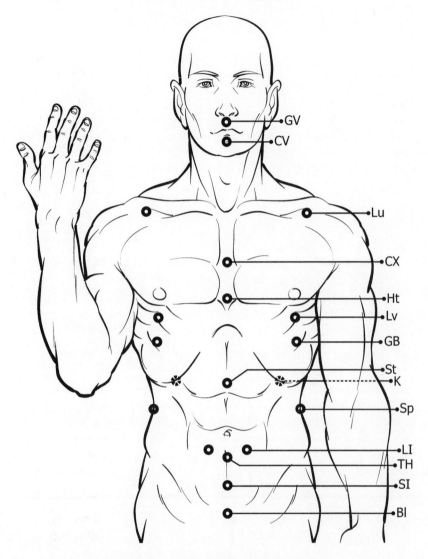

Abbreviations explained in Table 3.1.

Figure courtesy of Langdon Foss.

TABLE 3.2 KEY TO TREATMENT POINT ABBREVIATIONS

eb	End of the eyebrow (bladder-2, or Bl-2)
ie	Inside eye, just above and adjacent to the inner corner of the eye, (bladder-1, or Bl-1)
oe	Outside eye, just behind eye socket bone (gall bladder-1, or GB-1)
leb	Lateral edge of eyebrow (triple-heater-23, or TH-23)
ue	Under the eye, just on eye socket bone (stomach-1, or St-1)
un	Under the nose (governing vessel-26, or GV-26)
ul	Under the lip (central vessel-24, or CV-24)
or	Occipital ridge (bladder-10, or Bl-10)
uc	Under the collarbone, at the junction of first rib, clavicle, and sternum (kidney 27, or K-27)
ua	Under the arm, a palm width below armpit (spleen/pancreas-21, or Sp-21)
r	Rib (liver-14, or Lv-14)
t	Thumb, side opposite index finger in corner where nail begins (lung-11, or Lu-11)
if	Index finger, thumb side in corner where nail begins (large intestine-1, or LI-1)
mf	Middle finger, thumb side in corner where nail begins (circulation-sex-9, CX-9)
lf	Little finger, thumb side in corner where nail begins (heart-9, or Ht-9)
sh	Side hand, where crease ends when hand folded (small intestine-3, or SI-3)
g	Gamut spot, between fourth and fifth metacarpals, about two centimeters above knuckles (triple heater-3, TH-3)
ik	Inside knee, where crease ends (liver-8, or Lv-8)
Sore spot	A neurolymphatic reflex where the palm is placed for the Pledge of Allegiance (NLR)

hum a little of any tune,* count (say, to five), and hum again. Various practitioners have modified the 9G (Gallo, 2000a), shortened it (Gallo & Vincenzi, 2000), or eliminated it (Craig, 1998).

---

* A word of caution for those working with clients who report having been ritually abused by satanists. They say they have been abused on certain dates of the year that coincide with satanic "holidays," and the client's own birthday is one of the most important. Therefore, though we use "Happy Birthday" with most clients, we recommend something else as a song to hum during the nine gamut procedure, as it is likely to trigger traumatic memories. Clients usually have no trouble picking one.

4. After the 9G is performed, the original acupoint tapping sequence is repeated.
5. When the SUD rating is brought to 0 or 1, the client performs either the eye roll or the eer. For the eye roll, the client taps on the gamut spot while moving the eyes slowly from floor to ceiling. The elaborated eye roll is a variation devised by one of us (M. G.) (Gallo, 2000a, p. 115): While holding the head level, the client points the eyes down toward the floor as far as possible. Then, while tapping the gamut spot the client takes about 10 seconds to roll the eyes up as far as possible and holds them there. The client gently flutters the eyelids closed, takes a deep breath, relaxes the eyes, stops tapping, exhales, and opens the eyes when ready. Clients often report a floating sensation on opening their eyes. Frequently either eye roll will bring a SUD rating of 1 to 0.

As the client taps selected treatment points, the treatment points of an algorithm, the points of a comprehensive algorithm, or points diagnosed with muscle testing or voice technology, we note whether there is a significant reaction to the treatment of any point. There may be a sigh, twitch, shrug, repositioning, facial expression, or other indication that the point had particular effect. We might ask whether the client noticed any special effect from any point(s). If so, those points are used in subsequent treatment.

Selected Points

Our first level of intervention is often to select a meridian to treat based on the related emotion. For example, we might ask a client who brings up anger at his or her father to tap the little finger point while saying three times, "I forgive you Dad, you didn't know what you were doing (or I know you couldn't help it)."* In a surprisingly high number of cases, this alone is enough to lower the SUD score significantly.

Of course other points related to other emotions mentioned by the client or suspected by the clinician are often treated. Keeping with TFT tradition, we often add the collarbone point between each of the

* Most of the affirmations in Table 3.1 are infrequently used in practice, except those for anger, rage, and guilt. This variant of the affirmation is taken from the algorithm (see below) for treating anger. Similar variants exist for rage and guilt.

other points and at the end of a sequence. We may also have the client perform 9G and eye roll or elaborated eye roll.

Algorithms

If the selected point tapping has not been successful, then we usually apply an algorithm to the problem. Callahan discovered the first algorithms when he used his "diagnostic" procedure (see below) to determine which points to tap and in what order. He found that the same acupoint sequence (usually about three to five points) worked for a given problem. This held true for many problems, and many of the points coincided with the related emotions. To save time, therefore, rather than carry out the longer diagnostic procedure, Callahan would first try having clients tap the sequence related to their problem. Other practitioners have discovered other algorithms, either through the diagnostic procedure or by knowledge of the properties of the meridians. Lists of algorithms can be found in publications by Britt and colleagues (1998), Callahan (2001), Gallo and Vincenzi (2000), Galvin and Hartung (2001), Lambrou and Pratt (2000), and Nicosia (1999).

If selected point tapping or algorithms are not successful, there are treatments designed to be applied to any and all problems rather than to any specific targeted emotion, thought, or other problem. Some are "comprehensive algorithms" such as EFT (Craig, 1999), and Negative Affect Erasing Method (NAEM) (Gallo, 2000a), or BSFF (Nims, 1998), and another, which is not a tapping sequence, but a "chord" (Carrington, 1999), the Tapas Acupressure Technique (Fleming, 1999).

EFT has been presented in two manuals, numerous audiotapes and videotapes, and discussions on an Internet list and a Web site. Interested readers are directed to the EFT Web site (see Appendix B) where they can download the basic manual at no cost. The following presents the basics of the procedure: The client performs the MPR correction, then taps all points except the liver point (r). Differing sharply with Callahan, Craig claims that it makes no difference in what order the points are tapped, so to keep it simple he addresses the points in top-to-bottom order: eb, oe, ue, un, ul, uc, ua, t, if, mf, lf, sh. The client then performs the 9G, repeats the sequence, and performs the eye roll when the SUD score is 0 or 1.

It is possible to combine specific point treatment and algorithms. The following case example begins with some reversal treatment, goes through the EFT "recipe," and ends with some specific point work.

Case example:

A young woman came for treatment of chronic back pain and related aches in her neck and shoulders. She understood the energy model and mostly was interested in feeling better, as her pains caused significant disruption in her work and family life.

Therapist: Let's start by rating your pains on a 0 to 10 scale.

Client: Right now my back is an 8, and the aches are 5 and 6.

Therapist: What's your attitude about getting better?

Client: To tell you the truth, I don't really expect much. A friend told me about you because I just haven't been getting any relief, even though I see a physical therapist every week. My friend thought the energy stuff might work. But I don't know. I actually read a book on energy techniques and tried them but they seemed too odd, plus I didn't really notice any difference.

Therapist: What if we start by doing some energy balancing? Instead of checking with muscle testing, how about rubbing that sore spot near your heart while saying three times, "I accept myself deeply and completely with all my problems and limitations," and now with "I accept myself deeply an completely with all of this pain." [Therapist demonstrates on self]. Good. And now tap under your nose and say, "I accept myself deeply and completely even if I don't get over this pain." Good, and now tap under you lips and say, "I accept myself deeply and completely even if I don't deserve to feel better." That's really good. Does this all sound familiar to you?

Client: Yes, although I actually noticed a little shifting when I did the tapping, something I didn't experience when I was doing the exercises out of the book.

Therapist: OK. Now, let's just start by tapping the different points, beginning with your eyebrow, and notice what happens. Good, now side of the eye, under the eye, now collarbone, under the arm Good. Notice any shift in feeling as you tap. Now the side of the thumb, index finger, and notice what you feel. Now the middle finger point, little finger, side of hand, and now on the back of your hand on the gamut point. Good. Notice what you feel as you tap there.

Client: I feel sad. I'm thinking of my parents' death. They both died in the tornado. Now I'm wondering if that's when my pain began. Boy, this is very sad all of a sudden.

Therapist: That does sound like a very sad memory. It's OK to cry about this, you know. [The client cries for several minutes.] Keep tapping your hand. That's good.

Client: Boy, I didn't know that was there. I'm starting to feel better though as I tap. That's amazing. The sadness is going away. Now it's gone. Amazing.

Therapist: That point is often useful for sadness and grief. By the way, how is your pain now?

Client: Down a little. It's odd, but now I'm feeling ashamed that I wasn't with them when they died, like I'm not a good child.

Therapist: I wonder if you would now tap your index finger point again. That is a useful place for forgiving ourselves for things that we are ready to put in the past, but cannot just by trying to talk ourselves into being forgiven. As you tap, say this, "I forgive myself because I was not responsible for my parents' death."

Client: OK. Boy, that's hard to do. It's odd, because I know intellectually that I wasn't responsible, but I think I do feel responsible somehow, even though there was nothing I could have done. We didn't know it was coming. I didn't even live anywhere near them. I had my job to do. My family to take care of. Every day. Why do I feel so responsible?

Therapist: I don't know the answer to that. Would it be OK if you tapped that index finger point again? You will be able to tell if you can get further past this shame and guilt you feel.

Client: OK. But it doesn't sound true.

Therapist: We're just talking about energy. I'm not trying to talk you into anything that isn't true. You will forgive yourself, or not, only if the time is right for you. What if I start by tapping for you on my finger and you just listen to me and tap for yourself?

Client: OK. [Client listens and taps as the therapist repeats the affirmation, I forgive myself.] It's starting to sound like it might be true. I think I can say it now. OK, I'll tap myself and give it a try: "I forgive myself even if I was responsible for my parents' death." That's amazing. I feel better. And I don't feel my pain as much as before.

Therapist: Now I have something for you to do that may sound really odd. Would you be willing to try and see if you have been angry at your parents for dying?

Client: Well, that certainly sounds odd all right. I mean, they were victims of a tornado. How could I be angry at them for that? It was a work of nature.

Therapist: I agree that it sounds strange. Remember, we are talking about energy, about the unconscious, and about not very rational things. This occurs to me because a lot of people have told me that they have been stuck in their therapy work because they felt anger that they did not recognize consciously.

Client: OK. Let's try it. I guess it can't do any harm, can it?

Therapist: I personally have not known it to do harm. It either helps or does nothing, in my experience at least. OK, if you're ready, I'd like you to tap your little finger point just as I'm doing it—that's it—on the side of your little finger nail closest to your face as you look at your hand palm down, and tap while you see if you need to forgive either of your parents. It might sound odd, but you know how this energy stuff works.

Client: [Client taps] Mom. I need to say something to Mom.

Therapist: OK, now just tap and say, "Mom, I forgive you, because you couldn't have known how your death would have grieved me so."

Client: [*Client taps and tears resume and continue for several minutes.*] *Wow, that was hard. But I'm feeling better. Now I suppose I need to tap for Dad, huh?*
Therapist: *Go ahead and tap and tell Dad you forgive him too.*

Treatment continued in this manner for about 30 minutes. The client then reported feeling angry about events that occurred long before the tornado; forgave; asked for forgiveness; tapped again on the deserving point under the lips; and finally said, "My sadness has pained me for too long." We then did a modified type of Nims's (1998) early tapping version of BSFF. A SUD reading was requested then, and the client said all the pain had gone—a 0. She was asked to stretch, twist, and bend but still felt no pain. Two weeks later she called to say her pain relief had maintained and she no longer was visiting her physical therapist. She had achieved further insight into how she had used pain to deal with other sad feelings that she did not want to experience, and how growing up in her family had taught people to be stoic, no matter the somatic cost. (Therapists with a cognitive bent have already noticed how the simple EP work can produce a series of insights.) At the last follow-up, two months later, she said she still felt fine.

Our goal is not to put physical therapists out of business but to honor our clients' wish to heal. If there is a psychological component to their disorder, then it is in our area of expertise to help. If in the process our clients are able to put words not only to their healing experience but also to the etiology of their problem, so much the better. If in the process clients use fewer pharmaceutical or other drugs, or need fewer physical therapy visits, that also is acceptable. We cannot and do not predict or guarantee such changes, though we have learned to accept them when they are reported.

We sometimes have clients tap bilaterally, and EFT offers a good format for that, though bilateral tapping can be used with all techniques mentioned in this section. The therapist directs the client to tap one eyebrow point with a couple of fingers of one hand and the other eyebrow point with fingers of the other hand. The client does the same with the outside eye point, and so on through the "recipe." Note that there is only one central point under the nose and lip; hence it is impossible to stimulate bilaterally at these locations. It is possible to bilaterally stimulate the thumb, finger, and side hand points by having the client tap those points on the arm of a chair or some other object. Another option is for the therapist to alternatingly tap the points. Theoretically, the client could even tap the thumb point on the left hand against the thumb point on the right, and so forth through the hand points. Usually, however, we just ask the client to tap the points of one hand during the first sequence, and then, after the 9G, to tap the points on the other hand. Finally, the client can tap the back of one hand the first time the 9G is carried out, and of the back of the other hand, the next time, and so forth.

Bilateral tapping sometimes has a potentiating effect; clients who show little progress with tapping only one side of the body with one hand sometimes will respond to bilateral tapping. EP lore suggests that bilateral tapping is indicated in cases of dissociation, perhaps so that as many parts of the person can be stimulated as possible.

We likewise present only the basics of another technique, NAEM (Gallo, 2000a). The client taps just four points in this comprehensive algorithm, the "third eye" point (GV-24.5, one-half inch above a point midway between the eyebrows) un, ul, and the sternum where the "thymus thump" is given.

Nims (2001) has now developed BSFF to the point that it is no longer an energy therapy method but rather a sort of psychodynamic/hypnotic one. We continue to use his original four-point tapping sequence with affirmations: while tapping eb, "I am eliminating all the sadnesses in all the roots—and the deepest cause—of all this problem"; while tapping ue, "I am eliminating all the fears in all the roots—and the deepest cause—of all this problem;" while tapping lf, "I am eliminating all the angers in all the roots—and the deepest cause—of all this problem;" and at eb again, "I am eliminating all the emotional traumas in all the roots—and the deepest cause—of all this problem." By "deepest cause," Nims means the belief system that controls and directs the particular problem being treated.

In TAT, there is not a tapping sequence but rather a single pose. With one hand, the client touches one of the inside eye points with the thumb and the other with the fourth (ring) finger. The middle finger of that hand touches the "third eye" point. The palm of the other hand is centered across the back of the head with the thumb about one-half inch above the hairline. The client holds this pose until a subjectively significant change is felt (often a lowering of SUD score) or until four minutes has passed.

We, our trainees, and our colleagues have had considerable success with these comprehensive algorithms and TAT. We invite those who have not yet used them to try them out. We believe the reader will also be impressed with the results even using the very abbreviated descriptions above. If, nevertheless, the problem persists, the clinician may proceed to two other levels of acupoint therapy.

"Diagnostic" Level Treatment

Callahan developed the "diagnostic" level of TFT which uses muscle testing to determine treatment points. He conducts training (information available at Callahan Techniques Web site, see Appendix B) in the method, as do others. It cannot be learned simply by reading, but we very briefly review it here to clarify the concepts of TFT and to stimulate the curious to pursue training.

Callahan tests alarm points (see Figure 3.9) in this procedure. Three points are identical to their treatment points, governing vessel (GV), central vessel (CV), and Liver (9Lv). The lung (Lu) point is at the top outer side of the pectoral area; circulation-sex (CX) point is just below the center of the sternum; Heart (Ht) point just below the bottom of the sternum; Gallbladder (GB) points at the bottom of the rib cage; Kidney (K) points at the tip of the 12th rib on the lower back; stomach (St) point halfway between the bottom of the sternum and the navel; spleen (Sp) points on the side where we bend; thyroid (TH) point two finger widths below the navel; large intestine (LI) points one finger width down and one thumb width lateral from the navel; small intestine (SI) point four finger widths below the navel; and bladder (Bl) point one thumb width above the center of the pubic bone.

After preparing the client's energy fields, the therapist will have the patient hold a hand over an alarm point while thinking of the problem, and will then perform a muscle test. Testing continues until an alarm point tests strong, at which time the corresponding treatment point is tapped. The therapist then again asks the client to think of the problem, and performs muscle tests. If the muscle is weak, there is more to the "holon" or sequence, so testing of alarm points and tapping of related treatment points continues. When a strong result is obtained while the client thinks of the problem, the holon is complete. The client performs the 9G and then taps the "diagnosed" sequence again. The therapist elicits a SUD reading. If it hasn't dropped at least 2 points, the therapist addresses some block to treatment. Diagnosis and treatment of holons continue until the SUD score is 0 or 1. To complete treatment, the client does eye roll or elaborated eye roll.

Instruction and supervised practice are necessary for the clinician to gain proficiency in this method.

Voice Technology

According to Callahan, the most accurate level of TFT is the voice technology. Hypothesizing that disturbances in the thought field would be evident not only in muscle testing but also in other somatic phenomena, he constructed a machine that essentially tests the voice for treatment points. Treatment is conducted over the telephone. The client states a few simple phrases such as "I want to be over this problem," and the operator of the voice technology machine tells the client which points to tap. Success rates of 98% are claimed (see Chapter 2), but controlled, peer-reviewed research is thus far lacking. In spite of an unusually expensive price, over a dozen of these machines have been sold, and many practitioners (and many clients) are enthusiastic.

Treatment Blocks

In EP and EMDR, we have grown accustomed to such a rapid pace of treatment—often verified through periodic measurements including SUD—that when change is not occurring fairly rapidly, we notice and suspect that something is causing a block. Many other therapies work so slowly that we don't notice when they *aren't* working and consequently have not suspected the existence of treatment blocks. When treatment stalls in the process of EP, however, we quickly suspect blocks, and search for and correct them. We have already addressed neurological disorganization and massive psychological reversal in Step 4. There exist other psychological reversals and other types of treatment blocks.

Additional Psychological Reversals

Callahan identified the most common psychological reversals, the massive, mini, and specific reversals (Callahan & Perry, 1981). He also recognized the recurrent reversal which causes SUD level to rise after an issue has been partially or completely successfully treated. Finally, he discovered deep level reversal which is subtly different from specific reversal: Instead of testing "I *want* to get over this problem," the therapist tests for or corrects "I *will* get over this problem." Table 3.3 reviews these reversals, the affirmations used to diagnose them during muscle testing, and their corrections.

TABLE 3.3 PRINCIPAL PSYCHOLOGICAL REVERSALS

Type	Diagnosis: With muscle testing, Say, " . . . "	Treatment: Say three times:	Action
Massive	"I want to be happy/I want a happy life." vs. "I want to be miserable/I want a miserable life."	"I deeply (and profoundly) accept myself with all my problems and limitations."	Rub NLR (sore spot) or tap side of hand
Specific	"I want to get over this problem." vs. "I want to keep this problem."	"I deeply (and profoundly) accept myself even though I have this problem."	Rub NLR or tap side of hand
Mini	"I want to be completely over this problem." vs. "I want to keep some of this problem."	"I deeply (and profoundly) accept myself even though I *still* have *some* of this problem."	Tap side of hand
Recurrent	"I want to be completely over this problem." vs. "I want to keep some of this problem."	"I deeply (and profoundly) accept myself even though this problem keeps coming back."	Rub NLR or tap side of hand
DEEP LEVEL	"I will get over this problem." vs. "I will keep this problem."	"I deeply (and profoundly) accept myself even if I never get over this problem."	Tap under the nose

Note: NLR equals neurolymphatic reflex.

112

One of the most commonly occurring is the specific reversal. This blocks treatment of the specific problem being addressed. As with all reversals, its presence or absence can be ascertained by muscle testing, but little time is lost in simply applying the correction. The client rubs the neurolymphatic reflex (sore spot) while saying three times, "I deeply accept myself even though I have this problem." (Some clients prefer to specify—"this anxiety," "this grief," or whatever best characterizes the problem for them.) If previously blocked treatment then proceeds effectively, the most parsimonious conclusion is that a specific reversal existed and was corrected.

A mini psychological reversal (mPR) is suspected when treatment stalls after a period of effectiveness. This was seen in the client described in the Preface who used an affirmation with tapping on the side of the hand to enable therapy to resume. As in that case, the correction for mPR is usually successful. This reversal tends to reappear, however, and clinicians should be alert for it during subsequent treatment. Should it again be suspected, the clinician can easily reapply the correction.

As mentioned, muscle testing methods for identifying which reversal is present have been devised, and many practitioners prefer to perform them. The process is often quick and efficient, and reversals are identified and cleared in a minute or two. In addition, therapists learn something about what caused the blocks their specific client. (If we simply apply corrections, we're not always sure whether they were needed or not.) Sometimes, however, complexities arise in the process of muscle testing for reversals, and it becomes quite involved and time-consuming. Therefore, since the treatments for psychological reversals are quick and easy to administer, some therapists will forego testing and simply make an intuitive guess about which reversal is present and apply the corresponding correction. If the guess is incorrect, treatment will continue to be blocked, but little time has been lost and another correction can be tried.

For example, to diagnose a specific psychological reversal, the therapist asks the client to say, "I want to get over this problem." and then performs a muscle test. The phrase "I want to keep this problem." is then tested. If the response on second test is stronger than that on the first, specific reversal is suspected and can be corrected by the client either rubbing the "sore spot"/neurolymphatic reflex (NLR) or tapping the side of the hand while saying three times "I deeply (and profoundly) accept myself even though I have this problem."

TABLE 3.4 ADDITIONAL PSYCHOLOGICAL REVERSALS

Type	Diagnosis: With muscle testing, say:	Treatment: Say three times:	Action
Deservingness (Shame)	"I deserve to be (*completely*) over this problem." vs. "I don't deserve to be (*completely*) over this problem."	"I deeply accept myself even if/ though I don't deserve to be (*completely*) over this problem."	Tap ul, sh, or un
Safety	"(Deep in my unconscious) It is safe for me/or others to be (*completely*) over this Problem." vs. "(Deep in my unconscious) it is not safe for me/for others to be (*completely*) over this problem."	"I deeply (and profoundly) accept myself even if/though it's not safe for me/for others to be (*completely*) over this problem."	Tap sh or un, or rub NLR
Possibility	"It's possible for me to be (*completely*) over this problem." vs. "It's not possible for me to be (*completely*) over this problem."	"I deeply (and profoundly) accept myself even if/though it's impossible for me to be (*completely*) over this problem."	Tap sh or un, or rub NLR
Permission	"I will allow myself to get (*completely*) over this problem" vs. "I will not allow myself to get (*completely*) over this problem"	"I deeply accept myself even if/ though I will not allow myself to get (*completely*) over this problem."	Tap sh or un, or rub NLR

Motivation	"I will do what's necessary to get (*completely*) over this problem." vs. "I won't do what's necessary to get (*completely*) over this problem."	"I deeply accept myself even though/even if I will not do what's necessary to get (*completely*) over this problem."	Tap sh or un, or Rub NLR
Benefit	"Getting (*completely*) over this problem is/will be good for me." vs. "Getting (*completely*) over this problem is not/will not be good for me/for others."	"I deeply accept myself even if/though getting (*completely*) over this problem is not/will not be good for me/for others."	Tap ul, sh, or n
Deprivation	"I will not be deprived if I get (*completely*) over this problem/desire/attachment." vs. "I will be deprived if I get (*completely*) over this problem/desire/attachment."	"I deeply accept myself even if/though I might/will be deprived if I get (*completely*) over this problem/desire/attachment/impulse."	Tap sh or un, or rub NLR
Identity	"I will lose my identity if I get (*completely*) over this problem" vs. "won't lose my identity if I get (*completely*) over this problem."	"I deeply accept myself even if/though I will lose my identity if I get (*completely*) over this problem."	Tap sh or un, or rub NLR

Note: Italics indicate mini reversal versions of the reversals. So, for example, the therapist could perform a muscle test while the client says, "I will lose my identity if I get over this problem" or, if mPR is suspected, could say, "I will lose my identity if I get completely over this problem." The corrective affirmation is changed accordingly. NLR equals neurolymphatic reflex.

In addition to the reversals originally identified by Callahan, Durlacher (1994) identified others, and Gallo (2000a) and Nicosia (1999) greatly expanded the list. Grudermeyer and Grudermeyer (2000) have complied a list of over 100. These reversals relate to many issues familiar to clinicians. They can be identified by muscle testing, but again many practitioners simply follow intuition as to what reversal might be present, apply a correction, and resume treatment. If the correction is effective, a previously unsuccessful therapeutic exercise will be successful when retried. Table 3.4 shows the more common additional reversals and their corrections.

Workers in the field are currently identifying many types of reversals and developing and testing corrections for them. However, tailoring the affirmations and corrections to the client is generally preferred to prescribing a textbook list, both because the affirmations are personally relevant and because the client feels empowered by participating in the process. For example, one client identified 26 personally relevant corrections that she said she said on a daily basis to keep intrusive thoughts of childhood neglect from distracting her at work, including "I am not loving myself," "I am not sexually alive," "I am not reaching out in love," "I am not reaching out to love," and "I am not worthy of receiving love."

When administering corrections, the therapist should do the correction along with the client, for as Nicosia reminded us, "Treat yourself for *your* reversals before you treat your clients (because it's possible some of the problem is you!)" (1999, p. 46).

Toxins

If the clinician has ruled out or corrected neurological disorganization and psychological reversals, and treatment remains blocked, it may be that an energy toxin is the cause. Toxins, substances that interfere with the energy system, can include chemical and other entities that we come in contact with or ingest. Among the most common are detergents, which we keep next to our skin all day and all night since we apply them to our clothing and linens.

Another common energy toxin is nicotine. Many of our clients are unknowingly reversing themselves every waking hour with cigarettes. They are already aware of the negative effects on their physical health, but even when it is proved to them (through discussion or muscle testing) that smoking also causes psychological reversal and undermines therapy, they remain resistant to quitting. They are addicted, have a powerful habit, and are reversed about quitting.

It is well known that some persons are adversely affected by airborne substances. Many inhaled substances such as perfume, room "fresheners," and agricultural chemicals can have similar effects. These not only cause feelings of physical distress but also can interfere with treatment.

One client had a severely compromised immune system and was affected by many substances in her environment. For example, she was sometimes "knocked out all day" if she was home when the man in the next apartment sprayed deodorant. The substance caused both allergies and exposure to energy toxins. When she was affected in this manner, she hardly accomplished anything including keeping her therapy appointments. When she did come in, I (M. G.) would have to check and usually clear reactions to a variety of substances to which she was known to be sensitive, before therapy could proceed.

Some people seem to be affected by "sick building syndrome"—the very place they work (or live) contains noxious substances such as asbestos, plastic, Formica, and smoke.

Not everything to which someone is allergic or has a negative reaction will be an energy toxin. However, the reverse is true: there will be some sort of negative reaction to every energy toxin. We all ingest—knowingly and unknowingly—hundreds of additives and airborne chemicals that didn't exist at the end of World War II. They are found in Arctic ice, Saharan sand, and the cells of our bodies. Apparently most of us cope fairly well with them, but unfortunately some people are more sensitive and are affected physically and energetically.

Many foods can be energy toxins; common ones are wheat and corn. Any foods to which the client is allergic—or craves—should be investigated. Refined sugar, coffee, and alcohol can be culprits. Sometimes it may not be the foods themselves, but spices, herbs, or other additives in the food that are problematic.

Toxins can sometimes be identified and even neutralized by muscle testing and other techniques. These methods are described by various practitioners (e.g., Gallo, 2000a; Nicosia, 1999; Nambudripad, 1993) but are beyond the scope of this volume. Therapists can simply be alert to the possibility of clients being affected by elements in the environment. They can ask about allergies, sensitivities, or "feeling out of sorts" in certain situations or on exposure to certain substances.

They can determine the circumstances of the onset, worsening, or return of a particular symptom.

A client's therapy log can be very helpful. If a review of the week reveals that positive results suddenly reversed or the problem came back, inquiry should be made as to what happened just before the event. What had the client just become exposed to, eaten, or breathed? The answers will often lead to discovery of a toxic element. Clients who have trouble in the therapy session remembering back to the event should be encouraged to telephone the office. Although we often tell clients leaving a therapy session to call if they need, when trying to track down toxins, we emphasize that we *really* mean for them to call right away when an identified problem arises.

After a negative effect from exposure to a given substance or situation is determined, the client should try to avoid it. The client could use a different soap, detergent, perfume, deodorant, or cologne—or none at all. If treatment has been blocked because of influence of a toxin they cannot avoid clients can be treated during a "window of opportunity," when they are free of the toxin. For example, smokers can be given the first appointment of the day if they agree not to smoke until afterward. Treatment should be successful. Subsequent exposure to the toxin may again have adverse effects on the client, but often it does not usually undo the positive results of treatment.

Callahan has investigated many products that purport to counter the effects of toxins and now recommends methylsulfonylmethane (MSM) (see Appendix B).

If these methods are unsuccessful and the clinician still suspects a toxin, referral to a specialist in detecting and treating these conditions might be in order.

Electromagnetic Fields

The final block to treatment we mention is caused by the ubiquitous electromagnetic fields (EMFs) to which we are exposed—radio and television waves and microwaves; emissions from high-tension transmission lines; radiation from computer and television screens; and the like. If a client experiences symptoms in situations where EMFs are prominent but not in the therapist's office (assuming it is relatively free of significant fields), we may suspect that EMFs are a factor. Again, avoidance is a possible solution. For instance, a client could work at a laptop rather than in front of a CRT monitor. Or the client could wear a pendant designed to shield against or correct for EMF influences, both physical and mental (see Appendix B). However, even in a discipline used to concepts that stretch the paradigm, these pendants seem strange to some. Little research is available to support the use of these devices, but we are aware of a fair number of users who report significant benefits.

STEP 7: CLOSING THE SESSION

If the SUD rating for the problem addressed has been lowered to 0 or 1, treatment is considered successful, and we are ready to close the session. In keeping with a long (principally behavioral and cognitive) tradition for ensuring treatment continuity, we ask clients to take note of anything related to the work that might happen during the ensuing week. For this purpose we request that they always keep with them something to write on. If clients don't customarily carry a planner, appointment book, or personal data assistant (PDA), three-by-five index cards work well. At this point we also assign homework. This often includes a prescription for treatment of identified problems using methods chosen during the session. Specific points, an algorithm, or diagnosed points may be used to treat a recurrent problem, or a comprehensive algorithm may be suggested for whenever disturbing thoughts related to therapy (or other) issues surface. If clients are susceptible to neurological disorganization or a particular psychological reversal, corrections are recommended. We may ask them to practice whenever they feel the problem, to set their watch to beep on the hour and practice at that time, to practice every time they are stopped at a traffic light, or the like.

If treatment was not successful and the SUD rating remains above 1, we may try a brief procedure aimed at whatever disturbing emotion remains. We find TAT especially good for this process. Any upset that still remains can be handled in any number of traditional ways, including relaxation exercises, a visualization of storing the problem in the therapist's office, resting in the waiting room, and so forth. The client is told to call the therapist if an upset becomes especially high during the week.

Sometime early in the following session we review patient homework and make needed adjustments. We examine the client's journal of therapy-related events that occurred during the week, and, unless other more pressing issues have presented themselves, we resume work on unresolved problems.

Chapter 4

Conducting EMDR

In the first part of this chapter we review the 8 phases of EMDR (Shapiro, 2001a). Clinicians will find that EMDR produces positive effects about 40% of the time if they simply follow these 8 phases, providing bilateral stimulation during the desensitization phrase and encouraging clients simply to pay attention to what they are experiencing. By using advanced techniques, higher rates of success are possible, perhaps between 70% and 90% or more, depending on the overall competence of the therapist. These advanced techniques are introduced during Part I (formerly called Level I) training and further explained in Part II (formerly Level II). When the advanced techniques are insufficient, more experimentation is justified. Shapiro encourages innovation, but asks therapists to justify modifications by first showing that the original EMDR protocol is inadequate.

After reviewing the 8 phases we discuss our own innovations, and describe a model for applying EMDR differentially to overresponding and underresponding clients. Our motive is simple: in a book encouraging clinicians to combine the best features of EP and EMDR, we must first ensure that the best features are in fact evident, and that clinicians are using each approach optimally. We believe our model furthers optimal EMDR use.

THE 8 PHASES OF EMDR

Phase 1: Client History Taking

In addition to gathering detailed information about the client's presenting problem and history, the therapist completes the three-pronged past-present-future focus of EMDR by asking the client about possible manifestations of the problem at a later date, and how the client would like to envision the future. The therapist also carefully determines the readiness of the client for the potentially intensive EMDR experience and assesses the level of rapport. A client who wants to work on an isolated traumatic event, such as a near-death experience during an earthquake, and who does not seem to have any other history of trauma, can begin EMDR almost immediately. On the other hand, one who has been severely and repeatedly abused by a parent will likely require much more time to prepare for treatment, and the clinician should take special pains to assess the client's internal strengths, social supports, and so forth.

The therapist also screens for clinical signs of dissociative disorders. This is because of the ability of EMDR Phase 4 work to uncover dissociation, sometimes unknown even to the client. The signs, briefly, are a history of years of psychotherapy with little progress, symptoms of depersonalization or derealization, memory lapses, flashbacks and intrusive thoughts, Schneiderian symptoms (especially thoughts, feelings, and behaviors that seem to come from nowhere, and hearing voices), headaches and other somatic symptoms that are hard to explain, sleep disturbance, and depression. For more formal screening of dissociation, validated instruments can be used; the most popular and easiest one to administer is the Dissociative Experiences Scale (Carlson & Putnam, 1992).

Also in this phase the therapist reviews any history of substance abuse and warns the client of the possibility that initial EMDR treatment could temporarily increase the desire to use again. And the patient who wants to resolve a problem but whose growth might threaten others will need to talk about secondary gain prior to initiating treatment.

The therapist begins to assess the quality of rapport in this phase, ensuring that clients will feel secure and open enough to communicate openly what they are experiencing during difficult moments of treatment.

Phase 2: Client Preparation

The therapist-client relationship is further addressed in this phase. Since EMDR training participants are generally expected to be licensed psychotherapists, it is assumed that they already know how to establish a therapeutic relationships with clients. Nonetheless, trainees are encouraged to put special emphasis on the level of rapport because EMDR offers a profoundly moving treatment experience, and can produce immediate and powerful impact on the client. Such possibilities require, in turn, an extraordinary quality of trust and a "truth telling" agreement. It is essential that clients validly report what they are experiencing so the therapist can intervene appropriately. Clients who abreact need to be able to trust that the therapist will know how to guide them through that intense emotional experience. Clients who access forgotten experiences need to know that the therapist will not push them into remembering prematurely, and will accompany them on their memory journey. In cases where clients choose to stop the processing, they must know that the therapist will honor their request to stop. The therapist, in turn, needs to know how intensely a client experiences an abreaction as reported by SUD level, and how able the client is to withstand that experience.

Our belief is that generally the therapist-client relationship is necessary but insufficient for treatment change. We apply this principle to EMDR as well, and find that the relationship is in one sense even more necessary than usual, and in another sense even less sufficient. In the first sense, it is particularly important when the client is still deciding whether to undergo the possibility of a potentially distressing experience, and needs to feel assured that the therapist will be a good guide on an unknown journey. Once treatment has begun the relationship takes on greater importance, largely because abreactions are so common and the client may choose to continue through an emotionally upsetting experience largely because the therapist's credibility and attention provide a boost to the client's confidence and courage.

In another way the therapeutic relationship may also become *less* important than it is in traditional therapy because the method of EMDR is so powerful, and may overshadow the impact of the relationship itself. For instance, Wilson and colleagues (1995, 1997) found no differences in effectiveness among five therapists who conducted EMDR. Each of the five therapists was well trained, experienced, and friendly. They also had different styles, endorsed different theoretical paradigms, and came from several disciplines. Those who believe that "the relationship heals" would have to conclude from these findings that five therapists were virtually equal on the "healing variables" and that they were equally able to establish a healing relationship and to complete treatment within the 4½ hours allowed for each subject in the study. An alternative conclusion is that subjects in the study bene-fited not because of their relationships with their therapists but be-cause of the power of the EMDR method. In this sense do we say that the relationship between therapist and client is necessary (so that the client will initiate and continue with the treatment) but not powerful enough alone to heal the client. We concur with Lazarus (1998) who believed that healing does not take place primarily through the thera-peutic relationship, but that the relationship is the soil in which tech-niques and skills are planted and grow.

On the other hand, it is also clear from the data of Wilson and colleagues that even though the EMDR therapists were similar to one another in terms of overall effectiveness, each therapist worked with subjects who did not benefit in a statistically significant way. Might some of the non-responders have found greater benefit had more time been invested in the initial therapeutic relationship? To ask it another way, are there individual differences that might vary the impact of the relationship? It may be that with certain clients the relationship with the therapist is more important, more deserving of time and attention, more critical as a means of healing. Some of our clients, particularly longer-term patients with limited internal strength and resiliency, de-pended on us for motivation and encouragement. Our empathy for them, our initial attempts to tell them they were forgivable, and our willingness to stay with them in spite of their unpleasant and "putting off" behavior were essential in helping them to find the courage to con-tinue their therapy. It may even be that some of our acceptance of and respect for them was healing. These are questions for empirical study.

The following example shows how the factors just discussed can converge in an EMDR session.

Case Example:

A Catholic priest in a European country was required to undergo therapy to work on his "authority issues." He became intrigued after I explained EMDR, and he asked to use his therapy opportunity to resolve memories of having been homosexu-

ally assaulted as a child. After several hours of therapy on a memory of being raped by an adult caretaker, he associated that work to his authority problems with the bishop, then to issues with other authority figures, and finally to the physical abuse he suffered at the hand of his biological father. During one intense session he asked me to sit with him on the couch while he processed the grief of never having had a loving father. He borrowed an EMDR device from me which provided continual bilateral stimulation, and then, with his head on my shoulder, wept profoundly. The EMDR stimulation allowed him to focus on his own very personal memory of his father even as he rested his head on the father-figure of the therapist. For approximately 10 minutes the priest-client wept as he talked about missing the father he had wanted but never had. He then sat up and turned to me:

Client: I'm OK now. Thank you. You can move to your own chair now.
Therapist: OK. [I moved to my chair.] That was a lot of work.
Client: I don't know if I could have gotten that far if you had refused to sit with me. Thank you for that. For your trust. We had done so much work before on my feelings about my father, but I just couldn't seem to get through this. Even using this EMDR gadget and the energy work hadn't been enough. I think I finally got through that.
Therapist: How are you now?
Client: I'm much better. It feels like a weight was lifted. I feel at peace.

Could this have been accomplished if I had declined to sit next to him and had asked him instead to talk about his feelings of rejection? Possibly, though the point is not to claim that I needed to sit with the client. The point is only that this became an option because EMDR permits this kind intervention, and the risk does not seem as high as it is in therapies that depend more on the healing power of the therapy relationship or that consider transference issues to be more intimate than was the case here. Were there still transference issues, possibly of a homosexual nature, that I ignored? That is possible. Did they need to be talked out? The client indicated they did not, and I chose not to second-guess him. During the sessions that remained, he continued to process memories from childhood and then young adulthood and finally focused on future plans for being assertive with his superiors. He continued to use me to improve his relationships with his peers and parishioners.

Besides establishing a working therapeutic relationship, the therapist in Phase 2 gives the client enough information about EMDR so that the client can consent to treatment. What follows is a transcript of how the study by Levin and colleagues (1999) can be translated into lay terms and a metaphorical explanation of EMDR (see Chapter 2 to review this study in which brain changes following EMDR treatment were reported.)

Case Example:

Therapist: A very interesting study was conducted in Massachusetts that gives us some idea of what EMDR can do. First, let me show you why we do eye movements or why we use taps or sounds. Did you know that the brain is sort of wired backward? That is, the left side of the brain is working when I move my right hand, like this. And when I move my left hand my right side or right hemisphere is working. Does this sound at all familiar?

Client: Yeah, I remember something about that. So if someone has a stroke to the left brain, then they might have trouble using their right leg and arm. Is that right?

Therapist: Yes. Also, this side of the brain [therapist puts hand to left side of head] manages language for most people and is also generally where we process positive emotions. Meanwhile the right side processes negative emotions for the most part. So, as I put my hands up the sides of my head, I cover positive emotions with my left and negative with my right. Make sense?

Client: Yeah. Positive on the left, negative on the right. In everybody?

Therapist: Good question. Not in all people, but most. In any case, it's positive on one side, negative on the other. By the way, when you think about something pleasant, the two sides of the brain are more or less balanced, like this. [Therapist puts both palms to sides of head.] OK?

Client: Balance makes sense. Especially when I feel so out of balance sometimes.

Therapist: We all get out of balance when something old still bothers us. Let me show you what the brain looks like when you are talking or just thinking about something that bothers you. Like the memory you said you wanted to work on. And we're all like this, by the way. I'm not talking only about you, but about anybody who is still bothered by an old memory.

Client: That's good to hear. [Laughs.] So I'm not crazy or something.

Therapist: Not at all. This will probably not surprise you, but when we think of the old memory that still bothers us, this left side of the brain, where positive emotion seems to lie, has only a little activity [therapist touches left side of head with two or three fingertips], but the right side with its negative emotion has a lot of brain activity [covers right side with entire hand]. Also, there is only a little activity in the front, the most human part of the brain, and finally there is disruption in the inside part of the brain that warns us about danger. The result is that we think things are going to harm us when actually they are not dangerous.

Client: That sounds like me. Overreacting to things, then feeling guilty afterward.

Therapist: Right. It's really a matter of your brain being too alert to danger, even when there's none there.

Client: How do scientists know all that?

Therapist: They do a mapping of the brain while the person is thinking. Lots of devices have been invented to do this brain mapping. There are PET scans, which you might have heard of, and MRIs, and so forth. The study I'm going to tell you about used what's called SPECT. I can tell you more about it if you'd like, or I can give you a copy of a study, but essentially this is what happened: When a person in the study was just thinking about something rather neutral—for me that might be sitting here in my office—the brain registered like this [therapist puts both hands to both sides of the head.] But when the person thought of some old event that was still bothersome, this side became less active [therapist leaves three fingers on left side.] Remember what I was telling you about that?

Client: Yeah. Less positive emotion. But the same negative emotion.

Therapist: Remember what else the left side manages?

Client: You said that's where language is.

Therapist: Right. Less language, as if the person still hasn't put words to the experience in a way that really helps the person to think about it in a way that makes it feel finished. Perhaps the person can talk about it in a sensible way, but the emotions are still not connected with that sensible talking. And the final thing we talked about?

Client: You said the brain is wired for danger even when danger is not present.

Therapist: Right. It's as if the radar in the inside of the brain is too sensitive to things out there, even things that wouldn't hurt us.

Client: Yeah, sounds like me again. Certain little sounds can make me jump, even certain people who aren't really causing me any grief.

The information presented in the example can be adjusted according to the need of the client. Other clinicians might say that with trauma a past event can somehow get "stuck" in the nervous system, and EMDR can help it to get unstuck. The process of EMDR can also be compared to physical healing. Just as a physical wound can heal automatically, so can trauma heal itself; when it doesn't, EMDR serves to jump-start the healing process, but it is actually the brain and body that will do the healing.

During the informed consent discussion the therapist gives any information the client might need prior to initiating EMDR treatment. EMDR therapists have many kinds of information they can share with prospective clients, including copies of research articles, newspaper and magazine articles, and Web sites. Some clients will express fears about the process or about their own ability to manage abreactions. The therapist responds to these questions and teaches several strategies that the client can use to manage emotion, including use of a metaphor to normalize the process, a stop signal for interrupting an abreaction that is too intense, and an imagined safe place. It is during this phase that the therapist also teaches the mechanics of bilateral stimulation. As the therapist does hand movements, taps the client bilaterally, or provides bilateral alternating sounds, the client selects the preferred technique(s) with regard to speed, distance, and places where the client does or does not want to be touched. Therapists who use mechanical devices to produce the alternating stimulation demonstrate those at this point.

Phase 3: Assessment

A handy acronym, ICES, can be used to assess a traumatic memory—*I* represents image; *C*, cognition; *E*, emotion; and *S*, sensation. The image is a visual representation of the memory that is still bothersome. Cognitions refer to the beliefs of the client. A negative cognition accompanies the unresolved memory (such as "I deserve my misery"), and a positive cognition is the belief that the client would *prefer* to have about the memory (such as "I deserve to be happy"), but does not yet feel to be true. The terms emotion and sensation are thought of as body correlates of a traumatic memory, with emotion referring to what the person feels (e.g., anger, fear, sadness, and so forth) and sensation indicating where the person feels it (e.g., stomach, hands, chest). Sensation also refers to three of the senses: tactile, gustatory, and olfactory. As mentioned, visual stimuli are given separate attention in the image of the traumatic memory, and auditory stimuli are generally considered to be a part of the cognitive. During the assessment phase, two of the ICES factors are measured to set a baseline. The felt believability of the *positive cognition* is measured on a 1 to 7 rating scale that Shapiro (1995) termed "validity of cognition" (VoC). Number 1 means the positive cognition "does not feel at all true" and 7 that it "feels completely true." The negative cognition generally does not need to be measured. *Emotional* disturbance is measured on a SUD scale that Shapiro adapted from Wolpe. In his classic text *The Practice of Behavior Therapy,* Wolpe (1969) introduced the SUD as a subjective anxiety scale that ran from 0 to 100. In EMDR the scale runs from 0 to 10 and measures all emotions, not just anxiety. Because the sensation refers to "where the emotion is felt" in the body, it does not require additional measuring. The image is also unmeasured, as the impact of the image on the body is implied in the SUD rating.

Phase 4: Desensitization

At this point the active therapy work begins. The starting point for a selected problem is called a *node* or target. Issues associated with the node are seen to lie in "channels" that lead off from it and contain sequential information which is processed during treatment. When all the problems in one channel are processed, focus is returned to the original target. If disturbance is still present, there is another channel with material that remains to be processed. Similarly, there are layers of emotions so that when one is layer resolved, the next becomes accessible. The uncovering of a new layer—although sometimes distressing—is not failure but progress. The goal during this phase is to clear out negative thoughts and emotions, thereby preparing the client for the installation of positive substitutes in Phase 5.

Desensitization begins with the therapist asking the client to hold in mind the negative aspects of the ICES identified during the assessment: the image of the traumatic memory, the negative belief about oneself that accompanies that image, and the disturbing emotion and sensation. The therapist immediately begins bilateral stimulation, using one of the modalities chosen by the client during Phase 2. To produce eye movements the therapist asks the client to follow the therapist's hands moving from side to side in front of the client; auditory stimulation can be produced by the therapist snapping fingers or making other sounds, alternating from one side of the client's head to the other, with or without eye movements; and for tactile stimulation the therapist alternates tapping the two sides of the client's body (i.e., the backs of the hands, the knees, or the shoulders). There are many mechanical devices available which also can produce each type of stimulation. After a limited number of bilateral alternating stimuli, the therapist stops and asks the client for feedback. This instruction to the therapist to stop the stimulation from time to time distinguishes EMDR from the exposure methods to which EMDR has often been incorrectly compared (Perkins & Rouanzoin, 2002).

Approximately half the time, this stage will proceed fairly smoothly, and the therapist essentially repeats the process of stimulation and getting feedback and stays out of the way of the client's spontaneous processing. The therapist thus will witness what Shapiro called the innate and adaptive information processing system by which the client does the healing (see Chapter 1). The best EMDR therapists know when to keep interpretations and observations—however brilliant— to themselves, as a correct comment may prevent clients from getting to the same point on their own, and an incorrect comment will throw clients off track.

For clients who do not process smoothly, trainees are taught several advanced techniques to use when treatment stalls or a "blocked response" occurs:

- The therapist first changes the bilateral movements, either modifying the speed and direction of the hand movements or switching from hand movements to bilateral sounds or taps.
- The therapist can also ask, "What prevents you from working through this?" as a way to identify fears that need to be processed first.
- The use of a hierarchy can ease a client step by step through an emotionally upsetting memory or other trauma.
- Searching for "feeder memories" is a way to "untapped earlier memories that are contributing to the current dysfunction and blocking processing of it." (Shapiro, 2001a, p. 189).
- The therapist can investigate "blocking beliefs" that have been stalling treatment. Knipe (1997) developed a list of EMDR blocking beliefs, and recommended interventions or interweaves when a client's treatment stalls.
- Additionally the therapist can consult a series of troubleshooting tables (Shapiro, 2001b) that contain other visual, cognitive, and body-related techniques to help a client whose therapy processing has stopped.

EMDR trainees also learn about other strategies in advanced training seminars. One strategy useful in searching for feeder memories is the *floatback*, which has been discussed variously in the literature (e.g., the "affect bridge," Watkins, 1971). The client is asked to attend to a present symptom (emotion, physical pain, or other sensation) and then to journey back in memory to find a time when the client felt something similar. Induction-like language might be used: "That's it, just drift back into your earlier years. Perhaps you find a time when you felt this in high school . . . or in grade school . . . or perhaps before you began school. Just notice what comes up. You might consider this feeling (sensation) to be a kind of body memory, and what you are doing now is looking for the time, the place, the date when you felt this earlier . . . ."

M. G. has been using a technique called *trackback*, learned during his training in transactional analysis in the early 1970s, which gives a little more structure to the process. The therapist begins inquiry with a recent life stage, such as early in the marriage, and asks the client to search through that time period until the relevant symptoms "click into" a situation. That memory is then discussed until it is clear in the client's mind. The purpose is to make the retrieval of the next earlier memory easier. On occasion, a memory is so disturbing that it will inhibit further "backtracking" and so will need to be treated before the client is able to continue. The therapist then picks an earlier period, such as college, and asks the client to find a significant memory there. The work continues through high school and elementary school. The therapist continues asking for a memory "even earlier than that." This is repeated until the client, after some reflection, asserts that there is nothing earlier. Elementary school and earlier times most often contain the earliest memory which is considered to be the relevant "feeder memory." It is then thoroughly processed with bilateral stimulation. We suspect this procedure is more effective than just asking "When was the first time you felt like that?"

Dilemmas are often mentioned during history taking, and frequently appear in the midst of a treatment session. By attending to the somatic aspects of the dilemma or ambivalence and employing bilateral stimulation, a therapist can help the client to reach a deeper awareness of the two sides of the issue, tapping into sensory and emotional wisdom. More importantly, the client also begins to resolve the dilemma, perhaps by healing the anxiety related to approaching one decision, mourning the loss of the other, or facing some old beliefs needing to have it both ways. This simple technique is quite powerful and we use it frequently as a client gets to the edge of making a commitment or decision, then stops short because of the "yes but" with which we are all familiar. We have used the original Gestalt double chair technique extensively ourselves, but rarely have seen them produce the powerful changes this EMDR strategy provides. When combined with bilateral stimulation, this technique has been called a therapeutic interweave by Gilson and Kaplan (1999) and "The Two-Hand Interweave" by Robin Shapiro (2001). Greenwald (2001) was also a pioneer in the use of this technique. When the client reports changes, we accept those and continue with stimulation. If the client does not notice further change and does not yet feel resolved, we will become more specific with our questions: "Which hand is warmer/heavier/bigger?" Or, "Notice the index fingers; which one seems warmer?" The purpose is to help the client to become more aware of subtle clues to the nature of the dilemma and its solution. We do not make hypnotic suggestions, such as: "Notice your hand getting heavier," which some practitioners recommend.

In addition, Andrew Leeds (Korn & Leeds, in press; Leeds & Shapiro, 2000) developed a procedure, resource development and installation, to use with EMDR to help clients to strengthen inner resources. Gilson and Kaplan (2000) also wrote a clinical manual dedicated specifically to strategies called interweaves. We offer our own model for improving on the basic model in the second section of this chapter.

Through the years EMDR clinicians and trainers have added other suggestions from their own experiences and now the lore of EMDR strategies is quite extensive. Book titles such as *Extending EMDR: A Casebook of Innovative Applications* (Manfield, 1998) give a flavor of these contributions.

Phase 5: Installation

Once desensitization has brought the SUD reading to 0 or 1, work moves to the installation phase. As the client focuses on the traumatic event at the same time as the positive cognition the therapist initiates additional bilateral stimulation until the client reports that the positive cognition "feels true" at a 6 or 7 on the VoC (where a 7 feels completely true).

To explain how the same alternating movements serve both to eliminate the negative and replace it with the positive, Shapiro (2001a) refers to the principle of adaptive information processing: the inherent healing mechanism in a person resolves obstacles to optimal functioning, then strengthens features of that optimal functioning.

We noted earlier how the positive cognition is a hypothetical notion prior to desensitization. The thought "I deserve to be happy," for example, does not *feel* true to the client because the unresolved traumatic memory gets in the way, producing more of a negative than positive reaction. If desensitization is successful in helping the client clear out negative emotion, then a positive cognition can be installed and strengthened in this phase and will then *feel* true. Shapiro (2001a) concluded that the positive cognition is most valid if it can be felt to be true not in some abstract sense, but rather when paired in the client's mind with the original traumatic memory. Not to be able to strongly believe it signals that more of the negative residue from the trauma remains to be processed with EMDR.

Phase 6: Body Scan

Because of the nature of memory networks, it is assumed that the installation of positive features during phase 5 can trigger subtle physical protests within clients. To check for the possibility of any remaining negative material, a sort of body check is conducted on the assumption that "The body never lies." Clients are asked to hold in mind the originally disturbing incident along with the positive cognition. They then mentally scan their body and report any sensations they detect. Any sensations are then treated with bilateral stimulation. If the sensations are negative, they are processed further until the client can review the traumatic incident and link it with the positive cognition, conduct a final body scan, and feel only peace and calm. If the sensations are positive, they are further strengthened with bilateral stimulation.

Phase 7: Closure

This "good-bye" phase is done in one of two ways. If the session is considered completed (defined as a SUDS of 0 or 1 and a VoC of 6 or 7), the therapist debriefs the client, may assign homework with plans for the next session, and gives a phone number to call in an emergency. The debriefing includes telling the client about what might be expected between sessions: new memories may be revealed, triggers in the present might become more obvious, bodily reactions are common, and so forth. In other words, the processing may continue after the client leaves the office, and so even a completed session can lead to the uncovering of other traumatic memories and symptoms. All will be good news, the therapist says, because it means the client is continuing the work that motivated the initial call for therapy. The client is asked to briefly log relevant events during the week.

On occasion, however, time runs out before treatment is complete. "An incomplete session is one in which a client's material is still unresolved, i.e., they are still obviously upset or the SUD is above 1 and the VoC is less than 6" (Shapiro, 2001a, p. 31). In this case, the therapist chooses a technique, usually one that does not involve bilateral stimulation, to ensure that the client leaves the session in "a state of emotional equilibrium" (Shapiro, 2001a, p. 75). The clinician has options as to how to help the client achieve this stability: a relaxation procedure, a discussion about what the client accomplished so far, or an exercise from some other therapy mode that enables the client to leave with a sense of greater safety and confidence. The information that processing may continue beyond the end of the session, the request to keep a log, and the invitation to contact the therapist if need be are communicated.

Phase 8: Reevaluation

This very important phase, reevaluation, is often neglected by clinicians. It involves a careful follow-up in the subsequent session. EMDR practitioners discover with experience that successful processing of one memory frequently leads to other memories. Sometimes this uncovering is delayed; sometimes the newly recognized memories are positive but had been overlooked in the confusion of the traumatic experience. And sometimes they are negative, "forgotten" because they were relatively less disturbing, or hidden away because they were too threatening. These last often become accessible after the client has experienced some success in facing and resolving other pieces of the past: "I did it once, I can do it again" and "I don't have to be afraid of myself any more" are phrases that may describe the client's new optimism. If the client reports having become upset when thinking about the therapy work, the therapist can frame this as an example of self-discovery, rather than as a sign of treatment failure—the conclusion some clients are likely to draw. The therapist invites the client to examine all of these and other possibilities. Additionally, the therapist encourages the client to shift attention more and more to the future: EMDR is not only about healing past wounds, becoming whole, and being free of symptoms but also about being more, having dreams, and realizing them.

THE DECELERATING AND ACCELERATING TREATMENT MODEL: DEALING WITH OVERRESPONDERS AND UNDERRESPONDERS

In the remainder of this chapter we describe a model that can help clinicians to work more effectively and safely with their clients. The strategies that we describe are not necessarily original to us, but in many cases their origins have long been lost and we no longer know

to whom they should be attributed. In some cases, one or several clients might have happened on an idea which we used later with another client who was "stuck," and which we added to our list. In other
cases, students have volunteered ideas from their own practices during
the give-and-take of a training brainstorming. Some are taught during
EMDR training courses. We thank all the unrecognized individuals
who have contributed to this section: trainees, clients, and colleagues.

Clinicians who follow the 8-phase treatment process will safely and
effectively benefit most clients. As mentioned, simply following the 8
basic phases and asking clients to notice what they are spontaneously
experiencing will be sufficient for about 40% of the individuals who
seek treatment. By using additional techniques taught in Levels I and
II trainings, and depending on experience and skill, more clients can
be treated safely and effectively.

Not all clients respond favorably to the basic EMDR model, however, even when the clinician employs advanced techniques. When
problems occur, particularly during desensitization, they tend to be of
two types. One problem involves clients who have moved too quickly
or too intensely into memory work. These individuals may suffer an
intense abreaction as they relive an experience, find the experience to
be intolerable, and leave the session more distressed than when it began. The therapist may feel guilty for not being able to stop the abreaction. Sometimes the client decides the means is not worth the end, and
terminates EMDR treatment at that point. Sometimes the therapist stops
using EMDR, believing it is too powerful and inherently risky.

The other problem, less typical and less serious, appears when too
little change occurs in a session. Sometimes the therapist approaches
EMDR without much enthusiasm, stopping too soon when the client
shows any sign of distress and never really giving EMDR a chance to
do its best work. In other cases the therapist does not understand how
to use EMDR to activate the client's adaptive information processing
system. And in yet other cases, there may be blocks to the client's
processing of a given issue, with the result that the client feels too
little emotional distress and too little motivation to change. Clients
(and their therapists) in this case may also terminate EMDR treatment
early, concluding that the method is inherently weak and oversold.

These observations from our clinical experience are consistent with
the empirical psychotherapy literature. After reviewing the research
on psychotherapy effectiveness, Beutler (2000) proposed eight guidelines for enhancing efficacy. Number 7 reads as follows: "The likeli-

hood of therapeutic change is greatest when the patient's level of emotional stress is moderate, neither excessively high nor excessively low" (p. 1005). This guideline is not a prescription to work only with moderately emotionally stressed persons. Rather it represents a challenge to develop strategies to lower the emotions of those excessively stressed so that they can begin therapy, and to help those with low emotional stress to learn to feel more.

We have arranged these various concepts along a continuum of responsivity or level of distress. On the left side of the continuum we would locate Beutler's excessively emotionally stressed persons, those clients that we would call overresponders. Perhaps 10% to 50% of a clinician's clients would be found at this extreme, depending on the nature of one's practice. In the middle are persons Beutler described as moderately emotionally stressed. We would place here the approximately 40% of clients who respond to the basic EMDR protocol with a level of emotional distress that is both therapeutically useful, and emotionally tolerable. It could be said that clients in this range respond to basic EMDR procedures with appropriate and manageable emotion. On the right side of the continuum are Beutler's patients with excessively low emotional stress. Here we would place underresponding persons. The following continuum describes only the extreme ends, not the middle approximately 40% of clients who respond to EMDR with appropriate levels of emotion and who do not need any special intervention by the therapist:

CLIENTS WHO OVERRESPOND

On the left side we find clients who process too much, too fast. Abreactions are intense, SUDS levels are too high, and there is a heightened risk for dissociation. Some find EMDR work to be intolerably painful and may drop out of treatment prematurely to avoid further pain and suffering. It might be said that these clients are focused too much in the past and not enough in the present. They are too close to the past problem, too far from the present solution.

CLIENTS WHO UNDERRESPOND

On the right are clients who are unable or unwilling to process enough of their traumatic past, or who process it too slowly. In the therapy office they do not feel with enough intensity to allow EMDR to have an impact, even though outside therapy symptoms may be rather severe and disruptive. They may drop out of treatment, doubting that they can change. It may be said that they are focused too much in the present, not enough in the past.

The continuum implies variability, and allows for clients to move from one side toward the other as treatment progresses. A skilled therapist will be able to follow the client along the continuum and change interventions appropriately. Other psychotherapists have described this continuum as an approach-avoidance dimension, or as a matter of creating more or less distance for the client. We have not read about the concept elsewhere, however, so we offer our own version.

We think the most common and most unfortunate problems in using EMDR occur when clients overrespond (the left side of the continuum). When the therapist makes an error here, increased suffering is often the result. Both therapist and client are likely to be more fearful of continuing with EMDR. It is not unusual for both to turn to therapies that not only seem safer but also offer less hope for dramatic change.

Clients Who Overrespond

We first present three examples of clients who were overstimulated in an EMDR session, then we present one from our case files.

Case Examples:

- *An experienced, psychoanalytically oriented therapist began to work with a man who reported that a pastor had sexually molested him over a period of time some 20 years earlier. At first the therapist asked a more experienced clinician to do an EMDR consult, but then decided to conduct the session herself even though she had only recently completed Level I training. After five minutes of EMDR desensitization the man was in such an intense abreaction that both therapist and client panicked and stopped EMDR. The clinician's subsequent treatment report indicated that her client was too fragile for EMDR work, that she would use analytic therapy instead, and that the parish treasurer would need to free up an additional $10,000 for treatment. She later confided that the experience had convinced her that true change requires much time and much analysis. As it turned out, the client grew disenchanted with reliving his abuse hour after hour and eventually dropped out of therapy altogether.*
- *A veteran of a civil war agreed to EMDR therapy after being told that his memories of years earlier would likely not improve otherwise. Treatment began with a chronic pain the client had suffered for more than 10 years. The Level I trained therapist, an ex-soldier himself, had barely begun the first set of eye movements when the client said the pain was moving to his*

legs. The therapist, probably more connected with the client through his own war experience than he was aware, told his client to continue through the experience. After three more side-to-side eye movements, the client jumped up from his chair, his face white and sweaty, and refused to go further. He did not return for additional sessions.

- A male therapist sought a supervisory consult. He had been working with a female dissociative patient for about a year. After completing EMDR Level I training, he told his patient that she would finally be willing to work through memories of abuse, because he had recently learned a new method for treating trauma. The therapist said, "trust me," and began to move his hands for what he thought were the required 24 movements. The client blinked and was dissociated before the therapist completed three movements. The client was even more sensitive in subsequent EMDR sessions; just the mention of the procedure provoked a dissociative response. The therapist expressed guilt at having traumatized his patient, and wondered about the wisdom of using EMDR with his other patients, as it appeared that EMDR might be inherently dangerous.

- And the example from our files: Shortly after I (J. H.) learned Level I EMDR, I began to work with a severely traumatized and character-disordered offender living in a community corrections program. He was enthusiastic about working through a memory of his grandfather beating him on the head with a frying pan. He easily reenacted the memory but during the second session began to experience his hands swelling (not visibly, of course). I was still using EMDR with too much intensity (too long a set of eye movements, allowing abreactions to continue, not talking enough during the desensitization phase, and giving inadequate delays between abreactions and sets of eye movements). My client eventually decided that while the results were positive, the work involved in producing them was too demanding.

In each of these cases the client continued reliving a traumatic memory for too long and with too much intensity. After hearing many examples of this kind of problem, we made three adjustments to the EMDR model to help our students and their clients contain intense EMDR reactions.

First, it is important to consider slowing or even stopping bilateral stimulation when a client is recalling an intensely disturbing traumatic memory. This conflicts with what most newly trained clinicians learn: "When you're driving through a dark tunnel, keep your foot on the accelerator." In other words, continue bilateral stimulation to take the client through the difficult issue, rather than stopping and leaving them stranded in the middle of it. That's usually good advice—unless you can't see where you're going in the tunnel (i.e., the issue is too difficult to tackle head-on the first time).

Quite frankly, we have yet to witness any significant negative consequence as a result of stopping during an abreaction—as long as the work is resumed in a timely manner. With EMDR the therapist can restart the interrupted processing simply by asking the client to return to the target memory with its image, negative words, and body sensation. On the other hand, not stopping during an abreaction that the client cannot tolerate is traumatizing in itself, to both therapist and client. We know of many cases where clients refuse further EMDR treatment because they try to get through an abreaction, are encouraged to do so by the therapist, and then find they cannot continue. They stop in the midst of the abreaction, not out of caution but because they can no longer stand the pain. What they learn from the experience is to fear delving further into their traumatic memories. What matters is not always continuing or always stopping bilateral movements, but rather what the client wants and can tolerate.

A second adjustment is in the number of eye movements recommended for initiating EMDR treatment. Many EMDR clinicians have overlearned the instruction to "begin with a set of 24 eye movements." The number 24 is now a part of EMDR lore. Actually, the correct number is from 1 to 1,000 or so. And as we exemplify with the next case, sometimes 24 movements can be 23 too many. If EMDR clinicians can be more flexible in the number of movements during a set, fewer overwhelming abreactions would result and the issue of whether or not to stop during an abreaction would become less salient.

Third, clinicians should consider asking for a SUD rating during the movements themselves when they are unsure of how intensely the client is experiencing the EMDR work. There is an implication that asking for a rating during eye movements is always an interruption. Somehow the therapist is supposed to know how upset the client feels by reading body language or by trusting intuition. Unfortunately, therapist intuition can fail and clients cannot always be relied on to know when to ask for a break. Sometimes the SUD rating itself has been the only dependable way to detect a SUD score that is too high or to forecast a dissociative risk. We have yet to see a client affected negatively by a therapist asking for a rating during bilateral stimulation. Clients seem to report SUD levels truthfully under these circumstances.

Even though clients are taught a stop signal and can ask for processing to be suspended at any time, too often the client will not know when to use the signal. Some clients are not used to speaking up for themselves, and others have great difficulty predicting how one emotion can lead to another, especially if the subsequent emotion is abrupt, unsuspected, or intense. We might propose also that a particularly compelling therapist can convince a relatively compliant client to trust the therapist too much, and to assume that the therapist knows more about what the client needs than the client knows. A client under such a circumstance might well continue into an abreaction even when their intuition detects danger and warns, "I'm not going to get through this."

Lest this discussion of overresponsive clients seem too pessimistic, we end by citing a case with a positive outcome. An EMDR Part I training was held recently in a Central American country that had been shaken by the earthquake of January 13, 2001. I (J. H.) was demonstrating EMDR with a trainee who was still traumatized by memory of the earthquake. The trainee was far from being what we might call fragile or overresponsive. She was a respected and experienced therapist who was accustomed to earthquakes, and who had a wonderful sense of humor, a strong sense of self, optimism and love for the world, and the courage to volunteer to be treated in front of her professional peers. She rated her memory of the earthquake as barely a 3 on the SUD scale. She would be one person whom we would predict as being able to move through 24 eye movements and to tolerate whatever abreactive experience might arise.

Case Example:

Therapist: OK, Ana. You have said that this memory of the earthquake doesn't seem to be connected to anything else, but we'll just take it easy as we start, just in case. We've got plenty of time today. You have your image of the building swaying and the people in the street, and the thought, "I'm vulnerable." Just notice where you feel it in your body. Now I'll begin to tap your hands as we planned, but only four times each. [The therapist alternately taps each of the client's hands four times.] OK, good. Breathe deeply. Good. What comes up?

Client: Oh, God. It's awful. I feel already terrible. I see the buildings falling. People everywhere.

Therapist: Perhaps I'm going too fast. What number are you at from 0 to 10?

Client: 9.

Therapist: Do you want to take a break with your safe place?

Client: Yes, please.

Therapist: OK. Tell me about it if you wish.

Client: OK. I'm in my garden. Everything is green and peaceful. I feel at peace.

Therapist: How would you rate your upset now from 0 to 10?

Client: Oh, much better. A 3.

Therapist: Would you like to continue with hand taps?

Client: Yes.

Therapist: Perhaps I was going too fast. How would it be if I tapped your hands fewer times than before, let's say only once each so you don't process the memory too fast?

Client: Please. Yes. Just once each. Let's try it.

Therapist: OK. I'm going to start again. First, could you bring up the picture again?

Client: Yes, I'm back there.

Therapist: Words?

Client: I'm vulnerable.

Therapist: And now notice it in your body. What number do you give it now?

Client: 6.

Therapist: OK to begin?

Client: Yes.

Therapist: OK. As you focus on the picture, with the words "I'm vulnerable," notice the 6 in your body as I tap your left hand, there, and now your right hand, there, and now I'm stopping. Good. Blank it out if you wish. Take a deep breath. Good. Are you OK?

Client: OK.

Therapist: Should I tap your hands again, once each?

Client: OK. Yes.

Therapist: OK. Left, now I'll tap, and your right hand, and now I'm stopping again. OK. Good. Breathe. What do you get?

Client: Wow. I'm OK, but, God, these things certainly move fast, don't they?

Therapist: Yes, even though I'm tapping your hands only once each. Just one tap on your left hand and one tap on your right.

Client: I'm OK. We can continue.

Therapist: Two taps as before, or more?

Client: Two taps, please. That's enough.

Therapist: OK, here goes, left hand, right hand, and I stop. Good. Breathe. Blank it out if you wish. What do you notice?

Client: It's a 6 again.

Therapist: Two more taps?

Client: Yes.

Therapist: OK, I'm tapping your left hand, your right hand, and I'm stopping. Good, Breathe.

Client: It's a 7 now. The danger. I remember the danger.

Therapist: Continue?

Client: Yes.

Therapist: Two taps?

Client: Yes.

Therapist: OK, here goes, left hand, right hand, and now I'm stopping. Good. Breathe. Blank it out. What comes up?

Client: It's a 5. Let's continue.

Therapist: How many times?

Client: Try four taps to each hand.

Therapist: OK, here goes, one left, one right, two left, two right, three left, right, and four left, right, and I'm stopping. Good. Breathe deeply. Good. What comes up?

Client: I feel like laughing [laughs]. It's about a 3. The images are not so bother-some now.

Therapist: Continue?

Client: No. I think a 3 is about right.

EMDR has the potential to be overly disturbing to almost anyone. It is incorrect to assume that there are two types of clients, one being overly responsive and fragile and the other resourceful and resilient. It is also incorrect to assume that the former will always be vulnerable in EMDR, and the latter will always be able to tolerate any intensity of trauma work. It is better to be alert to the possibility that any client at any given time can overrespond to a particular memory, regardless of the client's overall resilience and ego strength. Overresponses cannot be easily predicted, even with a careful history. Using "decelerating" strategies under such circumstances requires that the therapist maintain constant attention to the client's experience. There is much more involved than simply doing basic EMDR slower than usual.

Case Example, continued:

I then asked Ana about her thinking that a 3 on SUD was "about right." I pointed out that there were no earth tremors at that moment, and I wondered if this might entail a blocking belief. After talking about her assumptions and fears, she said, "I'd love to get rid of that 3 if I could, but that isn't likely, is it?" I said that I didn't know, but that she could continue with EMDR if she wished to test out her question.

She said she came to the workshop to learn something new and decided to continue working. After about five more minutes of more EMDR processing, she ended with a 0 on SUDS and a 6 on VoC ("I'm safe" was her positive cognition). She said she could not believe completely (which would be a VoC of 7) that she was really safe while residing in an earthquake zone, and decided to end her treatment at that point. Over the next two days she reported that the memory she had worked on remained at a SUD score of 0.

This session lasted an hour and five minutes, including the brief history taking at the start. During the session we paused from time to time to discuss the experience with the rest of the trainees who were gathered around, as is our custom during demonstrations, so the actual EMDR session lasted about 45 minutes. It bears repeating that this trainee was a very healthy person, yet she clearly indicated that she was unable, or at least unwilling, to process the memory any more quickly than she had. Her face showed the fear she mentioned with the SUDS report of 9, and her laughter seemed to fit when she reported that the SUD was dropping. (EMDR therapists will note that the session was successful even thought the protocol for recent events was not used.)

It can be noted that the client stopped several times in the midst of abreactions, yet no particular negative consequence appeared. After a brief break, the client was easily able to pick up where she had left off. I used no special or advanced EMDR tools (such as cognitive interweaves from Level II training). Instead, the entire process involved basic Level I methodology. I had met the client only four hours earlier. Partly because the trust that existed between the trainer-therapist and the trainee-client was largely untested, and partly because I do tend to talk a lot when a client is feeling with such intensity, I was vocally active to ensure her that I would keep my promises ("your left hand" . . . "your right hand, now I'm stopping"). The words also were used to help her maintain contact with the present as she worked on her traumatic past. There was no apparent association with previous memories, no signs of any dissociative tendency, and no suspicion that she was fragile in other ways—yet she clearly indicated that she preferred a very slow pace. I can only conjecture what might have happened had I tried to keep her moving through her abreaction, but the point is this: Why run any risk if slow, even extremely slow, processing produces a benefit such as this? Slowing down does not mean stopping indefinitely. Some clients approach their trauma work too quickly, stir up too much too soon, and then need to take extended breaks—sometimes for weeks—before they feel recovered enough to try again. Slowing the pace can help the client to approach a traumatic memory a little at a time and actually resolve more in a session. Paradoxically, slower can sometimes result in faster.

By the way, we ask those energy-trained therapists who might be thinking, "I would have used energy techniques with this client," to bear with us. We will describe using energy techniques in cases like this in Chapter 5. While we would agree that energy techniques might have been useful as a decelerating strategy to help Ana contain her level of distress, here we concentrate on the utility of EMDR for the same purpose. We want to encourage EMDR practitioners not to give up too early on using EMDR, so that therapists have one more tool available for their clients. The choice is not *either/or* but rather *both/and*.

And now to the right side of the continuum.

Clients Who Underrespond

Underresponding is not as serious a matter as overresponding. Underresponders may drop out of treatment believing that EMDR will not produce the changes they wished for, but at least they do not leave feeling retraumatized and worse off than before. Nonetheless, the potential for healing goes unrealized. Here are three examples of treatment failure.

Case Examples

- *A man who was abused as a child by several males, allegedly "friends of the family," suffered such severe social phobia that he could neither date nor hold a job involving contact with the public. He sought help from an abuse counselor. The counselor specialized in group work for trauma victims and was planning only two individual sessions to prepare the client for the group. During the second session the client was informed that the therapist also practiced EMDR, and the client asked to try it. The therapist said that using EMDR could be a way to "scout" for trauma, and asked the client to focus on present phobic symptoms while the counselor led him in eye movements. The client remained stuck in his symptoms and did not move from his SUD rating of 8. After 20 minutes the counselor stopped and said, "We really shouldn't be using EMDR like this. I didn't think it would work, but it was worth a try, wasn't it? But you learned those unfriendly messages about yourself by hearing people talk to you,* so healing will require that you learn to hear different messages. In my experience, the only real way to work through abuse is to be in a long-term, supportive group." The client became increasing embarrassed at retelling his history in the group and after two sessions did not return. He later sought help from an experienced EMDR therapist, to whom he told this story.

- A teenage girl sought help for depression. She was becoming more and more isolated from her friends because she could no longer accompany them on outings; she was afraid of having panic attacks which were occurring more frequently. Her therapist tried EMDR for four sessions, but in the office the client felt none of the anxiety and choking sensation that so suddenly appeared outside. The therapist terminated treatment and referred the client for medication.

- A colleague, trained in both EMDR and EP, had a client who could not sleep because of pain in her legs, but she felt no pain during the daytime therapy sessions. The therapist said, "No problem. We'll just ask your body with muscle testing to give us information from your unconscious about what the SUD rating would be if you could report it consciously. We will then do energy work on that SUD rating, and see how things go." This would have been fine had the client consented, but she initially had specifically asked for EMDR work and refused to let the therapist treat her with any of the energy techniques.

To end this discussion on a positive note, we present a fourth case where the EMDR therapist knew what to do with his underresponsive patient.

Case Example:

The client, Karnik, was a plumber. He was highly motivated to resolve his fear of being trapped in a confined space. He was about to lose his job because his fear prevented him from entering crawl spaces under buildings. He realized the fear is usually irrational but could not shake the memory of being covered under tons of rubble six months earlier when an earthquake destroyed the village where he had been working. In the therapy office 300 kilometers away, he was humorous and articulate as he discussed his near-death experience. He said he felt absolutely no fear as long as he was with his kind and attentive therapist. Obviously, something would need to be done to enable the plumber to feel in the office some of the symptoms that were making his life unworkable outside. There was the option of going to the *earthquake zone to see if being at the site of the trauma might awaken some of his anxiety, but that was not feasible given the distance. Viewing media photos from the earthquake also failed to simulate any anxiety. The therapist, a wise and gentle soul, then asked if he could try an unusual procedure.*

Therapist: Might I be allowed to shake your chair?
Client: [laughing] Well, sure. But after bumping along in that old bus hour after hour, I doubt shaking my chair will do anything.
Therapist: OK, Karnik, let us begin, then. I would like you first to think about being trapped under the rubble. Go back to the village in your mind. Get a good picture of that memory, and tell me when you are back there. OK? OK. Now, Karnik, I am going to shake your chair. [The therapist shook the chair a few times, not very forcefully, until the client shouted out to him.]
Client: Stop! That's enough. I'm having trouble breathing.
Therapist: Good, you're back there. Now just follow my fingers. Slowly, slowly, and just notice what happens.
Client: Oh, man. It's all coming back.

After many sets of carefully conducted eye movements, Karnik resolved his traumatic memory and was able to resume work as a plumber with what he called "just enough fear to make sure I'm careful."

Some of the techniques exemplified in the cases just noted are taught in EMDR trainings, though they tend not be presented as methods specifically designed for decelerating or accelerating EMDR processing. Trainees tend to use the techniques somewhat randomly whenever their clients are "stuck," without a clear understanding of why, and at times with negative results. After trial and error many clinicians develop something similar to the model we propose below, but they often have to make significant mistakes with clients as they practice the strategies. Others become frustrated before they have understood the complexity and richness of EMDR, and abandon the method, thinking it has little value (or alternately, poses too much of a risk). The training and training manual should be fine-tuned to preclude many of these problems.

To take one example from the Part I training manual, we refer to the first of the flow charts called "pictorial flow" (Shapiro, 2001b, p. 39). The text reads, "When reprocessing stops," then offers two interventions: "scan for more upset," and "person w/o action." The first intervention involves returning the stalled or looping client to the target memory to see if other visual memories might stimulate further therapeutic movement. In our model this would be appropriate for a client who is *under*responding at that moment. The next suggestion ("person w/o action") involves asking the client to modify a visual memory so that a perpetrator is visualized without movement, on the theory that this will produce less disturbance for the client. In our model we consider this appropriate for a client who is *over*responding at the moment. But in the training no mention is made of this distinction, and the trainee is likely to leave without understanding how to use these ideas purposely. Clearly if one of the techniques were to be used when the other is indicated, the effect on the client would likely be ineffective, if not harmful. It seems to us that the emphasis is more on doing something to try to solve the problem before it has been understood.

In the Part I training manual (Shapiro, 2001c) the concept of the cognitive interweave also contains the principles of overresponsive and underresponsive clients, and the reference to "distancing strategies" (p. 9) is an implicit recognition of clients who are overresponding, or too close to their problem, and who need to remove themselves in some way from the intensity of their EMDR work. Our point is that this general notion is implicit in the training format, but needs to be made explicit so that trainees can use it to organize and select interventions.

We organize our model according to a TICES-BID acronym. In Phase 3 we introduced the ICES segment. We now add additional letters to account for other aspects of a client's functioning that can be a focus of treatment. The *T* stands for trigger, *B* for behavior, a second *I* for interpersonal aspects, and *D* for drugs and diet. A trigger is a stimulus in the present which causes a reaction that is not easily explained by present events alone, so is assumed to cue or provoke or trigger something in memory. The *D* includes both prescription and illegal drugs, exercise and other health-related factors, and the general biological and physiological functioning of the individual. We acknowledge our debt to Lazarus (1989), from whom we have modified the Multimodal Therapy structure that reviews behavior, affect, sensation, imagery, cognition, interpersonal, and drugs (BASIC I.D.).

Assessment of the Nature of the Treatment Block

When EMDR processing stalls it is essential to assess the reason or cause with the aid of something akin to the overresponding and underresponding continuum. Only then can the therapist choose the proper strategy and maximize the likelihood that the client will respond favorably. We suggest that adequate assessment led to the correct choice of interventions in the two successfully treated cases just summarized. Both involve trauma resulting from earthquake, and both show how a similar event might require two quite different interventions in therapy—hence, the need for assessing the therapy problem before trying to correct it. Ana was *over*responding in her treatment session and required a decelerating strategy from her therapist. Karnik was *under*responding, so his therapist needed to stimulate more feeling.

In this section we list a sample of the kinds of problems that will require the use of either a decelerating or accelerating intervention. The focus here is on assessment of the problem; in the next part we concentrate on interventions that can be used. The boxes that follow are organized according to the components of TICES-BID, with each component further organized according to assessment of problems in overresponding (left side of the page) or underresponding (right side). The examples cited are meant to attune the therapist to possible issues that can occur prior to or during that can lead either to an overresponse or an underresponse by the client. By keeping the possibilities of both underresponding and overresponding in mind, the therapist can stay alert for abrupt changes in the client's experience, and adjust interventions accordingly.

POSSIBLE PROBLEMS WITH THE TRIGGER

OVERRESPONDING	UNDERRESPONDING
Perhaps the client is processing too much, or too quickly, for example:	Or perhaps processing too little, or too slowly, for example:
• The real-life situation may trigger too much emotion. In agoraphobia, sometimes the simple act of leaving home and going to the therapist's office may trigger overwhelming anxiety.	• The situation of the therapy office may calm the patient and not allow for the anxious reactions that are common outside the therapy office where they seem to be triggered almost randomly.
• Some people have such fear of therapy that simply thinking of treatment creates panic. Some appear to be phobic of their own emotions, memories, or history.	• Some clients report vague complaints, as if unaware of what triggers their symptoms. They may be so afraid of their memories that they block them out.

POSSIBLE PROBLEMS WITH THE IMAGE

OVERRESPONDING

Perhaps the client is processing too much, or too quickly, for example:

- Visual flashbacks may be signs of being too close or processing too fast.

- Certain visual memories may cause the client to abreact too severely.

- Present-day visual stimuli in the client's environment may be overwhelming. Even the face of the therapist, or some other visual cue in the office, may provoke a reaction that the client cannot handle.

UNDERRESPONDING

Or perhaps processing too little, or too slowly, for example:

- Some adults and children cannot visualize well enough to stimulate a feeling.

- Some clients report traumatic events but are not upset at all by the visual memory.

- Some clients report unresolved trauma but are unaware of the causal event, so they have no way of offering a visual component which might remind them of the traumatic event that maintains their symptoms today.

POSSIBLE PROBLEMS WITH THE COGNITIONS

OVERRESPONDING

Perhaps the client is processing too much, or too quickly, for example:

- Some clients think about themselves in unfriendly ways that explain why they feel "stuck," perceiving themselves as unable to deal with the problem.
"I am powerless."
"I am weak."

- Some beliefs reflect borderline tendencies:
"I cannot stand it."
"I cannot control it."

- Some accompany depression:
"I am not good enough."
"I am not in control of."

UNDERRESPONDING

Or perhaps processing too little, or too slowly, for example:

- Some clients think about themselves in negative ways that reflect their fears of therapy and explain why they are not facing a problem, even though it may cause considerable trouble for them outside of the therapy office. One negative self-belief has to do with one's identify:
"Who would I be without this problem?"

- Another is related to fears of the unknown:
"I don't dare start to open up my past."

- Some reflect perfectionism:
  "I have to."
  "I'm not safe."
  "I can't make a mistake."
  "I can't succeed."

- And some indicate generalized anxiety:
  "I am not safe."
  "I cannot trust myself."

- Some clients think about themselves in ways that appear to be positive but that also reflect their fears of therapy and explain their "resistance," such as:
  "I'm OK as I am." (Not really.)
  "I'm OK, but I'm not so sure about the others." (Really, I'm not sure of myself.)
  "I'm in control." (Maintaining control and distance is the only way to protect myself.

POSSIBLE PROBLEMS WITH THE EMOTIONS

OVERRESPONDING

Perhaps the client is processing too much, or too quickly, for example:

- It may be that the client is in fact not processing too much but is reacting appropriately to a real event, such as ongoing danger. (First investigate the event provoking the appropriate response.)

- The client may be experiencing too many emotions at once, or the SUDS level is simply too high to initiate EMDR.

- The client may not know how to self-soothe or relax.

- The type of emotion felt may be too bothersome to the client, for example, when the emotion of rage provokes a wish to kill.

UNDERRESONDING

Or perhaps processing too little, or to slowly, for example:

- Sometimes a client is not able to identify an emotion, but simply states that a memory is disturbing in an intellectual sort of way. This is a form of emotional distancing.

- The tendency to overtalk an issue may be another sign of avoiding feeling, or it may be a habit left over from a history of having been a talk-therapy patient.

- Clients who intellectualize or rationalize may have learned to overvalue their ability to think through problems. Whether this signals fear, a learned/reinforced response set, or a deficiency in identifying emotions needs to be assessed further.

POSSIBLE PROBLEMS WITH THE SENSATION

OVERRESPONDING

Perhaps the client is processing too much, or too quickly, for example:

UNDERRESPONDING

Or perhaps processing too little, or to slowly, for example:

• It may be an appropriate response to a medical or organic problem. (Ensure that there is not a medical/organic explanation for the body sensation, especially if the client reports pain or numbness or seizure-like activity.) Sometimes a sensation can have both medical/organic and psychogenic components. Is it depression or anemia? Is it a psychogenic headaches? Or a tumor?

• Some clients try to process too many sensations at once, as when a client says, "I feel it throughout my body."

• Some clients cannot identify a sensation as they try to wok therapeutically on an unresolved traumatic memory, even though they can date the event, report negative self-beliefs, and identify emotions. An example would be a phobic person who cannot talk himself into "feeling" in the therapy office but is paralyzed by his phobia in the outside world.

• Some clients in the midst of EMDR processing will "lose" a sensation without having resolved it yet.

POSSIBLE PROBLEMS WITH THE BEHAVIORS

OVERRESPONDING

Perhaps the client is processing too much, or too quickly, for example:

• Some violent persons may seek help to reduce feelings of rage but will not agree to avoid their victim; they will use a spouse as a way to "vent anger" in some cases of domestic violence, blaming the victim instead of facing their own rage.

• Some clients seeking to learn to care for themselves better will continue to act carelessly and without regard for their own welfare. A simple example: a depressed person refuses to exercise.

UNDERRESPONDING

Or perhaps processing too little, or to slowly, for example:

• Frequently phobic people learn to avoid the cause of their fear—avoiding roads with bridges, for example, in the case of acrophobia. This brings relief from their anxiety but also reduces the motivation to confront and resolve their phobic response.

• Some addicted clients will try to maintain inappropriate distance from their feelings by continuing to use drugs to self-medicate. Their motivation drops as the drug numbs their distressing emotions.

POSSIBLE PROBLEMS ON THE INTERPERSONAL

OVERRESPONDING

Perhaps the client is processing too much, or too quickly, for example:

- Some people identify their social environment (marriage, friends, workplace) as the source of their misery but will not/cannot leave or confront the situation. Therapy will not be very successful as long as they remain in the traumatizing social situation.

- Transference: There may be something about the therapist's behavior or manner that provokes a reaction in the client. (EMDR can be used to work through feeder memories.)

UNDERRESPONDING

Or perhaps processing too little, or to slowly, for example:

- A socially phobic person could live alone and avoid people and the fear that social interaction produces. The person might then seek out only persons guaranteed to be safe and comforting, such as a psychotherapist.

- Transference: Some clients fear that changing their behavior will cause them to lose their therapist. (This fear needs to be discussed during Phase 1 or 2, well before commencing desensitization.)

POSSIBLE PROBLEMS WITH DRUGS AND DIET*

OVERRESPONDING

Perhaps the client is processing too much, or too quickly, for example:

- It may be an appropriate response. Perhaps the client suffers from a medical or organic condition that causes or aggravates an emotional response. (Ensure that you conduct a thorough history including medical factors. Allergic reactions that mimic emotional problems are not uncommon.)

- Clients who use drugs, prescription or not, may be experiencing upsetting reactions due to the drug use.

UNDERRESPONDING

Or perhaps processing too little, or to slowly, for example:

- The client may be taking a sedative that freezes feelings to the point where so little emotion is reported that EMDR work cannot be initiated. Under medical supervision, the dosage may be slightly reduced so that enough emotion is felt to allow EMDR to begin, with further reductions as the underlying traumatic memories are resolved.

- Some persons addicted to substances such as alcohol or tobacco

* See the lists of cognitions in Shapiro (2001a, 2001b).

• Diet may cause an emotional re-action. For example, some clients who drink excessive amounts of coffee may experience what they call an anxiety attack, but may only be reacting to the effects of caffeine.

may not be able to feel the urge to use unless they first smell or taste a cue substance. The cue substance may be something that has become associated with the addictive substance, such as coffee triggering the desire to smoke, or smoking triggering the desire to drink alcohol.

Headaches are sensations that may require special diagnostic attention. The therapist should thoroughly assess physical-medical conditions and refer the client when indicated. Headaches can also suggest resistance; look for secondary gain and assess for dissociative tendencies. The headache might suggest posttraumatic stress disorder. Headaches also can result from using eye movements. Have the client remove any eyeglasses (especially bifocals) or contact lenses, and use bilateral stimulation other than eye movements.

Determining the Appropriate Treatment Strategy

Once the nature of the treatment block is determined, the therapist selects an intervention strategy. Listed are strategies for intervening with a client who has stalled during Phase 4 of EMDR. The strategies come from the EMDR Part I and II trainings, from readings and reports of colleagues, and from our own experiences. Many of the ideas were originally developed by other schools of psychotherapy. The list begins with comments on the mechanics of EMDR and then follows the TICES-BID acronym. Towards the bottom of each section are strategies constructed from both ends of the decelerating-accelerating continuum. These examples take the form of a hierarchy, progressing from left (decelerating or less stimulating interventions) to right (accelerating or more stimulating). The term *hierarchy*, which we mentioned explicitly in the case study of Jerry comes from Wolpe's (1969) idea of systematic desensitization and reciprocal inhibition. He based his formulations on Pavlov's (1941) work on classical conditioning. Wolpe helped his anxious and phobic patients create a hierarchy of the stimuli that provoked anxiety in them, with the barely noticeable objects on the bottom of a scale and the most upsetting objects on the top. He would begin with the less provoking stimuli and desensitize the patient to them, then gradually move up the hierarchy. One of the assumptions was that as lower-end issues were resolved, the issues on the higher end would become less disturbing and more approachable than they had been initially.

In therapy generally, and EMDR specifically, clients occasionally cannot work through disturbing stimuli because they find the treatment targets too intense. Wolpe has taught us how to help these clients approach the target more slowly, in the manner of what he called "successive approximation"—which is to say, little by little until the client can face and tolerate the treatment target in its originally most disturbing form. This model is applicable to phobic objects (e.g., slowly approaching a bridge while processing each increasingly frightening experience) and can be applied with equal utility to disturbing memories. When clients are phobic to their own feelings and personal history, the therapist helps them to modify the target so that it becomes manageable—perhaps by thinking of only a part of a memory or by intentionally modifying how a memory is recalled—until they client can face or resolve the entire memory.

Therefore, the concept of hierarchy refers to strategies that help clients to progress from memories or objects that are tolerable to those that are more disturbing. It is also a process of moving from low SUD ratings to higher SUD ratings, which is how Wolpe did it with his original SUD scale.

Because a hierarchy always begins on the decelerating end of the scale, it can be represented graphically with arrows: $\Rightarrow\Rightarrow\Rightarrow$. Though hierarchies are presented in EMDR Part I, we find them underused as treatment interventions, perhaps owing to the training flaws we mentioned earlier, which imply that it is always better to go faster than slower. The idea of hierarchy is to start slower or lower on the SUD scale, and only later to consider going faster or higher on the SUD scale. So, how does a therapist decide to go slower or faster with a client? That decision follows from an accurate assessment according to the decelerating-accelerating continuum. If the client is already too close to the problem, use a decelerating strategy. And if the client is too distant or moving too slowly, employ an accelerating strategy. At times it really is as simple as it sounds.

The list that follows is not complete. You are encouraged to change and expand on it. Most of the items probably will be self-evident to EMDR-trained clinicians. Some of the ideas were in use in other therapies before EMDR was discovered, so persons not trained in EMDR will often find themselves in familiar territory. It also bears repeating that these strategies are not necessary with all clients: around half the time, according to Shapiro, the client will respond well if the clinician employs the original and basic EMDR protocol.

Cognitive interweaves are introduced in Part II training. These are subtle suggestions or questions that the therapist can use to hint at a solution for a client whose treatment is not progressing smoothly, or when time is at a premium and the therapist wishes to speed up processing, or at other times of special need. Shapiro (2001) suggests that these interventions serve to "weave together the appropriate neural networks and associations" (p. 249) and to jump start the adaptive information processing mechanism when it has gotten stalled. After the therapist has provided but a glimmer of possibility to the client, eye movements are done and the client usually continues the process that the therapist has initiated. EMDR-trained therapists will recognize that what is taught in training about the cognitive interweaves is relevant when using any of these decelerating and accelerating strategies. When the therapist decides to use more active interventions to help clients who are stalled, it is useful to keep in mind that the best suggestions we can make to clients are those that are offered subtly, and that allow the clients to continue the work under their own power. Then clients can accept and extend and expand and modify on their own as they process issues. The therapist will not get as much credit for providing brilliant insights, but clients will feel empowered: "I did it my way, and I can do it again."

EMDR MECHANICS AS DECELERATING AND ACCELERATING STRATEGIES

FOR DECELERATING

- EMDR processing can be slowed down simply by using *fewer* bilateral movements. We noted how the number 24 is frequently inappropriate. In one case example, a healthy and resourceful client could tolerate only one pair of hand taps while processing an earthquake memory. We have worked with some clients who asked for only one tap at a time to a hand or shoulder, that is one-half of one full bilateral movement, then a break, then a tap on the other side of the body. A dissocia-

FOR ACCELERATING

- EMDR processing can be speeded up by doing *more* bilateral movements. On the EMDR Internet list, several clinicians have reported that some clients require and can tolerate continuous alternating sounds being played in the background as therapist and client talk through an entire session. Continuous alternating bilateral stimulation produces ongoing EMDR processing and is particularly useful with well-defended clients; for persons with low-level but chronic malaise; late in therapy

tive patient could process provided she looked only to one side, then took a break to talk, then looked to the other side, followed by another break in processing. While we cannot explain why this should be effective neurophysiologically (assuming that it is alternating bilateral stimulation that is the key to processing), we find that it helps some clients to continue processing traumatic memories while protecting themselves with an exceedingly slow (but appropriate) pace of bilateral stimulation.

• Decreasing the *velocity* of the movements also slows processing. It helps to use soothing words with clients who require this slower pace. One very fragile client was able to process a particularly horrible memory by doing a single eye movement (from left to right and back to the middle of the visual field) over the course of one full minute. As always, the client's need determines treatment style.

• Some clinicians say that moving one's hand a very *short distance*, producing a narrow eye movement, will slow processing. This is often our experience, but we cannot say if it is the rule.

when relatively minor problems remain to be resolved; or with persons who are focusing on strengthening their positive thoughts, images, and feelings. Sometimes we will play the sounds over speakers, which we listen to along with our clients. If this is done, *it is critical that the therapist check the SUD level from time to time to ensure that if the client begins to abreact and the SUDS rises, appropriate care will be taken to protect him or her.*

• Increasing the *velocity* of the alternating stimulation accelerates processing. When using eye movements, the therapist needs to ensure that the increased speed does not cause eye strain or damage. Taps and sounds appear to be less risky. Generally, since increased speed increases the rate of EMDR processing, abreactions and dissociation risk need to be monitored with at least occasional SUDS checks. A *longer* eye movement (i.e., to the ends of the client's visual field) can produce faster processing but we do not know if this will occur with all clients.

Some bilateral movements can be placed in both columns because they can serve either a decelerating or an accelerating function. The therapist cannot assume either function based on history with other clients. Changing direction of eye movements (horizontal, vertical, diagonal, circular, or the infinity sign/lazy eight) may slow or speed processing, so every change needs to be planned, then checked with each patient. Some clinicians simply change directions when they feel like doing so, not seeming to realize that the change may have an unforeseen impact on the patient. For example, the vertical and infinity movements are often calming for some clients. For others, however, different movements will stimulate different intensities of emotion. Those who practice neurolinguistic programming tell us that when the clients look downward, for example, toward the bottom of the infinity sign, they are accessing kinesthetic memories, which in the case of EMDR clients processing sensory memories may well produce a more intense response than would eye movements upward or to the sides.

Likewise, changing from one mode of stimulation to another (the options are eye movements, bilateral visual stimulation while the client looks straight ahead, sounds, tactile stimulation, or a combination) could produce more emotional intensity or less. Again, we recommend checking with the client to determine whether the effect of the change is to decelerate or to accelerate processing.

Here now are two examples of hierarchical use of EMDR mechanics:

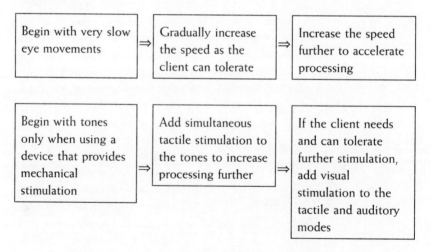

TRIGGER MODALITY

FOR DECELERATING   FOR ACCELERATING

• A clinician may treat agoraphobic   • Some clients need to be taken to
persons in their house at for the   the site of their triggers, such as a

initial session, thereby delaying the additional stimulation, or the more powerful triggers, involved with having to leave home to go to the therapist's office.

- A clinician can help a person afraid to face the triggering power of a specific memory to approach it metaphorically, or in segments. The clinician can also begin to work on relatively less troubling memories in the beginning of treatment.

- A clinician should ask about a client's "resistance" before judging it as inappropriate. Some clients should not begin therapy until issues of secondary gain are resolved.

- Sometimes it is necessary to work individually rather than with a spouse or other family member present who may provoke too intense a reaction in the client. The question of whether or not to involve others in a person's session is complex. (See Glang & Penner, 1996, for more information.)

- A clinician should check out secondary gain, as in the case of a phobia that allows a client to be excused from having to learn to become assertive and to learn to say no.

theater in the case of an actor with stage fright. This *in situ* or *in vivo* strategy usually produces emotions that do not appear readily in the therapist's office.

- Persons with symptoms that are not associated with specific memories can be encouraged to float back to early times to search for when they felt the same symptoms currently being reported. That earlier memory is then processed.

- Sometimes the client's "resistance" can be located in the body, connected with trigger words, or tied to a past experience, and processed with EMDR.

- A parent can be invited to a session to talk about a child's problem while the therapist treats the child with EMDR. The parent's narration will trigger emotions in the child that can be processed. (This is a complex strategy that requires training. See Lovett [1999] for specifics.)

- For vague complaints, a clinician can ask the miracle question (O'Hanlon & Weiner-Davis, 1989): "How would you know if overnight you had miraculously made these changes?" Then the clinician can use EMDR to install a future template, and desensitize any negative emotions, sensations, and images that arise.

Here are hierarchy examples for the trigger modality:

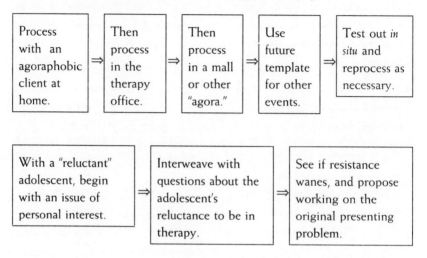

| Process with an agoraphobic client at home. | ⇒ | Then process in the therapy office. | ⇒ | Then process in a mall or other "agora." | ⇒ | Use future template for other events. | ⇒ | Test out *in situ* and reprocess as necessary. |

| With a "reluctant" adolescent, begin with an issue of personal interest. | ⇒ | Interweave with questions about the adolescent's reluctance to be in therapy. | ⇒ | See if resistance wanes, and propose working on the original presenting problem. |

IMAGE MODALITY

FOR DECELERATING

- Use EMDR on a single aspect of the traumatic image of a particularly disturbing memory ("fractionated" work).

- Consider developing and installing positive images as resources for the client prior to desensitization.

- Offer the client a device for simulation if the very sight of the therapist is too disturbing.

FOR ACCELERATING

- Return to the original incident and look for other aspects in the image that may have gone unnoticed but are disturbing.

- Some clients will feel more if they use a photograph or other visual stimulus instead of relying on images.

- Be aware that your placing your fingers in front of the client may be visually stimulating in and of itself.

Here are some ideas for using an imaginal hierarchy:

| Ask the client to imagine the perpetrator sitting quietly. | ⇒ | Ask the client to imagine a perpetrator in progressively more action. |

Use an imaginary glass protection between the client and the image of the perpetrator in a traumatic memory.	⇒	Slowly and "systematically," begin to remove the imaginary glass protector and process each new image.
Put the image in black and white or in colors not disturbing to the client.	⇒	Slowly add colors to the image as the client guides you, and process.
Have the client imagine being distant from the perpetrator, perhaps watching through binoculars.	⇒	Slowly the client imagines watching the perpetrator approach, or watching the traumatic picture come closer.
For children especially: use drawing, pictures, or other visual cues to create a sense of safety to develop.	⇒	Gradually introduce visual prompts to stimulate more emotion, all within the client's ability to tolerate.

COGNITION MODALITY

FOR DECELERATING

- Tell the client, "It's old stuff; you survived it; you're safe here in my office; it's over," or use other truthful and comforting words.

- Have the client role-play by comforting and assuring and advising a child or their own child ego state.

- Have the client role-play by advising another person regarding a problem similar to the client's.

- When a client makes progress, say, "Do you see that you can heal?" or

FOR ACCELERATING

- Use the Socratic method, asking, for example, "What do you think about . . . ?" or "Whose fault was it?" or "What if?" to stimulate further processing.

- Use role-play—"What if this had happened to your son or your daughter?"—to encourage looking at the problem differently.

- To stimulate a stuck point, ask the client to give a voice to it: "What would that feeling say about you if it could speak?"

"What does it say about you that you can heal?"

- Ask client, "Please *repeat* those positive words you just said."

- If client doesn't believe the original positive cognition, modify it down to a more "believable" form, for example, "I would like to believe [the positive cognition]."

- To stimulate a negative cognition, ask, "What does that [awful experience] say about *you*?"

- Ask the client, "Please *repeat* those strong negative words you just said."

- Ask, "What would you have to learn or believe about yourself for the validity of cognition score to go higher?"

To link both columns when a client is stuck on an old memory, encourage the client to "keep one foot in the past, one in the present." Another way to say it might be, "It is the child part of you that is feeling that old memory; the adult part of you knows that it is in the past. Notice that the child could not have done anything else then, and that the adult can now see it in better perspective." Or tell the client, "I'm confused. Are you saying that a 6-year-old child could have been responsible for what happened?" This will help the client see the problem from the vantage point of a mature adult, even as the client feels it from the point of view of an abused child.

Here is an idea for using the cognitive hierarchy:

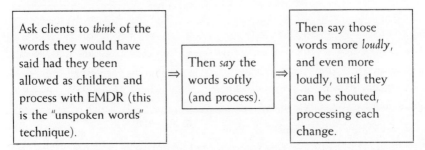

| Ask clients to *think* of the words they would have said had they been allowed as children and process with EMDR (this is the "unspoken words" technique). | ⇒ | Then *say* the words softly (and process). | ⇒ | Then say those words more *loudly*, and even more loudly, until they can be shouted, processing each change. |

EMOTION MODALITY

FOR DECELERATING

- When clients use a word suggesting strength or calm (e.g., "hope" or "wish"), ask them to repeat and to *feel* the word in their body, and do bilateral stimulation.

FOR ACCELERATING

- When you hear clients mention a strong emotion (e.g., "angry" or "scary"), consider asking them to repeat and *feel* the word while you do bilateral stimulation.

- Begin with a fractionated emotion. For example, begin with one memory that produces only moderate anxiety.

- Remind the client, "It is only a feeling you are having about the past," "It's only an emotional memory," or "It's over."

- Ask, "What might you feel if you had already resolved this problem?"

- For clients who "lose" feelings, ask, "What was that feeling you just had?" or "Where was it when you noticed it last?"

- Ask the client to pretend having a feeling such as anger over memories of abuse, and role-play a reaction to the abuser.

- Ask, "What might another person feel in circumstances such as this?"

The following strategy serves to decelerate initially, then frequently will stimulate and accelerate the processing of significant therapeutic issues.

Sometimes clients, for example, teens sent by a parent, will be willing to work with you, without admitting to harboring any residue from past trauma. After appropriate informed consent, suggest that clients recount their history while listening to continuous background bilateral stimulation (e.g., tones) and note any incident that still elicits a disturbance.

Here are some examples with the emotional hierarchy:

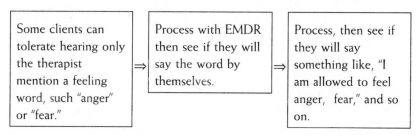

| Some clients can tolerate hearing only the therapist mention a feeling word, such "anger" or "fear." | ⇒ | Process with EMDR then see if they will say the word by themselves. | ⇒ | Process, then see if they will say something like, "I am allowed to feel anger, fear," and so on. |

Consider asking clients to use increasingly more stimulating words, processing with EMDR after they speak each new word, according to a hierarchy meaningful to the clients, such as in the following example:

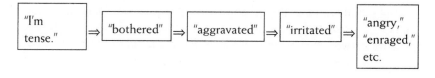

| "I'm tense." | ⇒ | "bothered" | ⇒ | "aggravated" | ⇒ | "irritated" | ⇒ | "angry," "enraged," etc. |

SENSATION MODALITY

FOR DECELERATING

- Install a safe place with a soothing aroma, such as the smell of pine needles.

- Focus on only one sensation at a time.

- Tapping the hands of some clients will soothe, perhaps in the tradition of healing touch.

- Ask clients to hold their hand over the part of the body where a sensation is felt, and process with EMDR only what is under the clients' hand.

- Not infrequently, clients recall unpleasant smells, tastes, and kinesthetic stimuli, or feel that they are gagging, being smothered, swallowing poison, being burned, etc. In such an instance, say, "It's only a memory," "It's in the past," etc. When a client reports a positive sensation (calm, peace), process with EMDR in order to install it further.

FOR ACCELERATING

- Some clients will "feel" a memory if they smell a substance associated with it.

- Focus on all sensations the clients feel.

- Tapping the hands of some clients will provoke a reaction as they recall a trauma of physical abuse.

- For clients whose SUD score is not changing, ask, "Where is that number in your body?" and resume processing after the response.

- When working with addicted clients, the therapist can stimulate the urge to use a substance by exposing the clients to the very substance (e.g., tobacco, alcohol, food) to which they are addicted. Then the therapist can process with EMDR as they report the urge to drink, smoke, overeat, etc.

- When clients report a negative sensation, ask, "What does that sensation say about you?" and process the response.

Ask for details about the sensation: size, color, weight, shape, temperature, texture, etc. While this may further *stimulate* (*accelerate*) processing for some clients, it also may serve to *contain* (*decelerate*) the experience for others. The therapist decides how the technique is intended to be used, and checks with the client to determine the actual impact.

Here is an idea for using the sensory hierarchy:

A highly motivated couple with sexual problems, already having resolved major traumatic memories, could be taught to use EMDR along with sensory focus techniques, desensitizing one another to any anxiety that appears when they touch each other in non-erotic and non-sexual ways.	⇒⇒	After becoming comfortable touching non-erotically, they can slowly begin sexual touching, using EMDR to desensitize any anxiety as it appears, and progressing to the more anxiety-producing touching only when they both have learned to feel calm and relaxed with the previous touching.

BEHAVIOR MODALITY

FOR DECELERATING

- Client can role-play assertive behavior.

- Client can practice smiling.

- Some clients should not begin EMDR processing until they have first learned to manage the physiological responses of anxiety and other unpleasant affect.

FOR ACCELERATING

- Client can hit a pillow to provoke anger.

- Client can role-play a depressed look.

- Many panic victims don't feel panic in the office, so consider having the client spin or hyperventilate, then process. (Note: special care needs to be taken with this technique.)

Here are two ideas for using the behavior hierarchy:

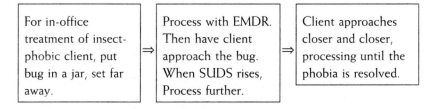

For in-office treatment of insect-phobic client, put bug in a jar, set far away.	⇒	Process with EMDR. Then have client approach the bug. When SUDS rises, Process further.	⇒	Client approaches closer and closer, processing until the phobia is resolved.

| For *in-vivo* treatment, client drives with the therapist to the phobic object (airport, bridge, theatre, etc.). | $\Rightarrow$ | As above, process each time the client reports an increase in anxiety, moving up the hierarchy of phobic stimuli. | $\Rightarrow$ | Continue until client is able to feel as desired and in a way that shows processing is completed. |

INTERPERSONAL MODALITY

FOR DECELERATING

- Clients are to be encouraged to expand and utilize their social networks.

- A supportive therapeutic relationship is important.

- The butterfly hug is useful in the group context.

- Clients can be encouraged to dialogue with their various ego states.

- Remember that some children will use EMDR more willingly if a comforting parent is present. Assess the child's comfort level with you first.

FOR ACCELERATING

- Sometimes the therapist's face, behavior, or proximity will provoke a transference response in the client. Instead of interpreting, process it with EMDR.

- Ask spouse or parent to join session to provide treatment targets.

- For children, ask parent to narrate a traumatic event while child processes.

- Some symptoms involving parent and child (e.g., school phobia) can involve treating both clients simultaneously, using speakers with tones in the background.

EMDR is used as an adjunctive resource in group therapy, for both decelerating and accelerating purposes.

In group treatment dependent largely on the therapist, two therapists are necessary. As past issues are provoked, the client leaves the group with one therapist and processes, using EMDR, then returns to the group to debrief. If all members agree to this system, the process of leaving for individual treatment is normalized and utilized routinely.

In a psychodrama group, the responsibility for conducting the group is shared, so EMDR processing can continue within the group.

Members of the group can take various roles. To accelerate process-ing, one person will purposely stimulate a second person in a way that provokes strong negative emotion, which can then be processed with EMDR. In some cases a third person will do the EMDR stimula-tion by standing behind and tapping the shoulders of the second person. At other times the first and third persons can assume sooth-ing and comforting roles to decelerate processing for the second person. The psychodrama director, trained in EMDR, can thereby in-struct other group members on the subtleties of using EMDR in this setting.

Here is an idea for using the interpersonal hierarchy:

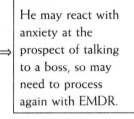

| A man with social phobia might be successfully treated for a fear of speaking in class. | ⇒ | He may react with anxiety at the prospect of talking to a boss, so may need to process again with EMDR. | ⇒ | Finally he can process the most fearsome task of all: asking for a date. |

DRUGS/DIET MODALITY

FOR DECELERATING

- Some clients need sedative drugs so as not to be overwhelmed by a traumatic memory.

- Some clients need to reduce their chemical stimulants, such as those who feel anxious from drinking too many caffeine-loaded beverages.

- It is a good idea to recommend aer-obic exercise so clients increase their levels of serotonin and other catecholamines.

FOR ACCELERATING

- Some clients need stimulating drugs to allow them to feel suffi-cient energy and motivation to work therapeutically.

- An intoxicated client will need to get sober, as the alcohol acts as a depressant and lowers emotion, creating distance from the prob-lem.

- Certain foods or chemicals can trigger a memory and can be used both to stimulate an abreaction and check effects.

Here are some ideas for using the drug/diet hierarchy:

Clients who take psychotropic medications can use EMDR to process the feelings that are accessible. As feelings are resolved, they can consider lowering their dosage, but only under medical supervision. (Careful informed consent is particularly important.)	⇒	As they lower their medication dosage, they will notice that new feelings arise. These, then, can be processed in turn with EMDR. (Close collaboration should occur between the therapist and the medical consultant.)
Therapists who work with substance addicts use EMDR to weaken the present-day stimuli that trigger the urge to use, beginning with the lease powerful triggers. EMDR can also be used initially to establish a sense of sobriety and well-being for clients.	⇒	As clients learn self-control and find that the strength of present-day triggers is weakened, EMDR can be used to target increasingly more powerful triggers, and eventually to target traumatic memories that fuel the urge to use.

We end this chapter with three cases that exemplify the use of decelerating and accelerating strategies with overresponsive and underresponsive clients, with reference to both assessment and treatment applications. The first case depicts a client who was treated inappropriately because the problem had not been assessed prior to treatment. The second is an example of an overresponding client who required decelerating interventions, and the third describes an underresponding client who benefited from accelerating strategies.

Case Example:

In this treatment session errors were made both in assessing the client's status and in using the appropriate intervention. A well-trained and licensed psychotherapist had worked with dissociative persons prior to learning EMDR. After completing EMDR Level I and Level II training and attending the specialty presentation on using EMDR in dissociation, he planned to use EMDR with a dissociative patient. He felt quite comfortable with this patient and with what he had recently learned, but wanted special consultation during the first EMDR session. He contracted with me (J. H.) to observe his session and provide feedback. During that session, he planned to use EMDR for the first time with a young woman diagnosed with multiple personality disorder (officially called dissociative identity disorder). This was to be her 30th session. To that point the therapist had worked well with her, and she seemed to trust him. She said she understood EMDR and was ready to use the new method. The therapist and I met prior to the session, and I suggested that he work very slowly. I then offered some EMDR decelerating ideas. It seemed that my therapist-consultee understood and appreciated the concept of decelerating strategies, so I went into the observation room and watched, with a clinical supervisor of the agency, through a one-way mirror.

The therapist began carefully, assuring that the different parts (what we used to call personalities) of the client were in agreement with proceeding with EMDR. A specific memory was targeted, cognitions were identified and measured, SUDS for the associated emotion was reported as moderate, a body sensation was localized, and desensitization began with the therapist moving his hand in front of the patient's eyes. The therapist did a sweep—but instead of doing it slowly, while asking for feedback from the client, and instead of stopping after one sweep as (I thought) we had agreed, the therapist continued (and continued, and continued) complying with what he had learned in EMDR training about beginning with 24 eye movements.

During that set, the SUDS zoomed to 10 almost immediately and the client, blinking her eyes, dissociated into a safe refuge. Unfortunately, the therapist failed to notice this and continued with more sets of eye movements. I will note that the therapist did everything according to the EMDR treatment manual, and exactly as he had heard it presented in training.

In the debriefing, I spent time recognizing the therapist for his obvious caring attitude, the quality of the informed consent, the preparation for EMDR during the previous 29 sessions, and many other qualities in the treatment relationship. I then said: "There was just one thing I noticed that did not seem to work. As you continued to move your hands, your client blinked and I think, dissociated." I then began to review the earlier discussion of decelerating techniques in EMDR treatment. At this point the supervisor volunteered that he had noticed the client's blinking. A useful discussion then took place among the three of us; it seemed that the therapist had to experience in a session the need for a decelerating approach before he could grasp what had been for him only an abstract concept.

Case Example:

Jon was an overresponder, already feeling too much emotion most of the time throughout his waking hours. Middle-aged and presently unemployed, he called for help to reduce his urges to use alcohol and cocaine, urges that had been increasing.

He said he had been in various kinds of treatment for decades, but his memories, and the urge to use substances that those memories triggered, remained upsetting during most of his waking hours. He had been attending Alcoholics Anonymous faithfully, but the longer he was sober, the more he found himself bothered by thoughts from the past, thoughts that he used to ignore by drinking himself into unconsciousness. He could not afford to get intoxicated again, as his probation officer had warned him that one more instance of drug use, whether it led to another crime or not, would get him housed in the penitentiary. He identified two of the memories that continued to haunt him: being beaten "black and blue" by his parents at age 10, and being raped at a youth crisis center while a foster family was being sought. He got the message that somehow the entire matter was his fault because he had "angered" his father previously.

He said that just thinking about these memories took him to a SUD score of 10. Assuming that EMDR processing would likely raise the client's emotion even more, but also wanting to help the client to work through some of the memory, I (J. H.) began with a relaxation exercise as an initial decelerating intervention until the SUD rating dropped somewhat, then I began with a very, very slow hand movement (the second decelerating technique).

Therapist: OK, Jon, we're ready to start. Now, I'd like you to look at the mental picture of your dad and mom standing there, and you black and blue. You say you can stand it if you put them far away from you, and without having them move [additional decelerating techniques]. How are you doing now?
Client: I'm OK.
Therapist: What would that be on the 0 to 10 scale?
Client: About a 6.
Therapist: OK, now I'm going to move my hand in a way we talked about before, very, very slowly, and I want you to tell me each time you notice that number 6 change, either going higher or lower. Remember we already agreed that we will continue unless your number goes higher than an 8. If it does, we will stop. OK? Are you ready?
Client: Yes. Go ahead. I'm OK.
Therapist: OK, here I go, now I'm going to move my hand very slowly first to your left side, very slowly, just like this, and when I get to the far left I'll stop. How are you doing? What is the number now?
Client: I'm still OK. About a 7.
Therapist: [Still moving slowly towards the client's left side] OK if I continue toward your left?
Client: Still OK.
Therapist: Now I'm getting to the end of this side and I'm going to move to your right side. OK?

Client: OK.

Therapist: OK, now I'm moving across the midline. How are you doing now? What's the number?

Client: It jumped a bit. It's up to an 8.

Therapist: Do you want me to stop, or can you handle a little more?

Client: Go ahead. I'll let you know.

Therapist: OK, now I'm going to your right side, very slowly, just notice what comes up, and tell me if you want me to stop.

Client: OK.

Therapist: Number?

Client: Still an 8.

Therapist: Continue or not?

Client: Continue.

Therapist: OK, I'm at the right side and now I'm going to move my hand back to the middle. OK, now I'm stopping, right here in the middle. [*Therapist stops after the one pass and slowly lowers his hand.*] Good. You can take a deep breath now . . . that's it. And blank out what you were working on if you want to. OK, what do you get now?

Client: Hmm. I seem to be OK. That's odd. I can still get the picture in my mind but it's faded now. And it doesn't bother me very much.

This kind of client could cause the therapist to wait too long to begin desensitization. His problem was long-standing and the initial SUD was relatively high. We are recommending that when there is a high SUD score (i.e., the client is assessed as being an overresponder), special strategies can be used to contain the emotional experience by "decelerating" or slowing down EMDR processing. This can be done mechanically (literally slowing and reducing the number of bilateral movements) or in other ways (such as talking the client slowly through the upsetting experience while doing EMDR movements).

If the therapist had not assessed the problem and determined that the client was already overstimulated, bilateral movements might have overstimulated the client further. Doing too many movements, or doing them too fast, could cause the SUD score to rise so high as to panic the client, stop processing and maybe end treatment prematurely, leave the client worse off than before, provoke feelings of helplessness and hopelessness, or lead to other unfortunate results.

Bilateral stimulation by itself can cause either harm or benefit, depending on how it is used. It is only a tool, and as with most tools, whether it is used effectively or not depends on the user. In the case of Jon the experience of the therapist was significant, as was the therapist's willingness to adjust the technique according to Jon's needs. Obvious too was the trust the client felt for the therapist. Recall that this client had been in treatment for decades, and was still suffering from memories that he had tried to resolve many times previously. Skilled EMDR therapists offer not only renewed hope that change is possible but also assurance that the client will be accompanied through the processing. Is this an element of the therapeutic relationship? We think so. Some of our colleagues tell us that "everybody has abreactions" and that we should not be so concerned with them. We strongly disagree with this view, as the case of Jon is one where a severe (and unnecessary) abreaction could well have retraumatized this man and caused him to bolt from treatment, again.

Case Example:

Jerry, a 50-year-old electrician, called for an appointment. As was the case with an earlier mentioned client, Jerry hated to enter crawl spaces under houses and his career was in jeopardy. He said he had always felt some fear in confined spaces but could not remember where it began. In the therapy session he was perfectly calm while discussing recent experiences in confined spaces, and reported no upsetting sensations that might lend themselves to EMDR work.

With the decelerating-accelerating model, Jerry would be assessed as an "under-responder" in that he did not feel enough emotion during therapy to allow EMDR to help him. Treatment, then, would need to be preceded by some strategy that would stimulate some of the fear he felt in crawl spaces. Since he was not able to engage in EMDR simply by talking about his experiences, I (J. H.) actually needed not so much to "accelerate" his therapeutic processing but to get it started. Together we devised a plan to stimulate the kind of fear experienced outside the therapy office. Jerry first agreed that he would enter a dark closet in my office until he felt claustrophobic and his SUDS level was elevated, and would then come into the main office where I would treat with EMDR. I used a "floatback" technique to find earlier memories that were triggered by this closet experience, and he immediately recalled crawling into a storm sewer with a childhood buddy and being locked in the trunk of a car as a "practical joke"—both memories were still quite upsetting to him. He then accessed and worked through each specific event successfully.

In the following session he reported that he still felt panic in confined spaces. But again, as he recounted the events of the previous week, he could generate no fear at all in my office. He volunteered to enter my closet again, this time with his face against the wall and the door shut to block out all light. When he returned, he told me he had remembered being smothered with a pillow—he did not want to tell me the details, so we did bilateral stimulation while he simply focused on the feelings. Eventually he felt less shame about the memory and was able to tell me that he had been smothered, when he was about six, by an older relative who wanted to keep

Jerry quiet while the relative sexually molested him. He had never told anyone about the sexual assault, about the fear of being smothered to death, or about the relative's threat. Working through this memory was also useful for him, but he felt fear again the next time he worked in a crawl space, though he then began to notice that he was afraid of bugs. "It's as if I lifted away the memory of being smothered and found the fear of insects underneath."

In the therapy session that followed, he again was calm as he recounted the latest fear experienced at work, so I needed to design another plan to simulate emotion for him in my therapy office. This time I followed the concept of hierarchy described by Wolpe (1969). To simulate the fear of insects, he agreed to bring a bug into the office. He had a colleague capture a harmless, nonpoisonous bug, bottle it, wrap the bottle carefully with fabric and newspaper, then place it in a paper bag. In the therapy office, I slowly uncovered the bottle while Jerry, on the opposite side of the office from the bottle, felt his SUD level rise. I had to place the closed bottle near an opposite wall so that Jerry could tolerate looking at it—feeling what he called a SUD rating of 5. We then used EMDR to lower the SUD. We continued to move the bottle closer by increments, stopping to use EMDR treatments, until he was finally able to let the bug out of the bottle and crawl on his arm with no fear reaction.

Treatment was successful because there was first an assessment of the problem of understimulation, and then the decision was made to use various accelerating strategies (namely, the dark closet, the face against the closet wall, and the insect in the bottle). Additionally, because one of the accelerating strategies proved too strong at first (the insect), the overstimulation and understimulation continuum was used in a progressive way, following the model of a hierarchy from less to more disturbing stimulation.

These cases illustrate how individual differences will cause clients to respond differentially to bilateral stimulation and how these variations in responsiveness will require adjustments in the therapist's interventions. While the therapist can rely on a careful history and assessment to predict client responsiveness to some degree, it is also necessary to conduct *ongoing* assessment throughout the desensitization process in Phase 4. No history taking can substitute for attention to the dynamic dialogue that should continue between therapist and client. Shapiro (2001a) wrote, "It is vital that the clinician read the client's nonverbal cues to determine whether the disturbing information has reached a new plateau and the set can be ended" (p. 176), and later referred to how the clinician should be able to notice "a new dissociation that is being triggered because the client has been pushed too far" (p. 178), in which case the set can also be stopped but for opposite reasons.

Chapter 5

EP Interventions in
an EMDR Session

Our motivation for introducing EP techniques into EMDR work comes not only from the usual propensity of therapists toward eclecticism and from our positive experiences with EP but also from Shapiro herself. According to Shapiro (2001a), EMDR is a synthesis of features from many therapies, including psychoanalysis, cognitive and behavioral therapies, Gestalt therapy, somatic therapies, and stress management training. The success of EMDR is due to the particular choice of elements and the way in which they are combined. Nevertheless, many other methods have been used effectively with EMDR in ways not catalogued in Shapiro's text: marital and family therapy (Glang & Penner, 1996), analytic psychotherapy (Grand, 1996), art therapy (Cohn, 1993), neurolinguistic programming (Popky, 1999), resource development and installation (Korn & Leeds, in press; Leeds & Shapiro, 2000), schema-focused therapy (Zangwill, 1988), and hypnosis (Gross & Ratner, 2002). Lawrence (1998) described EMDR as a special form of ego state psychotherapy. The EMDR training brochure notes, "Trainees from previous workshops have incorporated the EMDR method into their practices and paradigms as diverse as psychodynamic, behavioral, Gestalt, and Adlerian Life Style Analysis" (EMDR Institute, 2001, p. 3).

We endorse this attitude of both incorporating EMDR into existing frameworks and augmenting EMDR with other techniques and methods, even though we do not find all of the specific efforts at integration to be useful. We also concur with Shapiro (2001d) who cautioned clinicians against random experimentation without explaining how new protocols were chosen and without justifying claims that the original EMDR protocol had been proven inadequate. We also repeat the caveat: When you change the protocol, you are no longer conducting the EMDR that has been shown to be effective with a variety of disorders in a wide range of settings. You may indeed be improving on EMDR; on the other hand, you may be diminishing its power. In the continual effort to search for improvements, therapists need to preserve what is effective until they are sure they are replacing it with something better. In this chapter, we offer a limited number of suggestions for augmenting the EMDR protocol. We came to our conclusions only after lengthy experimentation with the basic EMDR model, and then only after becoming convinced, through repeated trials, that the hybrid treatment intervention would be more helpful to our clients.

In previous chapters we suggested ways to enhance the EMDR protocol from within. These advanced strategies have enabled us and our students to use EMDR more effectively. We now offer modifications from outside the EMDR model for those occasions when EMDR strategies have been exhausted and clients still are "stuck," do not respond, or overrespond. A final introductory thought: We do not suggest that the therapist in these situations stop using EMDR permanently. Quite the contrary, shifting from EMDR to EP will often allow treatment to return to EMDR again, and in this sense the EP techniques can be thought of as being "in the service of EMDR." Our outline follows the eight phases of EMDR.

PHASE 1: HISTORY TAKING

On occasion, the simple taking of a history can be upsetting for the client and EP techniques can be helpful.

Case Example:

One client who sounded quite agitated in her initial phone call was given an appointment the same day. Once in the office, she talked in a pressured manner about her history of therapy for an anxiety disorder. Archaic origins of her problem had been addressed in earlier treatment, but she believed more work needed to be done.

Her anxiety had become worse recently, progressing to panic attacks in public places. At the completion of the history taking, I (M. G.) described my practice and made a referral for a review of her prescription for anxiolytics.

Late in the session she still seemed as upset as when she arrived—maybe worse because of our review of her symptoms. I said that although little time remained in the session, we could try something brief that might provide some relief until the next session. I gave her information about the energy therapies. Though a little skeptical, the client nevertheless agreed to try a thought field therapy algorithm. Her SUD score was 10. I had her rub the "sore spot" while saying three times, "I deeply accept myself even though I have this anxiety." I then led her through a process of tapping under the eye, under the arm, and under the collarbone, followed by the nine gamut treatments and a repeat of the tapping sequence. I asked what the disturbance level was. At this point a look of astonishment crossed her face. "2." After another round, the SUD rating was 0, and the astonishment had progressed to happy relief. The time for the next meeting was set, payment was made, and as I stood to say good-bye, the client grabbed me in a hug and just as quickly departed.

Although EMDR is a very effective treatment for anxiety, it would not have been possible to help this client with EMDR in the initial 45-minute session—let alone the few minutes at the end of the session—since the preparatory phases had not been done. I was not willing to let the client suffer for another week or two the discomfort that had driven her to the office. Since the anxiety algorithm is so brief and is usually successful, I chose to implement it.

I did not believe that we had completely resolved her long-standing anxiety disorder in this one session, but the algorithm had resolved the disturbance related to at least one aspect of it. It had enabled her to safely leave the session and return to her daily life, and had been carried out at least as quickly as a relaxation procedure. She returned for subsequent EMDR sessions, successfully identifying and resolving related issues.

In addition to cases where levels of disturbance are unexpectedly elevated (such as the one just described), there are others where clients arrive for treatment wishing and expecting to begin work on troubling issues in spite of the fact that they will not be able to return for a second session in timely fashion. They may have heard of the considerable effectiveness of EMDR but not of the necessary preparation and follow-up. For these cases, we recommend that the clinician give a brief explanation of how EMDR requires a history and preparation and can bring up associated memories that may not be resolvable in one session, and extend an invitation to use energy techniques for that session.

In history taking, muscle testing can be used for clarification of various elements. For example, the client may present a problem whose details are nebulous. Since muscle testing can respond only to the dichotomous issue of "true–false," the therapist looks for an answer in a "20 questions" mode, narrowing down alternatives until reaching a conclusion.

Case Example:

A woman in her 40s presented for a fear of spiders but had no recollection of its origin. The "floatback" technique (see Chapter 6) might have been useful in preparation of the phobia protocol, but I (M. G.) decided to use muscle testing instead, partly because sometimes it is less threatening than asking the client to verbalize distressing life events, and partly because the issue was so well defined and it was suitable for the narrowing-down strategy. After determining that there were no psychological reversals or neurological disorganization that might interfere with muscle testing of the problem, I had her say, "The problem started before college," and tested her arm. The response was positive. I proceeded through the following statements, with the same result: "The problem started before high school," "The problem started before middle school," and "The problem started before elementary school." The response to "The problem started before age five" was negative, but to "The problem started at age five," it was positive. Believing I had determined the time frame, I searched for the participants. I tried "The problem has to do with a relative" and got a positive answer. The same result was obtained for "The problem has to do with a male relative," but the response to "The problem has to do with father" was negative. The responses of both the indicator muscle and the client to "The problem has to do with brother" were strong: she drew her arm away, "He thought it was real funny, but it scared me to death! I was sitting on the back steps and he came up behind me with his friend and put a big ol' daddy longlegs on me. I knocked it off and ran in while they were just out there laughing." We had identified the first instance of the phobia.

Phase 1 of EMDR includes instructing clients in self-control techniques, such as the use of a relaxation audiotape. Clients are to use these methods when disturbing material comes up between sessions. We have added selected energy techniques to the group, including the emotional freedom technique (EFT), Tapas acupressure technique (TAT), and the eye roll.

If history taking reveals dissociative tendencies or other issues that might destabilize the patient early in Phase 4, desensitization, the therapist might plan to begin with some energy work rather than

EMDR. Thereby, key issues can be targeted and disturbance levels lowered, decreasing the probability that abreactions or dissociations will occur later during EMDR.

PHASE 2: PREPARATION

If we haven't talked much with the client about EP in Phase 1, this preparatory phase is an opportunity for going into more depth. A relaxing technique, such as TAT, could be taught for increasing feelings of security and calm. Many clients report feeling more prepared simply by using Cook's hookups for two minutes or so. Other EP techniques can be introduced for use in addition to EMDR methods (e.g., imagined safe place), when treatment becomes too intense for the patient, and for many other purposes over the course of therapy. For some clients an energy technique will be easier to use between sessions than EMDR methods. Client need always dictates which to recommend.

For a client who asks to begin a session with EMDR and who is agreeable to using EP techniques as necessary, there are options for deciding when to introduce EP treatment. Some therapists will begin the desensitization phase with EMDR, then switch to EP if the client abreacts too severely, is at risk to dissociate, or wishes for processing to proceed with less intensity. A second option is to use muscle testing during the preparation phase to ask the body whether EP will be a viable alternative in the session. The clinician muscle tests while the client says something like "It would be best to begin with EMDR for this problem" or "Either EMDR or EP will be effective for this problem." If muscle testing produces a negative response to these two statements, the client might then try "We should use energy therapy to work on this problem." Whatever tests strongest should be honored, as long as the client is in agreement. This is a quick procedure that can be done at the opening of any session, and after the client is familiar with both treatment methods this testing usually proceeds rapidly.

Interestingly enough, muscle testing does not always indicate that EP treatment should be used. Sometimes it indicates EMDR; sometimes testing is equivocal, which may mean a psychological reversal or neurological disorganization is present; or it indicates that both methods should be used.

Should the decision be for EMDR, there remains the decision of whether the patient is ready for EMDR treatment of a defined problem. Muscle testing can supply another data point for consideration.

The clinician simply muscle tests while the client says something like "I am ready to begin EMDR treatment." The results of this test can be taken into account in making the determination of whether to continue with EMDR.

PHASE 3: ASSESSMENT

The first issue in assessment is to choose a target for treatment. When a client presents with many concerns, the therapist could certainly "start anywhere," since EMDR is very good at homing in on critical issues. But to save some time the clinician might again use muscle testing to help choose a target. The clinician can simply test an indicator muscle while having the client state, "I should work on issue X first," versus "I should work on issue Y first." Little is lost by moving directly into treating the problem testing stronger.

Choosing the most fitting negative and positive cognitions seems a straightforward endeavor but has proved the most problematic aspect of Phase 3. Therapists can accept phraseology that is inappropriate, and clients can have trouble finding any negative cognition related to their trauma or can come up with more than one cognition that is applicable to their target incident—especially if they are shown a list of possible cognitions. If the chosen cognition is inappropriate, treatment will often stall. Techniques designed to help a client find appropriate cognitions are discussed extensively in EMDR training sessions and manuals.

An option is to shift at this point from EMDR to EP by viewing or reframing the negative cognition as a psychological reversal instead of a stimulus for emotional processing. To treat the psychological reversal, the clinician asks the client to do a correction by rubbing the sore spot or tapping another of the reversal points and say, "I deeply and completely accept myself even though (or even if) I . . . [here the client states the negative cognition]." The negative cognition will still serve its purpose of stimulating a body response to the traumatic memory, but without the excessive emotional upset. This approach sometimes will resolve the issue completely, or decrease the level of cognitive disturbance, accelerating treatment when the clinician returns to the EMDR protocol.

Most EMDR therapists have had occasion to doubt the "truth" of numbers given to them by clients on the validity of cognition or SUDS scales. For example, a client may have done some very productive work but then report that the SUD rating has only lowered from an 8 to a 3, when it seems to the therapist that almost all—if not all—of the disturbance has been resolved. The EMDR therapist in such a case could suggest muscle testing, perhaps asking the client to say, "The level of my disturbance is a 3." If the indicator muscle tests strong, the therapist accepts the client's initial rating and says, "Think of that" or "Go with that," and reinitiates bilateral stimulation. If the muscle tests weak, the therapist, intuiting that the client's rating is high can try, "It's a two." If the response is strong, the therapist can reinitiate processing at that point. If the response is weak, "It's a 1" and "It's a 0" can also be tested, and whichever one tests strong can be followed up in the same manner. If none are strong, the SUD rating is probably above that reported by the client, and higher numbers can be tested and followed up.

If during assessment the SUD score is very high and the client either appears to be at risk to abreact or dissociate, or simply reports suffering too much, EP interventions should be considered. We usually direct the client through a treatment for the suffering—anxiety, grief, anger, or other disturbance—either using an algorithm or specific meridian points related to those emotions.

PHASE 4: DESENSITIZATION

EMDR desensitization has been characterized by terms such as "turbocharged free association" by therapists experiencing it in training or first using it with clients. EMDR processing is somewhat unpredictable and usually not a smooth progression from a high number on the SUDS scale to progressively lower numbers. It is more typical for the client's rating to move up and down on the scale during a session, sometimes up to a very high level; at other times the client will get "stuck" at a certain level, sometimes for an extended period. When these problems occur, EP techniques can be used with or without the decelerating and accelerating strategies we described in Chapter 4. We now describe some of the complications that appear during EMDR processing for which EP methods can help.

Looping

Looping is EMDR terminology for when therapy gets stuck—a client goes over and over the same issue without much progress. Often the SUD rating will be elevated for an extended period of time.

The simplest approach from EP would involve EMDR stimulation on a meridian point, obviously by using tapping. If eye movements, tapping, and tones have already been tried, and the client is still looping, she or he might try this procedure. While tapping on the backs of the client's hands, the therapist informs that she or he will be tapping at different sites, "where energy therapists say specific emotions are associated." After the client consents, the therapist continues: "What I would like you to do is simply pay attention as I change where I am tapping your hands. First, I'll tap here [gamut point] for a few seconds. What do you notice?" If the client reports a shift, continue tapping as the client reports the new awareness, and ask the client to notice accompanying body sensations. If there is no shifting, change to another meridian point, for example, the one for self-blame: "Now I will tap on the inside of your index finger. What do you notice now?" Change sites until something new is reported, and then continue with EMDR.

The therapist can also try using an EP algorithm for treating the specific problem being addressed.

Case Example:

A prison inmate was working through a memory of when a brother who had abused him for years put him into a closet. The brother threatened serious harm if the client came out. The rest of the family then entered the room and settled in; the client realized he would not be released for a long time. He panicked that someone would hear him, he would be discovered, and he would be beaten. He did indeed manage to remain quietly in the closet for hours. In the following years, he had nightmares and "flashbacks" of the incident. A couple of days before I (M. G.) arrived for the session, prison personnel had found the client asleep, tightly wedged between a wall and a file cabinet, reenacting his confinement in the closet.

I initiated desensitization which went well until the level of distress remained high and progress was not made in spite of many sets of bilateral stimulation. Rather than test for psychological reversals or neurological disorganization or employ a basic or advanced EMDR technique to deal with the impasse, I decided to try the TFT algorithm for trauma. I asked the client to tap the inside end of the eyebrow, under the eye, under the arm, and under the collarbone; to do the nine gamut procedure; and to repeat tapping of the four points. He became visibly calmer, and eye movement was resumed. The episode was then completely processed; the client no longer felt stuck in the memory. In subsequent sessions he reported that long-standing nightmares and intrusive thoughts had stopped.

We use this trauma algorithm fairly frequently, which is not surprising, since most disorders are trauma based. Also commonly used is the algorithm for anxiety. Almost every algorithm has proved useful in "unsticking" EMDR; the clinician determines (through intuition or asking the client) the emotion in question and applies the appropriate algorithm. At times diagnostic muscle testing is employed and points applicable to the problem are more specifically determined.

Sometimes looping reflects clients' fears about continuing to process a memory, what we already discussed as a kind of phobic response to the treatment process. Acrophobic clients, for example, will feel fear when thinking about crossing a bridge and feel better while walking away. In a similar way individuals who are terrified by their own history, memories, or the prospect of recalling a long-buried incident may simply refuse to address those topics. Clients will avoid the feared memory by stopping a treatment session that is about to expose them to what has become as much a phobic object as the bridge is to the acrophobe. The question is, what can therapists do to help clients to feel less fear in the presence of the phobic object? One answer is to use EP techniques for fear reduction. The clients focus on the idea of doing therapy on the identified issue, give a SUD rating to measure how uncomfortable that is, and are then directed in the use of some energy treatment, usually the anxiety or phobia algorithm. Most clients will then be ready proceed with treatment

Abreaction

One of our early—and still major—uses of EP treatment is in handling abreactions. In traditional therapy, when clients become distraught in a session, the therapist does everything possible to soothe and reassure them. The goal is to calm clients and relieve the distress. A hallmark of EMDR is that when clients are processing an issue and encounter distress, the therapist does not usually stop bilateral stimulation. Processing continues under the theory that clients are going through just what they need to; their adaptive information processing system is being aided by the stimulation, and with some perseverance, the process will lead to a positive resolution of the targeted issue.

When clients are in great distress reliving a very traumatic memory however, basic EMDR stimulation alone may not be enough. In fact, it may precipitate an abreaction. In terms of the phobia model just mentioned, EMDR clients processing too rapidly can be thought of as approaching the feared object (memory) too swiftly, with the result that the fear becomes intolerable. The panic and dread that clients report may reflect much more than the worry that "I am in danger of being harmed." Often it will imply a sense that "I am going to die." This response helps to understand why clients bolt from severe abreactions, sweating, flushed, and less likely to repeat that "therapeutic" experience. The experience of feeling "as if I was dying" is not rare. This is particularly true where clients relive a memory of childhood, when they were vulnerable, helpless, and perhaps even in great physical danger. As therapists we need to be especially careful not to trivialize the abreactive experience for clients who indicate in any way (use of the stop signal, heightened SUD score, avoidance behavior) that they are not prepared to continue with intense memory processing.

At moments when clients do not want to proceed, we can honor their wish to create distance from the heightened emotion while continuing treatment by using EP techniques. One of our favorite methods is TAT which addresses feelings of being traumatized and usually brings disturbance levels down quickly. The upset could also be targeted with EFT, be set free fast (BSFF), or other methods. In this way it is possible to create distance for the client and lower the intensity of the emotion without stopping the processing. The EP intervention simultaneously lowers the sense of dread while often treating the cause of that dread. After the EP intervention, EMDR can be resumed to determine what other elements of the target situation remain to be resolved.

It is worth repeating that some clients will not use the stop signal even when it would be in their best interests, and we therefore encourage therapists to consider asking for a SUD rating from time to time if there is any doubt about the disturbance level. If the reported SUD score is extremely high, therapist and client then have the option of slowing down the EMDR processing with strategies from Chapter 4, and/or intervening briefly with EP techniques.

Case Example:

A 43-year-old woman was referred for a consultation by her psychoanalytically oriented therapist of six years. He had recently been trained in EMDR and wanted to watch me work before using the method with the client. I (J. H.) spent the first hour, with her therapist present, getting a history of the client's problems and an overview of what they had accomplished in treatment, and talking about EP and EMDR. The client agreed to try both methods but wanted to start with EMDR. At the beginning of the second session all three of us were again present. I sat across from the client, and the other therapist sat about eight feet behind her. We had completed the preparation phase of EMDR. I asked where the client wanted to start:

Client: I think I want to start with that memory of having been raped by my father when I was five or six. It's the worst one on that 0 to 10 scale you gave me. It's probably about an 8 today. He did it a lot, the abuse that is, while my mom was sleeping in their bed, or at least that's what she told me later. Every time in the past six months that I have tried to talk about it, I get so physically sick that I want to throw up. Naturally I can't stand to keep thinking about it, but we can't go further in my treatment until I get past this, because it really gets in the way of everything else. I'm even afraid that my new job could be in jeopardy too.

Therapist: What does the memory make you think about yourself right now?

Client: Well, it's like "You S.O.B., Dad, you should have known better than to harm your own daughter."

Therapist: And what was the message you got about yourself. Imagine what a five-year-old might come to think about herself being treated like that. Remember, she's only five years old.

Client: Oh, God, awful. I feel awful. I can't get away. There's nobody to protect me. It feels like I'm still in danger.

Therapist: During our work today and next week I might ask that question again, "What does this seem to say about you as a person?" OK?

Client: Sure. I understand that. It's like what I got tricked into thinking about myself.

Therapist: Right. That's the idea. So what did you get tricked into thinking about yourself?

Client: I wonder if it might be: "You like it, little girl. You want this too. This is what love means." I think there's still some of that.

Therapist: OK. Let's start with that. And you know that it's not true, but something that you got tricked into believing about yourself. But it might still feel as if it's true. Does that make sense?

Client: Absolutely. False but true, true in how it makes me feel.

Therapist: Right. And we can keep talking about this during our work. OK. Are you ready to start with the hand tapping that you said I should use?

Client: I'm ready.

Therapist: OK. Now bring up that picture of being five or six . . .

Client: Oh God! I can't! I see his penis waving at me! [The client curls up into a fetal position on the couch where she is seated, weeping, and shaking.]

Therapist: OK. You know it's just a memory and yet you know how these memories can feel real. Would it be OK if I just tapped your shoulders once on each side?

Client: [*Through her tears*]: Yes. *Please!*

Therapist: OK, here goes. Once to your left shoulder, just like that, and once to your right, and now I'm stopping.

Client: [*Screaming now*]: Make it go away. I can't stand it!

Therapist: OK if I ask you to tap those energy points we talked about . . . Can you hear me? [*Client, weeping, nods.*] OK if I ask you to tap those energy points?

Client: I can't. I can't seem to move.

Therapist: OK if I tap them on myself?

Client: OK.

Therapist: OK. I'm tapping on my eyebrows now. Just tapping. Thinking about these terrible things that were done to you. I'm continuing to tap. How do you feel? [*I notice, by the way, that the psychoanalytic therapist just opened his eyes widely and shrugged his shoulders to me. I nod back.*]

Client: Hmmm. I'm suddenly feeling a little better. OK. What was that you said?

Therapist: I was tapping these points that are often helpful for times when we are working through terrible memories from when we were children. Can you tap your eyebrow points now?

Client: [*Sitting up*]: OK. That feels good. That really feels good. What am I doing?

Therapist: This is what I meant when I talked about balancing out your body's energy to help with your healing. It may seem strange, but you notice how you feel.

Client: Yes, better.

Therapist: OK. Can you also tap under your eyes, like this? Watch me.

Client: OK. Yes. Better.

Therapist: And now under your nose . . . under your lips . . . and under your collarbones. Good. And now under your arm, and the other side, about four to six inches below your arm. Good. And how do you feel?

Client: Better.

Therapist: Now if you wish you can try this. Tap your index finger. Good. Just like that. That's for the shame you feel even though you know that as a child you could not have done anything wrong.

Client: That's true.

Therapist: Now you might try this. Say, "I forgive myself . . ."

Client: [*Begins to tap, then screams*]: But it felt good to me I think. I think I wanted that form of love. [*Client falls into fetal position again and weeps*].

Therapist: OK if I keep tapping myself, and saying those words? [*Client nods affirmatively.*] OK. Just listen now. I forgive myself because I did the best I could. [*Client screams again.*] OK, just listen now as I say the words. You don't have to say them. "I forgive myself . . . I forgive myself . . . I forgive myself because I was

only five years old. I was just a child. I did the best I could. I really did. That's all I knew. It was their job to take care of me. I could not take care of myself any better than I did. So I forgive myself even though I didn't do anything wrong."
Client: *[Sitting up]:* *I really didn't do anything wrong, did I?*
Therapist: *What would you as an adult say to a five-year-old?*
Client: *You didn't do anything wrong, honey.*
Therapist: *Can you repeat that as I tap your hands now?*
Client: *Yes . . . You didn't do anything wrong. I didn't do anything wrong. I was just a child. We didn't do anything wrong.*

The session continued with EP work and the client was able to process this particular memory to a SUD level of 1. At one point I turned to the therapist and said, "The main thing here is to go slowly enough. Not too fast. There's plenty of time."

Might I have used other options? Yes. Let's review a few:

- I could have invited the client to return to her safe place, and allow her to embellish it for future use. I decided not to because returning to the safe place suspends processing, and I wanted to give the client a chance to keep processing.
- I could have continued processing with EMDR. I chose not to because the client's emotional distress seemed to intensify after only one pair of taps, and I did not know how much more intense the emotion would have become before it finally diminished.
- I could also have used other decelerating or distancing strategies from (see Chapter 4) or other techniques but again I wanted to continue the processing simultaneously with reducing her distress.

How often might such a situation present itself? For us, frequently, possibly because of our client caseloads and because we talk to therapists from around the world and may hear of their "worse-case scenarios." For therapists whose clients do not experience intense abreactions, EMDR may be more often sufficient and the use of EP less frequently indicated.

Sometimes an EMDR abreaction can be so intense as to produce paralysis. Whether we call this a severe abreaction, a form of dissociation, or another name, in some cases continued EMDR processing will have no effect in helping the person to recover. Rather than use hypnosis or a form of relaxation at such times, we are likely to try EP.

Case Example:

I (J. H.) was teaching EMDR once in an Asian country known for police torture and natural catastrophes. In a practicum a well-respected psychologist was working on what she thought was a case of mild trauma (being vicariously upset while doing EMDR with a torture victim) when she suddenly said she could not move her limbs. Her practicum facilitator, an excellent EMDR clinician, intervened to help her, but after 20 minutes of very creative EMDR work, she remained paralyzed. They then asked me to help out. All five persons in the practicum group looked quite upset, as did the six students in nearby groups who could not help but notice the trouble. The face of the paralyzed psychologist had a look of terror, and she was barely able to mumble, "Please help me. I am so very afraid."

Since I was doing the training and had no particular practicum responsibilities, I asked my colleague to continue supervising the other students but first to help me carry the woman to a private room away from the other EMDR participants. I then asked our local sponsor to join me so he could observe what I would be doing. "This is not EMDR, and we will not be teaching it in this course. But I want you to watch me so you can see what we do when EMDR techniques falter. This is rare, but when it happens we want to put the client first, even if it means going outside of EMDR. I also want you to be here because our student is suffering and I may need to ask you to help out."

I then told the student-psychologist that I thought I might be able to help her, but it would be something other than EMDR, and would that be OK with her? She whispered, "Yes. Please." The panic on her face was still intense, and she was still unable to move her limbs.

I then rubbed my sore spot and said I would be thinking of her as I spoke the affirmation, and then began to tap my meridian points. Her eyes relaxed ever so little. I then asked if I could tap the same points on her, and she said I could. I tapped two of her trauma points (eyebrows, under the eyes), skipping under the arms and the collarbones because I did not want to do anything that might cause her more discomfort, and then tapped her gamut point continuously. Within two minutes she was talking and said she felt better. She then was able to tap herself, and we did a combination of meridian points, corrections, and the TAT posture. Twenty minutes later her SUD rating was at a zero, she was smiling and laughing, and asked what I had done. "It's not EMDR," I said. "Maybe we'll talk about it later."

Dissociation

Some clients will escape from severe abreactions by journeying into a part of themselves where they have learned to be safe. In terms of the phobia model, they do not simply avoid a bridge that produces fear in them, but instantly psychologically leave the site of the bridge and enter a different interior reality, through the process called *dissociation*. They are still standing near the bridge, as it were, and an observer might wonder how it is that they just "spaced out," but are bothered neither by the bridge nor by the observer's perplexed response. The observer, in turn, not understanding the function of dissociation, may feel exasperated, angry, or, personalizing the scene, even hostile.

Our first definition of dissociation comes from the *Diagnostic and Statistical Manual of Mental Disorders* (American Psychiatric Association, 2000): "The essential feature of the Dissociative Disorders is a disruption in the usually integrated functions of consciousness, memory, identity, or perception" (p. 519).

An imprisoned sex offender gave the next description. We mentioned this case elsewhere (Hartung & Galvin, 2002) and repeat it here because it remains one of the most articulate descriptions of the dissociative experience we've seen.

Case Example:

Brandon was 42 years old when I (J. H.) began working with him in a medium-security prison for multiple pedophilia assaults. The therapeutic community where he is housed represents his fifth treatment effort. He is about to be terminated again for the same reasons he was discharged from the previous four programs: manipulation, tendency to shirk responsibility, defensiveness, and denial. He is viewed as particularly "resistant" to the heavy confrontation that is a core treatment modality in the therapeutic community. Prison staff asked me to work with him using EP and EMDR, to see if he could resolve enough of his resistance to treatment to be successful this time. The alternative would be to return him to the general population, where treatment was essentially unavailable.

The transcript that follows is from our fifth two-hour treatment session. The client is describing what he experiences when he is confronted too directly in treatment or when other triggers in his present environment remind him of an emotionally disturbing memory:

Client: I shut down . . . my eyebrows wrinkle . . . I hyperventilate . . . my face flushes . . . [I then asked him if he could tell me more about his internal experiences.] . . . tight chest . . . pain in my groin . . . no choices . . . run and hide . . . claustro-

phobic inside . . . like the whole building is collapsing . . . I put on a mask . . . [Here he is describing how he is seen by others] . . . my insides crumble . . . I numb out . . . I leave myself . . . I was sitting in the room but I left the room . . . I'm now looking in, I'm outside the room, I'm up in the corner of the room.

This brief description lasted many minutes, as it was the first time he was able to put his experience of dissociation (depersonalization) into words. Later in this session he talked about how he had been able to get to the point of understanding his dissociative tendency.

Client: I realized when I was working last week on that memory, the one about when I was tied up and raped by that group on the summer island, that I had stood up for myself by not trying to fight back. When you said, "That was smart," I suddenly realized I was doing the best I could. After all, all of those guys were big and a lot older than I was. I was just a kid. I'm thinking now in terms of being the victor.
Therapist: That sounds like a new idea.
Client: I had thought that I was responsible for the rape.
Therapist: What do you think now?
Client: They were responsible . . . I was just a kid . . . just like I'm responsible for hurting the kids who were my victims. I'm thinking in particular of one of those poor kids that I tied up, just like they had tied me up. I think I am beginning to know how he felt when I abused him.
Therapist: Do you want to work on this memory?
Client: Yes. But not yet. Let me talk a little more about what we did last week.
Therapist: OK.
Client: It's so odd. For the first time I was actually able to talk all the way through it. It felt bad, but not as bad as it usually has felt. I didn't have to go up into the corner of the room.
Therapist: I remember having a hard time figuring out just how troubling the memory was for you. Your face looked like you were not bothered at all, but when I asked for a number, you smiled and said, "It's a 10."
Client: That's why I've gotten in so much trouble with my therapy. I smile, my face is calm and smooth, but inside I'm churning. People think I'm being defensive, but it's like I'm facing death inside. There're all pissed off at me because they think I'm being too tough, but I'm already living in terror. They think I'm shirking responsibility. I'm just trying to stay alive.
Therapist: Do you remember what we did last week?
Client: You used the meridian taps. That brought the 10 way down. I think I had just left the room, in my mind, you know, and that let me come back into the room. Then you did the hand tapping, I think, that was the EMDR. I remember asking

you for EMDR because it lets me think more about those memories, and I want to remember them. Then I remember that awful headache. I think you switched to the meridian taps again; you had me tapping my face and hand. Then my headache stopped. Then I think we switched again to EMDR and I asked you to tap my hands again. And then I asked you to stop touching my hands because it was too painful and it reminded me of being tied up there. Then you waved your hands in front of my face. Then, I think it was then, I asked you to stop because your hand reminded me of my dad waving his penis in front of me when he first started to teach me about that sado-masochistic stuff. It was in the shower, those times he would assault me. Yeah. The assaults. I remember you then began to use that magic marker instead of your fingers and I was able to keep working through the memory. Magic marker. This stuff is like magic, isn't it? I've been thinking of you as a witch doctor. Powerful stuff that I don't understand yet. Then I asked you to keep the EMDR going again with tapping, my knees I think. My hands were still too painful. We did a lot of other energy work too, didn't we?

Therapist: *Yes. We did some corrections. You rubbed your sore spot next to your heart. I thought you might be getting stuck in the memory so I had you say that you accept yourself.*

Client: *Right. That was hard at first. Then it got easier. And then you had me tap under my nose and lips.*

Therapist: *Because you began to talk about feeling worthless.*

Client: *That was amazing. That really helped me to move on. I was stuck in the middle. And now I can trust myself. I can deal with whatever, given the last couple of weeks. Feeling like an object is just part of it. I'm thinking of a door, now, of all things. I don't know why. I'm more than an inanimate object used for the thrill of others. I don't exist for other people. I can give . . . I don't need to hurt other people . . . it's probably a 0.*

This is a small piece in our twenty-five hours of therapy during which we used EP and EMDR much as just described. He continued to work on memories of being a victim, which led to his reporting feeling empathy for the young men he had victimized. I then referred him to a colleague whom I had trained who works in the prison so that the individual work could continue. Therapists who work in similar settings realize that the short excerpt presented here represents only a fragment of what must be done if treatment is to be effective. Besides resolving traumatic memories, sex offenders must also learn how to manage masturbatory fantasies and anger, and how to behave in the pro-social ways that, hopefully, will eventually replace their past habits.

Let us summarize the work of one more dissociative client.

Case Example:

A 50-year-old woman who reported 11 different "parts" (what we used to call "personalities" in multiple personality syndrome) became my third client after I (J. H.) learned EMDR. She and I worked for about two years with EMDR, slowly but still with much switching from part to part, such that she had great difficulty resolving any specific memory. In the midst of processing she would often switch to a part where she would feel safe from the memory; unfortunately, the isolated part of the memory would not be processing so it would remain disturbing to the other parts of her personality.

After I learned EP, I began to use energy techniques whenever EMDR processing became too disturbing for her. She eventually was able to ask for EP when she felt that another part was about to take charge of her body. Sometimes a headache, sometimes a motion of her head, or sometimes a slight change in eye movements would signal that she was about to dissociate. We would use EP at that point until her abreaction subsided and her SUD rating lowered. Then we resumed EMDR. Several adult parts spoke fluent English but could not understand Spanish, and a child part, whom she called "La Mejicana," spoke only Spanish. In the process of her healing, the parts began to integrate, and the remaining parts became more bilingual.

The following transcript represents a session when she worked on an early memory of being sexually abused. I tend to use the word "parts"; my client uses "parts" or "personalities" when describing her dissociative experiences.

Client: A 10-year-old part wants to work. She's ten years old. [*Client shakes her head and switches.*]
Therapist: Welcome. And what is your name?
Client: Little Linda.
Therapist: Well, it's nice to have you here. Have you been in my office before?
Client: I think so. But a long time ago.
Therapist: Do you know what the other parts have been doing here? [*After Little Linda asks me to tell her, I then say that I have an agreement with the other parts to share information among the parts, and I then give a brief summary of the work we have all been doing. Little Linda then says she has been observing the use of energy tapping, and briefly taps her collarbone points. She then asks me to lend her a machine that provides simultaneous tactile and auditory stimulation in EMDR style, and she says she wants it to continue running. She seems to know how to use the machine and also ensures me that she will stop it, and the processing of her memory, if it gets to be too upsetting an experience. She also says that she will ask for energy tapping instead at that moment.*]
Client: I feel pushing. [*The client switches again, and the Spanish-speaking child arrives. The following is a translation of her next comments.*] I saw too much.

190

*They smoked, drank . . . They touched me . . . "Go and play" they would say, but
they never let me play. I drank coffee with the hobos on the tracks . . . I jumped
a freight once and got the beating of my life. I was trying to get away from me
. . . I didn't want to be big, I didn't want to be sexual . . . there was blood . . .
my mother would dress me in a white dress and then it would get blood on it . . .
and I would wash and wash it so she wouldn't find out, because whenever I tried
to tell her what they did to me she would beat me. I learned to be troublesome
because I wanted to survive. I remember, I was small, but my sister was smaller,
and I would sit on the stairs so that they would take me instead of my sister for
their sexual games. I hated it, but my little sister was too little. She wouldn't have
survived. I survived. [The client switches, and my adult client appears. She shakes
her head, shuts off the machine.] Oh, boy, look at the time. I sure missed a lot,
didn't I?*

Therapist: *Hello and welcome back. I don't know. Did you miss anything?*
Client: *Well, I think the little girl was here, wasn't she?*
Therapist: *Yes. Both the one who speaks English and the smaller one who speaks
Spanish.*
Client: *Oh, boy. And she worked on a memory. Something about blood. Something
about . . . was it the railroad tracks? She did a lot of work, didn't she?*
Therapist: *Yes. And it sounds like you were there in some way.*
Client: *Yes, it seems I was there. Holding her hand. She talked about the time she
protected her little sister, didn't she?*
Therapist: *Yes. And I thought it was a very rough memory. And yet she seemed
to get through it. She had said she would stop and use the energy techniques if she
needed, but she continued using the EMDR machine without stopping at all. I was
a little surprised.*
Client: *Oh, but she did use the tapping. My collarbones are as sore as can be. I
think she tapped too hard. I think it was the other little girl who was tapping.*
Therapist: *I didn't notice anything. She held the tapping device as far as I could
see.*
Client: *She was tapping. I know. [Laughs.] Boy, is my chest sore.*

EP practitioners may wonder if this is an example of intentional
tapping or surrogate tapping. According to my client, one part worked
explicitly on a memory while another part did some form of energy
work to keep the SUD score low, the abreaction contained, and the
EMDR memory work moving safely. My client then said she felt great,
and was able to get fragments of the work that had been done without
feeling disturbed. Since I had videotaped this sessions, she asked to
review the end of the tape before leaving. "But I can't speak Spanish!"
she said, to which I replied, "You never cease to amaze me."

Dilemma

Frequently a psychotherapy client will face a dilemma, a situation where two or more choices are equally attractive or aversive. Similar experiences are ambivalence, indecisiveness, confusion, or reluctance. When these appear, the EMDR therapist can use muscle testing as part of helping the decision process. The therapist simply tests "I should choose alternative A" and "I should choose alternative B" for true/strong and false/weak responses. This will probably only be useful when the client's energy system has some sort of knowledge on which to base the response. We cannot muscle test to determine, for example, who will win the Super Bowl. But if the client (or a part of the client) knows what is best, testing will be valuable.

Resistance

For about a century, therapists have struggled with what we call resistance, or what others call client opposition, defensiveness, defiance, foot-dragging, arguing, refusal to follow therapeutic advice, failure to complete homework assignments, or general contrariness. Some attribute resistance to the client not being motivated enough. EP and EMDR therapists find that it sometimes is sufficient simply to ask a client, "Would you be willing to do some work on that?" Many, even the most skeptical, will accept this invitation, perhaps because they think this is an opportunity to beat the therapist at the therapy "thing." Motive is not important, however, as long as they will either move their eyes or do an EP exercise. The resistance itself becomes the treatment target, usually with positive results. For more on working with a very resistant group, offenders, see Chapter 9.

The phenomenon of resistance can be conceptualized from the EP perspective as stemming from psychological reversal—or occasionally from neurological disorganization or an energy toxin. All the manifestations of resistance—contrariness, obstinacy, argumentativeness—can be the result of psychological reversal.

We very often begin Phase 4 with an application of the massive psychological reversal correction, the "setup" of EFT. On the theory that if the client is reversed, treatment will be blocked, and that if they aren't, the reversal correction takes little time, we ask the client to rub the sore spot while saying three times something like "I deeply accept myself with all my problems and limitations." We perform this—and all—corrections on ourselves at the same time because of the possibility that we are also reversed.

Correction of mini psychological reversal was one of our earliest uses of EP in EMDR work and remains one of the most frequent. When treatment has progressed well and then suddenly stalls, we suspect such a reversal. It is often addressed by having the client tap on the side of the hand, or under the lip, or rub the sore spot and say three times, "I deeply accept myself, even if I don't deserve to be *completely* over this problem."

On occasion when treatment stalls, the therapist will intuit that the client is generally ready for treatment but for some reason is not ready to work on the specified problem. This may occur before processing is begun, soon after alternating bilateral stimulation is initiated, or after work on one aspect or channel is completed and the focus shifts to another. Here the treatment is for the client to rub the sore spot while saying three times, "I deeply accept myself even though I have this problem."

Case Example:

Marty was devastated by how he destroyed relationships with women. In therapy he realized that his mother never loved him, and he therefore dedicated himself to finding unloving women and trying to get them to love him the way she never did. When they didn't, he became increasingly desperate and demanding in his efforts to elicit that love and eventually would alienate the objects of his affection. He had entered therapy with the expressed wish of changing so that he would be prepared for a healthy relationship, and agreed that his insight about trying to magically change his mother was relevant to his changing. Nevertheless, in spite of my efforts to keep him focused on resolving the relationship with his mother, he persisted in interrupting the processing and trying to turn the discussion toward strategies for getting women to return to him.

Knowing that mother's rejection had left him feeling unworthy, I [M. G.] asked Marty to tap under his lip while saying three times, "Even though Mom didn't love me, I deeply accept myself." He sat quietly for a time, then said, "If a person's own mother doesn't love him, who will?" Rather than engage in rational argument, I replied, "Go with that," and reinitiated bilateral stimulation. After a few sets, his reply to his own question was, "A lotta people! Mom didn't know how to love." Of course he "knew" that already. I had used logical disputation—as had his friends—in the past. I suspect that the reason the concept "got through" to him during this specific session was that the interfering reversal was corrected and treatment could really address the issue for the first time.

If the clinician guesses wrong and treats a given reversal while in reality another (or none at all) is involved, no harm is done, other than losing a small amount of time and perhaps generating a little frustration.

In addition to being alert to the possibility of psychological reversal, EMDR therapists should also be aware that neurological disorganization or toxins might be blocking treatment. If the patient seems confused or clumsy, a correction for neurological disorganization can be applied in a minute or two (see Chapter 3). They can be aware that substances toxic to the energy system can block treatment, and should ask about allergies, sensitivities, or "feeling out of sorts" in certain situations or with certain substances. They can investigate the circumstances around the onset of a particular symptom—in or outside the office—and help the client devise ways to avoid contact with toxic substances and situations.

Psychological reversal, neurological disorganization, and energy toxins can affect all phases, though they are most apparent in the desensitization phase. For example, during history taking they can cause resistance and problems with recall; in the preparation phase they can cause confusion in understanding the EMDR model; and during assessment, multiple blocks to focusing on and reporting on the target can emerge. We find them much less frequently during the installation, body scan, and closure phases. Of course, reevaluation will include questions aimed at determining whether these blocks have made a reappearance.

Incidentally, EP theory says that a psychological reversal blocks all treatment, including EMDR. How then do we explain the fact that EMDR usually works? The theory of PR also states that all of us go in and out of reversal during the day. It is probable that EMDR attempted while a client is reversed will be ineffective, but if the therapist is persistent, EMDR will be effective when the reversal disappears. We also conjecture that particular elements of EMDR are sometimes effective corrections for reversal. The direction of eye movement, for example, is changed sometimes from horizontal to vertical, diagonal, circular, or other configurations. Physical tapping on one side and then the other side of the body can be substituted for the eye movement, as can tones in one ear and then the other. Two of these modes of stimulation—or even all three—can be administered concurrently. Clients can be asked to change their focus of attention to different aspects of the situation being processed or to a past instance of the situation. It is possible that any of these, or other, EMDR techniques possess as-yet-undiscovered abilities to correct reversals.

PHASE 5: INSTALLATION

When the SUD value has come down to 0 or 1 and the VoC has risen to 6 or 7, the desensitization phase has ended and treatment proceeds to installation. However, the application of bilateral stimulation during the installation phase occasionally has the untoward effect of uncovering further material that needs to be processed. This in effect returns treatment to Phase 4, which is not a problem if sufficient time remains. But if the clinician suspects the possibility of such an occurrence, and there isn't enough time, the clinician can have the client do the eye roll or the elaborated eye roll (see Chapter 3) instead of bilateral stimulation. We have had good results substituting these techniques for bilateral stimulation. We ask the client to hold in mind the previously disturbing incident and the positive cognition, and carry out either eye roll technique. This takes about as much time as one set of EMDR stimulation but seems to be more efficient. One eye roll or elaborated eye roll can bring the VoC to "7+," with the addition of a pleasant relaxation effect. Either technique almost never brings up disturbing material and the consequent necessity to return to Phase 4.

PHASE 6: BODY SCAN

In the body scan phase, clients confirm the positive effects of treatment by involving the somatic modality. This process works well and we rarely substitute energy techniques here, though an algorithm could easily be used to treat disturbance and the eye roll or elaborated eye roll to strengthen positive sensations. Sometimes the choice will depend on how much time remains in the session.

PHASE 7: CLOSURE

The penultimate phase of EMDR is the Closure of a session. If things have gone well, the therapist alerts the client that things related to the session may come up during the week and asks that the log be filled in if they do, as we noted in Chapter 4. On occasion, however, time runs out before treatment is complete. In this case, the therapist can use these techniques to help the client achieve stability. As an alternative, we propose switching to an energy treatment.

Our clients usually are already familiar with EP treatment, since we describe both EMDR and ET during the informed consent procedure and introduce most to specific EP techniques. Therefore, when we need them in an EMDR session, we occasionally modify the standard

EMDR instructions for closing an incomplete session into something like "I'm afraid we're running out of time for today. You've done good work and we can do some more on this next time, but I'd like you to try some tapping to put things away for now. How does that sound to you?"

If a client has not experienced the tapping methodology, we say something along the lines of, "I'm afraid we're running out of time for today, and we can work on this next time, but I'd like you to try a little of that tapping I mentioned earlier to see if it will help. It might seem a bit strange but I usually have pretty good results with it, and we can talk about it later. Does that sound all right to you?" Refusal at this point is extremely rare.

Often we use an algorithm to quickly address an elevated SUD level. We identify the salient remaining emotion and lead the patient through the corresponding algorithm while the patient focuses on the remaining disturbance. Again we frequently use the trauma or anxiety algorithm. EFT is another common choice. The resulting SUDS level usually becomes low enough to safely end the session. On many occasions, the brief algorithm work has not only calmed the client significantly, but also decreased the SUD rating to 1 or 0.

Specifically for calming the patient, we will use the eye roll or elaborated eye roll or TAT. We avoid mention of the disturbing issue as much as possible, focusing instead on the promotion of stress reduction. These techniques are not only rapid but also very effective in enabling the clients to compose themselves and leave the session in good shape for driving and returning to their lives. We recommend that clients rely on TAT until the next session.

PHASE 8: REEVALUATION

Reevaluation can lead to work in any of the earlier seven phases, but usually assessment and desensitization become the focus of attention. In any case, the energy techniques just described can be applied.

During reevaluation, the clinician inquires about homework assigned during the previous session. There may be a review of the client's use of self-help procedures (discussed in Chapter 4). Failure to carry out a homework assignment is often due to a psychological reversal. So rather than try to unearth reasons for the resistance, the clinician can try to discern the type of reversal (e.g., deserving, possibility, motivation) and apply the corresponding correction. Determining whether the client did the homework the following week will show how effective the correction was.

Chapter 6

EMDR Interventions
in an EP Session

Sometimes during an energy treatment, the procedures are no longer suitable. For example, perhaps the SUD level has stopped lowering, or the client asks to cease the EP procedures, or the client makes a request (e.g., for insight or understanding) that the therapist believes will be best achieved through EMDR. In these situations, the therapist can use techniques specific to or adopted by the EMDR model. We list those techniques here.

Some of our suggestions for using EMDR in an EP session will already be familiar to EP practitioners, even those untrained in EMDR. Villoldo (2000), for example, in his book about the energy approaches involved in Andean shamanic healing techniques, wrote about the use of "an eye movement exercise that seems to recalibrate our neural networks" (p. 117). In *Energy Medicine* (1998), Eden described the use of the infinity sign to guide eye movements in a sort of installation exercise to imprint positive feelings in one's habit field. We leave it to the reader to decide if these examples are equivalent to what we will be discussing.

Many EMDR techniques are useful in EP sessions, but we do *not* recommend that anyone attempt adding EMDR alternating bilateral stimulation to their work without formal training. We have seen how powerful EMDR stimulation can be with clients who have regressed to early traumatic memories, and we must take a conservative stance in this regard. We strongly recommend EMDR course work and supervised experience before using alternating bilateral stimulation in trauma work, to avoid unnecessary risk to clients.

Our outline follows the seven steps described in Chapter 3.

STEP 1: RAPPORT

Though not original in EMDR, the principle of "truth telling," that the therapist know what the patient is experiencing in order to correctly intervene, is emphasized in EMDR but often overlooked in EP. It is equally important that EP patients give the "true" SUD number, not what they think they "should" give, or what will please the therapist. Although hoping for lower numbers, therapists need to have and convey an attitude of acceptance and inquisitiveness, rather than consciously or unconsciously impose any demand characteristics on the client.

STEP 2: INFORMED CONSENT

We have found nothing from EMDR to apply to this Step.

STEP 3: CLIENT HISTORY

The careful attention to personality dynamics in EMDR can prove useful in some EP cases in Step 3. Carrington and Craig (2000) reported the results of an informal survey of 250 therapists who used the emotional freedom technique (EFT) "and one other energy therapy" (p. 12). Of approximately 10,000 cases of trauma victims being treated by energy procedures, only 20 resulted in severe abreactions. In spite of this low incidence, a careful history might have avoided even some of these by alerting the therapist not to begin treatment before the client was properly prepared.

When more difficult cases are addressed, the probability of abreaction increases. Because some clients do not demonstrate their emotion clearly, inexperienced EP therapists (or any therapists, for that matter) can fail to notice a client abreacting or beginning to dissociate during treatment. These therapists should conduct an even more careful assessment of client history and resources, both to know the particular client's vulnerabilities and as an exercise in becoming more knowledgeable about risk factors. During EMDR trainings it is stressed that the practitioner screen for dissociation (see Chapter 4). Similar attention to signs of dissociation—with or without inventories such as the

Dissociative Experiences Scale (Carlson & Putnam, 1992)—is recommended to the EP therapist.

An important aspect of EMDR is that it entails a three-pronged approach, addressing present, past, and possible future manifestations of every problem (Shapiro, 2001a). This focus contributes to the effectiveness and long-term durability of EMDR treatment, and EP therapists can profit from this perspective. EP clinicians are very good at assessing difficulties with present situations or current distress about the past but often feel their work is done once the presenting problem is addressed and the initial SUD rating is sufficiently lowered. And often this is enough. In most cases, however, a further service can be provided by addressing all three time periods during history taking— not only how a client was and is, but how he or she would like to be. Past examples of a present issue—perhaps even the first instance—are identified, as are current manifestations of an old trauma. Finally, it is usually helpful to ask the client to identify times when the concern or situation might crop up again.

Case Example:

A man who used the anger algorithm to fairly quickly deal with current anger at a coworker described how his father used anger to deal with any upset—not only threat and disrespect but also disappointment, loss, and any stress. I (M. G.) worked not only on his early fear of father, but also on inappropriate displays throughout his life of behavior similar to his father's. During history taking, I had drawn on the EMDR three-pronged approach to ask about possible future occurrences of his problem of anger. At this point in treatment, I reminded him of an upcoming staff meeting where he and the colleague would have opposing interests. As he thought about the impending confrontation, the SUD level was lower than he expected. Treatment of the imagined conflict proceeded rapidly and he concluded, "No reason to get all wrapped around the axle; it's just a budget. He's only fighting for his folks like I am for mine."

STEP 4: PREPARING THE ENERGY
SYSTEM FOR TREATMENT

In EMDR, attention is not deliberately paid to the energy system and so no EMDR techniques are helpful here.

STEP 5: TARGETING THE PROBLEM

Part of the reason that EMDR is so successful is that it addresses several modalities at the same time, viz. image, cognitions, emotion, and sensation. In practice energy therapists usually focus on one distressing emotion. Many now also target irrational thinking but treat it separately. Although this strategy is usually successful, we believe that simultaneous work on multiple modalities is valuable.

It is a simple matter to assess during this step the image and body sensations related to the troubling affect. In addition, a negative self-statement and a corresponding desired positive statement can be obtained. The latter can be assessed with the validity of cognition (VoC) scale (see Chapter 4), before and after treatment, even if only the affect is directly treated. Positive changes in the VoC are almost always evident when the SUD has decreased to 0 or 1. If the VoC hasn't changed, it can be targeted itself.

Some clients have trouble identifying the source of their upset or finding words to describe it. They may have discomfort when they focus on a certain affect, for example, but have no image—no clear memory of either the origin or any of the subsequent occurrences of the trauma. Trackback and floatback methods (see Chapter 4 and below) are particularly helpful here.

With skeptical clients it may be useful to spend more time discussing and assessing the initial SUD (and VoC, if used) scores than is usual with EP treatment. These preliminary data can be used later to demonstrate to clients the changes experienced during treatment. This may counter the apex problem, the tendency for clients to undervalue their positive changes, because feeling good just "feels natural."

For example, with children and with persons who seem particularly skeptical about the likelihood that EP will be of value, we often determine baseline ratings visually and tangibly. We offer a handful of polished stones or pottery pieces and ask the client to arrange them according to how they represent the SUD (or VoC) scales. "Which one looks to you to represent the worse feeling [anger, sadness] you can imagine. Notice the color, the shape, and how it feels." After the client has chosen a stone or pottery piece, we say, "Let's call that a 10, the worse feeling you can imagine. Now, which one looks the most like no problem at all. We will call that a 0." Then, "now, arrange nine more of these from no problem to the worst problem you can imagine, thinking of the feeling you just mentioned." During treatment we then move the stones to represent changes in SUD scores, and leave them as graphic evidence of the changes the client has experienced. Some clients will stare at the "before" and "after" positions incredulously. It is difficult for them to deny what their eyes tell them.

Although one of the principal attributes of EMDR is that it does desensitize distress, in the process it often discovers other issues that need to be dealt with before the target is completely resolved. It is precisely this ability to locate and activate relevant issues that makes EMDR attractive to some clinicians trained in both methods. Some practitioners therefore prefer to use alternating bilateral stimulation to discover and activate problems, and then use EP tactics, which they deem more efficient, to desensitize and resolve them. It may seem paradoxical to abandon EMDR just as it begins to work, but the process can have a lasting benefit.

Of course, interrupting the bilateral stimulation once an issue is brought to the fore aborts the EMDR process of exploring and desensitizing channels (lines of association of the problem). One issue may have been quickly treated by EP, but the opportunity to discover related issues is lost. If there is enough time remaining in the session, and if the client is willing, the therapist can repeat the process, discovering and resolving (an)other issue(s). The therapist can focus either on the original target to see what else remains to be processed or on any of the issues that emerged during processing. EMDR therapists will find this an awkward way of dealing with all relevant problems, but the EP therapist will counter that treating one, or just a few, affords sufficient benefit.

STEP 6: TREATMENT

The Patient Is Processing Too Quickly

The question of what to do when clients become very disturbed during EP therapy is not addressed in most trainings (Britt et al., 1998; Gallo, 2000b; Nicosia, 1999). Treatment does not usually lead to disturbing (or insight-generating) issues. Usually, SUD scores diminish significantly with EP, but sometimes they diminish only a little or stay the same (usually because of a psychological reversal or neurological disorganization). Occasionally, however, the SUD level will increase with treatment after it has been decreasing for a while. This is almost always due to the uncovering of a new therapy issue or aspect. If this new aspect is especially troubling for the client, dissociation or abreaction might occur.

In other cases, clients who seem quite composed as the tapping begins feel their disturbance levels rise sharply when they get into their issue. It is not that they have discovered another aspect, but rather that they are startled by the intensity of the true emotional content of the original issue. Such an occurrence can also trigger dissociation or abreaction.

In psychotherapy practice EP work regularly lowers the SUD rating. For patients at the more troubled end of the spectrum, however, the uncovering of a new aspect or the shock of experiencing the true intensity of a targeted problem is very distressing, again possibly causing an abreaction or dissociation.

A technique used in EMDR that can benefit energy practitioners is the stop signal. On occasion, clients may wish to discontinue or temporarily pause treatment while working on an issue. Clients could simply stop tapping, but some are not assertive enough. Others may stop tapping and want a break but not be assertive enough to ask the therapist to stop pushing. Energy therapists can inform clients before treatment that they can stop the therapy process anytime they feel overwhelmed, either by using a prearranged stop signal or by otherwise indicating they need to take a break. The signal can be anything therapist and clients agree on, but usually clients simply hold up a hand, as would a traffic cop. When clients use the signal, even if the therapist has confidence that the issue can be successfully resolved if they persevere, the therapist should *not* insist on continuing. Doing so could exacerbate any abreaction and retraumatize the client. Failure to comply with the client's wish is especially damaging to trauma victims, since having control taken away is part of any traumatic incident. Therefore, the clinician should *always* discontinue treatment when the stop signal or other indication is given.

The imagined safe place, addressed in Chapter 4, is a good strategy to use during that break. Clients can recuperate as they visualize their reassuring scene, until they are ready to resume treatment or comfortably terminate the session.

When clients are dealing with especially traumatic memories or other issues represented by greatly elevated SUD scores, we often use "fractionated" work. For example, in working with a rape victim, we may not target the whole distressing event but rather choose to work solely with the moment when the client realized she was going to be attacked. That may be enough for one session, giving her some relief and confidence to continue working on other "fractions" of the experience.

Working with such traumatic targets in EP, we also use words designed to reassure the client even while reliving the event such as "It's only a feeling you are having about the past," "One foot in the past, one foot in the present," or "It's over," while the client is tapping, or even sometimes during testing or treating psychological reversals and neurological disorganization.

Many other decelerating strategies described in Chapter 4 can be useful when the client is overresponding, and the EP therapist can benefit from a proficiency in using a number of them. Especially helpful are the hierarchies, resource development and installation, and the use of cognitive strategies.

EP Work Stalls

After administering a treatment, the energy therapist usually asks clients to rate their SUD level, which will determine the next step. The level is usually lower, and work continues. Sometimes, however, it has not become lower, and rather than just treating a suspected mini-psychological reversal, the clinician might wonder why. On other occasions, the clinician might have noticed something in the client's demeanor during the treatment and wonder whether an insight or shift of focus has occurred. At this point, instead of or in addition to obtaining a SUD score, the therapist could employ an intervention often used after a set of bilateral stimulation in EMDR. This intervention entails asking the client to reveal what has become most salient at that moment and takes the form of a question such as "What are you getting now?" or "What comes up now?"

The client will usually give information about the aspect now at the surface. The clinician can use the information to decide on the next intervention. Often the client will mention a different troubling emotion from the one originally addressed, and the therapist will direct the client to tap on meridian point(s) related to that emotion, rather than persisting with earlier points. Or the client may have had a new understanding of the problem that takes treatment in a new direction. Other times, the clinician will conclude that neurological disorganization or a psychological reversal is present and will apply a correction. In all these cases, following energy treatment protocols would eventually have uncovered the relevant information, but simply using the nondirective, but penetrating wording of the EMDR questions can often save time and effort.

The same intervention can be used during muscle testing to determine treatment points. The therapist will usually ask for a SUD rating after each holon and level given will determine the next step.

At times, however, this diagnostic process can become very difficult and complex. The therapist may be unsure of the muscle testing results, whether a reversal is present and what type it is, whether a problem in polarity is present, or whether a toxin is interfering and what the toxin is. There exist EP methods for systematically ferreting out all these blocks to diagnosis and treatment, but using the intervention just described (e.g. asking "What are you getting now?" or "What has come up?") can be much quicker than energy therapy protocols.

When the SUD level does not drop in spite of continued treatment, or does not drop to the lowest level possible, a useful question often asked in EMDR is "What keeps it from being a zero?" The client's response usually reveals what is called a blocking belief, the client's belief that further progress is somehow wrong or inappropriate. Once the client has identified this belief, it becomes a target to be treated by energy techniques or EMDR.

An example often encountered by therapists who treat veterans is the belief that to heal from the traumas of battle would be to let down their buddies, some of whom never came home—"To drop the pain is to drop the flag." The energy therapist can at this point put on hold treatment of the original problem, to deal with the irrational belief. Once it is resolved, treatment of the original issue can resume.

Many other accelerating strategies from Chapter 4 are helpful, including use of hierarchy, focus on the body location of an issue, and repeating "strong" words.

It is hypothesized that the alternating bilateral stimulation of EMDR helps activate the adaptive information processing system. So, as have many other energy therapists (Benor, 2001), we have experimented not only with bilateral tapping, as described in Chapter 3, but also with tapping bilaterally in alternating fashion, producing a left-right, EMDR-like stimulation. For example, in doing a modified EFT, the client taps the left end of the eyebrow (eb) point once with two fingers of the left hand, and then the right eb point once with two fingers of the right hand, and continues alternating until each side is tapped a number of times. The client moves similarly through all the points, using strategies described in Chapter 3 to deal with central and hand points. As with simultaneous bilateral tapping, alternating tapping is recommended in working with dissociatives.

We also experimented with adding auditory tones to the tapping procedure.

Case Example:

While working through some childhood abuse, Arlene, a patient with Dissociative Identity Disorder (DID), had performed the EFT recipe several times, but on one iteration was suddenly "unable" to tap. She was struggling, as if there existed an invisible barrier between her tapping fingers and the points she wanted to tap on her other hand. She tried to tap, trembling, muttering disjointed sounds, having no success. I (M. G.) suggested trying EMDR and she readily agreed. We used the bilateral alternating tones tape (see Appendix B) played through earphones, and discovered that it enabled her to perform the tapping she had been struggling with. As the tones continued, she was able to work through the episode with energy techniques. After resolution of the issue, Arlene volunteered, "I could sense what we were trying to accomplish, and it [the bilateral stimulation] just gave me a clearer sight to get there anyway. And it woke me up in my head." Commenting on the fact that she had been "programmed" by a cult to "resist" any therapy, not to remember her abuse or heal from it, she added, "Also the resisting, not wanting to do it. It just kinda pissed me off—[I thought] 'I'll do it anyway.'"

With success in adding the tones to selected parts of EP sessions, we began experimenting with continuous alternating bilateral audio stimulation throughout a session. It can be provided through earphones or even loudspeakers, or through *pulsers* that provide alternate tapping to the hands, feet, or wherever one chooses to place the devices or both sound and tapping. (We do not recommend continuous *visual* stimulation because of the risk of fatigue and eye damage.) The TacAudioScan is only suitable for earphones, but tapes such as those produced by PsychInnovations or Biolateral (see Appendix B) can be used in either method. Keep in mind that when speakers are used, the therapist also gets treatment throughout the session. Therefore, it is especially important that the therapist have resolved significant therapeutic issues lest they be triggered by the tones.

With tones or tapping, or both, there are no "sets," as we do not stop to evaluate the client's status, but rather let the tones/taps run in the background while we provide EP or other therapy. Clients take in stride our suggestion that they don headphones or listen to speakers through most of a session. It often produces the phenomenon exemplified in the case example, wherein processing accelerates just after we start the tones.

The EMDR tones or taps often enrich the energy work, and in some cases enable it to proceed past treatment blocks. This simultaneous use of EP and EMDR techniques is fairly powerful and would usually be considered an "accelerating" strategy. For this reason it is recommended only for use later in treatment when the therapist already knows the client fairly well, when the client has already worked through the more severe traumas, and when there is no apparent dissociative risk. The technique, however, can function as a decelerating strategy, and the therapist must be continually alert in this regard.

Sometimes EP work stalls because the client is facing a *dilemma*, feels confused about several options, or is still not able to reach some important decision after EP work. In such cases we find the two-hand technique from EMDR to be especially useful (see Chapter 4). Two cases exemplify our version of the procedure. In the first, the client reported that EP was "still not helping me to be sure about what I should do."

Case Example:

Therapist: If you would like, you can try a special technique that often helps to uncover the reasons for the dilemma that you are talking about now. Do you want to hear more about it?

Client: Sure. OK.

Therapist: Imagine placing one side of your dilemma in one of your hands. You can choose either hand.

Client: OK. I'll put the "yes" part, the "I want to do it" part, in my left hand.

Therapist: Good. Now close your left hand on the "yes" part. And now imagine placing the "no" part in the other hand. Good. Now close that hand. OK, good. Now separate your hands and notice what you are feeling in each one. And follow my fingers. [I (M. G.) then did a series of hand movements.] OK. What do you get now?

Client: One hand seems to be heavier.

Therapist: Good. That's all you need to do, is just notice what is happening. Just follow my fingers again. [I did another set of hand movements.] What do you notice now?

Client: Nothing different.

Therapist: OK. Now, just notice which hand is warmer, and which is cooler. And follow my fingers again. [Another set of hand movements.] OK. Which one is warmer now?

Client: Well that's interesting. Actually, my right hand feels a little warmer now.

Therapist: OK. Now, just notice the difference, and follow my fingers again.

In another case involving a dilemma, I changed from tapping to the "classic" double chair technique and added EMDR.

Case Example:

A client was working on a decision about which she was "of two minds." (This isn't a case of multiple personality.) EFT failed to resolved the attendant low self-

esteem and anger. I handed her a small cassette player with earphones that provided the auditory stimulation of a PsychInnovations tape.

Therapist: *Since we're pretty stuck with this, I'd like to try something different. Let me know what you think. [The therapist sets out two chairs across from client's sofa.] When you're there [pointing to one of the chairs] you will be "I should quit," and when you are here [indicating the other] you'll be "I'll stay and fight him." OK?*

Client: *OK.*

Therapist: *OK. Put on the earphones, just clip that player on your waist for when you move over. Push the start button. Now, tell me why you should quit.*

Client: *[Switches chairs while hearing the audio bilateral stimulation]: I've tried everything I can with this company. If they won't deal with him in three years, they never will. I've done everything right. I could spend the rest of my life . . . like trying to get Dad's approval. You can get As and be a star but he never cares. Hell with that.*

Therapist: *Now over here. When you get there, you're the fighter part.*

Client: *Damned if they're going to treat me like that and get away with it . . . I have to show them they can't do that to people. Ha! Like Dad again; he never takes responsibility for what he did. Never will.*

Therapist: *OK. Back to deciding self [pointing to the sofa].*

Client: *Well, I still feel like someone should let them know what he's doing to people—and the division. But like I said—I tried. I've been deciding just to let Dad go, and I guess I'd better do it with [name of company]. It's not really being a quitter, you know. You give it your best shot—I gave it too long.*

Therapist: *So you'll go with [name of new company]?*

Client: *Well, maybe I was hanging in there too long, 'cause of like you said, trying to get Dad to love me by getting present people to. Still doesn't work [laughs]. Yeah, it's hard to give up when you're right, but I'm going to move on.*

Clients in both cases used variations of the dilemma technique to clarify the two sides of their issues, surfacing preconscious elements, and eventually processing them through to resolution.

At times, during energy work, EMDR treatment might seem especially indicated, in which case we will simply change to that method. Phillips (2000) and Lane (2001) describe such instances well. Usually we just ask the client to "go with that," after hearing what has come up for them, and initiate EMDR bilateral stimulation. Clients who have had EMDR in a previous session have surprisingly little trouble with the switch. The relevant emotion(s) and SUD scores will already have been established. The therapist can pause to assess the other elements of EMDR assessment—image, NC, PC, VoC scores, and body location—if clinical judgment is that they will be helpful and if time remains. However, we usually dispense with them and move right to sets of bilateral stimulation. Often treatment proceeds quite productively through a series of sets to a successful resolution.

Likewise, when the process of screening (by intuition or muscle testing) for neurological disorganization and psychological reversals stalls, or becomes excessively complicated, we sometimes switch to EMDR, either in that session if time permits or in the next. Treatment is usually successful.

The case of Amanda illustrates how EP and EMDR can be very effectively combined in therapy with children.

Case Example:

A therapist asked me (J. H.) to consult with her regarding an eight-year-old child she was treating.

Amanda had been adopted two years earlier from an orphanage in a country in Eastern Europe. When her prospective adoptive parents first saw her at age six, she was unable to speak any language and had undeveloped jaw muscles from having been fed a diet of soft gruel and having been silenced through most of her life. There were suggestions of physical and sexual abuse, though the parents had found nothing documented. They had sought therapy as part of an agreement with the adoption agency to help Amanda to transition to the United States and to resolve any "issues" that might arise. The therapist had been using both EP and EMDR and even though the parents and school staff were appropriately involved in treatment, the child had not improved much after eight sessions. Recently Amanda had started a second fire at her school and at times had been caught trying to twist the arms of the family's one-year-old biological son. She smiled continually and often would say, "Happy," but she did not seem to feel happy. For example, she did not initiate demonstrations of affection, did not play with other children, seemed unable to use any words suggesting negative emotion (mad, sad, scared), and often complained that her tummy hurt.

We decided to work as a group, two therapists, two parents, and Amanda. The original therapist had already done several brief EP and EMDR sessions related to the fire setting. As we began the first session, I suggested we switch gears somewhat by avoiding all talk about unpleasant things, and I asked the parents to talk instead about positive experiences they had been having, while the therapist and I would take turns tapping the child's hands. We played a kind of patty-cake that provided bilateral stimulation. The parents were also encouraged to talk about what it was like to have her in the home ("We love you; we are happy you are in our family"). We used EP and EMDR techniques together so the child would become used to this combination that we planned to use later for treatment.

In the second session Amanda was visibly relaxed, and as we talked about positive themes for about 15 minutes she would approach all four of us, touching appropriately, with her constant smile. I then asked Amanda if it would be OK for her parents to tell me a little about what they had heard about the orphanage. Amanda said it would be OK, but "not much." Using only a few words to introduce themes, the parents then mentioned the lack of food, the cold, and the isolation. Each time a new topic was barely introduced, the other therapist and I would use EP to reduce Amanda's anxiety as rapidly as possible, then switch to positive comments about the present. For example, when Amanda reacted with a look of panic after the parents mentioned "apples at the orphanage" (we never did understand the reference), we processed the negative emotion, then asked the parents to talk about the food available in their house, and then used a combination of EP and EMDR to install the thoughts of safety and nourishment that Amanda enjoyed in her present home. Throughout the session Amanda was encouraged to sit as near or as far from either parent as was comfortable, and we continued to discuss how we were all present to help Amanda to feel better about herself.

At the third session all five of us did several energy techniques, which the parents said were good for them too. Amanda was able to use a few words in this session. The only feeling word she would say was "happy," so we tapped using both EP and EMDR as she talked about things that made her happy: "eat, run, eat, TV, eat, come home." After about 20 minutes I asked for permission to talk about other words (sad, mad, afraid), and she agreed that I could mention them as long as she did not have to. I said that I would say each word only once during this third session and she could think about it if she wanted, but she would not have to say it. She also agreed to tap my hands 10 times, first one, then the other, after I said each word (to give her control of the EMDR processing). We closed with EP techniques until she said she felt good and was ready to go home again. We then debriefed the parents for another half-hour after this session, as they were not altogether sure that this approach would work. They also expressed some impatience in wanting to know why Amanda "kept setting fires," but eventually concurred with this new approach. We agreed we would meet again later in the same week.

In the fourth session we continued with slow pacing, and Amanda became able to say each negative word (sad, mad, afraid) herself. We then processed with EP and EMDR as before, until she was able to repeat each word without much negative emotion.

By the fifth session, she was willing to say words reflecting both positive and negative emotions several times, and we then asked her to mention events that might make her feel happy, sad, mad, and afraid. I ended my participation at this point. The plan for continued treatment was for the parents and therapist to introduce other events that needed to be discussed, including the fire starting, always with careful pacing, encouragement, and a blending of negative with positive so that the end of the session always involved a focus on the safe and secure present and an optimistic future.

The therapist consulted with school staff and treated each parent with EP and EMDR to help them deal with their frustrations. Amanda slowly began to talk more and threaten less. Though far from over, the treatment was working.

"Something Seems to Be Missing"

Whereas often EP can help reduce symptomatic disturbance without reference to the origins of the problem, for many patients simply focusing on the presenting complaint of anxiety, depression, or other upset is not sufficient. We believe this often occurs with the prescriptive EP approach when the therapist repeats an algorithm over and over. Sometimes the client may come to imagine (and we sympathize with this) that the therapist is trying to wear the symptom down by repeated applications, as if the problem were a foreign nuisance rather than a part of the client's life experience. I (J. H.) once watched an experienced EP trainer in an EFT demonstration repeat the exact same tapping sequence perhaps 30 times with a young man working on procrastination. As we watched what seemed to be a video replay, the SUD rating slowly dropped from a 7 to a 5 until the subject finally agreed that "it helped a little bit" and sat back down. While the procedure probably could not have been varied in this training situation because it was intended to be a demonstration of one specific EP technique, it would seem ludicrous to replicate this with a real client. Sometimes it is the therapists who become aware that they have become robotic. We once witnessed a trainer in an EP training stop an EP procedure and announce: "If I were in my clinic, I would switch at this point to EMDR, because obviously the EP has stagnated. However, since you paid for an EP course, and because I do not want to confuse issues here, I am going to try the EP procedure again." (The EMDR-trained clinicians in the room nodded their heads and said they agreed with *both* points being made.)

On a similar path, the client may say something like "I want to understand this better, where it came from, why it's stayed with me for so long. I would like some insight into my long-standing problem,

I want more than just to feel better about this." In other instances the client might seem to be improving but some of the symptom remains, as if it is still attached to an old trauma. At times we as therapists wonder if self-beliefs learned from a traumatic time might enrich EP work that the client reports as vague or abstract or incomplete, because it does not "feel like therapy."

Whatever the reason, whenever the EP process can be enriched (e.g., amplified, deepened, broadened, heightened, furthered) we will suggest procedures that we use frequently in our EMDR work, called floatback and trackback.

I (M. G.) have been using a technique called "trackback," learned during training in transactional analysis in the early 1970s, and which gives a little more structure to the process. The therapist begins inquiry with a recent life stage, such as early in the marriage, and asks the client to search through that time period until the relevant symptoms "click into" a situation. That memory is then discussed until it is clear in the client's mind. The purpose is to make the retrieval of the next earlier memory easier. On occasion, a memory is so disturbing that it will inhibit further backtracking and so will need to be treated before the client is able to continue. The therapist then picks an earlier period, such as college, and asks the client to find a significant memory there. The work continues through high school and elementary school. The therapist then asks for a memory "even earlier than that." This is repeated until the client, after some reflection, asserts that there is nothing earlier. Elementary school and earlier times seem most often involved. The earliest memory retrieved is considered to be the relevant "feeder memory" and is then thoroughly processed. We suspect this procedure is more effective than just asking, "When's the first time you felt like that?"

Investigation of feeder memories (see Chapter 4) often proves very productive, unblocking treatment—either EP or EMDR—and bringing insight.

Floatback and trackback (see Chapter 4) can also be used whenever the client wants to connect present symptoms with past events, or wishes to put a visual piece in what might be only a belief or body memory.

Ending the Step

The final procedure in many energy therapy protocols, after the SUD rating has been lowered to 0 or 1, is the eye roll or elaborated eye roll. As mentioned earlier, this process is analogous to the installation phase of EMDR. A difference is that the eye roll is seen as "sealing in" or reinforcing the treatment, whereas the purpose of installation is to "enhance the positive cognition and to link it specifically with the original target issue or event" (Shapiro, 2001a, p. 160). To accomplish this, we add a process not present in EP: The client is asked to hold in mind both the originally troubling image (or just "the incident" in general if the image has changed or disappeared) as well as the positive cognition, while the therapist provides bilateral stimulation. In EP, the client holds in mind only the originally disturbing affect or situation while doing the eye roll or eer, but the cognitive element is usually ignored. We often make use of the EMDR Installation procedure after energy work when we sense that some valuable cognitive work can be done. As with EMDR, however, installation is done only when the SUD is down to 0 or 1. If it is attempted at a higher SUD, it will probably not have the desired treatment effects, or the client may be unwilling to even try it.

If cognitive work has been part of the energy session, it can be brought into the installation procedure. When it has not, the therapist can help the client determine a suitable cognition or belief. The therapist then performs bilateral stimulation while the client thinks of the cognition and the originally troubling situation. With EMDR, progress in this phase is measured with the VoC, and we sometimes use this scale when doing Installation in an energy session. Usually, however, it suffices to ensure that the SUD rating reaches and remains at 0. In current EDxTM practice, once the emotional disturbance has been alleviated, the client is oriented to a positive outcome or core belief (Gallo, 2000b) measured on the positive belief score scale. Energy psychology techniques are then used.

An EMDR procedure for assuring that treatment is complete is the body scan. It incorporates the somatic component of therapy, which EP does not always take into account. In spite of EP's attention to meridians, the neurolymphatic reflex, and so forth, it pays less attention to such things as muscle tension. Therapists certainly address these variables when clients mention them, but the formal EMDR procedure for assessing this modality ensures that it is addressed before the successful session ends. The client is directed as follows: "Close your eyes, concentrate on the incident and the PC, and mentally scan your ENTIRE body. Tell me where you feel anything" (Shapiro, 2001a, p. 162). If any sensation is reported, the therapist can target it with EP or EMDR techniques.

STEP 7: CLOSURE

As a session closes, the client should be reporting a low SUD and a resolution of the problems that were the target of treatment. If not, the energy therapist will usually target the remaining disturbance.

If energy techniques have been unsuccessful at resolving the disturbance, another form of intervention is indicated. Many techniques such as relaxation and visualization have been developed over the years, and some are taught in EMDR trainings. It is recommended that therapists have a variety of such techniques at hand, not only for this step, but to add to the skills taught in Chapter 7.

Chapter 7
Client Self-Use and
Phone Consultations

It used to be that the psychotherapy patient depended on the therapist and the treatment session exclusively, and often for years. In this era of time-limited and innovative psychotherapy, therapists mostly concur that it is necessary and possible to transfer responsibility for therapy to the client, and as quickly as possible. Many benefits accrue: the cost is lowered, client dependence is discouraged, and the therapist is able to treat many more people.

EP FOR CLIENT SELF-USE

Two of the great advantages of EP techniques are that they are versatile and eminently portable. Part of the therapist's job is communicating that these techniques are to be used not only during the course of psychotherapy in the office but also as coping skills. They are strategies clients can use for the rest of their lives, on an as-needed basis. Clients can also teach the techniques to others. Clients and therapists find it reassuring to have available such powerful methods of self-care. They increase their confidence in tackling difficult issues. Three recently published resources on self-use of EP—Callahan (2001), Gallo and Vincenzi (2000), and Lambrou and Pratt (2000)—combine clarity with practicality and we recommend them. They lead

clients through treatments for many problems and give useful explanations of theory.

As Homework

Convincing clients (or ourselves!) to use EP techniques on a daily basis
takes some doing. Often in the early and middle parts of treatment
when clients mention a problem they had during the week, inquiry
reveals that they not only didn't apply an algorithm or other energy
tactic to the problem but also didn't even think of it. This presents an
opportunity to review how well clients have learned the technique
and to again encourage its use. We have clients recall the distressing
circumstance of the past week, and may conduct an assessment using
the TICES-BID format. We then ask the client to perform the energy
technique to treat the problem. Often they do not recall the steps,
even though they had left the previous session having practiced the
procedure and with the expressed intention of using it during the
week. They may even have taken with them a body map that we
personally drew showing the energy points, the emotions for which
each point can be used, and tailor-made affirmations for correcting
their personal energy reversals. Every so often, therefore, we have to
reteach all or part of a procedure, leading clients through the steps,
usually focusing on the emotional disturbance just identified.

This is an opportunity to reiterate that the techniques are there to
be used, that clients have something they can do on their own to deal
with distressful circumstances. There are many self-care techniques;
algorithms and TAT are among the most powerful. Gentle persistence
is required in this effort, but when clients "get it," they remain convinced. Normalizing the EP techniques will help many clients to use
them more easily. For example, almost everyone has seen someone
rub the points on the bridge of the nose next to the tear ducts, at
times of stress or fatigue. EP clinicians assume that this might be an
effort, conscious or not, to manage a traumatic feeling by treating ie
(inside eye, the bladder-1 point), the principal trauma treatment point.
Suggesting that the client rub these points intentionally when events
in the present trigger old emotions might then seem more "normal."
It may also help to remind clients that getting over a cold once does
not mean that they will never again get a cold (and so with recurring
emotional issues), and that exercising once a year will not make them
fit (and so with the value of having a daily routine for energy work).

These procedures, once learned, can be of great benefit between sessions—and after termination. Since they almost never lead to abreaction, they can be used safely during the week. Sometimes, however, as mentioned in Chapter 3, new aspects are discovered as clients use these treatments on their own.

Case Example:

One of my (M. G.) earliest EP clients reported that she was not sure she had confidence in the methods. When I asked why, she said that she had followed my advice, and when the fear we were targeting recurred during the week, she followed the EFT procedure we had practiced. She determined her SUD to be 7, and wrote it down. She then did the "setup," or massive PR correction, followed by tapping the 13 points (we were including the "rib" or liver point), the 9 gamut procedure, and the tapping sequence again. Encouraged that her SUD rating had gone down to a 5, she repeated the whole "round," but realized at the end that it had risen to 8. She dutifully logged the occurrence in spite of her distress, then calmed herself by listening to a relaxation tape and then going for a run.

I asked her to tune in again to the original disturbing issue and to redo the treatment she had done for herself. On attending to the point where her SUD had risen, she recognized that the distress was now a feeling of anger; the fear had in fact almost disappeared. We resumed EFT and the distress was soon rated 1. She realized that EFT had not caused the anger; the anger (at having been abused) had been there since the original incident, but only could be accessed once the overlying fear was resolved.

The appearance of underlying aspects at this level of intensity is rather rare when clients apply the techniques outside the office. Nevertheless, we now take care to describe the phenomenon when we introduce energy work, and encourage clients to be watchful for aspects and deal with them when they are uncovered. If clients know a comprehensive algorithm—such as EFT, BSFF, or TAT—they can apply it to the new aspect. If not, they can use an algorithm specifically for the new emotion.

A much more common occurrence, in the office and after hours, is that use of an algorithm will lower the SUD score fairly rapidly without complications.

If time runs out in a session while we are successfully working on a problem, we will ask clients to continue at home whatever we had been doing. If we have diagnosed treatment sequences, we will write them down for reference at home. Admittedly, if other sequences have to be discovered for the work to be complete, clients may not progress much beyond what was accomplished in the session. For this reason, we advise them to try one of the comprehensive algorithms if work gets stuck at home.

Work on other presenting problems can be prescribed as homework.

Case Example:

A client with a phobia of crossing bridges was assigned the task of standing at one end of a bridge and treating himself with the anxiety algorithm. When the SUD was brought below 2, he was to progress farther on the bridge and again treat himself when the discomfort level rose. He faithfully carried this out, and we debriefed the experiences in the next session. We treated related issues with EP and EMDR, including an episode where a fraternity brother threatened to and started to push him out of a second story window. Resolution of these issues and continued in vivo practice enabled the client to cross his target bridge without discomfort, and he was able to visualize crossing the bridges on an upcoming trip to the East Coast.

Some EP clinicians, particularly adept at using muscle testing accurately, report being able to use muscle testing to identify the best EP technique for a client to use as homework, the number of minutes it should be used, and the number of times it should be repeated per day. Clinicians who do not trust muscle testing can simply ask clients to do reversal corrections followed by an EP procedure of their choice from time to time during the day (e.g., morning, midday, and evening). One of our favorites is EFT, which has a high probability of success with whatever comes up. As its originator, Gary Craig, says, "Try it on everything!!" (1999). Other comprehensive algorithms include the TAT (Fleming, 1999, 2001a) and BSFF (Nims, 1998).

With TAT, we often recommend an earlier, simplified version for the client who is feeling traumatized. Rather than going through the preparation and seven steps of the current version, we advise simply writing down the SUD rating and then doing the TAT "pose." At the end of the short procedure the client writes down the final SUD score. Fleming (2001a) says the client can practice TAT up to 20 minutes per day. Finally, the client logs the procedure for review at the next session.

We have been using an earlier form of BSFF, which involves tapping four points and making accompanying affirmations. We are also impressed with the newest form (Nims, 2001) and will be using it with an increasing number of clients. In their work with BSFF we also advise clients to track the SUD score and write in their journal.

As we have noted, clients may need repeated instruction before they understand the energy paradigm well enough to take it seriously. When assigning EP homework, the therapist may need to go over the same information many times before clients get into a habit of daily EP practice. Noncompliance may simply mean that clients have not yet grasped the concept. It may also reflect psychological reversal or neurological disorganization. The correction of a reversal or disorganization is sometimes effective only for a few minutes during a session or for the duration of the session, but the negative condition returns once clients leave the office. Behavior, thought, and emotion can subsequently be negatively affected for the rest of the week. Clients who periodically apply the correction usually are happier and more successful in their lives. Interestingly enough, people who are chronically reversed are also reversed for doing the reversal correction. They report they "forgot" or "didn't feel like it." This "resistance" can be addressed—with EMDR or EP—in session. When reversal correction is assigned as homework, it is important to track it in therapy notes and be consistent about checking progress with clients. We often treat reluctance to do the homework as another target.

Insomnia

Sleep problems can exacerbate emotional problems, and treatment can be enhanced if the therapist suggests effective techniques and the client uses them. The ones we teach have only anecdotal support. We teach them in the office, but clients practice them at home when they go to bed or when they awaken during the night. One involves tapping or holding a point not usually used in energy psychology, point 7 on the heart meridian (Ht-7) on the radial edge of the inside of the wrist about where a wristwatch band would go.

Some practitioners report the following procedure as useful: Raise your open left hand to the left side of your head and reach behind your left ear with your middle and index finger tips, resting your fingers in the crevice just behind your ear, fingertips touching your head. Now imagine a line running over the top of your head from front to back, and with the four fingers of your right hand rest your fingertips at the top of your head along this line, little finger forward and index finger toward the back, cupping your hand slightly with the palm downward and slightly above your head. Hold for up to five minutes. Holding the position for longer can generate a negative kind of energy.

Addictive Urges

Offender clients have reported considerable success with the addictions algorithm, which is also the anxiety algorithm. They have been able to lower their urges to use drugs enough to stay "clean" until the next session. This ability is especially important to them since in some community settings they are given random drug screenings, and failure of a test is basis for a return to prison.

EP AND PHONE CONSULTATION

EP techniques are easily transferred to a telephone consultation. Therapists have always been able to be warm and empathic and to rebut irrational beliefs over the phone. They can analyze transactions and games and interpret transference. But the application of EP methods offers more substantial help, employing the same methodology used in the office. The client actually addresses the problem directly and usually notices the SUD decrease. Emotional distress can be eliminated rather than contained and held until the next session.

In our practices, most clients have already been instructed in the theory and mechanics of the EP procedures whether or not they are the focus of treatment. When they call, then, it is a simple matter to remind them of and talk them through a sequence to deal with the problem that occasioned the call. Of course, we often still engage in basic procedures including reassurance, identification of stressors, assessment of resources, and formulation of an action plan. Many times a simple lowering of the distress level is all a client needs.

We are encouraged by our success in handling after-hours calls and surprisingly receive fewer of them. This may be a result of a change we have made in our practices. We assure our clients that we are open to calls, but request that before calling they apply some tapping or other energy work. They know that when we talk to them, we will ask about the results of that work early in the call. Some have told us that they had forgotten to use the energy work to deal with their distress and became so upset they decided to call. On preparing to dial, however, they remembered our structure, applied the techniques, and found they had eliminated the need to call.

If clients still call after doing an energy exercise, we can try other EP techniques they may not have thought about. Common ones are the corrections for psychological reversal or neurological disorganization. Their application usually makes effective the algorithms that had not been working earlier.

Therapists do crisis work over the phone, teaching the points as part of the intervention. This sometimes occurs when the client is calling for an initial visit. Often things have gotten to an acute stage at that point.

Telephone work is so effective that some therapists conduct not only after-hours work but also part or all of their main psychotherapy practice over the phone. They usually mail out or post on their Web site instructions and diagrams of locations of the tapping, touching, and rubbing points. Diagnosis is carried out in various ways including therapist intuition, the Callahan Techniques voice technology (Callahan, 2001; Craig, undated), and simply attending to the client's complaint. Little research has been carried out on this modality, but anecdotal evidence suggests practitioners receive continuing referrals.

EMDR FOR CLIENT SELF-USE

EMDR also offers many techniques for client self-care. The eye movements themselves can be employed but with caution, since the same bilateral stimulation that helps resolve issues may uncover disturbing material and even lead to abreaction. If the client is employing eye movements for self-use and happens on a disturbing memory, the eye movements will likely stop, suspending the processing and leaving the client in the middle of a troubling episode. This could leave the client worse off than before the self-help EMDR. Such an experience could make the client wary of EMDR in subsequent office sessions. Therefore, only when the client and therapist are convinced that all potentially destabilizing historical and current situations have been effectively resolved is EMDR taught for self-use. It can then be employed for calming, and even to deal with minor upset.

We have occasionally found it beneficial to teach selective clients to use bilateral tapping, rather than eye movements, as a calming technique between sessions. The client is instructed to use the movements while focusing on a positive thought or image (to enhance the positive), rather than something negative (which could open the client up to further desensitization). A specialized adaptation of bilateral tapping, the butterfly hug, is a friendly and soothing self-use exercise (see Chapter 1) especially suited for this purpose. Although bilateral stimulation is intended to calm in this case, it always has the potential of stirring up serious processing, so therapists need to instruct clients carefully. For clients who will not use EP techniques between sessions (perhaps because of issues of face validity), these EMDR options are especially valuable.

Eye Movements for Sleep Problems

The eye movement exercise that follows was first brought to our attention by a prison inmate who said he read about it in a book on Buddhism in the prison library. Villoldo (2000, pp. 117–118) mentions something similar in his book on energy medicine of the Americas. Trainees from different countries also have described similar exercises. We introduce it here because it *looks* like an EMDR technique. The exercise can be taught as follows:

Therapist: I appreciate your having gotten that medical consult on your insomnia. Since your physician has found no organic causes to explain your trouble sleeping, and since you have already cut out caffeine and have changed your diet and exercise routine, it might help you to try a technique that I use myself when I wake in the middle of the night and have trouble falling asleep again.
Client: I'll try anything. What is it?
Therapist: Watch me as I demonstrate. While lying in bed you first move your eyes from side to side, like this, 10 times. All the way from side to side. Then vertically, like this, another 10 times. Up, down, up, down. Then diagonal, then diagonal in the other direction, like this, making an X with the other diagonal. Then a circle, and finally a circle in the other direction, each one 10 times. You can try it now. That's it . . . when you do the circle you might move your hands in an arc and follow them, that's it. Good. You don't have to do it 10 times today—you might fall asleep here in the office. Repeat it if you do not fall asleep within a few minutes.
Client: I'll try it. And what if it doesn't work?
Therapist: After trying it once, repeat it if you are not asleep in five minutes. Repeat it several times if you need. See what happens and tell me next time.

This exercise, according to client reports, works more often than it doesn't.

Mechanical Devices for EMDR Self-Treatment

Some clients buy or engineer devices that produce bilateral alternating stimulation for use at home (see Appendix B). If the client is fairly free of traumatic memories and other serious symptoms, the device can reduce stress or strengthen positive thoughts and feelings. Therapists often use devices for their own self-treatment, such as for mild stresses or upset.

The use of mechanical devices is a particularly risky proposition when severe traumas remain and can be triggered. As mentioned, when clients do self-treatment by moving their eyes voluntarily, the eyes will probably stop if clients begin to enter a particularly upsetting memory. Relying on a device to produce the stimulation (especially with auditory and tactile modalities), however, means that the stimulation will continue even if clients happen on an issue that provokes intense abreaction. It is possible that the continuing processing could traumatize them further or even provoke a dissociative reaction.

If precautions are taken, however, a device can be as valuable for clients as for therapists. We have received reports from clients who conduct their own machine-mediated EMDR processing with great benefit and no apparent liability. One man, a brilliant but distracted engineer with severe Attention-Deficit/Hyperactivity Disorder (ADHD), was able to get his mind back on his work after listening to bilateral alternating sounds over his headphones. Another man, an accountant, using a similar device was able to control his obsessive thinking, which, he said, was no longer necessary now that he was retired and away from the "numbers game." A third individual used mechanical hand stimulation to continue her work on a chronic history of childhood neglect and abandonment. A fourth, an accident victim with a closed head injury, used a combination of taps and sounds, both produced by a portable battery-powered gadget, to reduce the pain of the chronic headaches that are triggered since her accident by certain lights, molds, and temperature changes.

EMDR AND PHONE CONSULTATION

EMDR trainings stress the importance of therapists' being available for telephone contact between sessions. The EMDR desensitization process taught in the programs should not, however, be applied during such calls. Even if the client could apply the bilateral stimulation, the therapist would have difficulty determining when it should be started and stopped. Face-to-face contact is necessary to monitor changes in the client to manage treatment. In EMDR it is assumed that during phone contacts therapists will employ whatever techniques they used previously, as well as integrating the self-soothing techniques taught in Phases 1, 2, and 7.

COMBINED USE OF EP AND EMDR BETWEEN SESSIONS

On a given day a client may to come to the office and say, "I just can't get into that energy stuff when I'm alone. When I'm here in your office, I find it easy to follow what you're doing, tap myself, and feel better. But when I'm home and begin to feel that panic again, I either don't think to practice it, or else I remember but I don't believe it will help me. So I've started to use EMDR movements more and more. These just feel better to me."

On another day, the client may say, "I can use the eye movements OK at times, but what I really need is something to use in crisis—like when I sit in on a board meeting and I feel the panic rising. It has to be something that gives immediate effect. I can't do EMDR there." In this case we might teach the client to touch the point under the eye, nonchalantly and inconspicuously, until the anxiety diminishes.

The more self-use skills clients have, the more options they will have for different needs. Plus, given the nature of energetic and perceptual environments, sometimes a technique will work on one day but not on the next; alternatives will help to manage more contingencies.

LEARNING EP AND EMDR THROUGH INFORMAL MEDIA

It is possible for highly motivated persons to learn EP by reading a book. Then, with time and practice, they could treat themselves successfully and with virtually no risk for a variety of problems. It is also possible to go to the next step and to learn to become an EP clinician by reading about the theory and practice of the energy therapies, without ever taking a formal course. Though trainees often view supervised practice as very valuable, we presume that a novice could learn EP by studying a book closely and by practicing its content. The procedures are direct enough that they lend themselves to written description, and the liability (e.g., from abreactions) is minimal.

Trying to learn to use EMDR effectively through a self-study course is *not* recommended—in fact it is strongly discouraged. Though the procedures seem fairly straightforward when read or heard in lecture, they are not. Trainees who begin the practica often find themselves at a loss as to what to do. Learning EMDR comes from practicing the mechanics of the process, dealing with blocks which arise, and from the experiences of working through one's own problems and helping colleagues work through some of theirs, under the close and careful supervision that is provided during the training practica of both Part I and Part II.

We shudder at the prospect of a therapist witnessing a first-time EMDR-evoked abreaction in a therapy office without training in how to handle it. The prospect of the client abreacting, possibly being abandoned by the startled clinician who stops EMDR processing, and thus being retraumatized is an even more unpleasant thought. Yet we hear of similar stories in our work around the world. In one case a trainee seemed particularly reluctant to begin a practicum, so we asked why. The trainee answered:

I was in a university course several months ago where the psychology professor demonstrated the new therapy called EMDR. Someone in the class agreed to be a guinea pig. The professor asked the student to think about something that troubled him, and the student decided to reflect on a recent family reunion. The professor began to move his hand in front of the student and within a few seconds the student jumped back, sweating on his face and terror in his eyes. The professor looked bewildered, mumbled something about "it's not supposed to do that," and went on talking about trauma in the abstract as if nothing had happened! It was only much later that my friend, the guinea pig, told us that he was taken back to when he was 12 and babysitting his nephews. He got distracted playing soccer and a nephew drowned in the swimming pool. He still hasn't forgiven himself. Being at the reunion reminded him of the shame he still feels when he sees his sister and her husband, the nephew's parents. Even though they forgave him, he hasn't forgiven himself. Does that explain why I'm still a little nervous about all of this?

If a psychology professor can misjudge and misuse the power of EMDR, lay-people hoping to learn informally about the method and then to use it with themselves or others would likely pose an even greater risk for harm.

Chapter 8

Therapist Self-Care

Norcross (2000) has described clinician-endorsed and research-supported strategies that psychotherapists can use to deal with "moderate depression, mild anxiety, emotional exhaustion, and disrupted relationships" (p. 710), all of which can result from working with psychotherapy clients. In this chapter, we summarize some of the unique contributions to therapist self-care that accrue from EP and EMDR.

PRIOR TO A SESSION

In general, the most effective clinicians begin a therapy session long before the client does. Therapists who are reasonably free of troubling memories, who enjoy a balanced energy system, who think positively, and who feel optimistic will have a head start on being effective with clients. And therapists who feel effective are also likely to avoid burnout.

Although a training analysis is required in some programs, such as at psychoanalytic and Jungian institutes, there was a time when the majority of psychotherapy students were not required to undergo therapy themselves. We tried out a number of therapies in graduate school, but none of the faculties at our three alma maters (Ohio State University, University of Denver, and University of Florida) asked us to do so. The research and practice in those days led us to expect that psychotherapy would be drawn out with unpredictable results. We still feel regret as we recall our fellow students who dropped out of programs because they were too anxious to give a coherent public speech, concentrate on exams, or get rid of that awful burning pain in their stomachs. They found no solutions from us or their professors. We were pleased to realize that with EP, EMDR, and certain other brief therapy methods, we can help not only our clients but also ourselves! We join with those colleagues and those graduate school faculties who now have reason to recommend daily self-treatment for the healers.

Anyone who works in the field of trauma should be aware of the possibility of vicarious traumatization. This is as relevant for psychotherapists as it is for medical providers and police and firefighters. Unfortunately, most trauma workers do not take their own vulnerability seriously until they experience fairly dramatic symptoms such as sleeplessness, somatic pain, and violent behavior.

Whether or not a therapist's specialty is trauma, there is more and more evidence that most psychological problems for which people seek therapeutic services have a traumatic etiology. Self-help is not just a matter of finishing up old business, but also a matter of therapists continually renewing themselves and becoming untangled from the negative emotions and energies of those with whom they work everyday. Those who write specifically about the hazards of psychotherapy practice remind us that depression and anxiety, intrusive thoughts, emotional exhaustion, and troubled relationships are all-too-frequent results of work with distressed and distressing people (Brady, Healy, Norcross, & Guy, 1995; Norcross, 2000).

To resolve deeply troubling traumatic memories or other severe problems a therapist would be wise to seek formal psychotherapeutic help. On the other hand, mildly upsetting events—a problem with a family member, a financial worry, a challenging client, or a conflict with a colleague—can often be readily self-treated with EP and EMDR.

EP: Self-Treatment, Self-Testing

Most EP trainers mention the value of therapists' practicing good "energy hygiene." In our work, we sit hour after hour with people who present us with negative thought/emotion fields. If it is true that energy can be transmitted over space (Britt et al., 1998; Nicosia, 1999; Oschman, 2000), then we are being subjected to these negative influences throughout the day. Therefore, just as physicians will wash their hands between patients, it is advised that therapists similarly clear their energy fields.

Probably the most commonly used treatments are two corrections for neurological disorganization (sometimes called switching, the over-energy correction or "Cook's hook-ups," described in Chapter 3) and the three polarities unswitching procedure (Gallo, 2000a), as well as a correction for massive psychological reversal (MPR).

For the three polarities unswitching procedure one holds three fingers of one hand over the navel while tapping or rubbing the two collarbone points with the fingers of their other hand. With the hand still over the navel, one similarly stimulates under the nose, under the lip, and the coccyx.

In a training with Gregory Nicosia, I (M. G.) began to perform one of the practicum exercises with another participant. Though the steps were clearly delineated in the manual, I became confused after just a few seconds, losing my place, not knowing what to do next. Greg approached and tested me and the other participant; we were both neurologically disorganized. He said, "I wondered about that. I thought she was switched before you went over there." He pointed out that energy travels across space and we need to be mindful of our clients' influences on us. After the other participant and I performed a correction, the manual seemed easy to follow.

Since neurological disorganization and MPR are the two most common blocks to effective treatment, performing corrections for them is a quick way to make reasonably sure one is cleared from negative effects of a previous session. If neither were present, doing the corrections will cause no harm, and only a minute or two will have been spent. One can even do Cook's hookups while reading notes for the upcoming session.

Therapists suspecting that a specific emotion or belief is interfering with their effectiveness can use a tapping sequence to deal with it. Lambrou and Pratt (2000) designed different energy protocols for daily and weekly use, and a specific program for managing chronic and ongoing stress.

Some energy therapists who believe that electromagnetic fields harm the human energy field wear devices designed to shield against or correct for these.

Muscle testing can determine whether any correction—and which one—is necessary at any point during the day. The problem is that therapists must muscle test themselves, and it is therefore difficult to use an extended arm. Most energy clinicians use one hand to test the other. As one example, I (J. H.) can place one hand on a flat surface, palm down, index finger raised, telling my body that this index finger is my indicator muscle. With one or two fingers of the other hand, I then push down on the first finger to test strength in the clear (i.e., with my mind blank). I then ask my body to give me a "yes," push again, then ask for a "no," push, and notice the difference between the two experiments. To test for reliability, I say, "My name is ___," saying my true name, and push again. Since this is a true statement, my response should be for a "yes," usually strong. To cross-check I say a false name, push, and should get a "no" response. If the answers are equivocal, I can drink water, move physically, do an over-energy correction such as Cook's hook-ups, or correct a reversal, and retest. Once calibrated, the indicator muscle can then be used to check all sorts of information. A second popular method of self-testing involves creating a circle with the index finger and thumb of one hand, holding them together, then trying to open the circle with a finger of the other hand, either by pulling out from the inside of the circle or by opening the fingers forcefully. The body is instructed to consider the circle as the indicator muscle. Fleming (2001b) suggested using a response programmed into most humans, the habit of nodding the head vertically for yes and shaking it horizontally for no. One simply focuses on the question and notices whether there is a tendency toward nodding or shaking.

Durlacher (1994) described a number of techniques, including one Callahan taught him. One simply leans over as if to touch the toes. A true thought or "yes" enables one to lean farther. Craig (1998) performs self-muscle testing by extending his arm forward, then swinging that arm across his chest, with elbow locked; he reports that he can swing his arm farther when he is thinking or saying something true or positive. A great many other self-test methods, including pendulums, are in use and many have been cataloged by Wheeler (2001).

Self-testing is one of the most difficult EP skills to learn. It takes extensive hours of practice. One problem is that the tester/subject will know whether the statement (e.g., true name/false name) is true before performing the test, and will have to disregard this knowledge while attending to the subtle difference in muscle response. During this learning period, one may have to treat PRs (e.g., "I deeply accept myself even if I don't believe I can learn self-testing").

Using one's own body in this way for muscle testing is a handy and portable way to assess oneself prior to beginning a session, and with practice one can access various types of information. One can say, for example, "I am ready to begin with this client," and then muscle test. If the response is strong, one can proceed. If weak, further testing can be done to home in on the problem. As with other forms of testing, certain information is not available, such as who will win the next football game.

We muscle test frequently, both in sessions with clients and for our personal use, and find the procedure to be quite reliable for the most part. Usually the information we receive from muscle testing can be verified through independent testing by another person. At other times, however, we get contradictory responses. To increase reliability we have found an additional step to be useful.

First we make an affirmative statement such as, "I am ready to proceed with this client." Then we do a self-muscle test. The response should be strong if the statement is true. Then we put that statement in a negative: "I am not ready . . . ." The response to testing should then be weak. Finally, we state: "There is deception in this response." If testing for this is strong, we look for the reason for the deception. We consider drinking water, correcting for reversals, and doing an over-energy correction. We wonder about toxins and examine our attitude toward the client.

EMDR Self-Treatment

To self-treat with EMDR one can simply apply alternating bilateral stimulation (eye movements, tactile, auditory) to oneself, without doing the full setup recommended for clients. Let us say a therapist wishes to get free of an upsetting emotion left over from a difficult therapy session. To desensitize oneself in EMDR terms, it is often sufficient to focus on the upsetting emotion ("my anger," "my pessimism") or undesired thought ("I can't do it," "I'm a fraud") and then to commence the stimulation and to notice how the feelings and thoughts change. Some EMDR clinicians tap their knees alternately as they reflect on what just distressed them. Others lightly tap the sides of their bodies as they walk and swing their arms, while thinking about the session. Others sit in a chair and move their gaze from one spot on a wall to another, alternately stimulating their left and right visual field.

At other times the therapist may want to strengthen positive emotions and thoughts instead of desensitizing negative ones. In these instances it is usually sufficient to rehearse the positive ("I value this person as a growing human being," "I deserve to be effective"), then do a few short sets of alternating stimulation and notice changes.

A variety of mechanical devices has become available to provide bilateral stimulation. They include a bar with moving lights, vibrating hand-held buttons or rods, and headphones with audiotaped sounds, respectively producing visual/ocular-motor, tactile, and auditory stimuli. While the device is running, the therapist notices unpleasant thoughts and feelings left over from the day's events, or focuses on positive thoughts and feelings, that can be more deeply installed with bilateral stimulation. To repeat: This kind of self-help is limited to minor upsets, not deep trauma work. It is particularly important to be cautious when one is alone and using a device. It is feasible that the user could uncover a traumatic memory, begin to abreact, and either be distracted or forget to monitor the machine, which could then continue to stimulate EMDR processing.

We have also heard of prolonged use of a device by persons with no particular psychological liability. One psychiatrist friend inserts tactile stimulators in his socks and keeps them going through the night while he sleeps. He says that besides awakening refreshed, he has brilliant dreams. (We are only passing on what has been reported to us—not recommending this!)

DURING A SESSION

Sometimes a client will say or do something that triggers therapists in the midst of a therapy session, requiring them to take steps to resolve their own personal issue which could get in the way of their work with the client. Besides treating themselves on the spot for these unexpected interruptions, therapists also have the options with the new therapies to treat the triggers.

EP

We recommend therapists tap along with clients while administering treatments. This serves to demonstrate the exercise, allows the client to feel accompanied, may amplify the therapeutic benefit for the client, and provides maintenance energy balancing for the therapist. The excerpt that follows exemplifies how we use EP for ourselves.

Case Example:

The client is a middle-aged engineer who for years has struggled with depression which keeps him disabled and unemployed. He has seen psychiatrists, has tried most known antidepressants, and has been determined to be medically "treatment resistant."

He entered therapy to see if EP and EMDR might be of any use. In spite of all his disappointments, he still is eager to learn how to help himself, benefits from every therapy session, and agrees to do homework. At each following session, however, he reports that the benefits have been short-lived. He arrives pessimistic and worn down again. The content of one particular session feels like "déjà vu all over again." I, the therapist, have tried nearly everything I know. Today I catch myself glancing at the clock and thinking, "I really do not want to be here. This is hopeless. I've taught him just about everything I can, and still none of the benefits hold from one session to the next."

These thoughts trigger a reaction in me: "Now just what in hell was that all about? This fellow has to be one of the most motivated clients I saw today. He struggles and makes improvement in every session, only to slip back again after a few days, sometimes just a few hours. Look, right now he's listening to alternating EMDR sounds as he talks about that old memory of horrible abuse—for about the 20th time, unfortunately. How can I be criticizing a man who works so hard, and whose pain I can only imagine? Easy for me to point fingers. Talk about blaming the victim. Good grief. Know thyself Mr. Physician. This probably has a lot more to do with me than with him."

I reach as inconspicuously as I can toward my heart and rub the NLR (sore spot), saying to myself, "I accept myself deeply and completely even though I don't want to be here with this client, . . . even though I am doubting that I can help him, . . . even though I am feeling little interest in him, and even though I catch myself blaming him."

I then touch my index finger point and think, "I forgive myself because I'm doing the best I know how" and I then hold my little finger point while thinking, "And I forgive my client because he may well be doing the best he can too."

Because from time to time I have an old issue with feeling intolerant of other people, I touch my thumb meridian point and think, "My intolerance, my impatience with others, my tendency to look down on people who are different from me," and then I feel myself smiling, lighter, relieved. I go on to think, "I accept the goodness I have received from the world and I feel thankful, and I share this with my client who is struggling so much, and who, were I able to walk for a while in his shoes, would become completely comprehensible to me." I do all of this silently as my client listens to the EMDR tones and occasionally says something.

Is the shift in my attitude due to treatment of the NLR and meridian points? Is it a function of positive self-talk? Right now it doesn't matter. I then notice that I am leaning ever so slightly toward my client, feeling re-energized to work again. And I ask myself: "What energy reversal might I have missed with my client? Maybe we could try the taps for hopelessness, or worth, or . . ., or maybe I'm simply trying too hard. I'll ask him what his hunch might be."

Therapist: Sam, what do you think is going on?

Client: I'm actually feeling a little better. It always feels good to be able to talk and to know you will listen. I just wish it would last. I feel better for a day or so after leaving here, then I slip back. I forget to do the exercises. I get tired. I get lazy.

Therapist: What do you think we're missing, Sam?

Client: Sometimes I wonder if there's any hope for me.

Therapist: What energy point does that sound like, Sam?

Client: Index finger? No. I can't remember. Let me look in my notebook. Here it is [laughs], right under my nose, so to speak. It's the point under my nose. [He begins to tap under his nose on the governing vessel point]. I accept myself even if I don't get better. And even if this doesn't last. [He reads from his notebook]. And even if my problem comes back again and again. Which it does, of course.

Therapist: That sounds good to me. How about tapping all those points again?

Client: [Client repeats the taps]. I'm feeling better. How come it doesn't work this well when I'm alone?

Therapist: Good question, Sam. I can't say that I have an answer for you. What do you think you'll need next time you feel fatigued and doubtful that you can help yourself to get out of the doldrums?

A discussion then ensues. The client makes a list of exercises that he agrees to do daily and will report on in the next session. He also plans to buy a book on affirmations that he will rehearse with both energy taps and EMDR stimulation (tapping his shoulders alternately). He asks about making an audiotape of bilateral alternating sounds and using it to maintain treatment gains. I encourage him to make the tape but ask him not to use it on his own yet, and I remind him how self-use of the tape could trigger emotions that might make him feel worse rather than better. The client agrees that many memories of childhood abuse still remain and that he does not want to open them up outside of the therapy office. As the session ends, we both feel energized and more optimistic.

EMDR

Sometimes clinicians who use EMDR may purposely accompany their clients by playing alternating tones on speakers, with chairs arranged in such a position that each will hear the tones bilaterally. At other times therapists may be unaware of how EMDR processing in their client affects them. For example, they might use tactile stimuli in EMDR, such as when they tap the client's hands with their own, and not be cognizant that they are stimulating not only the client but also themselves. In fact, while the client experiences only sensory (tactile) stimulation, the therapist's sensory (from the touch) and motor (from the hand movements) modalities will be stimulated. This phenomenon is not always mentioned in EMDR training. If the therapist has re-solved significant life issues fairly well, this secondary processing may be experienced as relatively comforting and strengthening. On the other hand, if the emotional issues that the client is working on hap-pen to remind the therapist of his or her own unfinished business, the therapist may rather abruptly and unpredictably begin to feel much of the same emotion and level of intensity that the client is experiencing. The emotional impact of countertransference can be multiplied many times in EMDR. In such a case, the therapist should attempt to take note of the issue, isolate the associated thoughts and feelings from the session, and work on them as soon as convenient after the session. It is not advisable for the therapist to use the EMDR stimulation in the session to "work along with the client" on issues, as the therapist's course of treatment (or channels to be followed, in EMDR terminol-ogy) is almost certainly not that of the patient.

Chapter 9

Specialty Applications

B asic courses in both EMDR and EP prepare a trainee to become skilled in and comfortable with the core principles of the method. Thus prepared in either method, the practitioner will have a high degree of success. For those practicing in specialty areas, additional instruction is available in all EMDR Part II trainings and many EP trainings. Specialties include work with children and adolescents, forensic populations, dissociation, eating disorders, obsessive-compulsive disorders, addictions, performance enhancement, and couples therapy.

In EMDR trainings, Shapiro cautions that "EMDR is not a cookie-cutter" (2001a, p. 381), by which she means that it is relatively easy to learn the basic procedure, but only with practice do therapists learn to use it well and with a wide range of clients. The method must be tailored to the client and complaint. She also warned against employing EMDR with a client population therapists have not treated prior to learning EMDR. Her message is that EMDR will help clinicians be more effective in areas where they are already reasonably competent, but it will not make them immediate experts with children if they had never treated children, nor would they likely use it safely with a multiple personality disordered client if they had not yet worked effectively in the field of dissociation.

We would add that the same should be said of energy work in spite of the fact that EP courses have not stressed the issue as specifically.

Assuming, then, that clinicians are prepared in a given specialty area, we offer a few suggestions:

- When beginning work and when in doubt, use the basic protocol from EMDR and one of the simpler strategies in Step 6 of EP.
- Break down complex problems into specific TICES-BID elements. For example, instead of treating "a borderline," identify and deal with the pertinent symptoms (anxiety, obsessive thoughts, "losing my temper"), triggers ("when I think about his family"), and contributing memories ("My Mom threw the ironing board out the window when my boyfriend was there"). Then target the issue with the basic EMDR protocol, or use a selected point or algorithm treatment.
- Make appropriate use of consultation—especially medical when indicated—and similar resources such as study groups.
- Remember that expertise in one specialty area does not qualify a therapist to enter another without appropriate training.

Given these cautionary statements, we now offer models for working with two specialty groups with which we are familiar, to exemplify how the basic EP and EMDR protocols can be adapted, modified, or adjusted. The following is a fairly basic presentation of the models, and is not by itself sufficient to prepare a clinician for forensic or performance enhancement work.

EP AND EMDR WITH OFFENDERS

Perlman (2001) wrote that in the process of becoming a patient one admits to having failed, acknowledges being helpless, examines and confronts oneself, self-discloses, and indicates an intention to change. These qualities do not characterize offender-clients, who often are ordered by the court or resign themselves to therapy in exchange for some other benefit, such as release from a closed institution. Reluctant to begin with, they may behave in ways usually taken as signs of "resistance": skepticism, lethargy, denial of responsibility, blaming, provocation, hostility, and threats of violence. Offender-clients may also belittle treatment efforts on the part of others, or fake interest to meet requirements, or mock the therapist. In addition, offender-clients often have suffered severe and long-standing traumas and dissociative tendencies, with limited education and work skills, spotty job histories, and significant relationship conflicts. Given these characteristics, more than a few therapists on learning EMDR and EP wondered if these new methods might be applicable to the forensic population that has been generally overlooked in traditional psychotherapy.

When EMDR was first becoming popular, a number of recently trained clinicians began to treat offenders in a community corrections program in Colorado Springs. A working premise was that offenders begin acting out because they have been mistreated, and continue to act out because the trauma is not resolved. Resolving their traumatic memories, then, would remove what had precipitated and what was maintaining criminal behavior. Sometimes when EMDR was used, the results were indeed positive and extraordinary. At other times an apparently constructive EMDR session would provoke later that day an intense sense of abandonment and despair in the client; more than once a client threatened suicide after such a session, suggesting that the EMDR session was too powerful and in itself traumatizing. It was as if EMDR had taken the clients' only identity (as a "ne'er-do-well" or "victim") and left them empty. In other cases the EMDR session was obviously too intense, causing many to drop out of treatment early. Soon the word spread that EMDR was dangerous, and inmates as well as program administrators began to shun this new treatment.

In 1998 I (J. H.) was asked to consult on a state-sponsored clinical-research project on the effects of EMDR with an offender population. The subjects were male and female felons living in the community correctional setting, generally with extensive rap sheets involving the three major categories of crime: crimes against persons, crimes involving property, and substance abuse. Virtually every subject reported a childhood and adult history of being abused or neglected. All had failed previous attempts at rehabilitation. The goals of the treatment study were to help these clients to reduce the emotional power of traumatic memories, to correct thinking errors, and to produce prosocial behavior, that is, an increase in positive behavior at the treatment center, increased rates of employment, assertiveness, and the like. Longer-term measurements would come from tracking recidivism through reoffense records.

A quick review of the history of EMDR with the Colorado offenders indicated that as many as half of the clients referred for EMDR
might refuse, and of those who did begin treatment, some would terminate it prematurely, while others would experience the negative reactions just noted. The abreactive experience so common to EMDR
was a central reason for the high refusal and dropout rate.

For the study, then, I decided to introduce EP techniques as well.
One of my assumptions was that EP could help the clients to initiate
some of their trauma work; EMDR would be used subsequently after
the power of certain traumatic memories is reduced and the worry of
abreaction diminished. I also believed that EP might serve to reduce
some of the clients' reluctance and resistance to even agree to undergo
therapy, in this case EMDR. I wondered, too, whether the negative
transference of the client toward the therapist might be diminished.
As the study began, M. G. joined the research and treatment teams.

There are ongoing programs for domestic violence and substance
abuse clients (the actual criminal record of any individual is likely to
include other crimes as well). In addition, clients in the control group
engage in specific educational programs, job training and placement,
recreational groups, chemical-use monitoring, polygraph tests, and
group counseling. Members of the "enhanced treatment" group engage
in these activities and treatment with EP and EMDR. Each client in
the enhanced treatment group is expected to complete three EP/
EMDR sessions, and is then given the choice to continue after that.
We cannot honor strict random assignment to groups, so an unknown
degree of selection bias is at work. Though it is too early for definitive
outcome data, some preliminary findings are intriguing, as our colleagues Fisher & Shelton (2000) reported.

The great majority of the enhanced treatment clients began with
EP; less than 15% of clients wanted to try EMDR in the first session.
As time went on, more and more clients used EMDR. This was consistent with our expectations that EP would prepare a client for EMDR,
and in this regard we began to think of EP not only as a treatment in
itself but also as a resource "in the service of EMDR." Also interesting
is that certain clients who had already felt benefit from EP later opted
to add EMDR when it was offered.

We heard from many staff persons that the EP/EMDR clients often
responded more appropriately to other aspects of the comprehensive
treatment program. For example, the group therapist who conducted
the educational course for domestic violence offenders said that earlier

her clients would actively dispute her comments, blame their victims, and diminish their own responsibility for as much as the first 30 hours of a 36-hour course. When clients began EP/EMDR sessions at the same time that they started in her group, they were ready to work cooperatively after about 6 hours. These anecdotes paralleled higher staff ratings for the enhanced treatment group on measures of positive motivation during the treatment program. We also have some early indications that EP/EMDR clients were rated higher on compliance with residential program structure and stayed longer in the program, two important factors given that longer times in the program are correlated with lower reoffense rates.

We will be looking at long-range impacts, so it is too early to know whether the positive changes we have seen so far will continue as future groups enter treatment. We also do not know whether positive changes during the program will produce lower recidivism rates and increased prosocial behavior in the open community. However, based on the early positive experiences with the clinical-research project and our individual work in prison settings, we describe a few strategies that could be useful to other clinicians who work in either community settings or closed correctional institutions.

How to Introduce EP and EMDR to Offender-Clients

In general, the processing of traumatic memories with offenders needs to be more contained, less abreactive, and less likely to provoke dissociation or some other adverse response. For these reasons we emphasize EP over EMDR initially.

We like presenting the concepts of EP and EMDR in a group setting, with the number of participants ranging from 4 to 10. We might first talk about why we are offering this new treatment. In Colorado a useful metaphor is the backpack. "Hikers, no matter how fit, might not make it to the top of Pikes Peak if they are carrying 80 pounds of out-of-date junk. And individuals trying hard to make it through life may have to struggle too much, and perhaps fail, if they carry the equivalent amount of stuff from the past in a memory backpack." At this point in the introduction one or more members will talk about past efforts to change, and how it feels "like I'm carrying this load from the past." From here we talk about trauma and how the new therapies are particularly helpful in lightening the trauma load. The first part is as short as possible. If there are persons in the group who endorse conservative religious views, we might swing the discussion

away from acupuncture and more to Pert's work with the neuropeptides. It is also possible at this point to talk about the science behind
EMDR. Fairly quickly we offer to do a demonstration of EP.

Virtually always someone will volunteer to work with us in front
of the group since we say they can work on anything from the distant past, something recent, an event from today that still bothers them,
and the like. Sometimes an individual will want to work on the urge to
smoke, sometimes on a physical pain, sometimes something more intimate. We get some idea of the problem while respecting confidentiality,
and with their permission, write a SUD number on a board. We then
talk about the body's energy system and do muscle testing. This demonstration is often quite impressive and usually gets the attention of any
participants who are drifting off or looking skeptical. We test for and
correct psychological reversals or neurological disorganization. We can
also invite other group participants to be muscle tested.

Then we either treat the client, perhaps with EFT, or invite everyone to think of a problem, allow us to write SUD scores on the board
for each participating member, and suggest that everyone use the
Tapas acupressure technique posture to treat their identified problems.
We guide the group through the treatment, writing down SUD
changes as they are reported. Before the end of the group session, we
explain EMDR in greater detail. Generally, following this 45-minute
introduction one or more members of the group will sign up for an
individual session, which we then conduct right afterward.

All of the strategies in Chapters 3 and 4 are relevant with this population. We repeat that it is particularly important not to allow processing of traumatic memories too soon or too rapidly.

Transference and Countertransference

The offender-clients we treat have typically felt abused by authority
figures, by the legal system, by therapists—by the world. Much of
their "resistance" is an effort to protect themselves from further abuse.
One motive for using EP initially is to reduce fears and defensiveness.
If the therapist is respectful of the client's effort at self-protection, and
paces the course of treatment according to the clients' needs, trust will
develop and form a basis for treatment.

With this in mind, the therapists on our team initiate EP during the
very first treatment session. Since only three sessions are required,
"relationship building" becomes part of the treatment process itself.

It helps if we as therapists can have empathy for the client, recognizing from time to time that this individual was undoubtedly dealt a very bad hand in life and probably had a bad run of luck with it. The person in the opposite chair is more than just a stalker or batterer or pedophile. Though we work on early trauma, we eventually turn to the issues that brought the offender into the program to ensure that our therapeutic work is touching the causes of past offenses as well as present-day symptoms. To address the offenses too early can exacerbate the defensiveness. Clients usually become less defensive as we help them work through early memories of victimization. We were very pleased to discover that frequently, as clients resolve their own trauma, they begin spontaneously to express empathy for their victims or even for the persons who had abused them.

Character Disorders

A survey of 2,000 residents in the Colorado Springs community corrections program (Hartung & Philbrick, 1997) indicated that 90% had elevated scores on one or more of the character disorder scales of the Millon Clinical Multiaxial Inventory (Millon, 1977). Rather than being cause for alarm, these data can suggest treatment targets for EP and EMDR.

Millon (1981) wrote compassionately about the troubles that burden persons who meet the criteria for character disorders. Much of his early writing reminded us that the first impression of character-disordered (or "personality-disordered") individuals can be quite deceptive: The might be viewed initially as bad or sick, but it would be more productive to see their beliefs and habits as ways of handling overwhelming pain and threat. Beginning early in life, they think of themselves and the world in a way that helps them manage everyday problems (like the rest of us), but since their problems are extreme, their actions and ways of thinking are also extreme. Their goal is to survive, and extreme measures seem reasonable and justified to them.

Consider, for example, persons diagnosed as "narcissistic," which included 58% of our sample. Their tendency toward self-aggrandizement, entitlement, carelessness with the truth, failure to take feedback and learn from mistakes, and lack of empathy can be seen as protection from deeper feelings of worthlessness, shame, emptiness, and ultimately, the fear of nonexistence. Their early experiences of being told they are perfect are rarely replicated in later life, and their reaction to

this hard reality is to retreat into fantasies where they might reexperience specialness.

A therapist who understands the client's diagnosis, history, and motivation can hypothesize about the belief systems that are likely supporting the individual's emotion and behavior. Early in treatment the
therapist would not likely confront these beliefs but rather use them
to pace interventions and look for treatment targets. Thinking of a
narcissistic person as fearing failure, for example, would guide the
therapist to begin working on a very small issue, with one eye to the
"fear" and another to the possibility of "failure." In this case both EP
and EMDR could produce a fairly rapid reduction in generalized fear
and anxiety, and when combined could give the client an experience
of success while facing little risk.

With time and additional treatment successes, the therapist could
confront the narcissistic beliefs bit by bit. Sometimes a gentle accelerating strategy is to ask a client to repeat specific self-statements. In
this case they might be "I am an ordinary guy," or "I know what it
feels like to be a victim," or "I am going to follow orders all day long
today." As the client reports an emotional response to these challenging thoughts, either EMDR or EP is used to reduce the emotion. An
option is to use the floatback technique to take the client back to
memories of early events that shaped the narcissistic style.

Let us mention one more character disorder, which we found among
35% of our sample: "antisocial." In this case the superficiality, lack of
loyalty, manipulative interpersonal habits, irresponsibility, and criminal versatility can be thought of as defenses against the same behavior
that is feared and expected from others. Most in this group who use
aggression and deception might well be defending themselves against
the threats that originally taught them to become as they are. In this
sense, again, their behavior can be seen as originating in fear and then
becoming reinforced and habitual—because it works for them (though
not very well). The part of them that is capable of remorse, con-
science, and empathy remains, however well hidden. Relatively few
offenders we have seen are truly psychopathic in the sense of being
unreachable and unteachable.

Persons with this diagnosis might be seen as fearing deception, control, and abandonment. An early target might be a childhood memory
that taught them, as the song goes, "to do unto others before they do
it unto you." Let us look at an example of a young man diagnosed

"sociopathic" (antisocial) in the domestic violence program. He was in his first session.

Case Example:

Therapist: OK, Jeremy. You said you have no further questions about the enhanced program. We also agreed not to talk just yet about the charges your wife made that brought you into the program. You also say the idea of carrying a backpack felt true to you. This incident that you mentioned, about getting written up last week after that phone call from your mother—do you want to do some work on that?

Client: Well, yeah, 'cause it looks like I'm back to prison if I don't get this together.

Therapist: What happened?

Client: I got this call. I hadn't heard from my mother in years, but she heard I was here and called, said she wanted to help. She said she is getting her own life together. Said her treatment program is finally taking. Or at least so far.

Therapist: What kind of treatment?

Client: She's used coke for years. Years. It got her into bad stuff just to pay for the stuff. Prostitution, robbery, scams. Spent time in prison herself. Just hearing her on the phone got me all mixed up with feeling sorry for her, then angry. I really blew it in the program for a few hours.

Therapist: You know how we do the work with these new techniques. How would you like to try to chip away at some of the memories that are making life harder for you these days? Perhaps one old, early memory that the phone call got boiling up in you.

Client: Maybe the time Mom left us alone in the shack in Pennsylvania.

Therapist: OK. You can tell me as much as you want.

Client: I was about 12. No, maybe 10. I don't know. My little sister and brother were there too. The lights had been cut off and we were in the dark. No food. I was baby-sitting. But Mom had said she and Dad would be back in a few hours. Now it was a few days. We had no food left. And we were afraid to go out because of the neighborhood. It makes me crazy just to think about it.

Therapist: How would you like to do a little work as you continue to talk about it?

Client: OK.

Therapist: First, how bad does this memory make you feel? Zero to 10. Ten is the worst. Zero is no bad feeling at all.

Client: It's got to be a 10. No, maybe a 9.

Therapist: That sounds like a very tough memory. OK. What would you call the feeling you are having?

Client: Not sure. Mad.

Therapist: Any sad feeling? Think about the 10-year-old and his little sister and brother.
Client: Probably sad too.
Therapist: Scared at all?
Client: Not now.
Therapist: OK. Of those techniques we just did in the group, which one seemed to work for you?
Client: That hand thing. Let's try that. Where you put your fingers on your face and head.
Therapist: That's called the Tapas technique. Show me what you remember about it. [I help the client get the TAT position, which he then holds for two minutes. The SUD level drops to a 2.]. Good job. What do you think about this?
Client: It seems to work [Laughs], but will it last?
Therapist: I don't know, but you are probably already whittling away at the memory so it won't bother you so much in the future. You can remember it, but it will be less and less able to make you feel angry or some other feeling you don't want to have anymore.
Client: That would be good. Sometimes I think I want to stay angry at my mother, but then I remember that she is trying to get her life straightened around and she probably didn't have it so great growing up either.
Therapist: Do you want to keep doing work on it?
Client: Let me try that hand gadget, will you? I heard from a roommate that it really takes you back.
Therapist: OK. That might be a lot more powerful, so I'll be asking you from time to time how you feel. I also want you to be in charge of the controls so you can make it go faster or slower, or just stop it if it gets to be too much. We can always use the Tapas technique to help you get back to being in control of your feelings again.

   The client processed the memory successfully during the session. In future hours he volunteered for sessions, wanting to work on his guilt at having beaten his wife, saying that he was beginning to understand that he was wrong, even though he still said that she had some part in what had happened. When EMDR treatment stalled, I would use either EP or cognitive interweaves that might lead him to the blocking beliefs (called "thinking errors" by the cognitive therapists in the program) that were interfering with his treatment. (See Knipe, 1997, for a list of EMDR blocking beliefs, and recommended interventions.)

Behavior Is Multidetermined

From time to time we hear or read of an EMDR or EP therapist who has treated an offender who then has not committed another criminal offense for a given period of time. The implication is that the EMDR or EP treatment caused the client to reform, and that this success can be replicated with similar clients.

We find these anecdotes to be quite misleading. They are rarely presented as careful single-subject designs, which means that the client may go straight for other reasons. Also, without long-term follow-up, initial positive results may not hold. The graduates of programs designed to help domestic violence offenders, for example, tend to behave appropriately during and for several weeks following treatment, then reoffend violently at relatively high rates.

The impression is also given that EP and EMDR can be independently effective with an offender population, whereas our experience is that a comprehensive treatment program is required (as suggested in the case of Brandon treated in a prison setting). Simply treating a repeat offender for traumatic memories, for example, will target only one of the likely causes for that person's crimes. While it is true that some persons engage in illegal activity as a function of unresolved trauma, others do so for pleasure, power, or greed; because they lack discipline; to prevent starvation; under the influence of judgment-mitigating chemicals; in response to peer influence; and so forth. In the case of sex offenders the crime may be more a function of anger than sex, in that gratuitous force was used; may be more a sexual act than an angry act; may reflect the individual's social inadequacy; may be occasioned by substance use; and so forth. Without conducting a careful behavioral analysis of the client prior to treatment, the therapist may well target an irrelevant issue and may ignore the true factors that are likely to precipitate a reoffense.

Maintaining Treatment Benefits

Many of the offenders we work with have habits that might be toxic to their energy systems (e.g., smoking, use of chemicals). They may also work in caustic settings (e.g., with chemicals, metal dust, petroleum products) may have peers who promote resumption of old negative habits, and may have not yet practiced alternative ways to feel good, to support themselves, and to experience a sense of self-importance. These and other factors interfere with treatment benefits and make it difficult for clients to continue enjoying their success.

We stress using EP exercises for self-care, and recommend aftercare in group settings where clients can be reminded to repeat their self-care until it becomes a habit. Some will take treatment point charts, and refer to them when they feel particularly upset or tempted. Nonetheless, we do not know just how long term the effects of treatment are, especially after a client is discharged from a program or relationship that has provided a monitoring value. As we gather data from our community corrections project, we will try to answer these issues.

In summary, offenders are more like the rest of us than they are different, which makes the earlier sections of this book applicable. On the other hand, this population carries more trauma baggage, has fewer external and internal resources, and has more disruptive habits than average, so the various cautions we have suggested (e.g., about containment and decelerating strategies, about using EP to complement EMDR) are even more salient.

EP AND EMDR WITH HIGHLY PERFORMING INDIVIDUALS

So far in this text we have directed our attention mostly to those whose past traumas and present symptoms interfere with their day-to-day performance. As noted, some of these persons barely survive in the community. For treatment, we have focused on healing the past and eliminating the barriers to success, and only then have we discussed how to introduce the positive.

In this section we take the opposite approach. We focus on persons already performing at high levels who are concerned with improving in the future. Simply attending to the positive and to the future, however, is no guarantee that unresolved past issues will not appear in some form. In this sense, what we have discussed is relevant for working with persons who are already relatively successful, optimistic, and symptom free. Nonetheless, our emphasis here will be on applications of EP and EMDR for what has been variously called peak performance, performance enhancement, and the development and installation of internal resources—in essence, improving on what a person is already doing well.

We first learned the use of EMDR in performance enhancement from Sandra Foster and Jennifer Lendl (1996), EP from trainings with Fred Gallo, and the combination of the two methods through our experiences as executive coaches. We each spend part of our work hours in clinical practice and part in leadership training. Over the past 15 years we have taught, given feedback to, consulted with, and coached over 3,000 men and women in positions of leadership. They came from approximately 50 countries, representing a wide range of companies, campuses, governmental entities, and foundations. Most were executives or managers. Others excelled in sports or academics or were high achievers in the arts and sciences. We found more similarities than differences among these various samples. Our contact times with these individuals have included one-hour feedback sessions, consults of four hours or so, trainings of several days in succession, a several-month psychotherapy treatment contract, long-term coaching relationships, and periodic contacts over several years. Mostly we have worked in one-on-one sessions. When we work with a group, we find the optimal size to be from 2 to 12 participants, depending on the objective of the contact.

An initial impression is that high-performers are both innovative and matter-of-fact individuals. They tend to accept the premises of both EP and EMDR because they are open to new ideas and intrigued by the results that these two methods offer. The prospect of experiencing tangible change, fairly quickly and with reasonably stable results, fits easily into the value system of most high-performers. We find that we are introducing EMDR or EP techniques to more and more of our high-performance clients. Sometimes an entire team convenes for the expressed purpose of learning the tools of EP.

It has not always been this way. When we began to work as executive coaches, which was prior to learning EP and EMDR, we relied solely on traditional management theory and shied away from bringing up the dreaded *T* word (i.e., *Therapy*) for fear we would offend. The therapeutic options then available required more time and self-analysis than most of our clients found comfortable, so we tended to recommend cognitive and behavioral strategies only. This attitude is still widely endorsed in executive coaching. For example, we frequently use and recommend the particularly well-written and thorough *FYI: For Your Improvement* (Lombardo & Eichinger, 2000). This book, now in its third edition, contains close to a thousand specific development tips for learners, managers, mentors, contributors, and citizens, and as far as it goes, it is excellent. Yet one searches in vain among these many tips for any reference to therapy, meditation, emotional healing, or the like. The suggestions made in the book are directly extracted from the assumption that highly achieving individuals will overcome personal burdens through sheer effort, willpower, or perseverance. Hence, for stage fright one is told to breathe deeply and to drink water. To develop composure, the individual is encouraged to count to 10. For managing emotional reactions the suggestions are to recognize early signs of fidgeting, then to ask a question to buy time, and then somehow to recover from the undesired agitation (how this recovery is accomplished is not indicated). These are perfectly useful techniques, high-performers learn them quite well, and we teach them. However, the strategies are also quite limited in that they imply that the best one can do is to control undesirable emotions and impulses. An individual is taught to view anxiety, anger, and self-doubt as if they were disagreeable in-laws: Since they are going to remain in your life, you might as well learn to live with them. With patience and tenacity, and lots of time, you may weaken their impact but cannot expect ever to dismiss them.

When such persons experience EP or EMDR, they may well feel and show an immediate increase in performance. Already successful in spite of their emotional baggage, they may now report that they are finally approaching the peak of their potential. Some may speak of a sense of lightness. Some of greater freedom and choice. Some will turn to spiritual themes and switch their focus to future goals that go beyond measures of tangible signs of success.

On the other hand, there are those who evidence the apex problem in EP. In EMDR training it is described as a sense of change being so rapid and seemingly natural that it taken for granted, its significance unrecognized or discounted by the client. It may be useful, by the way, to see if this reaction to sudden change presents an additional treatment target or opportunity for growth. One might look for the blocking beliefs of EMDR (Shapiro, 2001a) or the psychological reversals of EP (Grudermeyer & Grudermeyer, 2000) such as "I must not linger or savor the present," "Idleness is the devil's workshop," "To live is to be active, to rest is to die," "I am OK only if I am accomplishing something," and "I don't deserve to win." Searching for these possibilities will present some clients with the opportunity to resolve further unfinished business or to examine the lack of balance in their lives.

With regards to the consultant, we have found that professional coaches who combine EP and EMDR with established management consultation strategies significantly increase their coaching tools and effectiveness and eventually broaden their range of influence.

We need to recognize at the same time that not all high-performance individuals are appropriate for EP or EMDR work. We remind ourselves first of those persons who are simply too uncomfortable when they step outside of their traditional methods of performance enhancement, which is to say the cognitive-behavioral tools of management theory, visualization methods for athletics, or the habit of overlearning that characterizes some artists. We must be judicious and not ask clients to stretch too far beyond their comfort level, not to attempt too radical a paradigm shift. Likewise, EP and EMDR will not be endorsed by every high-performer any more than they will be by every therapy client or, for that matter, by every psychotherapist. This is not as salient an issue when we enjoy an extended period of time to get to know and to work with an individual, but the more usual arrangement with high-performance clients (at least for us) involves a very brief encounter with the client, without the possibility of follow-up, and with the expectation that the coaching will follow a rather conventional set of procedures.

The briefness of the consult raises the related issue of the relationship we have with the client. In some ways the relationship in a time-limited coaching-style session is even more critical than in a therapy setting. When a therapy client arrives, we can assume that we have permission to be fairly intrusive in asking about history, unconventional in suggesting solutions, and confrontational when exploring noncompliance. We cannot necessarily make these assumptions when we are asked to coach on a specific performance issue. Even with a relatively open-minded person, it can be quite risky to move from traditional coaching (as exemplified in *FYI*, for example) to a discussion of EP and EMDR. To repeat: These are persons who generally think that they can overcome personal disability through willpower and perseverance. They tend to overemphasize the future and to ignore the past. How will they react if what we suggest for them in any way implies that their present troubles are rooted in their history? What if, in spite of our efforts to avoid mentioning the word *therapy* they hear us suggesting that there is something psychologically wrong with them? And what if we err in our initial assessment, and what appeared to be an isolated matter of public speaking anxiety is intimately tied to an intense fear of abandonment? Unless we have unquestionable trust with our client, unless our client has high confidence in our ability and goodwill, and unless we are fully focused on the welfare of that person, we would be better advised to leave the EP and EMDR material for another day.

In spite of appearances, a well-performing individual might harbor deep and unresolved trauma and might also have to manage other complications that we may not be able to detect in a brief consult: medical or organic conditions, issues of secondary gain, and dissociative tendencies are among the factors that can complicate an EP or EMDR intervention. While we might introduce EP or even EMDR as a fairly efficient and direct tool for reducing stress, eliminating specific phobias, or containing other undesired affect, informed consent guidelines require that we talk about how other matters may arise, such as how prior events in one's life may appear at any time during treatment and may require further and unforeseen attention. It is important not to oversell either EMDR or EP, or to trivialize a person's previous struggles and suffering. Contrary to behavioral premises, it is not always the case that a dysfunctional behavior or emotion is simply a bad habit left over and now totally isolated from one's past. It may be tempting to assume that a person who has achieved a highly visible position, for example, no longer experiences any self-doubt or stage fright or a sense of being a fraud. Or that a high-performing person must have been spared significant trauma. Or that a person who overcomes failure will always be resilient. In reality, such individuals may simply have learned to better compensate for feelings of dread and memories of failure. Other high-performers can deal with most challenges but are susceptible to specific triggers in their environment. Practitioners need to examine all of their assumptions about the burdens high-performers might or might not be carrying, and remind both high-performers and themselves that everyone is vulnerable in some way.

At this point we would like to offer our most sincere appreciation to all those persons who have confided in us the secrets they so often and effectively keep from the rest of their public. They have taught us about striving, about recovery from adversity, about excellence. They have also reminded us of the commonalities of the human experience through their willingness to reveal their private shame and fears. What we have learned from them allows us to write about these concerns and, we hope, to enable more of their colleagues to have access to healing opportunities.

In the remainder of this chapter we describe five increasingly complex levels of performance enhancement interventions. Readers may find more or fewer levels of complexity in their own work. At the least intrusive level is a self-help resource, such as a book. At a slightly more risky level we can refer the person to an EP or EMDR practitioner for follow-up assistance. Next is very brief one-on-one EP training within the context of a contracted consultation. The fourth option involves working at the group or team level in response to a specific request for EP skills training. At the most involved and time-demanding level is individual treatment with EP or EMDR, or the two in combination.

SELF-HELP RESOURCES

At the least complex and intrusive level are interventions involving use of a self-help resource on EP (we do not recommend EMDR for self-use unless assistance simultaneously available from an EMDR practitioner). Clients who might benefit generally complain of a specific behavior, which is most commonly anxiety based, such as a fear of public speaking, nervousness in the presence of a particular person such as a superior, or some other phobic response. In some cases a client may wish to improve behavior without recognizing or mentioning that anxiety is present. Others will speak of "hesitation" or "reluctance" to risk a certain behavior, again without awareness that anxiety may be the prime factor. Practitioners can introduce the EP paradigm with one of the formulas mentioned in Chapter 3. To increase motivation, they might suggest that the client call or email them within a month or so to follow up on progress.

This strategy is also recommended when working with persons notably skeptical of the concepts of EP. We have found that some clients are swept up in the enthusiasm of the moment during a consultation, especially at an off-site location, only to lose interest on returning to work, whether in a corporate office or gym. We know of a few individuals who have later complained about having felt tricked into a development plan without having had the implications explained. If there is doubt about a client's sincerity or commitment, consultants can simply refer them to a book, tape or the like. There will not likely be much complaint from a client who has simply been given the name of a resource available in most bookstores. Clients can then work at their own pace with the assigned materials. Many subsequently return for extended work, having become convinced of the utility of the methods.

If the client is open to some experimentation and if time is available it may be useful to conduct muscle testing briefly, or even to demonstrate a specific thought field therapy algorithm. This serves to introduce and normalize the material that will be found in a self-help book such as mentioned in Chapter 7.

Case Example:

I was asked to consult with a school superintendent who had recently been hired to turn around a failing school district. A competent and attentive leader, she had resigned from her previous job a year earlier and was still so upset by that experience that she was having trouble focusing on her present tasks. She had thought the previous position would involve another turnaround assignment, something at which she was an expert. Instead she found herself in the midst of a community deeply divided along racial (white and black) lines, and as an African-American she could please no one. When the five white board members refused to renew her contract (with the four black members dissenting), she confronted them all: "I was explicitly hired to improve academic scores, which is something I can do. I also seem to have been implicitly hired to resolve your long-standing dislike for each other, which is something I cannot do." No one disputed her allegation.

In spite of the obvious setup for failure, which she understood intellectually, she could not seem to shake the sense of failure and shame that followed her. We had the following conversation during our two-hour consultation:

Consultant: As far as I can tell from your psychological data and feedback results, you are continuing to take care of other people while costing yourself dearly in terms of self-esteem and joy. You tend to underrate yourself quite a bit on the feedback forms, and you say on one of these instruments that you don't trust yourself very much these days even though others find you extremely trustworthy. It all creates this general impression of a person who would be well advised to take care of herself as well as she takes care of others.

Superintendent: That's absolutely true. It's hard for me to believe my reports and peers rated me so highly. That last experience was dreadful, frankly. The hate mail, with the subtle comments about knowing where I lived, where I drove my car. I kept as much of that from my family as I could, but I couldn't keep it from myself. I know I'm safe now, but I still think of the fear I felt then. It was the worst experience of my life. The rage in the board meetings. The hostility in the streets. The conflicts in the school. All fueled by the divided board. I don't think I solved any problems while I was there.

Consultant: After all this time a lot of it is still with you.

Superintendent: I think I've been making headway, but I have a long way to go.

Consultant: Tell me what you have been doing that has been helpful.

Superintendent Mostly self-talk. You know, the stuff they teach us in leadership courses. Self-talk. I have to say that it is hard work for all the benefit I get. What ideas do you have that could help me get through this?

Consultant: I've got some, but they might sound kind of weird to you.

Superintendent: I'm game. I wouldn't have asked you if I weren't serious. What do you have?

Consultant: Well, first tell me what you've heard about acupuncture.

The superintendent talked about Asian medicine but didn't know anyone who had used acupuncture. I gave a brief overview and then mentioned how psychologists have learned to use some of the same points that acupuncturists use to reduce physi-

cal pain. It was a short step from here to recommending a book on EP, which she bought and read. A month later she wrote that she was doing EP exercises twice daily, was "almost" free of the terrible wrath and fear and shame, and was able to concentrate again on work. The teachers in her new school were responding, and she is working harmoniously with the board of education.

Although these materials are popular and we often have success with them, there are relatively few people with the motivation and perseverance necessary to use a self-help book or tape optimally.

REFERRAL TO ANOTHER PROFESSIONAL

At a slightly more intense level is referral to another EP or EMDR practitioner. Having a professional therapist, coach, or consultant is likely to be more motivational than a book alone. However, one also runs some additional risk by suggesting that the client is in need of more intensive assistance. Here is where we would encourage practitioners to avoid speaking of therapy. It is accurate and useful to distinguish EP and EMDR from the traditional psychotherapy model, which many people believe, and correctly so, requires a rather major investment in terms of time, expense, and self-analysis.

We tend to refer to professionals who use both EP and EMDR and who are known to us personally, if possible. We have heard of referrals where the alleged consultant/coach/clinician had learned EP or EMDR and was even on a list of referral sources but no longer practiced either. We have also made referrals to practitioners who once used EMDR or EP but had since switched back to relying on traditional talking methods without informing us. Both we and the client feel deceived when that happens, so we try to update information periodically.

BRIEF TREATMENT DURING CONSULTATION

Sometimes it seems preferable to treat a problem during the consultation itself. We are referring, of course, only to EP treatment under such conditions. EMDR is not appropriate under circumstances where the consultation is time limited and where there is no allowance for follow-up, conditions akin to an emergency situation such as discussed in earlier chapters.

Before attempting an EP intervention, we would need to assume both a high level of motivation on the part of the client and a strong relationship of trust between client and coach. The coach is essentially redefining the nature of the contracted services, and there is always the possibility (slight though real) that the EP exercise will not be productive. It is critical that the coach use timing and clinical intuition to best prepare the client and to ensure that the client is truly ready to try what will probably be a fairly radical experience. Because the client did not initiate a request for this additional assistance, it is also essential that the coach be especially experienced in the use of EP and confident in its efficacy. This is *not* a time for the coach to experiment with a new EP technique.

Having said this, we add that so far we have had no negative experiences when we introduce an EP intervention in the context of a traditional coaching session. Let us describe three examples to give a sense of how EP techniques can be taught within a brief consultation and with minimal fanfare.

Case Example:

A businesswoman was at risk to plateau in her position as communications director of a software company because of her visible anxiety during meetings with superiors. She had already been told that she did not exhibit "executive demeanor," and her many efforts to overcome her anxiety went unrecognized by upper management who had let her supervisor know that they were interested only in results.

During a one-day consultation related to a recent performance review, she told me about her history of anxiety in the presence of authority figures. I asked her if she would like to learn about a useful technique, warning her that it was quite far outside of the field of traditional management theory and practice. She indicated that she had nothing to lose, and noted that in the following week after this consultation she was to make a major presentation on her previous year's work to the same superiors who had caused her to feel such terror in past encounters. Because of the seriousness and immediacy of this task, she agreed to spend 30 minutes learning EP techniques during that very consultation session. I first explained EP according to the Pert studies (see Chapter 3), then demonstrated muscle testing, and finally taught her TFT algorithms specific to phobia and anxiety. She then visualized future meetings, continued to work on the anxiety these images provoked, and finally was able to reduce her SUD score to a 1 ("I haven't proven I can do it yet," she said, "so it can't be a zero"). I then drew a meridian chart that she could refer to when practicing her EP tapping. The entire EP discussion and demonstration took about 20 minutes.

The consultation ended, she returned to her work site in another state, and there was no word from her for two months. Then this email appeared one morning:

Thanks for the work you did with me in our meeting a couple of months ago. Has it really been that long? Sorry for being so late in checking in. The presentation that we worked on together went really well. As you probably can guess, I was overprepared as usual, and since I felt none of that old terror I was really able to be myself—even my jokes went over well. The visual props were good, and I had none of that cottonmouth I had told you about. I didn't even have to change my clothes before dinner that night (remember how I used to sweat?). Senior management was there with tough questions. I don't know if they were more pleased with the information I could give them or the time I answered one of their questions with, "I don't know. But I'll get back to you by the end of the day with the data." Amazing being able to say "I don't know" without getting that knot in my stomach. After my presentation an HR guy approached me and asked if I would consider being company spokesperson for the next year or so while they launch a new product. Nothing significant, just a promotion, salary increase, and some exotic international travel! Thought you might like to know.

Best regards, _____.

Case Example:

In an ongoing coaching relationship on the telephone, I had worked with an executive on many issues including staffing problems, developing a motivating leadership style, and dealing with negative feedback, so he had developed a comfort level with me. During our third call, he revealed that he had a secret, something that made his business life difficult. His job required a lot of travel, but he had always had a fear of flying. Every flight was an ordeal, as there were days of increasing dread as the day grew nearer, and at the airport, he would usually head to the bar to treat his anxiety. I said I knew a procedure that was a little strange but that might help if he were willing to try; he agreed. I gave a very short introduction, mentioning acupuncture, and then described and helped him locate the sore spot and the eye, arm, and collarbone points. He was able to vividly imagine boarding the plane and the take-off roll, his most fearful times, and gave a SUD of 8. I directed him in the specific psychological reversal correction: he rubbed his sore spot and said three times, "I deeply accept myself, even though I have a fear of flying." He then tapped the three points. Without using the nine gamut treatments, we were able to get the SUD to 0 in three rounds. We finished with the rest of our business, and I didn't hear from him until our next call, about a month later. He started off with, "I didn't want to call until I was sure, but I've taken two trips, with no problem! By the way, my mother has the same fear; do you know anybody in Philadelphia who does these treatments?"

There are other occasions where the benefit of EP treatment can be even more immediate. Sometimes a coaching client wishes to learn a new behavior that can be applied in the training itself. One individual, for example, was being triggered by another participant and used a brief TFT algorithm to reduce her anger with this person. Another learned the anxiety algorithm and was able to speak up more easily among his 23 peers in the workshop. At times the motivation to use EP arises initially from a source other than the client. We have been asked during a group training session (as the next case exemplifies) to work with specific individuals whose antagonistic behavior was disrupting the group process. In a situation such as this we will set up an individual feedback session with the person and begin by talking about how the person's behavior ostracizes him from his group, how it could possibly jeopardize his present employment or future promotions, and how his present symptoms must surely be as unpleasant to him as they are to others. We then might invite the individual to try out a technique for containing emotion. After informing the client of the EP model and gaining consent, we then conduct a brief treatment session. It is important in these cases to keep in mind the comments in Chapter 3 about the nature of the "therapy relationship." Usually it does not take great effort to convince these individuals that their disruptive behavior will do them a disservice unless they modify it, since they are already fairly well selected as persons committed to improvement and success. At this point, it is useful to draw on one's clinical experience. We do not recommend that a nonclinical industrial consultant, for example, attempt an intervention that will likely be more of a clinical nature than a purely technical demonstration of energy techniques.

Case Example:

A scientist studying to become a manager of fellow scientists was in a week long training course with 19 of his peers from the same company. I was consulting with the group during their training sessions. The scientist had been consistently argumentative both during lectures and in small-group activities. On the third day, I met with him for an hour in a one-on-one session. The following is a very abbreviated version of our discussion:

Consultant: *Thanks for your time, Hal. I know we had promised that this hour would be set aside for a break, but I thought it was important for us to talk.*
Client: *I was half expecting it.*
Consultant: *How's that?*
Client: *It's pretty clear I don't think much of this training course.*
Consultant: *Gosh, Hal, if that's all there was I wouldn't have asked for this private time with you. Actually I wanted to talk about what your peers have been*

saying to me. Four of the 19 have now approached me to complain about your being so combative with them. They feel that no matter what they do or say it's not good enough for you. I told them all to go back and talk with you directly, but they said they had already tried. Two of them said you have been acting the same back at work for the past three months. "Hard of hearing" was what one of them said about you.

Client: Turkeys.

Consultant: [Laughing] Turkeys?

Client: My reports back home. They should all be replaced.

Consultant: What if we just focus on what's happening this week. With your competent peers. You do admit the people in this course are pretty amazingly competent.

Client: Well, yeah.

Consultant: So just between you and me—and this is 100% confidential—what's going on this week, Hal? It's like you're shooting yourself in the foot. I'm concerned that news of your combativeness this week will get fed back to the organization. It's like you're purposely setting yourself up for failure.

Client: [After a very long pause]: I'm dying.

Consultant: I'm sorry, I don't understand, Hal.

Client: Three months ago I was diagnosed with a bad heart. I could have a heart attack at any time. I've been so depressed I can't think straight. I know it comes out in anger, but it's like I don't care about anything or anyone any more. I treat my wife and family the same way.

Consultant: Who knows about your medical condition besides your wife and family?

Client: Just my M.D.

Consultant: Why not tell your colleagues? Friends? At least your boss?

Client: And make things worse? Then I'd never get a chance to become a manager. Who wants to invest in a guy whose days are numbered?

Consultant: So you've been feeling anxious and scared—and depressed—and people have been interpreting it as combativeness—anger. I guess.

Client: I guess that's right. I tell you, things just come over me, like a chemical washing over my entire body, and before I know it I'm saying nasty things. I hate myself for it, but I don't see it coming. To apologize would only set me up to make promises that I know I couldn't keep.

Consultant: Hal, it's like you're living out a trauma.

Client: But one that never ends.

Consultant: You remember when I was first introducing myself and I talked about my other hat, the one I wear when I work with trauma victims? How would you like me to show you some of the techniques I teach other people, to see if you might get more control of what you call that chemical washing over your body?

Client: What have I got to lose?

Consultant: That's a good question. In my experience, there is not much risk, so this will probably be helpful to you, or it won't do anything at all. If it does turn out to be helpful, you will probably notice benefits that you can use during the remainder of this course. It might even help you to put a little less pressure on your heart.

Client: My doctor says I should do something to relax. Will it help me there?

Consultant: Quite possibly. The best way is to try it and see what happens.

Client: Let's go.

Consultant: OK. I appreciate your motivation. First, let's start with some kind of baseline to see if this is going to be of value to you or not. What if I asked you to give me some kind of rating on how you feel right now?

Client: I'm feeling pretty shitty. Angry. Upset. Mostly upset with myself.

Consultant: Let's say I gave you a scale numbered from 0 to 10. Zero would mean you don't feel shitty or upset at all. Ten would mean the most you could even imagine being upset. Where are you right now?

Client: About an 8. No, a 9. Not the worst I've ever felt, but pretty bad.

Consultant: OK. By the way, how much do you want to know about what I'm going to teach you now, before we actually begin?

Consultant: Well, that seems like a kind of luxury right now, given that we have so little time. Look, Doc, You've convinced me that you know a lot of stuff. And I trust you. So if what I don't know isn't likely to hurt me, you don't have to tell me just yet. Maybe just a little information, OK?

Consultant: Like what?

Client: Like, is it hypnosis?

I then gave a brief overview of EP, demonstrated muscle testing, and found he was disorganized. He agreed to do Cook's hook-ups, we retested, and he tested organized. We then found and corrected several PRs. Following this I taught him several algorithms. I then asked him to treat himself with energy point sequences for anxiety, followed by TAT for several minutes. His SUD score decreased steadily until it reached a zero. He said he was amazed. Since this entire procedure lasted only 45 minutes, he then worked on specific memories using what he had learned, and was able to resolve traumatic memories from a light plane crash, a public criticism by a boss, the memory of having been diagnosed with a weak heart, and the thought of having to return in a few minutes to face his workshop peers. He practiced EP for the rest of the course. During an exercise involving a hierarchical leadership task, he volunteered to be the CEO "so that I can see if I have what it takes to be a good manager." The task didn't end in complete success, but his team members participated with a spirit of collaboration, and they applauded him at its *completion (and later kidded him with relatively good humor at a celebration dinner, voting him "most improved"). At the end of the training seminar he gave a short speech to his peers, apologizing for his behavior during the first two days. He also apologized for not having had sufficient trust to tell them earlier of his medical problems. In response, one of his peers said that it was not essential to be perfect, just resilient. Another said that he had learned from Hal how to admit to mistakes with grace.*

Effective EP therapy is clearly not simply a collection of techniques. Without having shown this scientist respect for three days in spite of his constant complaining and without his willingness to trust me, I would not even have attempted the intervention. But had I stopped without introducing EP, Hal would likely have left the seminar feeling even worse than before; I doubt that I could have helped him in any significant way by simply talking to him. About all I would have accomplished would have been to heighten his awareness of his problem. This is a specific case of what we mean when we say that both the relationship and the method are necessary, but neither is sufficient by itself.

WORKING AT A GROUP OR TEAM LEVEL

A more complex intervention involves training an entire team in EP techniques. In a way this is less risky than the brief one-on-one intervention as the invitation comes from the team. On the other hand, there is greater exposure for the coach, who must now demonstrate the EP model, treat high-functioning individuals convincingly, and do so while being observed by persons with fairly high standards. Another risk factor is that some of the participants may have been ordered to attend the session. Questions to raise in such a case are as follows: Should the reluctance be discussed first? Or would this be an opportunity to treat the reluctance as if it were a PR? What is the likelihood that the skeptical or reluctant person could lose face in front of colleagues? Will laughter be bonding or humiliating?

Earlier we presented some ideas on how to demonstrate EP in a group setting and with reluctant clients. One might also review Chapter 10 on training. In all of our trainings in EP or EMDR we demonstrate the technique by treating some of the participants publicly. In this sense, psychotherapists and other healers attending an EP or EMDR training can be considered high-performing individuals seeking to improve themselves even further. What works in teaching other EP and EMDR practitioners (assuming one demonstrates as we suggest) is usually adaptable to EP demonstrations for high-performing teams.

(We know of some high-performance trainers who begin a typical training program by having participants do a few exercises for "mental hygiene." The exercises look remarkably similar to the EP procedures for PR correction, to EFT, and to TAT! Another begins with the butterfly hug. So far we have not replicated their pioneering efforts in our own work.)

INDIVIDUAL TREATMENT

Our final option with high-performance individuals is to offer work very similar to our usual therapy combining EP with EMDR. To give a flavor of how such a therapy session might proceed, we offer three brief case studies.

Case Example:

A company president, successful for most of her career, had recently suffered a setback. The national economy was down as were sales for her company. She was feeling less depressed and anxious while on Prozac, but she said her life was "tiresome and sad," her parenting was enjoyable neither to her nor to her two children, and she and her spouse seemed to criticize each other a lot. The chief operating officer she had hired to manage daily matters for the company had asked her to begin attending staff meetings again, but she was so distractible that she opted simply to be absent. Turnover on all levels was high, and morale was low.

My client had been in psychotherapy before and so was comfortable with the idea of self-analysis and change. What she was not so comfortable with was the idea that change could be relatively speedy. I explained EP according to Pert's design and then tied it in with acupuncture. For EMDR I gave her a copy of the Wilson, Becker, and Tinker articles (1995, 1997) and the SPECT study (Levin, Lazrove, & van der Kolk, 1999). For the first treatment session (the second appointment) we did energy corrections, then classical EMDR. She felt better, but a week later she reported ongoing anxiety, particularly having been triggered by a staff meeting. This time (the third appointment) she held tactile stimulators for about a half hour while talking about early childhood memories of being criticized by her parents. Again the hour was productive. We did EMDR again in the fourth session. Toward the end of that hour the following exchange took place:

Therapist: You say the turnovers at work are particularly tough for you.
Client: When people leave I take it personally. Like I've failed.

Therapist: What does that remind you of from your past?

Client: I'm not good enough. I'll never be good enough, whether it's in this job, as a child to my father . . .

Therapist: Anything in particular?

Client: Thousands of times. "Why did you get an A minus instead of an A?" "How could you have been so stupid as to spill your milk?" "You missed a spot." Do you get the idea? I was never able to please them.

Therapist: How about taking these tactile stimulators, hold them in your hands as you did before, and just repeat, "I'm not good enough". That's it. Good. Over and over. And notice what you feel. . . . When did you feel that before?

Client: I'm not good enough. I'm not good enough. I remember something very bad. I was with my younger brother. We were both very young. I don't remember who got in bed with whom but we took our clothes off. And my mother caught us . . . God, did she scream.

Therapist: How much does that bother you now, from 0 to 10?

Client: It's a deep sadness. About an 8.

Therapist: OK to continue?

Client: OK.

Therapist: What did you learn about yourself then?

Client: I'm unredeemable.

Therapist: Just repeat that and let the gadget stimulate your hands, back and forth.

Client: I'm unredeemable . . . I'm unredeemable . . . I'm unredeemable. It's very sad for me. It stays stuck in my chest again. I don't notice much change.

Therapist: Since we have only a little time left, I wonder if you could put that hand tapper to the side and just tap that place in the center of your chest. It's said that's where your thymus point is, the place you touch when someone calls your name and you respond with "Who? Me?" Just tap that, fairly forcefully. Use several fingers. What do you notice?

Client: Odd, but it feels energizing, and I begin to feel lighter. That's really odd.

Therapist: Now since you are on what's called the heart chakra, how about doing a little work with that chakra? Or call it a bundle of neuropeptides if you wish.

Client: [Laughing] Yeah, I guess I asked for that, didn't I? Me and my scientific skepticism.

Therapist: Whatever seems OK for you. Now with your hand open, just watch me and imagine a giant corkscrew, and you are going to turn it so it pulls negative energy out of your chest. Turn it the other way, imagine it being a corkscrew.

Client: Oh, I get it, like this, counterclockwise.

Therapist: That's it. A circle about as wide as your body. Hand close to your body. Do that circle a couple dozen times until you notice something.

Client: Wow, that's amazing. Like I'm actually pulling out some of the negative stuff.

Therapist: Now reverse the circle, and make it go clockwise, and put positive energy in.

Client: That's really nice. This shouldn't really work for me you know [laughs], skeptic that I am. But I feel lighter. But I also am having trouble breathing. What's going on there?

Therapist: Maybe it has to do with believing you are not redeemable. How about tapping your index finger point and saying, "I forgive myself. I did the best I could?"

Client: OK . . .

Therapist: And now, tap your little finger point and say, "Brother, I forgive you too. We were both very young."

Client: OK. . . . That feels right. I think I had held him responsible. He was two years older.

Therapist: Now try, "I'm redeemable" as you use the hand tapper again.

Client: OK. I'm redeemable. Feels good. I'm redeemable. I am redeemable [laughs]. Even that felt good. It feels like it's going up. In a positive direction I mean.

She continued to work on her history of trying to become perfect to please her parents, and how that connected with her present troubles at work, and she slowly began to trust others on her team to work with her. EP and EMDR are not miracle therapies, and she still had to work at finding other investors for her company, becoming profitable, learning to delegate, and giving up control. As is the case with all businesses, there is no guarantee of success. She also had to find energy to remain positive with her husband when their relationship seemed to offer little to either of them, and to keep communicating when she wanted only to avoid. The issue of balance remains salient, and she still does not get enough sleep. She has stopped taking Prozac, however, substituting the odd exercises she learned in the therapy office.

Case Example:

A brilliant academic was about to lose his university teaching post because he could not finish his dissertation, and without a Ph.D. his temporary appointment would not be renewed. We had three hours of sessions before he had to return to face his thesis advisor, who reminded him—believe it or not—of his parents, also brilliant academicians. We first talked strategy for approaching the task of writing, then made plans for presenting a proposal to his advisor, and in the final hour did a dilemma procedure with EMDR, which went as follows:

Therapist: As you listen to those bilateral alternating tones, notice that memory you just mentioned about growing up.

Client: We're living in an apartment in New York. Everybody is brilliant. And crazy. Loud. Screaming. I feel intense fury. Helpless. Prickly in my throat. Electricity in my chest. That's all.

Therapist: What does that feeling in your throat seem to be saying?

Client: It's a minor feeling. I felt silenced by my parents' rage. It seems that I've always had this feeling, a feeling of not being allowed to have my own words. Not being who I am.

Therapist: OK. What else?

Client: When I talk now, I feel lighter. When I am who I am, I feel light-hearted. But then comes the old feeling of "Don't be who you are." I think that's what's happening with my thesis and my advisor. I don't fit the mold of a mathematician and I don't feel like that's OK with them.

Therapist: How about putting part of that idea, like the "I am who I am" in one of your hands, you can pick the hand, then close your hand on that thought. Good.

Client: Right hand for that thought.

Therapist: OK. Now in the other hand, the opposite thought, which is . . . ?

Client: Left hand. I cannot be who I am.

Therapist: OK. Now, what do you notice in the right hand?

Client: It's really hard for me to say it. Because . . .

Therapist: Because . . . ?

Client: I don't know.

Therapist: OK. Now the left hand.

Client: Don't be who you are. That's not OK. Shut up. You have no ideas worth hearing.

Therapist: What does that hand feel like?

Client: Cold. Heavy. Electric. It makes me hard to be seen. Hard to be heard.

Therapist: Now the right one?

Client: It's hard to find a place to be myself so I lose track of me.

Therapist: Left again.

Client: Feels different. Lighter.

Therapist: Right?

Client: Also lighter. I can say that I want to be me. I can be me. That's OK. Hey, that really is OK.

We continued until he had resolved his dilemma enough to be able to discuss his fear of his advisor. This brought up new fears, so we went through some EP procedures (TAT plus several PR corrections) that lowered the SUD to a zero, even as he visualized his advisor. He decided to practice these EP exercises just before the interview with his advisor the following week. He ended the session saying he could think about the advisor and not feel the anticipatory fear anymore. "But that might be for now. I'll have to wait until I actually lay eyes on him—that is, if I can look him in the eyes. But for now I feel pretty good. I think this has to do with not believing my ideas are worth listening to. My math department is very high level, you know. They only want to hear topics that will change the world, at least the math world."

This was a matter for follow-up so I referred my client to an EP and EMDR clinician in the city where he would continue his doctoral studies. Last report: "So far, so good."

Case Example:

Andrea was a professional cyclist. She was never more graceful than when humming down a mountain pass on her 12-speed. Along with her team, she sometimes won and sometimes lost. Generally she was able to take her experiences with success and failure in stride—except in one event. For eight years in a row she had trailed the leader in an annual road race through the mountains surrounding her birthplace. Not once had she come in first in this race that had such importance in the region. She approached me the day before the latest annual event. I was surprised at how nervous she was after so many years of experiencing both success and failure in other places.

Client: I know you do energy work. I wonder if you might help me in my race tomorrow.
Therapist: Who knows? It probably wouldn't hurt to try.
Client: I would just love to win this race. It would be really important to my family if I could do it. Important to me too. Eight years of losing are looking like a pattern, though.
Therapist: I might be willing to do some work with you. But let's talk first about your motivation. It sounds like you've got a lot of personal investment in this win.
Client: I've gotten to hate seeing the leader's butt.
Therapist: I wonder about your competitive spirit. I know that's necessary, but could it be that it's started to hurt you in some kind of paradoxical way?
Client: You know, I've thought about that myself. Sometimes I've wondered—no matter who the winner happens to be that year—if my wanting to win so badly actually worked against me.
Therapist: I've got an idea. What you might do is talk to yourself in certainly friendly ways while I have you do some energy exercises.
Client: OK. Let's do it.
Therapist: OK. Let's start by rubbing a sore spot near your heart. Find it? Good, now rub clockwise—no, the other direction. That's it. Good, now say, "I accept myself deeply and completely even though I have this competitive spirit."

Client: What? But that's good, isn't it?

Therapist: This sounds kind of illogical, doesn't it? Don't worry. It's not about what you believe, but about what your energy system needs. Just try saying it. Good, that's it. Now keep rubbing and say, " . . . and even if I don't win the race tomorrow."

Client: OK, I get it . . . I think. Anyway, . . . even if I don't win tomorrow.

Therapist: Very good. Now, say some friendly things like this: "I am resilient. I am strong. I recover from pain." That sort of thing.

Client: OK. I am resilient.

Therapist: Now, as you say these friendly things over, tap on these points. First on the beginning of your eyebrow . . . [We do a complete EFT procedure.] Very good. Now try it yourself, and add things as they occur to you.

Client: OK. I am resilient. I am strong. I am stronger than the leader is . . . .

Therapist: That sounds like that competitive stuff again. Just in case that stuff is getting in your way, how about gently taking yourself back to yourself. Just yourself, all alone, with yourself, no one else. You are not competing with them; you are not even competing with yourself. You are simply being at your best—strong, resilient, powerful.

Client: Yeah. That's a totally different way of looking at it. OK. I am strong, eyebrow. I am resilient, side of the eye. I have trained well and I am a serious bicycle rider, under the eye. This feels good. I feel my pain, and hear it, I recover, under the nose . . .

Therapist: Nice job. Good. Now try this: "I deserve to do my best. I endure." Good. Continue, and consider rehearsing the same phrases tomorrow when you are riding.

At the annual mountain race on the following day Andrea earned the gold medal. I was reluctant to make too much of the brief EP work she and I had done, and reminded her that she had been training for years for the event. She reminded me that while that was true, she had never come in first before. I asked her what she thought helped her this year, and she said, "I'm pretty sure it was the energy work. As I was coming to the finish line I was in second place, and all of a sudden I heard myself saying over and over, 'I am strong, I am resilient.' Then I began to say, 'I feel my pain. It makes me strong.' None of that old competitive stuff came up. And then, 'I manage my pain, the pain makes me stronger, I recover from my pain,' and the oddest thing happened—I really did feel stronger and it was as if my pain began to dissolve, and I found myself flying past the finish."

(A question here for those who have their clients rehearse competitive thoughts: Let us imagine a running event where all 10 sprinters have their own EP coaches, and every coach is encouraging the runner-client to say something like, "I am better

... stronger ... faster than the others." What sense would there be to such an exercise since only one can land in first place?)

Andrea's next goal was to try out for her country's team for the 2000 Olympics in Sydney. We did four sessions of EP, and when she would come across a feeling of anxiety, we would use the EMDR floatback technique to uncover feeder memories, which we would then process with EMDR, EP, or the two in combination. She seemed to grow much less nervous when contemplating the Olympic tryouts, and was fairly diligent in her use of the treatment point chart to guide her EP practices. At the tryouts she came in one place short of qualifying for the Olympic team. She was very disappointed. Yet she continued to use the EP techniques and stayed on her personal training regimen to improve her cycling strength and strategies.

As of this writing (2001) she has set three records for her country. Had she been at this level of fitness (physical and mental) prior to the Olympics, she would have made the team.

How much of this can be attributed to her EP and EMDR work? These are her words: "The energy exercises definitely made me less anxious. The trick for me is to sustain my level. Breaking three records is one thing. Can I now repeat that performance? Just thinking about it makes me wonder again."

As the cabbie said to the visitor who asked how to get to Carnegie Hall, "Practice, practice, practice."

Maintenance of Effects

Work with high-performing individuals tends to be even more short term than with other clients, which makes the use of EP and EMDR even more appropriate. It also means that follow-up is more difficult, and we must leave it to the client to determine if the benefit is sufficient and being maintained. We find EP techniques to be excellent in the short run, but frequently a client will complain that the benefits eventually eroded and the old self-doubt arose. In these cases we encourage the use of EMDR, often using the floatback or trackback procedure to track down earlier memories that are triggered by competition, public performance, and failure.

The use of visualization is particularly powerful, as many of our clients already know. For those unfamiliar, we remind them of the studies where a person had the strength of his index fingers measured, and then over a period of time ignored one finger but *visualized* pushing down with the other. At the time of the second measurement the strength of the finger that was visualized as being exercised had increased, whereas strength of the ignored finger remained as before.

Further investigation showed that the muscles were unchanged, but the nerve pathways between the motor cortex and the visualized finger had become more efficient and complex.

Visualizing a future activity and then using alternating bilateral stimulation or EP techniques, or both, seems to amplify the power of the visualization. It will be interesting to see if the brain-limb neural connections can be shown to develop even further with this enhanced intervention.

Chapter 10

Training

F or those seeking to be trained in EP and EMDR, we suggest how to find a trainer. For those interested in teaching, we outline several ways to become prepared as trainers. The suggestions for course content and process have been tested in various countries and with diverse populations.

EP TRAINING

EP is defined in so many ways that it is difficult to make very many general statements about what one might expect from an EP training course. We focus, instead, on our own model for training.

Choosing a Trainer

In general, the marketplace determines who teaches EP methods, as there are few restrictions on trainers. No overall body certifies trainers or trainings. Those who wish to learn or be credentialed in a specific approach can do so; in Appendix B we provide Web sites for further information. Some trainings are for very specific techniques reflecting a particular school of psychotherapy (sort of like a brand name) and it can be assumed that the trainer has been screened and mentored for those approaches. Anyone wanting a more generic training in EP methods should ask previous trainees about the quality of any given trainer. Most EP trainers offer several types and levels of training, making the selection that much more complex.

Format and Curriculum

The training format we follow is largely based on meridian theory. While we use other aspects of the energy field in our clinical work, we do not include much beyond meridian-derived techniques in our trainings, as we hope to teach effective treatment techniques (utility) that are economical and efficient (simplicity) and acceptable to both therapist and client (face validity). We rarely need consultation or treatment assistance, so our experience tells us that although there are many effective and innovative treatments in the field, what we describe is a very effective armamentarium. Should new approaches that meet our criteria of utility, simplicity, and face validity come to our attention, we will likely learn them as well. Currently, however, we believe we are at the point of diminishing returns for adding further techniques.

Trainees in our EP courses have included psychotherapists in the United States, indigenous community healers in Guatemala, crisis intervention specialists in Mexico, psychiatrists and psychologists in Argentina, medical practitioners in Ecuador and Colombia, Nicaraguan counselors working with a Women Against Violence network, researchers studying trauma work with Turkish earthquake victims, trauma workers in Indonesian refugee camps, and a clinical/research trauma treatment team in El Salvador. Their previous therapy experience and formal preparation have varied widely, and as we have adapted our training format we have found ourselves offering different energy courses to account for preferred learning modalities and cultural distinctions. It is feasible to design an EP course with special emphasis on pain management, forensic considerations, medical issues, dissociation, children, crisis intervention, or any number of other special interest areas.

After much trial and error, we have found that our students seem most content with a single two-day EP course of about seven hours each day. This is a relatively economical way to learn the basics of EP. Trainees are encouraged to continue their studies through posttraining meetings with colleagues, reading, and experimentation. We share information about alternative training resources in addition to what we teach. Our two-day course covers certain content and experiences.

First we summarize the history and theory of the energy systems and energy psychotherapies, and the science underlying the theory if the group is interested (not all are). Then we briefly cover some issues related to therapist variables (e.g., "attitude of the EP practitioner," factors that facilitate and impede using EP) and client variables (e.g., "attitude of the EP client," including the apex phenomenon). Then we present the seven steps of treatment (see Chapter 3) in order:

1. Rapport.
2. Informed consent, including ways to introduce the EP model.
3. Client history.
4. Preparing the energy system for treatment.
   a. Use of muscle testing to assess for psychological reversals and neurological disorganization, with practice for trainees.
   b. Procedures for correcting psychological reversals and neurological disorganization, with practice in correcting both.
5. Targeting the problem.
6. Treatment, with several practice sessions.
   a. Introduction to the meridians (with meridian charts) and the specific treatment points on each meridian that will be used in the course.
   b. Selected treatment points.
   c. Algorithms.
   d. Diagnostic level treatment (optional).
   e. Additional psychological reversals (here or at end of course).
   f. Positive and negative emotions and affirmations related to each meridian.
   g. Thought field therapy, (Callahan & Callahan, 1996) with meridian point legend and specific algorithms, with practice.
   h. Comprehensive systems (single procedures designed to treat most problems)—emotional freedom techniques (EFT) (Craig, 1999), be set free fast (BSFF) (Nims, 1998), Tapas acupressure technique (TAT) (Fleming, 1999)—with practice of each system if possible.
   i. Toxins.

      j. Several demonstrations by the trainers before and after the practica.

7. Closing the session.

During the introduction to meridian theory, students become familiar with the underlying principles of EP and can often invent the very sequences that we later teach as algorithms. As they create their own sequences of meridian points in response to the needs of a particular client, they seem both to learn the EP concepts better and to feel more empowered after the course ends. It is as if they have created their own approach, generating a greater sense of ownership. By the time we reach the specific methods of TFT, EFT, BSFF, and TAT, the students are familiar with energy concepts, and these models seem less like prescribed recipes.

A two-day course limited to this curriculum allows several opportunities for students to practice muscle testing, to assess for and correct psychological reversals and neurological disorganization, and to treat each other. The trainer also demonstrates each method with volunteers who work on personal problems in front of the class.

Students may be asked to invite to the seminar any of their clients who are not responding to their usual treatment; the trainers may then treat these clients, or trainees may treat the clients under supervision of the trainer. These situations can be challenging but also provide a special opportunity for all of us to learn more. We take care to inform the client beforehand that while the experience will feel like a therapy session, it will also be an educational experience for the students, which means that we will interrupt the process from time to time, write discoveries on the board (e.g., psychological reversals, corrections, meridian points, algorithms, SUDS levels) and engage the client in ongoing debriefing. So far these experiences have been positive and successful, even though some clients arrive quite skeptical and with an extensive inventory of psychological reversals and blocking beliefs. When student-trainees or outside volunteer clients are treated publicly, it is especially important to ensure that they have given consent for treatment and know of the option to stop treatment at any time. Sometimes these demonstrations are videotaped, and the tapes are left for the students to view in ongoing study groups. If sessions are videotaped, we offer to make a copy for the client and ask the client again if she or he will allow the video to be used as a teaching resource, and, if so, under what conditions. Sometimes clients will agree to having a video of their sessions viewed in countries other than their own, for example.

The practica are critical learning opportunities and often determine whether a trainee actually uses EP therapy after the course. Close supervision is important, so the trainee-trainer ratio should be optimal: we recommend a maximum of 15 persons per trainer. It is possible to increase the number of trainees if advanced students can be conscripted to monitor their classmates' muscle testing and treatment. When students have particular trouble with the model, or when those working on an issue do not have time to complete their work, we often remain into the evenings to continue a demonstration or treatment session. We find this both necessary and practical given that we conduct many of our trainings in other countries and on an irregular schedule that does not allow for close follow-up.

We have already mentioned that originators of schools of psychotherapy seem to practice only their own methods. Each of the founders in energy therapy also teaches his or her method to the exclusion of other models of psychotherapy—and with great success; we remain impressed when we watch these masters in action. So why do we choose to teach so many variations? Primarily for the same reason we teach EP as well as EMDR: to give our trainees more choices and to make the workshop feel richer. Although the founders of EP methods can make their own models work for them exclusive of other interventions, we often cannot get only one method to work exclusively for us. The same holds true for our students. Questions that occur to us are these: Is there some special intentionality that a founder brings that makes his or her personal approach more powerful? Is there an additional layer of expectancy or placebo that causes a client to respond more favorably when a treatment is being conducted by its inventor? Could it be that the person who discovered the approach is better at using it than the students might ever be? Are they somehow specially suited to practice it? We do not know how to explain the phenomenon.

As a caveat, our emphasis on the meridian system as a preferred treatment focus may cause us to understate the value of the chakras, aura, and other energy systems in EP. While we use the chakras minimally—the TAT posture, which utilizes the sixth chakra being the notable exception—chakra clearing can be quite helpful when a client continues to loop in spite of all of our efforts with EMDR and meridian-based interventions. In some of the trainings that we conduct with international co-trainers, a colleague may choose to teach chakras in an extended EP course, or in a seminar where we teach the integration of EMDR with EP techniques. There are also techniques for working with the biofield (or aura), but generally we do not use any of them. Eden (1998) described a number of very useful EP techniques derived from other energy systems.

Optional Course Content

The curriculum we just summarized comprises a complete EP course. One could teach each of the approaches separately. EFT or TAT, for example, might be more appropriate for a shorter course, or when a group of healers wanted to learn a technique for immediate use under emergency conditions. We have seen Gary Craig teach a complete EFT course in a morning session, and have watched Tapas Fleming deliver the basic concepts of TAT in two hours. Often we are able to introduce clients to one or another of these approaches in just a few minutes when we have run out of time in a session and the client still reports high levels of distress.

The main problem we see with teaching only a ready-made set of sequences or procedures is that the trainee more often than not gets bored with the resulting monotony of the course, as what is required is the fairly constant repetition of the same basic recipe. Professionals complain that there is something too "easy" about the process, and that their experience and skills are no longer relevant. Some professionals and paraprofessionals report that they find the process impersonal, and that if they as trainees are feeling disengaged in the learning process, their clients will also likely begin to feel disengaged in therapy. We do not argue in response, but rather follow our guiding principle, which is to respond to the needs and preference of the clients.

We have taught the TFT diagnostic procedure at times but do not have a lot of requests for follow-up. Our informal surveys reveal that surprisingly few of those who learn it use it very often. Nevertheless, there are those, especially Callahan, who believe "diagnostics" should be the principal focus. The course offered by Britt, Diepold, and Bender (1998), for another example, is a three-day training focusing on diagnostics. They teach algorithms only briefly toward the end of the program. We consider the diagnostic procedure an excellent backup for when everything else fails, however, and we continue to look for ways to incorporate it.

Whatever the training format, we have found the teaching of EP methods to be particularly appropriate with paraprofessional groups, as we have mentioned several times. The main issues to emphasize are those that professional therapists take for granted: take a careful clinical history, get to know the client, establish rapport, give information about the procedures that will be used and ensure that the client gives consent for their use, and ensure that the client is safe and respected at all times. These comments are particularly important in a public training course, which tends to give short shrift to history taking and, because of the way demonstrations are done efficiently, can make EP therapy appear facile and purely technical. We find it useful to remind our trainees that there is a certain expectancy effect present in trainings that may be absent in a clinical office, and the latter setting may require much more preparation prior to beginning EP treatment.

Adaptations Outside the United States

We have found the teaching of EP methods to be adaptable cross-culturally. At the end of this chapter we discuss general issues in cross-cultural work.

Limitations

EP can be the target of ridicule if it is presented too mystically. Generally skeptics in EP training courses are doubtful of the nature of energy itself and on the lookout for concepts that are presented unscientifically. We find it helpful, then, to begin the course with a review of the science behind the model and to avoid mentioning concepts that sound metaphysical or magical. Demonstrations are probably the best way to sell the EP product. The practica also need to be closely supervised, as persons intent on discrediting the course may (inadvertently or not) fail to practice the EP procedures as taught, and their resultant failure to help a colleague in a practicum may stem from a misuse of a technique that could be easily corrected by a supervisor.

TRAINING IN EMDR

For those wishing to become trained in EMDR, we provide suggestions on selecting a trainer. For those already trained, the ideas in Chapters 4 and 6 will help in using EMDR more effectively. We have participated as trainers and facilitators in some 50 training courses in over a dozen countries, so the ideas that follow reflect our own experiences as well as feedback from many students representing varied cultural contexts and realities.

How to Choose a Trainer

When Shapiro first began teaching her innovative method to others, she called it EMD, eye movement desensitization. A complete training consisted of a two-day workshop that she first gave single-handedly in 1990. With time she added client safety factors and other specific guidelines, introduced new therapeutic concepts based on her experience and feedback from trainees, and gradually expanded the training into a two-part format, 34 hours overall, accompanied by comprehensive manuals. She added the word *reprocessing* to describe the positive cognitive changes that accompanied clients' resolving traumatic emotions. Whether in its original (EMD) or current (EMDR) form, the method is powerful not only in producing positive change but also in triggering unfinished and upsetting memories. To prevent harm to clients at the hands of undertrained clinicians, Shapiro kept strict tabs on who would be trained and on who would conduct the trainings.

Eventually she published the content of her model in a textbook (Shapiro, 1995), which provided enough information for any EMDR-trained and reasonably skilled therapist to teach EMDR.* She then transferred authority for training standards to an independent body called the EMDR International Association (EMDRIA). This democratization of EMDR calmed the emotions of certain critics who claimed that Shapiro's motivation for keeping EMDR in-house was self-interest rather than client oriented. It also created certain problems, not the least being a loosening of standards for both trainer selection and for oversight of the trainings themselves.

EMDRIA now certifies all trainers. Shapiro's group, from the EMDR Institute, is on the same level as all other EMDRIA-authorized trainers. In reality, however, these groups of trainers are far from equal.

At the EMDR Institute, those wishing to become part of the training team must first become facilitators. The main function of these

---

* However thorough the text, study of it alone does not prepare one to use EMDR. Shapiro repeatedly stressed that *supervised* practice is especially important with this method. It seems deceptively simply, but we see it misapplied over and over, both in the practica (where errors should be exhibited and corrected) and in demonstrations and practice.

instructors is to supervise the clinical practica, which are an important part of the trainings. The process of becoming a facilitator is extensive, involving a kind of apprenticeship with other persons who have been selected, trained, and mentored by Shapiro. Facilitators-in-training follow a course of study including reading a standardized manual and other written materials, classroom instruction, supervised exercises, observation of experienced facilitators, and finally supervision by them. They are required to attend ongoing seminars to keep their skills current. By working in a team they can exchange feedback, correct errors, and hone facilitation skills. The assumption is that there are certain "best practices" worth passing on to new generations of facilitators, and that these tried-and-true practices are important both in clinical applications and as fidelity checks for research. Neither the model nor the training format is yet in final form so we can expect improvements in future years.

Certain facilitators are invited to become trainers, where a similar process of mentoring takes place: observation of more experienced trainers, practice sessions where the trainee presents portions of the training format under supervision, and so forth. A person who has completed the additional steps to become a trainer will cotrain with an experienced trainer for a least a year prior to working solo.

Compared to Shapiro's rigorous selection criteria, EMDRIA's standards are less exacting. Applicants must be EMDRIA-approved consultants, which guarantees a good level of knowledge of the material. They agree to teach what is contained in Shapiro's textbook, provide examples of the training materials, and inform EMDRIA about other training procedures. Their presentation and teaching skills, and ability to communicate the EMDR model, however, do not seem to be evaluated. Whereas the EMDR Institute trainers spend several years in a structured curriculum, no such oversight and accountability is required of non-Institute trainers. This does not mean that persons outside the Institute cannot train effectively, only that they have not been monitored to ensure that they do. We therefore can recommend training courses sponsored by the EMDR Institute (we provide information on how to find them in Appendix B). For all other EMDRIA-approved trainers the principle of "caveat emptor" must guide: the consumer will need to discover who is a decent teacher by asking other trainees about their experience.

Goals, Curriculum, and Levels

In Part 1 (formerly called Level I) training the student is taught to trust the power of the basic EMDR model and the spontaneous healing resources of the client. The trainee is encouraged to be relatively nondirective. The principle is a variation of one that has been tested and found to be true in many settings: "Don't do for the client what the client can do for him/herself." It may seem odd to the uninitiated, but perhaps half of all clients will benefit from therapy if the therapist simply does a form of bilateral stimulation; then stops and asks the client, "What do you get now?"; and then after the client has responded, says, "Go with that" and resumes bilateral alternating stimulation. Though a few other comments and instructions are also made, this basic three-step procedure is often all that is required. We feel compelled to repeat, at this point, that the foregoing does not constitute training in EMDR, nor does it even equip the reader to experiment with the technique. During much of the basic training, the student is encouraged to fight the urge to repeat or "actively listen" to what the client says, to interpret, to analyze, or to interrupt the spontaneous processing of the client in any other way. The bilateral simulation activates the client's adaptive information processing system, which is thought to work toward health and personal evolution and activation of which is often sufficient for the client to heal. An additional benefit is a sense of empowerment the client feels after having resolved a troublesome issue with apparently no noteworthy assistance from the therapist.

All trainees work as therapists and clients during several practica. These are fine opportunities to witness the power of the method and to learn to avoid unnecessary interventions. It is an especially important time for therapists who have felt distressed by their apparent irrelevance to the therapeutic process; they begin to learn that their role is very important, though different from what they had learned in graduate school.

The training model is fairly effective in teaching cautions and safeguards. Skilled facilitators observe the practica, guiding therapists-in-training and helping out when patients relive an experience more intensely than had been expected. Follow-up is provided for trainees who need further help before leaving the program. The use of EMDR with special populations is introduced, e.g., with persons with recent traumatic events, anxiety, and relationship problems. Trainees are also taught to use EMDR for treating one's own stress and minor upset. As a result, most trainees leave Part 1 with sufficient skill to work with most clients.

In Part 2 (formerly Level II), students are encouraged to become more active in cases where clients are not able to process traumatic memories solely through activation of the adaptive information processing system. The cognitive interweave is introduced as one technique to add adult perspective when the client is stuck in the memories of childhood. Certain distancing strategies are introduced to help the client contain overwhelming emotion. Trainees also learn about applications of the EMDR model to additional special client populations: people with obsessive-compulsive disorder, addictions, dissociation, or eating disorders; those wanting performance enhancement; and children. Students are encouraged to try out these new skills during Part 2 practica. However, since the basic techniques from Part 1 are sufficient to handle most issues presented by trainee-clients during the practica, the advanced techniques are infrequently practiced. Too many graduates of a Part 2 course return to their offices not yet ready to apply the advanced techniques to deal effectively with their more challenging clients.

Our trainings follow the EMDR model, though we rewrite the training manuals to meet the changing needs of our students, and to account for cultural contexts. In a given year we may use several revised editions. As a result, the training manual has become very practical, more a clinical manual than a training textbook.

We tend to work with small groups, from 15 to 70 trainees rather than the several hundred more common in the United States. This makes it feasible to conduct demonstrations of the method with live clients—generally trainees from the course but frequently outside clients. When time permits, we also offer supervised client treatment in addition to the practica. This is particularly useful if we are not able to return to a training site regularly, and where trainees are not experienced in psychotherapy generally.

In Chapter 4 we suggested a number of adjustments to the way EMDR is usually used. Those comments are also applicable to this chapter as examples of how we think EMDR training could be improved. For example, we now teach the decelerating and accelerating strategies to our trainees. We also noted that we would introduce an exercise designed to help EMDR trainees begin to examine personal traits that might enhance or mitigate the effect of their EMDR work. We are referring specifically to the therapist's attitude toward abreactions, as many of the problems in managing abreactions reflect the therapist's discomfort or impatience more than the client's readiness.

The exercise described next can be added both to EMDR Part 1 (prior to the last practicum) and Part 2 (prior to the first or last practicum) trainings. It should be conducted in the practicum group of nine participants, led by the facilitator, rather than by the trainer in the entire group of participants. Even if limited to 15 to 20 minutes, the experience can be positive and useful.

Trainees are asked to think about how they reacted to a client's abreaction while the facilitator encourages a nonjudgmental atmosphere. Trainees might volunteer different issues, or the facilitator might suggest some to start the discussion. First, reference can be made to qualities that characterize a hesitant therapist: "Some therapists discourage processing by the client. If you feel abreactions are inherently dangerous, you might notice that you slow down clients, even those ready to work harder. Some clinicians notice that a client issue taps into their own unfinished business, and may feel upset. If that therapist then stops using EMDR, would it be to protect the client or the therapist? Most recent trainees feel some discomfort, which is normal. How much time do you think you will need before you accept a client's abreactions as natural and potentially healing? What about the difficulty therapists might have letting the EMDR model 'in' because it is so discordant with what they have always done? Does that sound like you?"

And then some thoughts for therapists who hurry unnecessarily: "Do you ever feel impatient with a client, and might that feeling cause you to push a client into an abreaction? What do you do when you do not like a passive-dependent person? Might you overlook legitimate fears and go too fast? How do you look at dissociation? Could you underestimate the terror clients feel that causes them to dissociate?"

These are suggestions; it is better to wait until the trainees speak up: "When I heard that client wailing in the training room, tears welled up in me. I think I'm going to have trouble with clients who cry intensely." Or "I tend to think that people should just get through an abreaction, so I might not stop when I should, or might not ask them if they really want to continue."

Training Outside the United States

The professional therapists we train in countries outside the United States tend to be bright, successful, and good-natured. They generally find value in the EMDR model, provided we adjust the model and our teaching style to fit local customs and psychotherapy context. The extra work involved in restructuring a course is more than offset by the adventure and enjoyment of working within another culture: part of the reason we train internationally is for the splendid opportunity to work with excellent colleagues from other locales. We indeed feel fortunate.

In some countries there are relatively few professionally trained clinicians, so the model and our teaching style have to be adjusted even further. We have not taught EMDR to entire groups of nonprofessionals, but we have included carefully selected individuals without formal psychotherapy training in seminars attended mostly by professionals. Physicians, acupuncturists, natural healers, and self-taught persons who have had extensive experience in working with trauma victims are among our students.

In a recent article, Kaplan and Van Ommeren (2001) wrote about teaching EMDR to paraprofessionals in Nepal. They make an articulate case for training selected nonprofessionals in areas where few professionals live (noting that Nepal has only one psychiatrist per one million people, for example). They observed that one specific focus of the EMDR training there was on affect management. As we remarked earlier concerning decelerating strategies, affect management is worth emphasizing for professionals and nonprofessionals alike, and because even professionals frequently have trouble managing their clients' emotions and abreactions, paraprofessionals using EMDR should be even more sensitized to this issue. It is particularly important for EMDR paraprofessionals to have access to formally trained clinicians for any critical situation that may arise.

Whether the trainees are professionally trained or not, it is critical to provide ongoing follow-up and consultation to trainees. In a number of countries we were the first to teach EMDR and have seen firsthand how complex, even incomprehensible, the EMDR model can seem to the first group of initiates. We encourage them to contact us or other EMDR clinicians by e-mail, but we find there is no real substitute for returning from time to time to offer follow-up conferences, additional trainings, and simply moral support.

Limitations

A limitation (and strength) of EMDR arises from a single source: the fact of abreactions. This phenomenon places EMDR training out of reach of nonprofessional helpers, who are not likely to know what to do if a client begins to abreact, runs the risk of being retraumatized by another unresolved traumatic experience, and even dissociates to escape the pain.

Nonetheless, I (J. H.) have been involved in a pilot project for teaching EMDR to select persons who have an interest and a natural skill in healing but who are not formally trained as psychotherapists. The pilot project is going slowly and well, and so far enjoys the financial support of an international organization that sees training nonprofessional helpers as a solution to the underavailability of professional psychotherapists.

Another limitation arises from the format the most trainers follow. Even the best EMDR trainers we have observed tend to present Shapiro's concepts in a somewhat disorderly fashion. Students can leave with a less-than-optimal understanding of how to use EMDR and even with what we consider to be certain bad habits in implementing the method. EMDR is a robust methodology. Clinicians can commit minor errors and still find EMDR to be a powerful healing force. Some errors, however, will render it ineffective or result in clients feeling stuck or even overwhelmed. We believe many post-training misapplications of EMDR can be avoided through improved training. The strategies presented in Chapter 4 will improve trainings. A course combining EMDR and EP techniques advances training goals further.

TEACHING EP AND EMDR TOGETHER

We recommend that a person first learning EP and EMDR take the courses separately. We tried to combine the two models in a pilot project several years ago and found that students left confused by the different theoretical concepts. However, once a person has become familiar with both approaches and with the theories that distinguish them, and has solid experience with both in clinical practice, a workshop in which EP and EMDR techniques are taught and demonstrated in combination is useful.

It is not necessary to offer formal trainings combining the two approaches, as a clinician trained in both methods can eventually figure out combined uses through trial and error or with the help of a book such as this one. On the other hand, formal training does speed learning and it is particularly helpful in demonstrating exactly how one can move from the techniques of one method to those of the other. Here we are speaking of mixing techniques, not seeking a unifying theory of cause and effect, and we are combining tools or skills within one's therapeutic repertoire, not creating a brand new and cohesive theory of psychotherapy. The two theoretical bases, as we have suggested, are not easily blended.

Curriculum

It is possible to teach a one-day course combining the two approaches, provided that participants are already trained in EMDR and at least familiar with the EP concept. One working format is the following:

1. Review of advanced EMDR strategies with an introduction to the decelerating and accelerating dimension.
2. An overview of EP (similar to the outline noted earlier for the regular EP course; this will be a review for some of the trainees, new information for others).
3. Using EP during EMDR sessions (content is determined by time available, and is taken from Chapter 5 in this book).
4. Using EMDR during EP sessions (content is determined by time available and preference of the students, and is taken from Chapter 6 of this book).
5. Special discussions, as time allows, on resistance, performance enhancement, paraprofessional training, and use of both methods in groups.
6. Practicum (mostly limited to muscle testing).
7. Demonstrations as time allows.

The demonstration of EP and EMDR in combination tends to be extremely complex, as the clients who volunteer for this are likely to have tried both EP and EMDR (and other therapies) to resolve a problem, and the fact that they are still distressed after so much effort suggests deeper interference with healing than we usually meet in daily practice. For many reasons we recommend that this course be taught only by persons who are very comfortable treating clients publicly, who have already taught both EP and EMDR extensively, and who are able to handle failure.

We offer three brief case studies of how these demonstrations might proceed.

Case Example:

A psychologist in an integration workshop asked for help with chronic pain that she felt mostly in the evenings, and requested that I (J. H.) begin with EMDR. We were working in an open classroom in the tropics. A breeze was cooling us, flower scents filled the air, and the sounds of birds surrounded us. "This is odd," she said, "because in the evenings the pain is so bad that it does not let me sleep. Maybe my pain has gone away for now because I have been practicing some of the training techniques today. Maybe it's because of this setting." Though she had asked to begin with EMDR, we decided it would be awkward to do so because her SUD at that moment was at a 0, leaving us with no emotional target. Instead, we agreed to begin with muscle testing to ask her energy system what the number might be. I first asked her to think about her usual pain level and to write the SUD number on a piece of paper without showing me. We then muscle tested. The muscle testing reading and the number she wrote were both 6. This demonstration supported the validity of muscle testing for the participants, and also suggested for me that I was neither psychologically reversed nor neurologically disorganized.

We then began to use EP techniques to see if her SUDS level might drop to a 0. We began with meridian tapping:

Therapist: What are you thinking about as you tap?
Client-student: Only this: "Where did it all begin?"
Therapist: Good question. What is your hunch?
Client-student: No idea.
Therapist: Would you be willing to switch back to EMDR now and try to find out?
Client-student: That's why I'm here. Let's go for it.
Therapist: OK. You know about feeder memories. Notice what you are feeling right now.
Client-student: Actually, nothing in particular. That's been part of the problem. I cannot track much about my pain until I'm already feeling it intensely, and then it's too late.
Therapist: OK. Where do you usually feel the pain at night?
Client-student: In my right foot, in my arch.
Therapist: OK. Just put your attention on that place now. That's it, you can touch the arch if you would like. Good, take off your shoe. OK, now as you touch the place where you usually feel the pain, what comes up for you?
Client-student: Oh, oh. It's a memory of when I was slightly overweight as a kid. I got criticized for it by both parents. They seemed more interested in how I

looked to the public than in who I was as their daughter, as a person. [Client begins to cry.] It still makes me very sad.

Therapist: Well, good work in figuring this out. Now, would you like to do some more work on it?

Client-student: Yes, please.

Therapist: OK. You're an excellent EMDR therapist, I know, so let me just ask you what procedure you would like to use.

Client-student: Could I use that machine, the one that taps my hands?

Therapist: Sure. Set it as you like. Good, now just notice what comes up.

Client-student: Where did this all begin?

We then agreed to use the floatback technique to find the memory that was feeding her present-day anxiety and distress. She quickly found an early memory of having been criticized for being overweight, which led to another memory of having felt lazy in matters of physical exercise, which led to a memory of having gained weight during pregnancy—all of which we then processed, at her request, with EMDR. Subsequent muscle testing suggested that her pain level was then at a 0. That evening she felt pain at a SUD score of 1 and was able to sleep soundly for the first time in weeks.

Case Example:

A psychiatrist asked to be treated for stage fright. He was a professor at a medical school, highly regarded and skilled, but had never been able to overcome his anxiety at being in front of a group. He reported that he had been in psychoanalysis for seven years prior to this workshop, had tried EMDR for a year, and had been using EP techniques for the past six months—all with little benefit. At the moment, in front of 50 other trainees, he felt anxiety, at a score of 6.

I asked what might be the origin of his stage fright. While thinking, he put his hand to his chin as if to reflect on his answer.

Therapist: You know from the course so far that you are touching the last point of your central vessel. And that it may have to do with worth. How does that sound to you?

Client-student: Yeah. That's been lifelong. Or at least as far back as I can remember.

Therapist: How about tapping the point and saying, "Even though I have this problem with public speaking anxiety, I accept myself deeply and completely."

Client-student: After all these years, it's true that I still have that problem. In spite of that, I accept myself deeply and completely.

Therapist: And now, "Even though I continue to hassle myself for not having gotten over this yet, I accept . . ."

Client-student: Man, that's tough. But it's true that I am my worst critic. Even though . . .

Therapist: That idea came from you, you know.

Client-student: I guess I wear my heart on my sleeve, don't I?

Therapist: And I thank you for it. Otherwise how would I know what to do to be of use to you?

Client-student: I think you just paid me a compliment.

Therapist: Tried to, at least. How about this as a final: "I deeply accept myself even though I tend to notice myself more when I am making mistakes than when I am doing well."

Client-student: [Laughter from the class, which contains some of his former students. Client then turns and raises his voice in mock horror]: Will you all still love me after knowing this about me?

Someone in the audience: We already knew it and still loved you. Why should we change our minds now? [More laughter.]

Therapist: Looks like you're in good hands today. What's coming up for you?

Client-student: An old memory. It's the one where this all began.

Therapist: OK. Tell us about it if you wish, or you work on it.

Client-student: I'd rather just work on it. You know, that conflict in me between doing well and doing poorly is pretty chronic.

Therapist: Have you ever used the EMDR dilemma procedure?

Client-student: Don't think I ever heard of it.

Therapist: Here's what you could do if you wish. Put one side of that conflict in one hand, the other side in the other hand.

Client-student: OK. The "good me" in the right, the "bad me" in the left. Like that?

Therapist: That's it. Now I'm going to lend you this gadget which stimulates one hand, then the other. Hold each of these two pieces in a hand, now regulate the machine. That's good. OK. Now with the machine running just notice your hands. First, what's your right hand like? . . . Now your left?

The procedure continued, and with help from the therapist the client began to process an extended list of memories of having failed when trying to be "visible" in the world. He reported feeling changes in the weight, sensations, size, and temperature of his hands as he processed his memories. From time to time a psychological reversal appeared, having mostly to do with hopelessness and unworthiness; he corrected them with EP techniques. After about 50 minutes he said he could not find any more upset feelings. He returned to the memories he had worked on and found all of them to be "interesting, but as if they were no longer significant." I then asked if he would field questions from the audience and he agreed. I sat in the back of the room as he *talked with the group for another 20 minutes. Some of his students said they had never seen him so calm in front of a group. He seemed to have found peace in being visible.*

To what do we attribute the effect? The loving acceptance of a group of 50? The expectation that something could happen that had not occurred before in his therapy? Demand characteristics from the therapist? A specific combination of EP and EMDR techniques? Or was it a coincidence that all the effects of his previous therapies happened to converge at that moment in time? We cannot say for sure, can we? But we do have the hunch that it was somehow due to the impact of the EP and EMDR interventions, and that both the treatment and the therapeutic effect could likely be replicated.

Case Example:

A psychologist-trainee, skilled in both EP and EMDR, wanted to do some work on improving her performance as a professional. She had specific challenges she was about to assume that caused her to feel quite angry. In her country men tend to be granted favored status, so she felt she had to be much better than her colleagues simply to be considered for promotions and recognition. I was hoping to be empathic:

Therapist: And the bad news is that a similar condition exists around the world. We men tend to get more than our share, I am afraid to say.
Client-student: I might as well tell you that that pisses me off too. Here we consider that all of you in America are fairly well off, women and men alike. The way you define poverty there means that you have to drive an older car and rent a room. I don't mean to be combative, but—well, I guess I am being combative, aren't I?
Therapist: I don't know if this is related to what you wanted to work on today, but would you be willing to take on this issue, since it happened to come up here?
Client-student: What am I getting in to? [Her colleagues are laughing along with her at this point.]
One of her friends in the group shouts, "Go for it, Sinita."
Therapist: Remember, that it is always up to the client. You can choose to focus on this or not. You don't have to do anything you don't want to do.
Client-sudent: Well, now, that would certainly be a new experience for me, wouldn't it? [More laughter as she turns and grins toward the group.]
Therapist: Hey, I'll take acceptance whenever it's offered to me.
Client-student: OK. Me too. Let's work on it.
Therapist: Well, you said you wanted to use EP to increase your sense of efficacy. Still want to start there?

Client-student: Yes.

Therapist: OK. You know how it works. How about getting a nice image of yourself performing well in the future, notice the feelings, and find a friendly thought about yourself to go along with that.

Client-student: Like, "I can do it." Or maybe, "I deserve to do it." God, that hurts.

Therapist: It looks like that's touching you personally, huh? How about if I give you the option of continuing with tapping or switching to some EMDR work?

Client-student: Let me tap for a while. That's better. It seems that when I tap on my stomach point here under the eyes I feel better. Anxiety, huh?

Therapist: So they say. How about the index finger point too?

Client-student: Yeah. I forgive myself because I'M DOING THE DAMNEST THAT I CAN.

Therapist: Might be a piece in there related to your little finger point too. What do you think?

Client-student: [Taps little finger nail on the heart meridian point, then rubs her temples for rage] BUT I DON'T FORGIVE THOSE BASTARDS FOR KEEPING ME STAKED TO THE GROUND WHILE THEY TIGHTEN THEIR STRANGLE HOLD ON POWER AND RESOURCES. YOU FUCK HEADS!

Therapist: I don't now who all you're talking to right now [what sounds to me like nervous laughter from the group; client laughs back, for a very long time] but it sounds like good work. Go ahead and tap for as long as seems right to you. What do you notice?

Client-student: I notice, first, that I want to tell you, "I don't need your permission to tap. What's it to you?" Then I notice that it's not important if you give me permission or not. It's not about you, it's about me.

Therapist: Repeat that as you tap, would you?

Client-student: What?

Therapist: When you said, "It's about me."

Client-student: It's about . . . Oh, God, I can't do it. [Client begins to cry deeply.]

Therapist: Can you keep tapping?

Client-student: No. I feel so sad. It is about me, after all.

Therapist: Would it be all right if I tapped myself for you?*

Client-student: No. This is something I have to do for myself. This is about me. I've got to stop putting it on other people.

---

* This is an advanced technique called *surrogate tapping*. We teach it in some advanced trainings, but because it is even more outside the traditional paradigm than the client's own tapping and rubbing, we are judicious in assuring it will be received in an open manner.

Therapist: What do you choose to do right now?
Client-student: Could I ask you just to tap my hands, back and forth, and let me do the work?
Therapist: Sure. Like that? [I stand next to the client. She extends her hands and I tap the backs as she continues processing.]
Client-student: Yes. And please continue. Just let me cry. I'll tell you when to stop.

After about 40 minutes of laughing, crying, and shouting (at one point she said, "Thank God we're in this isolated place"), the client was able to forgive people with whom she has been angry for so long, and tapped her little finger point as she forgave. She then asked forgiveness for herself for having passed her anger on to others, as she tapped her index finger point. Finally she turned to the group.

Client-student: Thanks for being here with me. I know some of you have had to put up with a lot of rage from me, lots of anger, lots of blaming. I apologize for that. I get a sense that I have been inflicting you with some of the same oppression I have felt for so long from the people I keep blaming for all of my problems. Sorry. I guess I realized today—at what we call a gut level—that misery and oppression and injustice will always be here, and that it is up to me to move on in spite of it. Light the candle instead of cursing the darkness. Now I get it. I finally get it.

The response from the group was immediate and affectionate. Hugs and kisses all around. Another reason why we take these trainings to other parts of the world.

Optional Training Format

A three-day course is preferable, with a review of EMDR one day, a review of EP the second, and the combination course the final day. Review of content is emphasized to correct deficiencies in a particular training group, and the combination course designed according to the trainees' interests. One group, for example, was composed mostly of alternative healers, including many sufferers of chronic pain. Another was dedicated to crisis intervention with victims of natural disasters.

GENERAL COMMENTS ABOUT INTERNATIONAL TRAINING

In almost every instance, we train internationally in response to a request for an EMDR program. EMDR seems to have greater credibility than EP, in large part because of its face validity (EMDR *looks* more like psychotherapy). In addition, certain funding groups appreciate the accountability that accrues from the scientific support that EMDR enjoys. We then introduce EP for any number of reasons, but mainly because our hosts eventually ask us to teach techniques that can be used by paraprofessionals, under emergency conditions, when time is limited, and as additional tools to reduce the severity of abreactions and dissociation.

Wherever we train we work with our sponsor and trainees to establish local resource teams. These groups function best when they are composed of persons who have credibility within their professional community, a history of community service, and the time available to nurture a new professional group. It is also desirable to seek linkage with university professors so that research can be conducted. In a spirit of solidarity, we continue to cotrain with these local teams even after they have become able to function on their own. It is essential to help these colleagues develop resources in their own languages and with attention to their own cultural context. Locally recorded videotape sessions to demonstrate the procedure, case studies relevant to local conditions, and economically reasonable training and supervision are a few of the considerations.

Our ultimate goal wherever we train is to identify the best among our trainees and invite them to join the international team, traveling with us as appropriate. They are selected for their strong clinical skills, organizational savvy, sense of service, and ability to get along with other team members. They become practicum facilitators, then equal partners with whom we cotrain. Eventually they will replace us.

Some of our trainees reside in indigenous communities that practice traditional shamanic healing; some have already studied other energy methods used for centuries in their countries; others endorse fairly conservative religious dogma. We are fairly convinced that differences among clients *within* a given group (a geographic region, a religious persuasion, a professional discipline) are much more salient than are differences *between* groups or cultures. This being said, we also recommend that those who work in other cultures do some preliminary research on the customs and mores of their hosts. One book we have found accurate and practical is *Kiss, Bow, or Shake Hands: How to Do Business in Sixty Countries*, by Morrison, Conaway, and Borden (1994).

Perhaps the best overall attitude for working in cultures other than one's own is that of a sensitive therapist: listen carefully, show respect, and above all, ask frequently for feedback from students. In one EMDR training, for example, I (J. H.) was talking in Spanish about being unable for the longest time to help a client during an abreaction.

When I noted, "I couldn't get him to stop," I was quite unwittingly using the colloquial phrase for "I couldn't get it up." The very proper trainees did their best to suppress their smiles but it was obvious that I had committed some *faux pas*. One of them eventually helped to clarify the error, to the great delight of the class. In one EP training in a Moslem country, the students said it did not sound right to tap the little finger meridian point while saying "I forgive You, God, for You always do what is best for me," because Allah never deserves one's anger, no matter how hypothetical; another student in that course joked that if one did try to forgive Allah for something, that person would immediately have to tap the index finger and seek forgiveness for oneself! We modified this affirmation, which students in other countries had recited with nary a protest. In a third setting, a woman volunteered to work in front of her training colleagues on memories of being a domestic abuse victim. After a successful EMDR session she asked for additional time to debrief her fear that her ex-husband, a member of the ruling military class in her country, might find out about her disclosure of his violence. She gave us permission to use the videotape of her session for training purposes, but only outside her own country. As a fourth example, we were told in one country that the position of the fingers in the Tapas acupressure pose (Fleming, 1999) was the signal of a local (and unpopular) political party. Finally, as occurred in the United States during the Vietnam War, controversies abound in countries where civil wars rage or are still recalled— Guatemala, Turkey, Lebanon, El Salvador—and we have found it particularly important to focus on the human suffering of war victims while taking great pains to avoid any appearance of taking sides.

Given these examples of cultural and regional sensitivities, it is remarkable how open our students are in trainings in widely dispersed venues. With some adjustment for beliefs and cognitions to make our techniques more easily endorsed in a given society (e.g., some people think it boastful to talk about oneself too positively, as in "I deeply accept myself") and with allowance for cultural differences in defining emotion, both the EMDR and the energy models seem widely acceptable in the different places we have taught.

The issue of language is particularly salient when working cross-culturally. Some languages simply do not have words to express EMDR and energy concepts. A back translation from the Mayan language of Quiche, for example, describes EMDR as follows: "When you have suffered from some hurt in the past, and you begin to move your eyes in a certain way, you can begin finally to feel better and to think better about the world and no longer feel so sad about what happened." There is not an easy way to express either "desensitization" or "reprocessing" in Quiche. The concept of "cognition," particularly positive or negative cognitions, is particularly unfathomable in certain cultures. The energy concepts generally are easier to translate and to understand. This may be because we limit our trainings mostly to meridian theory, and because in most of our energy seminars there are trainees who had already studied some other form of energy healing.

Whether using EMDR or EP, we encourage our clients to think, remember, and process in their language of origin as much as possible. The words first associated with an event are more powerful in eliciting emotion and sensation than are translations. The EMDR or EP therapist does not need to know exactly what the client is experiencing from moment to moment. Clients can then report what they experienced in the language of the therapist. One person who had been born in Brazil and was being treated by an English-speaking EMDR therapist reported the following experience: "It was more realistic to think through that memory in Portuguese. It was like I was actually there. When I first began to process in English, part of me was here translating for you. But English was not the language I used when I went through that event, so that made it harder, less real." Santiago-Rivera and Altarriba (2002) discussed the role of language representation and emotions and the implications for treatment with clients who speak both Spanish and English.

DIFFERENCES BETWEEN TRAINEES AND PATIENTS

Strengths and liabilities of typical clients are often heightened during training demonstrations, for better or for worse—but mostly for the better. Virtually all of the persons we treat in front of other trainees improve significantly, whereas not all of our clients improve at such a high rate. This requires trainers to dissuade trainees from assuming that all of their clients will also improve within a relatively short period of time (usually less than an hour during the trainings). This distinction offers an opportunity to talk about nonspecific effects in psychotherapy.

In an article written for psychologists about the process of becoming a patient, Perlman (2001) noted how persons who become psychotherapy patients are different from those who do not, even though many of the latter would probably benefit from doing so:

The act of becoming a patient, with its component parts of acknowl-
edging helplessness, admitting failure, and overcoming pride, can signal
a whole new way of looking at oneself. This opens the path to further
self-examination, self-disclosure, and self-confrontation, which may not
necessarily be a product of the psychologist's activity. (pp. 283–284)

Perlman then described how expectancy and placebo effects within
the therapy relationship, intention to change, self-fulfilling prophe-
cies, and expectations on all sides can effect therapeutic change.

While our premise is that therapeutic techniques are more powerful
than the therapy relationship, we believe the notions in this article
deserve attention. It may be that the issues Perlman mentioned are all
relevant with trainees who volunteer to be treated publicly—after all
it is quite a commitment to show one's flaws and foibles to this mini-
world in the hope that something new and positive is about to occur.
Add to these qualities a sense of drama and possible psychodrama
elements (since the volunteer will likely interact with many of the
other trainees subsequent to the training), and we have a potent formula for treatment expectancy, if not demand characteristics.

Sometimes a demonstration can be for the worse, for a trainee may
also bring in and exaggerate the negative qualities of being a client,
mainly issues of secondary gain such as (possibly unconscious) wishes
to prove the trainer a fraud, reluctance to disclose adequately, or a
belief that special attention comes only if one remains dramatically
damaged. The risk of failure under such conditions is valuable because
it will be accompanied by the opportunity for the trainer-therapist to
try out advanced treatment techniques, and to discuss with trainees
our attitudes about failure.

I (J. H.) once taught EP at a conference in Central America attended by psychotherapists from several different countries. The trainees were accomplished and confident, so I asked if we might compare
therapies by treating the same person with several techniques, until
one had an effect. We agreed to focus on a problem where treatment
changes could be observed, and settled again on the social phobia
called public speaking anxiety. The discussion that ensued was quite
stimulating, though only one of the trainees—Jorge, a friend and competent psychologist—was willing to work in front of the very large
group. He said he would use the phobia procedure from neurolinguistic programming (NLP) with a volunteer. A very quiet and very nervous woman then raised her hand and softly walked to the front.

Jorge began by asking the client about her previous efforts to eliminate her phobia. She surprised us by saying that she had already been in NLP treatment to no avail, but said she was willing to try it again. Jorge then did a nice job with the classical NLP phobia procedure, but the client remained nervous and would not so much as turn and face the group. She seemed, in fact, to become increasingly embarrassed that she was not being a successful client. I allowed more time than Jorge had requested, but we finally agreed to suspend the NLP part of the session. The EP procedure that followed was quite impactful within 10 minutes. The young woman got to a SUD score of one, then, at my invitation, began a little speech about herself. I finally had to interrupt her. "I can tell you're enjoying this, but I'm afraid it's time for a coffee break." The client: "Now that I'm finally able to talk, I'm going to take advantage of the opportunity to tell my story!" Participants laughed loudly, along with us.

But the point of this story is what to do with failures. After Jorge stopped doing NLP, he and I had a rich discussion with our audience about how the NLP procedure is often effective but, as is the case with all therapists and therapies, not always. We were later able to talk about how this would have taken a different focus if the EP procedure had not been useful to the client either. In all of these situations, having the client talk about her or his experience, whether it met expectations or not, can be especially enriching.

Chapter 11

Conclusion

The title of this chapter signals only the end of this book, not by any means the end of what will be said about EP and EMDR. Gallo entitled the final chapters of two of his books "Beginnings" (1999) and "The Future of Energy Psychology" (2000a). Gary Craig (personal communication, October 21, 1997) is fond of saying on his Internet list (see Appendix B), "We are all on the ground floor of a major healing high-rise and we need to learn from each other." This reflects the attitude of many of us who work not only with EP but also with EMDR. With all the advances that have been made, still we sense we are just feeling parts of the elephant, mistaking them for the whole, unable to explain our colleagues' different explanations for the parts they hold. Yet we are making progress, striving for an ultimate understanding of the animal.

Both methods are now backed by growing international associations staffed by enthusiastic, dedicated people. These groups are well organized with solid finances and are promoting the ethical use of the methods. They sponsor annual meetings that attract a growing number of participants to a variety of presentations displaying not only improvements in current theory and technique but also innovations that show neither method has yet found its boundaries. It is safe to say that EMDR and EP are here to stay.

COMMENTS ON TREATMENT AND RESEARCH

EP

Lambrou and Pratt (2000) predicted that by the year 2010, EP fundamentals will have become incorporated into many therapies and will have become standard treatment in health care, business consultation, athletics, coaching, and in the teaching profession. We cannot disagree given that we have seen growing applications in these situations in our own work.

There is a danger, however, in promoting EP too quickly. On the one hand, we do not wait for empirical research findings before trying out additional EP applications, and find the experimental attitude of the EP community to be refreshing. On the other we are cautious in promising impressive benefits before we have at least clinical assurance that we can deliver. EP practitioners too often use the word *cure*, when what is described is no more than relief from symptoms. EP research is particularly absent of peer-reviewed follow-up and maintenance data, and the data we do have simply do not allow us to say if the positive effects from an EP intervention will last or if they are temporary respites. Some of the studies we cited clearly caution against believing too much in the enduring effects of EP work. Unless and until research documents the stability of EP treatment, we will earn more respect from other professionals if we make more modest claims about the efficacy of EP methods. We also believe that there is growing interest in research: while some of the EP originators ignored and even discredited empirical investigation, as if their results were self-evident, more recent practitioners have begun to do their own clinical research (as evidenced in several studies in Chapter 2).

The relatively low quality of EP research can be related to two factors that are simultaneously causes and effects of this situation. First, traditional university campuses seem to eschew EP as a research topic. Of the 12 studies on EP we cited in Chapter 2, none was carried out on a university campus known for its scientific leadership. Furthermore, many of the studies were funded by the investigators themselves. This is not to say that nothing is being done on university campuses or in scientific laboratories, only that the EP field has been largely ignored.

Related to this is the second factor, that being the breach between scholar and practitioner, which we discuss below.

EMDR

Owing mostly to Shapiro's unrelenting insistence on good studies, EMDR has succeeded in building a firm base. But trainings in EMDR were popular before the research was in, and the reason was that clinicians were getting results considerably better than what they had experienced before, and they were telling their colleagues. While research can validate clinical experience, most therapies began in the clinic, not in the laboratory.

THE SCIENTIST–PRACTITIONER RIFT

In spite of efforts to promote a scientist-practitioner or academician-clinician model in psychotherapy, the fact is that the standards for academic research do not overlap easily with those respected by clinicians. At least some of the controversy apparent in Chapter 2 reflects this conflict.

Clinicians may find laboratory-confined, variable-controlled, random-assignment research to be interesting but not practical. First, in the reality of clinical work clients are not assigned to a particular treatment protocol but rather choose their own therapist. Second, the rigidity of academic science, while necessary to tease out specific components that make a therapy effective and that allow for comparison between therapies, does not hold much interest for a clinician who would grow bored repeating a prescribed method day after day according to the dictates of a clinical manual. Clinicians follow their career partly to be helpful, partly to make a living, and partly to be creative. This assumes some allowance for flexing, modifying, innovating—taking a working method and then changing it to see if it might work even better, or might allow for new applications, or might simply allow the work to feel novel and evolutionary.

The disputes between scientists and practitioners can become quite heated, as in the October 2001 issue of the *Journal of Clinical Psychology* cited in Chapter 2. In one fell swoop, Richard McNally of Harvard University took both EMDR and EP to task. Regarding the form of EP called thought field therapy (TFT), he (2001) wrote:

> TFT therapists . . . continue to tell their patients how to tap and hum their troubles away. Baffled by their faith, I am reminded of Tertullian,

the Early Church Father who famously proclaimed, "I believe because it is absurd." (p. 1173)

On the same page McNally wrote about EMDR:

EMDR is the most thoroughly studied psychotherapy for PTSD. However, despite repeated attempts, researchers have been unable to provide any convincing evidence that its novel, defining element—eye movement—enhances the effectiveness of traditional imaginal exposure . . . . Hence what is effective in EMDR is not new, and what is new is not effective.

EP clinicians might well object to the accusation that what they are doing is based on faith alone, and EMDR practitioners might well wonder how one can read all of the EMDR research (see Chapter 2) and still believe that EMDR is no more effective than exposure therapy. The larger point is that until the academic-scientific and clinical communities can communicate, the future growth of both EP and EMDR will be hampered.

In the same issue of the journal, Lohr (2001) criticized the study by Sakai and colleagues (2001) (of TFT in an HMO setting) because the researchers tested TFT in an applied setting before going through the earlier steps of carefully controlled, restrictive research endorsed by academic researchers. Lohr further wrote:

Treatments that purport to be novel or extraordinary must be accompanied by extraordinary evidence. The nature of the "evidence" must not be based on clinical testimony, on vivid case studies, or on numerous clinical applications. . . . The evidence should rest upon strong experimental tests using control conditions that can identify the effects of procedural artifacts and nonspecific factors that are common to various social influence processes. (p. 1233)

Here we see another example of the gap between academicians and clinicians. We support the need for controlled studies and agree that the promotion of EP methods outstrips the available scientific evidence. However, this is not the only kind of evidence that guides people. For example, it is difficult for us to imagine a clinician waiting for scientific evidence before trying a novel treatment purported to reduce human suffering. The "evidence" that accrues from vivid and numerous case studies is probably more moving for an applied practitioner than are statistical effect sizes.

The experiential context of field clinicians and academic researchers (i.e., the world in which we live and work) may be part of the problem that makes it so difficult for communication to occur between persons with such different perspectives on psychotherapy. For example, in the study on the use of TFT in treating Kosovo trauma victims, Johnson and colleagues (2001) spoke of five separate trips to the site where atrocities had been committed for a total of 10 weeks, during which they linked up with physicians already in the area "whose positive reputation among the people made it possible to access patients in the remote villages that had been totally destroyed in the war" (p. 1238). These physicians used their own knowledge of the population to determine who was most in need of outside assistance, and referred them for treatment. The atrocities, by the way, had taken place the previous year, and those referred were still considered to be traumatized. The authors then spoke of the horrible suffering of the survivors who had been gang raped, had witnessed the slaughter of their spouses and children, and had faced the possibility of death themselves. Taboos ruled out the possibility of using the word *trauma*, so the therapists listened to whether their patients used negative or positive emotions to talk about their traumas to determine the level of suffering. In addition to relying on self-reports before and after treatment, the authors described other signs that the treatment was successful, including

> their spontaneous expressions providing confirming clues. People gave that look of astonishment, hugged, put their palms to their temples, and looked up to the heavens in gratitude—looked up from the very yards, outside the homes, where family members had fallen to a firing squad. Also, it was typical for them to feel great energy, then disappear long enough to return with a bag full of peaches or nuts. (p. 1239)

These reports remind us of ones we have heard, and we would tend to believe their reports and expressions of suffering. We also accept what they say and demonstrate after their healing, and if they have been obviously suffering for a year or more before we treat them, we attribute their reports of healing to the treatment they have just received.

We now quote Rosner (2001) who reviewed the article by Johnson and colleagues from the point of view of a careful scientist writing in a peer-reviewed psychotherapy research journal. Rosner depicted her fantasy of what might actually have taken place in those Kosovo villages:

> Important people from the main city, accompanied by doctors from afar, come to remote villages. The villagers are treated with a treatment that they do not understand. The healers provide unknown and strange procedures, and these procedures look, therefore, even more magical. The treatment happens in the presence of half of the village inhabitants.
>
> A scenario like the one depicted would trigger expectancy effects and make it almost impossible for the person to say the treatment was not really helpful. (p. 1243)

Two very different perceptions of the same event, each viewer perhaps feeling a different part of the elephant. A solution might be for more clinicians to befriend university professors and to visit laboratories; and for more academicians to accompany clinicians into the field to view the relieving of symptoms. The ultimate goal of us all—applying knowledge and skill in the service of healing human suffering and promoting human welfare—may eventually bring us together.

THE FUTURE OF INTERNATIONAL TRAINING

EMDR is enjoying the kind of scientific credibility that makes it marketable around the world, but so far it has been confined to professionals. Since we cannot expect to meet human needs if trainings are confined to professionals, we laud recent efforts to adapt the EMDR model. Of course, with the greater risk involved, greater precautions, follow-up, and supervision will be necessary. We trust that we have made our own modest contribution with our suggestions in Chapter 4. This approach to training paraprofessionals is consistent with the value of international organizations, so funding for pilot projects should be readily available.

EP is immediately appropriate for nonprofessional training but does not have the face or scientific validity necessary to provide it with credibility and recognition. The emphasis here needs to be on more, and more careful, research.

The bottom line is that we believe we are now providing more help to more clients than ever before. A judicious combination of EP and EMDR provides effective treatment of human suffering in a wide range of settings. It is very rewarding, and we have become reenergized in what Norcross (2000) said is "often a grueling and demanding calling" (p. 710). We believe we are now able to help people as we had hoped we would when our pilgrimage led us to graduate school. We hope the present work will help and encourage those who accompany us on similar paths around the world.

References

American Psychiatric Association. (2000). *Diagnostic and statistical manual of mental disorders* (4th ed., text revision). Washington, DC: Author.

American Psychological Association. (1992). Ethical principles of psychologists and code of conduct. *American Psychologist, 47,* 1597–1611.

Artigas, L. A., Jarero, I., Mauer, M., Lopez Cano, T., & Alcal, N. (2000, September). EMDR integrated treatment protocol and the butterfly hug. Poster presented at the EMDRIA Conference, Toronto, ON, Canada.

Baker, B. L., Cohen, D. C., & Saunders, J. T. (1973). Self-directed desensitization for acrophobia. *Behaviour Research and Therapy, 11,* 79–89.

Bandler, R., & Grinder, J. (1979). *Frogs into princes.* Moab, UT: Real People Press.

Bassett, C. A. L. (1995). Bioelectromagnetics in the service of medicine. In M. Blank (Ed.), *Electromagnetic fields: Biological interactions and mechanisms* (pp. 261–275). *Advances in Chemistry Series 250.* Washington, DC: American Chemical Society.

Bassett, C. A. L., Mitchell, S. N., & Gaston, S. R. (1982). Pulsing electromagnetic field treatment in ununited fractures and failed arthrodeses. *Journal of the American Medical Association, 247,* 623–628.

Baule, G. M., & McFee, R. (1963). Detection of the magnetic field of the heart. *American Heart Journal, 66,* 95–96.

Becker, R. O. (1990). *Cross currents.* New York. Putnam.

Becker, R. O., & Seldon, G. (1985). *The body electric.* New York: Morrow.

Benor, D. J. (2001). *WHEE (wholistic hybrid of EMDR and EFT)* [On-line]. Available at: http://www.emofree.com/benor.htm

Berne, E. (1972). *What do you say after you say hello?* New York: Grove Press.

Beutler, L. E. (2000). David and Goliath: When empirical and clinical standards of practice meet. *American Psychologist, 55,* 997–1007.

Beutler, L. E. (2001). Editor's introduction. *Journal of Clinical Psychology, 57,* 1149–1151.

Beutler, L. E., & Harwood, T. M. (2001). Antiscientific attitudes: What happens when scientists are unscientific? *Journal of Clinical Psychology, 57,* 43–51.

Boèl, J. (1999). The butterfly hug. *EMDRIA Newsletter, 4*(4), 11–13.

Brady, J. L., Healy, F. L., Norcross, J. C., & Guy, J. D. (1995). Stress in counselors: An integrative research review. In W. Dryden (Ed.), *Stress in counselling in action* (pp.1–27). Newbury Park, CA: Sage.

Brady, K., Pearlstein, T., Asnis, G., Baker, D., Rothbaum, B., Sikes, C., & Farfel, G. (2000). Efficacy and safety of sertraline treatment of posttraumatic stress disorder: A randomized controlled trial. *Journal of the American Medical Association, 283,* 1837–1844.

Brighton, D. T., Black, J., Friedenberg, Z. B., Esterhai, J. L., & Connolly, J. F. (1981). A multicenter study of the treatment of non-union with constant direct current. *Journal of Bone and Joint Surgery (America)*, 63A, 1–3.

Britt, V., Diepold, J., Jr., & Bender, S. (1998). *Thought field therapy: A comprehensive workshop*. Montclair, NJ: Authors.

Cahill, S. P., Carrigan, M. H., & Freuh, B. C. (1999). Does EMDR work? And if so, why? A critical review of controlled outcome and dismantling research. *Journal of Anxiety Disorders*, 13, 5–33.

Callahan, R. J. (1985). *Five minute phobia cure*. Wilmington, DE: Enterprise.

Callahan, R. J. (1987a). *Stop smoking now!* Indian Wells, CA: Callahan Techniques.

Callahan, R. J. (1987b, winter). *Successful treatment of phobias and anxiety by telephone and radio*. Shawnee Mission, KS: Collected Papers of International College of Applied Kinesiology.

Callahan, R. J. (with Trubo, R.). (2001). *Tapping the healer within*. Lincolnwood (Chicago), IL: Contemporary Books.

Callahan, R. J. & Callahan, J. (1996). *Thought field therapy and trauma: Treatment and theory*. Indian Wells, CA: Thought Field Therapy Training Center.

Callahan, R., J. & Perry, P. (1991). *Why do I eat when I'm not hungry?* New York: Doubleday.

Carbonell, J. (1996). An experimental study of TFT and acrophobia. *The Thought Field*, 2(3), 1 & 6.

Carbonell, J., & Figley, C. R. (1999). A systematic clinical demonstration of promising PTSD treatment approaches. prevention and treatment. *Traumatology* [On-line], 5(1), Article 4. Available at: http://www.fsu.edu/~trauma/promising.html

Carlson, E., & Putnam, F. (1992). *Manual for the dissociative experiences scale*. Lutherville, MD: Sidran Foundation. Available at: http://www.sidran.org/des.html

Carrington, P. (1999, January). The use of energy chords for stress reduction. Paper presented at the winter Brain-Mind Conference, Palm Springs, CA.

Carrington, P. (2001, May). Annual energy psychology research update. Presentation at the third annual International Comprehensive Energy Psychology Conference, San Diego, CA.

Carrington, P., & Craig, G. (2000). Emotional freedom technique (EFT): A meridian based intervention for trauma. *Bridges (the ISSSEEM Magazine)* 11, 10–12.

Chambless, D. L., Baker, M. J., Baucom, B. H., Beutler, L. E., Calhoun, K. S., Crits-Christoph, P., Daiuto, A., DeRubeis, T., Detweiler, J., Haaga, D. A. F., Bennett Johnson, S., McCurry, S., Mueser, K. T., Pope, K. S., Sanderson, W. C., Shoham, V., Stickle, T., Williams, D. A., & Woody, S. R. (1998). Update on empirically validated therapies II. *Clinical Psychologist*, 51, 3–15.

Chemtob, C. M., Tolin, D. F., van der Kolk, B. A., & Pitman, R. K. (2000). Eye movement desensitization and reprocessing. In E. Foa, T. Keane, & M. Friedman (Eds.), *Effective treatments for PTSD: Practice guidelines from the International Society for Traumatic Stress Studies* (pp. 139–155) New York: Guilford Press.

Cho, Z. H. (1998). New findings of the correlation acupoints and the corresponding brain cortices using functional MRI. *Proceedings of national academy of sciences*, 95, 2670–2673.

Clevenger, T., Jr,. & Halvorson, S. K. (1992). *Converting the PRCA-State Version 2 to the Speaker Anxiety Scale*. Unpublished manuscript, Florida State University, Department of Communication, Tallahassee.

Clinton, A. N. (2001a). *Seemorg matrix work Level 1 manual* (3rd ed). Princeton, NJ: Energy Revolution.

Clinton, A. N. (2001b). *Seemorg matrix work Level 2 manual* (3rd ed). Princeton, NJ: Energy Revolution.

Clinton, A. N. (2001c). *Seemorg matrix work Level 3–5 manual* (3rd ed). Princeton, NJ: Energy Revolution.

Clinton, A. N. (2002). Seemorg matrix work. In F. Gallo (Ed.), *Energy psychology in psychotherapy: A comprehensive source book.* New York: Norton.

Cohn, L. (1993). Art psychotherapy and the new eye treatment desensitization and reprocessing (EMD/R) method: An integrated approach. In E. Dishup (Ed.), *California art therapy trends* (pp. 469–534). Chicago, IL: Magnolia Street.

Craig, G. (1998). *Steps toward becoming the ultimate therapist.* Sea Ranch, CA: Author.

Craig, G. (1999). *Emotional freedom techniques: The manual* (3rd ed). Sea Ranch, CA: Author. Also available on-line at: http://www.emofree.com/downloadEFTmanual.htm

Craig, G. (n.d.). About voice technology [On-line]. Available at: http://www.emofree.com/about.htm

Cummings, N. A. (1999). Comment on L'Abate: Psychotherapist future shock. *Family Journal: Counseling and Therapy for Couples and Families, 7,* 221–223.

Darby, D. (2001). *The efficacy of thought field therapy as a treatment modality for individuals diagnosed with blood-injection-injury phobia.* Unpublished doctoral dissertation, Minneapolis, MN: Walden University.

Dennison, P. E., & Dennison, G. (1989). *Brain gym handbook.* Ventura, CA: Educational Kinesiology Foundation.

Derogatis, L. R. (1992). *SCL-90: Administration, scoring and procedures manual.* Baltimore, MD: Clinical Psychometric Research.

Devilly, G. J., & Spence, S. H. (1999). The relative efficacy and treatment distress of EMDR and a cognitive-behavior trauma treatment protocol in the amelioration of posttraumatic stress disorder. *Journal of Anxiety Disorders, 13,* 131–157.

Diamond, J. (1979). *Your body doesn't lie* (Original title: *BK behavioral kinesiology*). New York: Warner.

Diamond, J. (1985). *Life energy.* New York: Dodd, Mead.

Diamond, J. (1988). *Life energy analysis: A way to cantillation.* Valley Cottage, NY: Archaeus.

Diener, D. (2001). A pilot study of the effect of chakra connection and magnetic unruffling on the perception of pain in people with fibromyalgia. *Healing Touch Newsletter, 1,* 7–8.

Diepold, J. H., Jr. (2000). Touch and breathe: An alternative treatment approach with meridian based psychotherapies. *Traumatology, 6,* 109–118. Also available at: *Electronic Journal of Traumatology, 6*(2): http://www.fsu.edu/~trauma/v6i2/centv6i2.html.

Dossey, J. (1993). *Healing words: The power of prayer and the practice of medicine.* San Francisco, CA: Harper.

Durlacher, J. (1994). *Freedom from fear forever.* Tempe, AZ: Van Ness.

Eden, D. (with Feinstein, D.). (1998). *Energy medicine.* New York: Jeremy P. Tarcher/Penguin Putnam.

Eden, D., & Feinstein, D. (2002). Energy medicine for energy psychology practitioners. Post-conference workshop presented at the fourth annual International Energy Psychology Conference, Litchfield Park, AZ.

Ehlers, A. (1999). *Posttraumatische Belastungsstörung.* Göttingen, Germany: Hogrefe.

EMDR Institute. (2001). 2001 *EMDR July-December Level I training schedule.* Pacific Grove, CA: Author.

Farrelly, F. (1989). *Provocative therapy.* Cupertino, CA: Meta.

Figley, C. R., & Carbonell, J. (1995, August). The active ingredient project: Preliminary findings. Paper presented at the annual conference of the American Psychological Association, New York.

Fisher, B., & Shelton, D. (2000, September). Enhanced EMDR treatment with domestic violence offenders. Paper presented at the annual EMDRIA conference, Toronto, Canada.

Fleming, T. (1999). *You can heal now: The Tapas acupressure technique (TAT).* Redondo Beach, CA: TAT International.

Fleming, T. (2001a, May). Tapas acupressure technique (TAT). Presentation at the third annual Comprehensive Energy Psychology conference, San Diego, CA.

Fleming, T. (2001b, October). Material presented in the Train the Trainer Course. Redondo Beach, CA.

Forte, K. (1999). Group EMDR therapy in young children. *EMDRIA Newsletter,* 4(3), 20–22.

Foster, S., & Lendl, J. (1996). Eye movement desensitization and reprocessing: Four case studies of a new tool for executive coaching and restoring employee performance after setbacks. *Consulting Psychology Journal: Practice and Research, 48,* 155–161.

Fröhlich, H. (1968). Bose condensation of strongly excited longitudinal electric modes. *Physics Letters, 26A,* 402–403.

Gallo, F. (1999). *Energy psychology: Explorations at the interface of energy, cognition, behavior, and health.* Boca Raton, FL: CRC Press.

Gallo, F. (2000a). *Energy diagnostic and treatment methods.* New York: Norton.

Gallo, F. (2000b). *Energy diagnostic and treatment methods training manuals I–IV.* Heritage, PA: Author.

Gallo, F. (2001, May). Getting on the same page: The big picture. Presentation at the third annual Comprehensive Energy Psychology conference, San Diego, CA.

Gallo, F. P., & Vincenzi, H. (2000). *Energy tapping.* Oakland, CA: New Harbinger.

Galvin, M. (1995). Generalization of treatment effects. *The Thought Field. 1*(2), 2 & 4.

Galvin, M., & Hartung, J. (2001). *Manual of meridian-based psychotherapies.* Colorado Springs, CO: Authors.

Gerbode, F. (1989). *Beyond psychology: An introduction to metapsychology.* Palo Alto, CA: IRM Press.

Gilson, G., & Kaplan, S. (2000). *The therapeutic interweave in EMDR: Before and beyond. A manual for EMDR trained clinicians.* Tarzana, CA: Authors.

Gismondi, M. (2000). Energy medicine in a new key: Influencing the neuropathways of trauma via "neuro-active" psychotherapy techniques. *Bridges (the ISSSEEM Magazine), 11,* 8–11.

Glang, C., & Penner, C. (1996, June). Integrating EMDR with marital and family therapy. Paper presented at the annual EMDRIA conference, Denver, CO.

Gorman, W. (2001). Refugee survivors of torture: Trauma and treatment. *Professional Psychology: Research and Practice, 32,* 443–451.

Goulding, R., & Goulding, M. (1997). *Changing lives through redecision therapy.* New York: Grove Press.

Grand, D. (1996). Integrating EMDR into the psychodynamic process. *EMDRIA Newsletter, 1,* 16.

Greenwald, H. (1989). *Direct decision therapy.* Capitola, CA: Meta.

Greenwald, R. (1999). *Eye movement desensitization and reprocessing (EMDR) in child and adolescent psychotherapy.* Northvale, NJ: Jason Aronson Press.

Greenwald, R. (2001, December). Celia's capsule and Robin's two hands. *EMDRIA Newsletter* (Special Edition) 18–20.

Gross, L., & Ratner, H. (2002). Use of hypnosis and EMDR combined with energy therapies in the treatment of phobias and dissociative, posttraumatic stress and eating disorders. In F. Gallo (Ed.), *Energy psychology in psychotherapy* (pp. 219–231). New York: Norton.

Grudermeyer, D., & Grudermeyer, R. (2002). *The energy psychology desktop companion* (2d ed). Del Mar, CA: Willingness Works.

Handlesman, M., & Galvin, M. (1988). Facilitating informed consent for outpatient psychotherapy: A suggested written format. *Professional Psychology: Research and Practice, 19*(2), 223–225.

Hartung, J., & Galvin, M. (2002). Combining energy psychology and EMDR. In F. Gallo (Ed.) *Energy psychology in psychotherapy* (pp. 179–197). New York: Norton.

Hartung, J., & Philbrick, P. (1997). *EMDR in the treatment of offenders: A guide for those who work with traumatized, addictive, dissociative and personality-disordered offenders.* Colorado Springs, CO: Comcor.

Herbert, J. D., & Gaudiano, B. A. (2001). The search for the holy grail: Heart rate variability and thought field therapy. *Journal of Clinical Psychology, 57,* 1207–1214.

Hover-Kramer, D. (2002). Incorporating chakra and biofield concepts into energy psychotherapy. In F. Gallo (Ed.). *Energy psychology in psychotherapy* (pp. 135–151). New York: Norton

Ironson, G., Freund, B., Strauss, J., & Williams, J. (2002). Comparison of two treatments for traumatic stress: A community-based study of EMDR and prolonged exposure. *Journal of Clinical Psychology, 58,* 133–128.

James, M., & Jongeward, D. (1971). *Born to win.* Reading, MA: Addison-Wesley.

Jarero, I., Artigas, L., Maurer, M., Lopez Cano, T., & Alcala, N. (1999, November). Children's post traumatic stress after natural disasters: Integrative treatment protocols. Poster presented at the annual meeting of the International Society for Traumatic Stress Studies, Miami, FL.

Jarero, I. (1999). *El abrazo de la mariposa.* Available at: http://www.amamecrisis.com.mx/articulo/06_apendice_c.htm.

Jensen, J. A. (1994). An investigation of eye movement desensitization and reprocessing (EMD/R) as a treatment for posttraumatic stress disorder (PTSD) symptoms of Vietnam combat veterans. *Behavior Therapy, 25,* 311–325.

Johnson, C., Shala, M., Sejdijaj, X., Odell, R., & Dabishevci, K. (2001). Thought field therapy—soothing the bad moments of Kosovo. *Journal of Clinical Psychology, 57,* 1237–1240.

Kaplan, S., & Van Ommeren, M. (2001). A model for training in low income countries: Nepal. *EMDRIA Newsletter, 6*(2), 4.

Kendall, H. O., & Kendall, F. M. P. (1949). *Muscles—testing and function.* Baltimore, MD: Williams & Wilkins.

Kessler, R. C., Sonnega, A., Bromet, E., Hughes, M., & Nelson, C. B. (1995).

Posttraumatic stress disorder in the national comorbidity survey. *Archives of General Psychiatry, 52,* 1048–1060.

Kluft, R., & Fine, C. (1993). *Clinical perspectives on multiple personality disorder.* Washington, DC: American Psychiatric Press.

Knipe, J. (1997). Identifying hidden blocking beliefs. *EMDRIA Newsletter, 2*(6), 10–11.

Korkmazlar, Ü, & Pamuk, Ş. (2000, October). Group EMDR with child survivors of earthquake in Turkey. Paper presented at EMDR clinical applications with children: A cost-effective treatment tool, Westminster, England.

Korn, D. L., & Leeds, A. M. (2002). Preliminary evidence of efficacy for EMDR resource development and installation in the stabilization phase of treatment of complex posttraumatic stress disorder. *Journal of Clinical Psychology, 58*(12), 1–23.

Lambert, M. L., Okiishi, J. C., Finch, A. E., & Johnson, L. D. (1998). Outcome assessment: from conceptualization to implementation. *Professional Psychology: Research and Practice, 29,* 63–70.

Lambrou, P., & Pratt, G. (2000). *Instant emotional healing: Acupressure for the emotions.* New York: Broadway Books.

Lane, J. (2001, May). EMDR and EP. Presentation at the third annual international Comprehensive Energy Psychology conference, San Diego, CA.

Lawrence, M. (1998). EMDR as a special form of ego state psychotherapy. *EMDRIA Newsletter, 3*(4), 7, 13–15, 24–25.

Lazarus, A. (1989). *The practice of multimodal therapy.* New York: McGraw-Hill.

Lazarus, A. (1998). Practicing psychotherapy briefly without cutting corners. Keynote address for the Brief Therapy conference, New York. (Available on audiotape through the Milton H. Erickson Foundation, Inc., Phoenix, AZ.)

Leeds, A. M. (1998). Lifting the burden of shame: Using EMDR resource installation to resolve a therapeutic impasse. In P. Manfield (Ed.), *Extending EMDR: A casebook of innovative applications* (pp. 256–281). New York: Norton.

Leeds, A. M., & Shapiro, F. (2000). EMDR and resource installation: Principles and procedures for enhancing current functioning and resolving traumatic experiences. In J. Carlson & L. Sperry (Eds.), *Brief therapy strategies with individuals and couples* (pp. 469–534). Phoenix, AZ: Zeig/Tucker.

Leonoff, G. (1996). Successful treatment of phobias and anxiety by telephone and radio: A preliminary report on a replication of Callahan's 1987 study. *The Thought Field, 2*(1), 3–4.

Levin, P., Lazrove, S., & van der Kolk, B. (1999). What psychological testing and neuroimaging tell us about the treatment of posttraumatic stress disorder by eye movement desensitization and reprocessing. *Journal of Anxiety Disorders, 13,* 159–172.

Lipke, H. (1999). *Response to Herbert, Lilienfeld, Lohr, Montgomery, O'Donohue, Rosen & Tolin.* Unpublished manuscript.

Lohr, J. M. (2001). Sakai et al. is not an adequate demonstration of TFT effectiveness. *Journal of Clinical Psychology, 57,* 1229–1233.

Lohr, J. M., Lilienfeld, S. O., Tolin, D. F., & Herbert, J. D. (1999). Eye movement desensitization and reprocessing: an analysis of specific versus nonspecific treatment factors. *Journal of Anxiety Disorders, 13,* 185–207.

Lombardo, M. M., & Eichinger, R.W. (2000). *For your improvement: A development and coaching guide for learners, supervisors, managers, mentors, and feedback givers* (3rd ed). Minneapolis, MN: Lominger.

Lovett, J. (1999). *Small wonders: Healing childhood trauma with EMDR*. New York: Free Press.

Manfield, P. (1998) *Extending EMDR: A casebook of innovative applications*. New York: Norton.

Marcus, S. V., Marquis, P., & Sakai, C. (1997). Controlled study of treatment of PTSD using EMDR in an JHMP setting. *Psychotherapy, 34,* 307–315.

Marzano, R. J., & Marzano, J. S. (2001). *A meta-analysis of the effects of EMDR on specific dependent measures.* Unpublished manuscript.

Maxfield, L., & Hyer, L. (2002). The relationship between efficacy and methodology in studies investigating EMDR treatment of PTSD. *Journal of Clinical Psychology, 58,* 23–41.

McCroskey, J. C. (1970). Measures of communication-bound anxiety. *Speech Monographs, 37,* 269–277.

McNally, R. J. (1999). Research on eye movement desensitization and reprocessing (EMDR) as a treatment for PTSD. *PTSD Research Quarterly, 10*(1), 1–7.

McNally, R. J. (2001). Tertullian's motto and Callahan's method. *Journal of Clinical Psychology, 57,* 1171–1174.

Mentgen, J., & Bulbrook, M. J. (1996). *Healing touch Level 1 notebook* (2d ed.). Carrboro, NC: North Carolina Center for Healing Touch.

Mentgen, J., & Bulbrook, M. J. (2001). *Healing touch level 2 notebook.* (3d ed.). Carrboro: North Carolina Center for Healing Touch.

Millon, T. (1977). *Millon Clinical Multiaxial Inventory, manual,* Minneapolis: National Computer Systems.

Millon, T. (1981). *Disorders of Personality: DSM-III; Axis II.* New York: Wiley-Interscience.

Modena, I., Ricci, G. B., Barbanera, S., Leoni, R., Romani, G. L., & Carelli, P. (2001). Biomagnetic measurements of spontaneous brain activity in epileptic patients. *Electroencephalography and Clinical Neurophysiology, 54,* 622–628.

Monti, D. A., Sinnott, D. C., Marchese, M., Kunkel, E. J. S., & Greeson, J. M. (1999). Muscle test comparisons of congruent and incongruent self-referential statements. *Perceptual and Motor Skills, 88,* 1019–1028.

Morrison, T., Conaway, W. A., & Borden, G. A. (1994). *Kiss, bow or shake hands: How to do business in sixty countries.* Holbrook, MA: Bob Adams.

Muris, P., & Merckelbach, H. (1999). Traumatic memories, eye movements, phobia, and panic: A critical note on the proliferation of EMDR. *Journal of Anxiety Disorders, 13*(1–2), 209–223.

Nambudripad D. S. (1993). *Say goodbye to illness.* Buena Park, CA: Delta.

Nicosia, G. (1997). Integrating the power therapies: TFT & EMDR. *Thought Energy Synchronization Therapies Network Newsletter, 1*(1), 2–3.

Nicosia, G. (1999). *Test Dx: Thought energy diagnostic and treatment procedures (manual for thought energy synchronization therapy training).* Pittsburgh, PA: Author.

Nims, L. (1998). *Be set free fast: Training manual.* Orange, CA: Author.

Nims, L. (2001). *Be set free fast: Training manual.* Orange, CA: Author.

Nims, L. (2002). Be set free fast: Power in your subconscious mind will set you free. Paper presented at the fourth annual International Energy Psychology conference, Litchfield Park, AZ.

Norcross, J. C. (2000). Psychotherapist self-care: Practitioner-tested, research-informed strategies. *Professional Psychology: Research and Practice, 31*(6), 710–713.

O'Hanlon, W., & Weiner-Davis, M. (1989). *In search of solutions: A new direction in psychotherapy.* New York: Norton.

Omaha, J. (1998, July). Chemotion and EMDR. An EMDR treatment protocol based upon a psychodynamic model for chemical dependency. Paper presented at the annual meeting of the EMDRIA, Baltimore, MD.

Oschman, J. L. (2000). *Energy medicine: The scientific basis.* Edinburgh, U.K.: Churchill Livingstone.

Pallesen, S., Nordhuis, I. H., Havik, O., & Nielson, G. H. (2001). Clinical assessment and treatment of insomnia. *Professional Psychology: Research and Practice, 32,* 115–124.

Pavek, R. (2001). The tribulations of a trial: Proving the biofield exists. *Healing Touch Newsletter, 1*(3), 4–5.

Pavlov, I. P. (1941). *Conditioned reflexes and psychiatry* (W. H. Gantt, Trans.). New York: International.

Perkins, B., & Rouanzoin, C. (2002). A critical evaluation of current views regarding eye movement desensitization and reprocessing (EMDR): Clarifying points of confusion. *Journal of Clinical Psychology, 58,* 77–97.

Perlman, L. M. (2001). Nonspecific, unintended, and serendipitous effects in psychotherapy. *Professional Psychology: Research and Practice, 32*(3), 283–288.

Pert, C. (1999). *Molecules of emotion: Why you feel the way you feel.* New York: Simon & Schuster.

Pert, C. (2000). *Study guide to your body is your subconscious mind* (two audiocassettes). Boulder, CO: Sounds True.

Phillips, M. (2000). *Finding the energy to heal.* New York: Norton.

Pignotti, M., & Steinberg, M. (2001). Heart rate variability as an outcome measure for thought field therapy in clinical practice. *Journal of Clinical Psychology, 57,* 1193–1206.

Pitman, R. K., Altman, B., Greenwald, E., Longpre, R. E., Macklin, M. L., Poire, R. E., & Steketee, G. D. (1991). Psychiatric complications during flooding therapy for posttraumatic stress disorder. *Journal of Clinical Psychiatry, 52,* 17–20.

Popky, A. J. (1999) *DeTUR (desensitization of triggers and urge reprocessing), a new approach to working with addictions* [On-line]. Available at http://www.emdrportal.com/clinical_applications_notes/DeTUR.htm

Pulos, L. (1999). Thought field therapy: Clearing emotional circuitry. *Shared Vision Magazine,* May, 36–37.

Richards, D. A., Lovell, K., & Marks, I. M. (1994). Post-traumatic stress disorder: evaluation of a behavioral treatment program. *Journal of Traumatic Stress, 7,* 669–680.

Rosen, G. M. (1999). Treatment fidelity and research on eye movement desensitization and reprocessing (EMDR). *Journal of Anxiety Disorders, 13*(1–2), 173–184.

Rosner, R. (2001). Between search and research: How to find your way around? Review of the article "Thought field therapy—Soothing the bad moments of Kosovo." *Journal of Clinical Psychology, 57,* 1241–1244.

Sakai, C., Paperny, D., Mathews, M., Tanida, G., Boyd, G., Simons, A., Yamamoto, C., Mau, C., & Nutter, L. (2001). Thought field therapy clinical application: Utilization in an HMO in behavioral medicine and behavioral health services. *Journal of Clinical Psychology, 57,* 1215–1227.

Sandmeier, M., & Cooper, G. (2000, September/October). Telling it like it is: Be prepared to back up your therapeutic claims. *Networker,* 13–18.

Santiago-Rivera, A. L., & Altarriba, J. (2002). The role of language in therapy with the Spanish-English bilingual client. *Professional Psychology: Research and Practice,* 33, 30–38.

Schoninger, B. (2001). *TFT in the treatment of speaking anxiety.* Ph.D. diss., Union Institute, Cincinnati, OH. Manuscript in preparation.

Seto, A., Kusaka, C., Nakazato, S., Huang, W. R., Sato, T., Hisamitsu, T., & Takeshige C. (1992). Detection of extraordinary large bio-magnetic field strength from human hand. *Acupuncture and Electro-Therapeutics Research; The International Journal,* 17, 75–94.

Shapiro, F. (1989). Efficacy of the eye movement desensitization procedure in the treatment of traumatic memories. *Journal of Traumatic Stress,* 2, 199–223.

Shapiro, F. (1995). *Eye movement desensitization and reprocessing: Basic principles, protocols, and procedures.* New York: Guilford.

Shapiro, F. (2001a). *Eye movement desensitization and reprocessing: Basic principles, protocols, and procedures* (2d ed.). New York: Guilford.

Shapiro, F. (2001b). *Level I training manual: Part one of a two part training.* Pacific Grove, CA: EMDR Institute.

Shapiro, F. (2001c). *Level II training manual: Part two of a two part training.* Pacific Grove, CA: EMDR Institute.

Shapiro, F. (2001d). The challenges of treatment evolution and integration. *American Journal of Clinical Hypnosis,* 43(3–4), 183–186.

Shapiro, F., Vogelmann-Sine, S., & Sine, L. (1994). Eye movement desensitization and reprocessing: treating trauma and substance abuse. *Journal of Psychoactive Drugs,* 26(4), 379–391.

Shapiro, R. (2001, December). The two hand technique. *EMDRIA Newsletter* (Special Edition), 15–17.

Shaw, P. (2002, May). CHART and the chakras. Paper presented at the fourth annual international Energy Psychology conference, Litchfield Park, AZ.

Spielberger, C., Gorsuch, R., Lushene, R., Vagg, P., & Jacobs, G. (1983). *Manual for the State-Trait Anxiety Inventory.* Palo Alto, CA: Consulting Psychologists Press.

Teeguarden, I. M. (1996). *A complete guide to acupressure.* Tokyo: Japan Publications.

Tinker, R. H., & Wilson, S. A. (1999). *Through the eyes of a child: EMDR with children.* New York: Norton.

van Etten, M. L., & Taylor, S. (1998). Comparative efficacy of treatments for post-traumatic stress disorder: A meta-analysis. *Clinical Psychology and Psychotherapy,* 5, 126–144.

Villoldo, A. (2000). *Shaman, healer, sage: How to heal yourself and others with the energy medicine of the Americas.* New York: Harmony.

Wade, J. F. (1990). *The effects of the Callahan phobia treatment technique on self concept.* Ph.D. diss., Professional School of Psychology Studies, San Diego, CA.

Walther, D. S. (1988). *Applied kinesiology: Synopsis.* Pueblo, CO: Systems DC.

Watkins, J. G. (1971). The affect bridge: A hypnoanalytic technique. *International Journal of Clinical and Experimental Hypnosis,* 19, 21–27.

Watkins, J., & Watkins, H. (1997). *Ego states: Theory and therapy.* New York: Norton.

Wheeler, M. (2001, June). Muscle Testing 101. Presentation at the Energy Psychology conference, (Southeast) Highlands, NC.

Whisenant, W. F. (1990). *Psychological kinesiology: Changing the body's beliefs.* Austin, TX: Monarch Butterfly.

Wildish, P. (2000). *The book of ch'i*. Boston: Journey Editions/Tuttle.

Wilson, S. A., Becker, L. A., & Tinker, R. H. (1995). Eye movement desensitization and reprocessing (EMDR) treatment for psychologically traumatized individuals. *Journal of Consulting and Clinical Psychology, 63*, 928–937.

Wilson, S. A., Becker, L. A., & Tinker, R. H. (1997). Fifteen-month follow-up of eye movement desensitization and reprocessing (EMDR) treatment for posttraumatic stress disorder and psychological trauma. *Journal of Consulting and Clinical Psychology, 65*, 1047–1056.

Wilson, S. A., Tinker, R. H., Hoffman, A., Becker, L. A., & Marshal, S. (2000, November). A field study of EMDR with Kosovar-Albanian refugee children using a group treatment protocol. Paper presented at the annual meeting of the International Society for the Study of Traumatic Stress, San Antonio, TX.

Wolpe, J. (1969). *The practice of behavior therapy*. New York: Pergamon Press.

Wolpe, J., & Abrams, J. (1991. Post-traumatic stress disorder overcome by eye movement desensitization: A case report. *Journal of Behavior Therapy and Experimental Psychiatry, 22*, 39–43.

Wylie, M. S. (1996). Going for the cure. *The Family Therapy Networker, 20*(4), 20–37.

Zangwill, W. (1998) Integrating EMDR with schema-focused therapy. *EMDRIA Newsletter, 3*(4), 16–17.

Zimmerman, J. (1990). Laying-on-of-hands healing and therapeutic touch: A testable theory. *BEMI Current, Journal of the Bio-Electro-Magnetics Institute, 2*, 8–17.

Zimmerman, J. E. (1972). Josephson effect devices and low frequency field sensing. *Cryogenics, 12*, 19–31.

Zimmerman, J. E., Thiene, P., & Harding, J. T. (1970). Design and operation of stable rf-biased superconducting point-contact quantum devices, and a note on the properties of perfectly clean metal contacts. *Journal of Applied Physics, 41*, 1572–1580.

Appendix A.
Information For My Clients

John Hartung, Psy.D.

Depending on the problem(s) you wish to work on in therapy with me, you might be interested in knowing what previous clients have reported. I list below the persons I treated in 2001, noting the main problems they came to resolve. The numbers do not include couples or family therapy, nor those persons (about six) continuing to work with me. The numbers represent about 500 hours of therapy, 88 clients, and 106 different problems. Under the N column I note the number of people I treated for each problem. I then give the average number of hours we spent working on each problem, and finally the benefit that they said they experienced. Benefit is based in part on the final number the client reports on a 0–10 scale where 0 means "no problem left" and 10 means "this is the worst I can imagine feeling now." Another way to determine benefit is to ask the client to report changes in feelings, thoughts, and behaviors after treatment. In some cases family members, physicians, and others help to determine benefit. A person would get a "high" rating on public speaking anxiety, for example, only after actually giving an effective speech in public and feeling good about it. On the other hand, a person continuing to need medication for depression would not be given a "high" rating, no matter how much better s/he felt. "Unknown" includes two groups: persons I did not follow up with long enough to tell if the treatment benefits continued (for example, someone wanting to stop an addiction); and those who dropped out before completing the treatment I recommended.

I use various treatments, including cognitive-behavior methods. Techniques that I find to be especially helpful are EMDR and therapies from a field called "energy psychology." Please ask any question you might have about anything we do in treatment. Page 3 of this handout tells you more specifically about your rights as a client.

About 60% of these clients are male. These data are on children, teens, and adults. My clients list a wide range of cultural, religious, and life-style preferences.

The numbers are averages. While they are useful for predicting future results, your experience may differ from previous patients' experiences. Also notice that different presenting problems are likely to produce different benefits. Now some details:

Addictions are complex and require additional treatment that I do not offer (such as 12-step treatment, family therapy, medical attention, residential treatment). EMDR and EP are often helpful in reducing the urge to use, and in working through the trauma that often keeps the urge alive. The final category, "unknown," represents those who dropped out of addictions treatment.

Depression includes chronic depression that requires medication. It is easier to recover from depression that is a part of post-traumatic stress.

Dilemmas are situations of ambivalence where two or more choices are equally attractive or equally unpleasant. This can cause procrastination, resistance, and indecisiveness.

Pain refers to physical pain, of any cause. Auto accidents resulting in closed-head injury and headaches are the most difficult to treat, though often a person can learn to limit the resulting pain using both EMDR and energy techniques at home.

Performance problems interfere with success using a skill one already has. Clients in this group include executives, artists, musicians, actors, athletes, and other high achievers.

Phobias include fear of animals, fear of public speaking, height phobias, and so on.

PTSD means the trauma that results from a life-threatening experience. Last year my clients were victims of accidents, assault, natural disaster, and civil war.

Stress usually refers to a person's worries that cause body aches and pain and distract the person significantly from work and relationships.

Miscellaneous in 2001 included sleep problems, procrastination, concentration problems, and dissociation.

CLIENT PROBLEM	N	Length of treatment		Benefits of Treatment Reported			
		TOTAL HOURS	AVERAGE	NONE	SOME	HIGH	UNKNOWN
Addiction	7	1 to 10	4.3	1	2	2	2
Anger	8	1 to 20	6.6	1	3	3	1
Depression	5	3 to 20	8.0	1	2	2	0
Dilemmas	6	1 to 3	2.0	0	1	5	0
Pain	6	2 to 4	3.0	1	3	2	0
Performance Problems	9	1 to 6	2.2	0	1	7	1
Phobias	10	1 to 4	1.9	0	1	7	2
PTSD	32	1 to 21	4.4	0	9	23	0
Stress	7	3 to 12	6.4	0	0	7	0
Miscellaneous	16	1 to 30	6.1	1	8	7	0
% TOTALS				5%	29%	60%	6%

Appendix B: Resources

The following sources provide information and tools for those interested in exploring EP and EMDR further. Practice in both methods is evolving and resources supporting practice are increasing. Although organizations and trainers are generally reputable, there is no consensus on most of the products. Internet discussion lists, Web sites, and local study groups will keep you up to date.

ENERGY PSYCHOLOGY

Association for Comprehensive Energy Psychology: 800-915-3606, ext. 21, http://www.energypsych.org

Training

Be set free fast: 714-771-1866, http://www.BeSetFreeFast.com

BDB Group: 973-746-5959, http://www.tftworldwide.com

Callahan Techniques/TFT: 800-359-2873, http://www.tftrx.com

Colorado Consulting Group: 719-634-4444, DrGalvin@earthlink.net

Emotional freedom techniques: http://www.emofree.com

Energy diagnostic and treatment methods: 724-346-3838, http://www.energypsych.com

International College of Applied Kinesiology: http://www.icakusa.com

Tapas acupressure technique: 310-378-7381,
http://www.tat-intl.com

Thought energy synchronization therapies: 412-683-8378,
http://www.thoughtenergy.com

Information

Durlacher: 800-529-8836,
http://www.freedomfromfearforever.com

Institute for Meridian Psychotherapy and Counseling list: send
blank e-mail to IMPC.Forum-subscribe@listbot.com

Energyspirit1 email discussion list (moderated by Phil Friedman,
Ph.D.): PilF101@aol.com,

Nambudripad allergy elimination technique: 714-523-8900,
http://www.naet.com

Energy therapy home page:
http://home.att.net/~tom.altaffer/index.htm

PsychInnovations: http://www.psychinnovations.com/y1inner.htm

Materials

EMF PROTECTORS

BioElectric shield: http://www.advancedliving.com

Q-Link pendant: 800-603-0339, http://clarusproducts.com

METHYLSULFONYLMETHANE

Freelife: 800-882-7240, http://www.freelife.com

Rich Distributing: 503-761-7450,
http://www.richdistributing.com

EMDR

EMDR International Association: 512-451-5200,
http://www.emdria.org

TRAINING

EMDR International Association: 512-451-5200,
http://www.emdria.org

EMDR Institute: 831-372-3900, http://www.emdr.com

INFORMATION

EMDR news: http://www.emdrnews.com

EMDR portal: http://www.emdrportal.com

David Baldwin's trauma information pages:
http://www.trauma-pages.com

MATERIALS

Biolateral (audio stimulation tapes and CDs, book, videotape):
516-826-7996, http://www.biolateral.com

Neurolateral (software for stimulation by computer): 866-666-
0166, http://www.neurolateral.com

Neurotek (EyeScan, Tac/AudioScan, LapScan): 303-420-8680,
http://www.neurotekcorp.com

PsychInnovations (Phased lateral synthesis audio stimulation
tapes and information on EP and EMDR): 303-654-2557,
http://www.psychinnovations.com

SchmidtWerks (TheraTappers): 210-561-7881,
http://www.theratapper.com

Index

Abrams, J., 18
abreactions (in EMDR), 16, 38
  in client self-use, 219, 221
  in EP, 197–98, 200–202
  EP with, 180–85
  fractionated, 27, 158, 161, 201
  lay risk of, 223, 278, 279
  minimizing chances of, 39, 40, 44, 134–143
  in offenders, 236
  pregnancy and, 41
  therapist's attitude toward, 277
abuse, xx, 83, 121, 143, 170–171, 182, 204, 231, 235, 238
acrophobia, 58–59, 150, 158, 180
acupoints, 10
acupuncture, 3, 57–58
adaptive information processing (AIP), 15, 16, 38, 39
addictions, 42–43, 121, 150, 151–152, 162, 218, 236, 310
affect management, see abreactions
affirmations, 10, 92–93, 104n, 112, 114, 216
see also algorithms
agoraphobia, 37, 147
algorithms (TFT), 5, 6
  for anxiety, 174, 180, 195, 216, 252, 254
  client self-use of, 214, 215, 243–244, 249
  conducting, 105–110
  impact of selected, 24
  for phobias, 83, 84, 252
  for trauma, 82, 179, 180, 195
alarm points, 102, 110
allergies, 41, 117, 151
Altaffer, T., 81
Altarriba, J., 289
American Association of Humanistic Psychology, 7
American Psychiatric Association, 4, 53, 186
American Psychological Association, xix, 22, 32, 66
anorexia, 32
antisocial disorder, 240–241
anxiety, 36–37, 40, 82, 252, 258
apex problem, 21, 22, 199, 246, 268

Artigas, L., 29, 48, 49
aspects, in EP, 82–83, 89, 200–201, 202, 215
Association for Comprehensive Energy Psychology (ACEP), 9, 20, 23, 58, 63, 313
asthma, 41
attention-deficit/hyperactivity disorder (ADHD), 221
attention span, children's, 48
auditory tones, 203–205, 206
aura, 2, 7, 9, 65–66, 271 (see also energy fields)

Baker, B.L., 58
Bandler, R., 71
Bassett, C.A.L., 56
Baule, G., 55
Beck, A., xiv
Becker, L., 67, 258
Becker, R.O., 8, 57
behavior:
  accelerating/decelerating, 163–165
  as multidetermined, 242–243
  problems with, in EMDR, 150
beliefs, 45, 129, 141, 210, 240, 242, 246
Bender, S., 5, 43, 64, 271
Benor, D., 8, 203
Berne, E., xviii
be set free fast (BSFF), 38, 105, 108, 109, 181, 216, 217, 268, 313
Beutler, L.E., 59, 66, 134, 135
bilateral stimulation, 14, 38, 88n
  accelerating/decelerating, 154–155, 170–171
  benefit or harm, 169–179
  client self-use of, 219–220
  direction of, 155–156
  empowerment of, 275
  EP, during, 203–204, 211
  mechanical devices for self-treatment, 221, 229
  overview of, 128
  stopping, 137–138
  SUD during, 181–184
  tapping, 108–109
  velocity of, 155
  visualization combined with, 265